INNOVATIVE STRATEGIES FOR HERITAGE LANGUAGE TEACHING

INNOVATIVE STRATEGIES FOR HERITAGE LANGUAGE TEACHING

A PRACTICAL GUIDE FOR THE CLASSROOM

MARTA FAIRCLOUGH and
SARA M. BEAUDRIE, Editors

Foreword by Ana Roca
Afterword by Guadalupe Valdés

Georgetown University Press / Washington, DC

Library of Congress Cataloging-in-Publication Data

Names: Fairclough, Marta Ana, editor. | Beaudrie, Sara M., editor. | Roca, Ana, writer of foreword. | Valdés, Guadalupe, writer of afterword.
Title: Innovative strategies for heritage language teaching : a practical guide for the classroom / Marta Fairclough and Sara M. Beaudrie, editors ; foreword by Ana Roca ; afterword by Guadalupe Valdés.
Description: Washington, D.C. : Georgetown University Press, 2016. | Includes bibliographical references and index.
Identifiers: LCCN 2016001905 (print) | LCCN 2016006089 (ebook) | ISBN 9781626163386 (pb : alk. paper) | ISBN 9781626163379 (hc : alk. paper) | ISBN 9781626163393 (eb)
Subjects: LCSH: Heritage language speakers. | Native language—Study and teaching. | Language and languages—Study and teaching.
Classification: LCC P51 .I47 2016 (print) | LCC P51 (ebook) | DDC 418.007—dc23
LC record available at http://lccn.loc.gov/2016001905

∞ This book is printed on acid-free paper meeting the requirements of the American National Standard for Permanence in Paper for Printed Library Materials.

17 16 9 8 7 6 5 4 3 2 First printing

Printed in the United States of America

Cover design by Naylor Design, Inc. Cover image by michaeljung/Shutterstock.com.

To the memory of my beloved mother, Marija Tomljanović Duić.
Her infinite kindness and wise words are deeply missed . . .

—*Marta Fairclough*

To my twin sister, Silvia, for her positive energy, unconditional support, and amazing friendship throughout these years, and to my older sister, Adriana, por tu apoyo constante aunque estemos tan lejos.

—*Sara M. Beaudrie*

Contents

Illustrations

FIGURES

TABLES

Foreword

Ana Roca
FLORIDA INTERNATIONAL UNIVERSITY

Professors Sara Beaudrie and Marta Fairclough have thoughtfully brought together an exciting, must-have, important collection of cutting-edge essays written by distinguished researchers and practitioners on current practices in heritage language (HL) teaching in the United States. This timely co-edited volume is an additional contribution to Beaudrie and Fairclough's other recent and well-received *Spanish as a Heritage Language in the United States: The State of the Field* (Georgetown University Press, 2012), which exclusively addressed issues in Spanish HL instruction, theory, and practice.

Expanding the subject range in their new publication to include the full range of HL instruction found in the United States, Beaudrie and Fairclough address other minority languages—rather than just the largest, Spanish—as a heritage language. This publication is based on the most current and varied voices in the field of heritage languages in educational linguistics and pedagogy. The essays in this co-edited volume explore a number of important questions in minority language education. The collection of essays moves the field beyond descriptions of the current state of HL education in the United States, offering a welcome and solid contribution of innovative ideas as well as proposing an optimal instructional model and practices that are well informed by the most current thinking drawn from sociolinguistic, psycholinguistic, and pedagogical research on bilingualism and language learning and teaching. As such, this volume, ideally suited for a number of courses in linguistics and language education, stands as a welcome, much-needed, and up-to-date compilation of overview essays that are useful to both new or inexperienced practitioners and more experienced scholars and instructors interested in the growing topic of HL education in the United States within the wider contexts of educational linguistics, bilingualism, and bilingual education.

The book you are about to read presents useful and thought-provoking information in both theoretical and applied linguistics; it asks questions about learning and teaching and about language acquisition, literacy development, and issues and possibilities in formal instruction that we can apply in schools and colleges or in community schools, where both young and adult learners receive HL instruction.

As we read the following essays, we also cannot help but consider the role of heritage languages in the historical context of US bilingualism. We realize that numerous other issues are vital in any discussion or consideration of the past, present, and future place of heritage languages in the United States, given the need and continuous calls for more advanced competency in more than one language. These include societal and economic issues related to attitudes toward heritage languages, the role of politics and language policies, power struggles in educational models, the effects of twenty-first-century immigration patterns and projected minority population growth, the impact of globalization on our bilingualism readiness, and the enormous need for better public awareness and community engagement in order to more effectively demand appropriate funding for bilingual and HL programs. By definition, the creation of appropriate programs includes changes in K–16 language requirements and, at the US college/university level, changes in language department offerings, professional development, and teacher preparation programs.

Although all minority/heritage languages are important, that "sleeping giant" in the room we used to talk about more than thirty years ago is no longer "sleepy." The "giant" of heritage languages in the United States now represents a very large Spanish-speaking presence that continues to expand, a population to contend with in towns and cities alike. Many cities now have Hispanic mayors, just as states have Hispanic representatives or senators, and the Supreme Court has a female bilingual Puerto Rican judge. In popular culture, singers like Ricky Martin, Juanes, Gloria Estefan, Marc Anthony, Shakira, and even Presidential Medal of Honor recipient Dr. José Greer, have become successful bilingual role models for younger generations. In whatever language combination, these heritage speakers will likewise cross over, back and forth, between languages and cultures; we wish them all to be successful in English without being pressured to lose or neglect their heritage language.

The US Hispanic population continues to grow not just in terms of numbers but also in terms of political and economic power; they identify with the English language and the United States without necessarily giving up their Spanish language, traditions, or hybrid US Latino/Hispanic identity. Because the Spanish-speaking population is the largest HL group on which the most research has been published, much has been learned that is applicable to other heritage languages, but much can also be learned from other heritage languages in the United States—benefiting all of us involved in HL education. The concept of "who" or "what" is an American has already been changing—and rightfully so—for some time. Now we need to ask ourselves, what are the optimal conditions for HL education, and what does it take to offer these and to foster the best educational practices at all levels, K–16?

Social media is part of our "shrinking" and "merging" world through our ability to communicate instantly via FaceTime, Twitter, Facebook, Google, Tumblr, and Skype. This has connected bilinguals and monolinguals alike at a rate, level, and speed that would never have been possible until the last few decades. Now a global view can be obtained in the palm of one's hand as bilinguals can change keyboards on an iPhone or simply speak to Siri in English or Spanish, for example—until she is better programmed to interact in Spanglish, too, and to code-switch as easily as bilinguals naturally do—reflecting the reality in our bilingual homes, schools, and communities, whatever the language combination. Our US population is rich with HL combinations to be nurtured—whether they be Chinese, Tagalog, Vietnamese, Korean, German, French, Russian, Hindu, Arabic, or American Sign Language, to name just a few of the many heritage languages we are fortunate to have in the United States.

Based on what we have learned, it is clear that in teaching heritage languages we need to approach our classes with low-anxiety, interactional, content-based, and task-based approaches that are flexible and open to a variety of student-centered, creative projects; high-interest, theme-based readings and discussions; and learning activities in and outside of the classroom (such as the Abuelas Oral History Project, started in Spanish but effective for any other language; service-learning assignments; film viewing; discussion analysis; formal written reviews; lectures and panels in the heritage language; and Internet and other research). In the end, HL learners can become more comfortable in their heritage language, developing more advanced abilities in a wider range of discourses and registers appropriate to different environments and circumstances. To achieve this, HL learners first need to be "hooked" on the desire to monitor and direct their own HL learning as a lifelong endeavor, to seek opportunities beyond the classroom, to learn to love reading in the heritage language, and to seek cultural activities and experiences where they can hear and use the heritage language, in order to continue developing it in so many necessary aspects.

The teaching, maintenance, retention, and development of literacy among heritage speakers and the challenges we face and solutions we can implement as instructors and curriculum planners are a focus of this anthology. There are now many more educators and linguists interested in, doing research on, and writing instructional materials for heritage languages in the United States. Unlike decades ago, dissertations are being written on these topics, and articles, special interest groups, conference panels, keynote addresses, workshops, blogs, associations, and so on are appearing. We have indeed been moving the field forward due to the dedication of faculty, students, institutes and centers, and projects like this wonderful publication that will certainly advance the field even further and stimulate its growth.

I am sure that the material in this volume on best and universal practices or guidelines for teaching heritage languages will advance the field in the

United States. This much-needed collection can and will be used for years to come in language education and applied linguistics classes. I am sure that its readers, both students and instructors, who are as caring and passionate as I am about minority linguistic rights will also appreciate the admirable and careful work that the co-editors have undertaken, both in their own writings and in their thoughtful selection of contributors, who must also be congratulated for their work.

INTRODUCTION

Heritage Language Education in the United States

Marta Fairclough and Sara M. Beaudrie
UNIVERSITY OF HOUSTON AND ARIZONA STATE UNIVERSITY

The importance of heritage language (HL) education is now widely acknowledged. As the report of the first Heritage Language Research Priorities Conference states, heritage languages are an invaluable resource whose preservation "is a matter of urgency not only for the nation, but also for individuals, families, and communities. The urgency involves matters of cultural understanding, identity, equitable access to social services, and social justice as well as cognitive issues related to the achievement of higher level competencies" (UCLA 2001, 6). HL education has as its primary aims to help learners regain, develop, or maintain their heritage language while gaining deeper understanding of their cultural heritage. Preserving and developing linguistic proficiency among heritage speakers stands to benefit both the individual (by helping maintain connections with family and the home language community) and society at large (by strengthening national linguistic and cultural resources).

While HL education has existed in the United States in various forms for more than three hundred years (Fishman 2001, 2014), it was not until the turn of the twenty-first century that the field of HL education gained the attention of a wide group of researchers, policy makers, administrators, and practitioners. New initiatives have been very influential in the growth of the field, including the National Heritage Language Resource Center (at UCLA), devoted to HL education and research, the *Heritage Language Journal*, the Alliance for the Advancement of Heritage Languages at the Center for Applied Linguistics (in Washington, DC), and conferences and workshops devoted to HL issues, along with many journal articles, books, and dissertations. This volume presents insights into the research on HL education over the last two decades and aims to take the HL education field a step forward, positioning it at the forefront of innovative and transformative educational practices in order to benefit all learners who choose to continue developing or maintaining their heritage language in an educational setting.

HERITAGE LANGUAGES AND HL LEARNERS

In the US context, the term "heritage languages" refers to minority languages (i.e., languages other than English). Despite initial criticism of this term (see García 2005; Wiley 2001), it has now been widely adopted by US academics. It is a relatively "neutral and inclusive term" that lacks the stigma attached to terms such as "minority," "indigenous," "immigrant," or "ethnic" (Hornberger 2005, 102). As we did in the volume *Spanish as a Heritage Language in the United States: The State of the Field* (Beaudrie and Fairclough 2012), we will use the term "heritage languages" throughout this book. This choice fulfills the dual purpose of using the term that most scholars and educators in the field embrace as an alternative to stigmatizing terminology while at the same time promoting language learning and, in some cases, reversing language shift (Wiley 2001).

Defining "heritage language learners" has proven to be more difficult, as a variety of definitions have been proposed (e.g., Draper and Hicks 2000; Fishman 2001; Hornberger and Wang 2008; Polinsky and Kagan 2007; Valdés 2001; Van Deusen-Scholl 2003). We agree with Wiley's statement, that "heritage language learner" and similar terms "attempt to apply a single label to a complex situation (Wiley 2001, 29); these terms mean different things to different people and thus we currently lack definitions upon which all agree." Determining who is included under this term, however, has crucial implications for issues of identity as well as inclusion and exclusion (Wiley 2001). Most of the proposed definitions have focused on two key characteristics: a personal connection to a particular cultural/ethnic group (i.e., Fishman, 2001) or proficiency in the language acquired naturalistically rather than through classroom instruction (i.e., Valdés 2001). These two types of definitions have been labeled broad and narrow, respectively (Polinsky and Kagan, 2007). For pedagogical purposes, several researchers have argued in favor of a proficiency-based definition (e.g., Kagan 2005; Carreira and Kagan 2011) because a certain degree of proficiency is deemed necessary to justify the separation of second or foreign language learners from heritage learners on linguistic grounds. Thus, in this volume, we follow Valdés's definition, which defines a heritage language learner as an individual "who is raised in a home where a non-English language is spoken. The student may speak or merely understand the heritage language and be, to some degree, bilingual in English and the heritage language" (Valdes 2000, 1). This definition includes learners at the lowest level of the bilingual continuum—that is, receptive bilinguals (see Valdes 1997) as well as learners who possess more advanced levels of language proficiency and may come near the highest levels of the bilingual continuum.

Heritage Languages in the United States

From its inception, language diversity has been a defining characteristic of the United States. This diversity is a result not of recent immigration but of the country's rich history of a multilingual population (Wiley et al. 2014). The top thirteen non-English languages spoken in the United States as of 2011 are listed in table I.1 with their corresponding number and percentage of speakers (Ryan 2013).

Interestingly, this diversity increased 158.3 percent from 23,060,040 speakers of non-English languages in the United States in 1980 to 59,542,596 in 2010 (Ryan 2013). These numbers should not be interpreted as a sign simply of language maintenance but rather of the continuous influx of new immigrants, which creates a false impression that heritage languages are being maintained. In fact, heritage languages continue to be lost, generally over the course of three generations. Fishman (1964) proposes a model of intergenerational language shift in which the first generation is typically monolingual in the heritage language, the second generation is bilingual in the heritage and dominant languages, and the third generation is monolingual in the dominant language. This general pattern is well documented among immigrant communities throughout US history (see Balestra, Martínez, and Moyna 2008; Potowski 2010; Veltman 1983). HL education has the critical role of altering this natural pattern of loss of heritage languages since its main objective is to achieve HL maintenance or even reverse language

Table I.1: Non-English Languages Spoken in the United States (2011)

Language	Number of speakers	HL population speaking that language (%)
1. Spanish or Spanish Creole	37,579,787	62
2. Chinese	2,882,497	4.8
3. French or French Creole	2,055,433	3.3
4. Tagalog	1,594,413	2.6
5. Vietnamese	1,419,539	2.3
6. Korean	1,141,227	1.9
7. German	1,083,637	1.8
8. Arabic	951,699	1.6
9. Russian	905,843	1.5
10. Italian	723,632	1.1
11. Portuguese	673,566	1.1
12. Hindi	648,983	1.1
13. Polish	607,403	1.0
All other languages	8,309,361	14
Total	**60,577,020**	**100**

Source: Ryan (2013), using data from 2011 American Community Language Survey.

loss. However, as a new field of research and practice, it presents HL educators with many instructional and administrative challenges, including the following:

1. How do we define heritage learners as a group in their own right as opposed to defining them in contrast to other groups or in terms of characteristics they do not possess?
2. What should be the goals of HL education in the twenty-first century?
3. How should HL instruction prepare HL learners and teachers to understand the sociolinguistic context of learning minority languages?
4. As the demand for quality HL programs intensifies, how should new HL programs be designed?
5. How do we prepare HL teachers to meet the pedagogical demands of serving a diverse group of students with unique needs in a single classroom?
6. What are the most effective pedagogical approaches to HL instruction?
7. What are the best ways to help learners acquire a standard dialect of their HL for use in professional and academic settings?
8. How can critical language pedagogy be implemented in the HL classroom?
9. How do we help HL learners become multiliterate in the postprocess era of literacy instruction?
10. How should HL learners' skills be assessed for placement in the appropriate course level?
11. What does technology have to offer to HL instruction?

Teaching professionals play a major role in HL maintenance and revitalization. The purpose of this volume is to provide teachers with the knowledge and pedagogical tools to answer these important questions and overcome the obstacles that interfere with trying to implement them in the classroom. It is our hope that this information will better equip teachers to help reverse language shift.

OVERVIEW OF THE VOLUME

Innovative Approaches for Heritage Language Teaching: A Practical Guide for the Classroom reviews state-of-the-art practices in HL teaching in the United States based on cutting-edge knowledge drawn from recent research. It goes beyond describing the present state of HL pedagogy and seeks to move the field forward by introducing innovative ideas that are optimal for this population. The goal is to advance a working model for HL classroom instruction that is informed by linguistic, sociolinguistic, and educational research on heritage languages. It also describes the challenges of transferring research findings to teaching practice and suggests solutions to overcome practical problems associated with the implementation of innovative teaching approaches. The volume seeks to include all heritage languages by reviewing research and perspectives from multiple heritage languages in each chapter. As the most widely spoken heritage language in the United States and the one that has received the widest attention from research, Spanish is unquestionably more heavily represented throughout the book.

But what exactly does innovation mean to HL teaching professionals and to the field of HL pedagogy? A quick search through dictionaries and on the Internet offers general definitions of innovation as something original, groundbreaking, pioneering, or improved. The innovation could be an idea, a process, a product, or something else, but it has to add some new value. Steven Maranville (1992) views innovation as the application of better solutions to meet new, existing, or unarticulated needs. If we were to choose just one concept to convey the meaning of innovation in the HL education field, we would propose "student involvement"—that is, students' active participation in the HL learning process. The student should always be at the center of curricular, assessment, and administrative considerations in HL instruction. Within this context, the construct of *involvement* could be operationalized mainly in terms of the agency students gain via heightened sociolinguistic knowledge and critical language awareness (chapters 3, 4, 8), capitalization on technological advances (chapters 5, 11, 8, 9), and stronger connections with their home community (chapters 2, 8, 10). Ideally, the degree of student involvement would increase gradually, eventually leading to individual engagement or commitment to promoting HL maintenance, to developing stronger ties to the HL community, and finally to becoming a citizen of a multilingual world.

Innovation = Student Involvement → Commitment

In order to facilitate this process, HL professionals need to (a) be informed about the latest research on HL learner profiles and needs (chapters 1, 6, 7, 10), (b) be flexible about modifying course content (chapters 3, 7, 8, 9), (c) learn new ways to design and implement programs and curricula (chapters 5, 8, 10), and (d) be familiar with advances in pedagogical approaches and new ways of delivering instruction (chapters 4, 6, 7, 11).

This introduction summarizes the innovative ideas presented in this volume as well as the challenges and opportunities the profession of HL teaching will face in coming years. The contents of the eleven chapters inevitably overlap because the various aspects of HL pedagogy need to intersect to create a strong, unified model of HL instruction. The chapters are divided into two parts, as described in the following subsections. The volume ends with an afterword from the viewpoint of expert Guadalupe Valdés regarding current innovations and future possibilities in HL education.

Part I: Foundations in Heritage Language Teaching: Essential Notions in Curricula, Teacher, and Program Development

"Innovation" appears in chapter 1 in the form of a "prototype model" that characterizes HL learners' proficiency in terms of basic-level cognition and implicit knowledge. The author, Eve Zyzik, highlights the difficulty of defining and characterizing HL learners due to the broad variability within the group. After briefly explaining such variability from the traditional "bilingual continuum" perspective, she presents her prototype model, which stresses learners' implicit knowledge of their heritage language. Following Jan Hulstijn's (2011, 2012) dichotomy between basic-level cognition (BLC) and higher-level cognition (HLC), Zyzik argues that the prototypical HL learner's linguistic proficiency is characterized by BLC. Whereas HLC is mainly developed in academic contexts and often includes metalinguistic awareness, BLC is shared with native speakers of the language and primarily consists of implicit knowledge. Drawing on research contrasting the explicit knowledge of second language (L2) learners versus the implicit knowledge of HL learners, Zyzik illustrates how materials designed for L2 students fail to tap into HL learners' implicit knowledge. In sum, Zyzik's prototype model of an HL learner includes the following gradient characteristics: (a) proficiency (BLC) in the HL, (b) ethnic/cultural connection to the HL, (c) dominance in a language other than the HL, (d) implicit knowledge of the HL, (e) bilingualism, and (f) early exposure to the HL in the home. The chapter ends with some pedagogical implications derived from the model and examples of how to implement them in the classroom. For example, L2 materials will have limited applicability for teaching grammar to HL students because they target the explicit base of knowledge that HL students lack, but for teaching vocabulary, L2 materials and methods can be effective.

Drawing from a number of empirical studies and reports, chapter 2, by Glenn Martínez, begins with a description of the National Standards for Foreign Language Learning (NSFLL) developed under the leadership of the American Council for the Teaching of Foreign Languages and intended to apply to all language students, including HL learners. The standards center on linguistic competency (i.e., what a student is able to do with the language) and, although they outline "Five Cs" of language (communication, cultures, connections, comparisons, and communities), they focus mainly on communication. Less attention has been paid to culture while the communities standard has been described as "the lost C" (Glisan et al. 2010). Martínez explains that, for these reasons, HL educators have come to realize that the NSFLL does not reflect the unique circumstances and needs of HL students and their communities, and therefore they have proposed different goals (Beaudrie, Ducar, and Potowski, 2014). The author lists and reviews the seven goals for HL education and underscores the essential role of the community in accomplishing each one. He also discusses how connecting HL learners with HL communities benefits both student and community. For HL education, the author proposes a groundbreaking pedagogical framework based on the notion of "capabilities" (Nussbaum 2011; Sen 1992, 2000), which considers personal abilities in the context of the environment (in this case, what an individual can *do* and can *be* within the HL community). The "capabilities" orientation is better suited to HL learners because it takes into account competencies within the social, political, and economic environments, making community engagement an essential part of HL education. In the last part of the chapter, Martínez operationalizes the capabilities approach by presenting several examples of community-based pedagogical initiatives (i.e., service learning) that promote language development through community involvement. The fact that, according to Martínez, the connection between HL education and the community is not optional but "an imperative that must be pursued" places significant responsibilities on HL teachers.

In chapter 3, Jennifer Leeman and Ellen J. Serafini call for the incorporation into the HL classroom of a broad range of sociolinguistic topics that they consider of paramount importance to both students and HL educators. Current research supports the promotion of "critical language awareness" that makes students aware of the sociopolitical and ideological aspects of language and gives them some agency to resist language-based discrimination, and the promotion of "translingual and transcultural competence" among students. Leeman and Serafini discuss how many forms of linguistic variation (e.g., geographic, contextual)—including language-contact-related phenomena such as code-switching, borrowings, and calques—are the norm in HL classrooms. They strongly reject the "standard language ideology" that views one variety as superior to all others and reject the notion of "appropriateness" as justification for linguistic variation. The authors propose a "critical translingual model" that, in addition to promoting acquisition of multiple dialects in HL instruction, prepares students to understand linguistic variation from many perspectives and empowers them to make their own linguistic choices in specific situations. The last part of the chapter presents several examples of incorporating this model into the classroom. Among the suggested activities are reading scholarly research, analyzing different types of texts, and collecting and analyzing data from family, peers, and community members.

In chapter 4 Sara M. Beaudrie offers comprehensive practical guidelines for designing, developing, and evaluating an HL program. After briefly describing the different types of HL programs (school-based, higher education–based, and community-based), the author proposes a sequence of steps for building or redesigning an HL program: (1) gathering information and building an argument for the creation of an HL program; (2) gathering resources for program building; (3) providing teacher development in HL instruction; (4) deciding on program structure and preliminary course content; (5) identifying HL students; (6) placing HL students in appropriate course levels; (7) promoting the program and recruiting students; and (8) evaluating the program. For each step Beaudrie highlights frequently encountered challenges (e.g., limited funding, resources, and expertise) and suggests ways to overcome them through a number of initiatives, resources, and activities and collaboration among students, instructors, administrators, researchers, and the community to achieve optimal results. The final section of the chapter offers successful examples of each program-building step from HL programs nationwide. The concluding remarks emphasize the importance of continuous program evaluation to improve current programmatic and curricular practices to ensure that HL learners receive education of the highest quality.

In chapter 5, Manel Lacorte presents recent advances in the professional preparation and development of HL instructors in community-based programs as well as in K–12 and higher education. To begin, the chapter outlines the current second language acquisition (SLA) perspective, which views language as a social practice situated in a specific historic, cultural, and sociopolitical context. After a brief description of recent trends in L2 education and teacher preparation, Lacorte proposes an "ecological model" for L2 and HL teaching and learning. In addition to several dimensions that should be part of the knowledge base and skills of HL teachers (e.g., knowledge of general pedagogical approaches to teaching HL learners and pedagogical strategies for use in mixed HL and L2 classrooms), Lacorte lists and explains seven key aspects of an ecological approach to HL teacher development:

- *Ideological*: Adopting language beliefs and attitudes about teaching that may lead to teacher/institutional ideologies such as the promotion of standard languages versus the acceptance of multiple dialects.
- *Cultural*: Understanding students' cultural baggage and their motivations for studying their heritage language.
- *Socio-affective*: Being aware of students' identity issues, confidence, self-esteem, and social interaction with others as well as their affective practices, such as expressions of feelings or attitudes.
- *Linguistic*: Understanding of the distribution of HL proficiency and the differences between L1, L2, and HL acquisition; knowing the sociolinguistic issues surrounding minority languages.
- *Curricular*: Being familiar with administrative practices such as the evaluation of pedagogical material, placement and assessment procedures, and the development of community involvement activities.
- *Pedagogical*: Training in different language-teaching approaches and a variety of classroom strategies.

- *Professional*: Studying issues of interest for instructors working either exclusively with HL learners or with L2 and HL students in mixed courses. These include a variety of professional development experiences related to HL education, including HL methods courses, workshops, and attendance at professional conferences.

Part II: Strategies, Techniques, and Approaches in Heritage Language Teaching

Innovative pedagogical proposals are also found in each chapter in part 2 of the volume. María Carreira's contribution, chapter 6, focuses on the use of macro-based, or bottom-up, approaches to HL teaching as well as essential principles, strategies, and tools for supporting this approach. Carreira favors placing HL and L2 learners in different classes whenever possible, due to the wide gap in the functional abilities of the two student populations, especially at the lower levels of instruction. After comparing macro- and microbased approaches in the different teaching domains (e.g., grammar, vocabulary), she underscores the importance of personal relevance, particularly in HL education, where it strongly relates to ethnic identity. Carreira explains how macro approaches more effectively address identity issues and promote language development in HL students. To illustrate best practices in macro-based HL teaching, she describes two college-level programs: "Medical Spanish for Heritage Learners," at the University of Texas, Pan-American (Martínez 2010), and an advanced-level, mixed course taught at Harvard University (Parra 2013). Carreira proposes designing macro-based curricula and activities within a "From-To" model (Kagan and Carreira 2015) that uses scaffolding strategies (Vygotsky 1978) to build upon students' existing knowledge (e.g., progressing from home-based register to general and then academic registers). She illustrates the model using STARTALK, a high school program for Chinese HL learners (Wu and Chang 2010).

In chapter 7 Marta Fairclough endorses an additive language-learning process for the HL classroom. The mechanisms of acquiring a second language (SLA) or a second dialect (SDA) would seem similar since both entail learning new lexical items for the same referents or learning either adaptation or correspondence of phonological and grammatical rules between the two languages (L) or dialects (D) (Siegel 2010). However, whereas SLA is always additive (L1 + L2), SDA can be either subtractive (D2 replaces D1) or additive (D1 + D2). Although there is a common belief that SDA should be easier and faster than SLA, it appears to be more difficult and to occur at a slower rate (e.g., Wolfram and Schilling-Estes 2006). Sometimes the small linguistic distance between the two varieties can make it harder to notice and master the differences between them (Schmidt 1992). After reviewing the concepts of language, dialect, register, and style, and explaining some of the main commonalities and differences between SLA and SDA, the author applies SDA principles in an attempt to better understand how HL students in an academic setting add a new language variety to their linguistic repertoire. Due to the paucity of research on SDA in educational contexts (recent exceptions are Clachar 2005; Fairclough 2005), the goal of the chapter is to shed light on the acquisitional mechanisms and on the social and linguistic factors that contribute to the process. The second part of the chapter presents a multidialectal pedagogical model grounded on the notions of linguistic variation and contrastive techniques. The model includes concrete examples on how to apply SDA principles in the HL classroom.

In chapter 8 María Luisa Parra examines applications of critical pedagogy in the HL classroom. Critical pedagogy was introduced by Paolo Freire in the early 1970s and developed by Henry Giroux and others more recently (Freire 1970a, Giroux 1991). It is mainly concerned with social injustice and oppression both inside and outside the classroom, and its ultimate goal is to guide students to become agents of social change in a time when socially responsive frameworks are replacing traditional prescriptive teaching models. After an overview of the main theoretical and pedagogical issues of critical pedagogy, Parra elaborates on the relevance of three key critical pedagogical frameworks for the teaching of HL students: critical language awareness that incorporates sociolinguistic knowledge, multiliteracies, and service learning in communities. The author underscores the importance of critical awareness in teacher training and development and suggests activities for all three frameworks that can be tailored to the specific needs of the HL classroom. By aligning materials and lesson planning with the critical pedagogy model, Parra presents numerous examples of how to engage in critical dialogues about constructs such as "native speaker," "translanguaging," or "standard language"; to analyze linguistic landscapes (e.g., commercial signs, street names); and to compare linguistic variation through research projects (either diachronic or synchronic). She devotes a major portion of the chapter to a multiliteracies approach to culture, which uses many of the new socially constructed literacies (e.g., email, blogs) along with longer-standing ones (e.g., videos, advertisements, music) to develop critical language awareness and foster critical thinking. Finally, Parra promotes service learning in the form of internships or volunteer work, offering specific suggestions of how to implement these in ways that benefit both students and the community.

In chapter 9 Malena Samaniego and Chantelle Warner examine in depth the notion of multiliteracies to serve as a model for developing literacy in HL speakers. HL pedagogy has historically focused on the development of academic writing, mainly because HL students are perceived to lack advanced literacy skills in their home language. In contrast, the authors propose a framework—which has already been used in L1 and L2 education—that embraces the multiplicity of languages used in the HL classroom. Samaniego and Warner describe the progress of writing instruction in HL education over the past few years. From "process-oriented" approaches, in which the emphasis is not on the final product but on the act of composing, the field has moved to "postprocess" or "genre" approaches, which stress patterns specific to particular genres and incorporate guided focus on form to facilitate students' writing development. After this overview the authors briefly discuss the background and origins of the concept of multiliteracies and offer some definitions of the term. They underscore that one of the main objectives of the multiliteracies approach is to prepare students to adapt to the evolving nature of literacy. Key notions of this approach are the social and multiple nature of literacy; the role of genre and genre continua in connecting culture, content, and language; the understanding of meaning making as an act of "design"; and the incorporation of critical thinking as an essential component of language use. Finally, for implementing the multiliteracies approach in the HL classroom, the authors present a model consisting of four interconnected and overlapping curricular components, each with subcategories. The authors use the components to guide a sample lesson based around a television advertisement, illustrating how to implement the multiliteracies model in the HL classroom. The chapter ends with practical recommendations for adopting the model.

In chapter 10, Gabriela Ilieva and Beth Clark-Gareca present a strong argument that L2 assessment tools have little utility for HL learners due to the many fundamental differences between the two student populations. The chapter begins with a general introduction to language testing, including definitions, theoretical frameworks, and uses and implementation of assessment in educational contexts. The authors then explain why exams such as ACTFL's Oral Proficiency Interviews and computer-based selected-response tasks do not effectively measure linguistic gaps, achievement, and proficiency in HL learners. They underscore the need for specific guidelines and performance descriptors in HL education. After a summary of some key recent developments in HL testing, the authors propose an "organically integrated model" for designing diagnostic and placement exams as well as summative and formative evaluations for the population of HL learners. They offer several examples to illustrate the different types of tests and their uses. This organic model includes background questionnaires to help understand HL learner profiles and recommends testing HL learners using "multiple-measures" tests and "performance-based, contextualized, student centered" assessments that allow students to demonstrate their language abilities in the HL. Ample feedback from many sources (the student, peers, instructors, and the local and global community) is essential for student success. The authors suggest conducting large-scale empirical studies to identify HL learners' weakness and abilities in order to better understand their linguistic and cultural needs and to contribute to the development of better assessment tools and teaching practices.

In chapter 11 Florencia Henshaw highlights the benefits and limitations of technology in HL instruction. Henshaw points out that research on computer-assisted language learning (CALL) has focused on L2s, while the integration of technology in HL classes has mostly been unexplored. Henshaw describes some studies on the benefits of incorporating CALL techniques such as asynchronous text-based discussions and online blogging, which appeared not only to increase HL students' lexical and grammatical knowledge but also to reinforce their cultural and linguistic identity while reducing the anxiety they typically feel in face-to-face encounters. She lists other advantages, which include allowing program administrators to maximize resources (e.g., through course scheduling or serving both L2 and HL learners in a mixed course through differentiated instruction). Among the challenges of integrating technology in HL instruction, Henshaw cites the nonstandard spellings that frequently appear online, limitations of computerized assessment tools, lack of a sense of community among learners, and paucity of online ancillary textbook materials. In the second part of the chapter Henshaw endorses some technological tools for both asynchronous and synchronous communication and explains the many benefits of using them in HL instruction. She suggests ways to use social media sites, content curation sites, free tools for creating digital projects, web-based videoconferencing, and text-based chats as the basis for communicative, sociocultural, and literacy activities in HL courses. She suggests the following best practices for incorporating technology: (a) favor instructor-graded tasks over computer-graded quizzes; (b) foment electronic literacy by embracing learner autonomy; (c) use tools that allow learners to convey meaningful content to real audiences; and (d) capitalize on the text-based nature of online materials.

CONCLUSION

Earlier in the chapter we equated innovation in HL pedagogy with student involvement in the learning process. Instructors promote student involvement by expanding students' linguistic repertoires and giving them agency through the development of a sophisticated sociolinguistic understanding that allows them to choose when and how to use a specific language or language variety. Student involvement also involves their taking an active role in literacy practices and computer-based communication rather than just being passive repositories of information owned by the instructor and "deposited" into their knowledge bank (to use Freire's metaphor [1970b]). Students should also be integrally involved in curriculum planning, pedagogical instruction, and student assessment. Another way of involving students in their linguistic development is through experiential learning outside the classroom. Such experiences can begin with projects that bring learners closer to their families and community. By means of scaffolding, projects can expand out to the broader community through service learning, which one hopes will lead to increased commitment to the community and to promotion and subsequent maintenance of the heritage language.

Although some HL programs and instructors are beginning to implement the models, strategies, and practices described in this volume, it is important to recognize that many continue to follow old traditions, often out of habit or lack of knowledge of pedagogical trends described in recent publications (see Beaudrie 2015). In order to continue developing the HL education field, we need to adapt and accept innovative practices and to professionalize instruction.

As editors of the volume, we encourage HL practitioners to leave traditional practices behind and dare to try the innovative ideas that leading scholars in HL pedagogy so carefully present in the following chapters. We started this project with the philosophy that HL learners deserve nothing but the best instructional practices and that we can achieve these only when we question our current practices through reflection and critical examination of existing research with the goal of finding common ground that benefits not only students but also teachers, administrators, and the HL field as a whole. We predict that the field of HL education will continue to grow exponentially, and we thank each of the contributors to this volume for leading the way with their truly exceptional contributions.

REFERENCES

Balestra, Alejandra, Glenn A. Martínez, and María I. Moyna. 2008. *Recovering the US Hispanic Linguistic Heritage: Sociohistorical Approaches to Spanish in the United States*. Houston, TX: Arte Público Press.

Beaudrie, Sara M. 2015. "Approaches to Language Variation: Goals and Objectives of the Spanish Heritage Language Syllabus." *Heritage Language Journal* 1, no. 1: 1–21.

Beaudrie, Sara M., Cynthia Ducar, and Kimberly Potowski. 2014. *Heritage Language Teaching: Research and Practice*. New York: McGraw-Hill.

Beaudrie, Sara M., and Marta Fairclough, eds. 2012. *Spanish as a Heritage Language in the United States: The State of the Field*. Washington, DC: Georgetown University Press.

Carreira, Maria, and Olga Kagan. 2011. "The Results of the National Heritage Language Survey: Implications for Teaching, Curriculum Design, and Professional Development." *Foreign Language Annals* 44, no. 1: 40–64.

Clachar, Arlene. 2005. "Creole English Speakers' Treatment of Tense-Aspect Morphology in English Interlanguage Written Discourse." *Language Learning* 55, no. 2: 275–334. http://dx.doi.org/10.1111/j.0023-8333.2005.00305.x.

Draper, Jamie B., and June H. Hicks. 2000. "Where We've Been, What We've Learned." In *Teaching Heritage Language Learners: Voices from the Classroom*, ed. John Webb and Barbara Miller, 15–35. New York: American Council on the Teaching of Foreign Languages.

Fairclough, Marta. 2005. *Spanish and Heritage Language Education in the United States: Struggling with Hypotheticals*. Madrid, Frankfurt: Iberoamericana Libros and Vervuert.

Fishman, Joshua. 1964. "Language Maintenance and Language Shift as a Field of Inquiry: A Definition of the Field and Suggestions for Its Further Development." *Linguistics* 2, no. 9: 32–70. http://dx.doi.org/10.1515/ling.1964.2.9.32.

———.2001. "300-Plus Years of Heritage Language Education in the United States." In *Heritage Languages in America: Preserving a National Resource*, ed. Joy Kreeft Peyton, Donald A. Ranard, and Scott McGinnis, 81–99. Washington, DC: Center for Applied Linguistics.

———. 2014. "Three Hundred-Plus Years of Heritage Language Education in the United States." In *Handbook of Heritage, Community, and Native American Languages in the United States*, ed. Terrence Wiley, Joy Kreeft Peyton, Donna Christian, Sarah K. Moore, and Na Liu, 36–44. New York: Routledge. http://dx.doi.org/10.4324/9780203122419.ch4.

Freire, Paulo. 1970a. "Cultural Action and Conscientization." *Harvard Educational Review* 40, no. 3: 452–477.

———. 1970b. *The Pedagogy of the Oppressed*. New York: Herder and Herder.

García, Ofelia. 2005. "Positioning Heritage Languages in the United States." *Modern Language Journal* 89:601–5.

Giroux, Henry A. 1991. "Postmodernism as Border Pedagogy." In *Postmodernism, Feminism, and Cultural Politics: Redrawing Educational Boundaries*, edited by Henry A. Giroux, ch. 8. Albany: State University of New York Press.

Glisan, Eileen, W. J. Phillips, H. Allen, A. Abbott, and T. Sauer. 2010. "The Lost C: The Communities Goal Area." Paper delivered at the American Council on the Teaching of Foreign Languages Conference, Boston, MA, November 19–21.

Hornberger, Nancy, ed. 2005. "Heritage/Community Language Education: US and Australian Perspectives." Special issue *International Journal of Bilingual Education and Bilingualism* 8, no. 2–3.

Hornberger, Nancy H., and Shuhan C. Wang. 2008. "Who Are Our Heritage Language Learners? Identity and Biliteracy in Heritage Language Education in the United States." In *Heritage Language Education: A New Field Emerging*, ed. Donna Brinton, Olga Kagan, and Susan Bauckus, 3–35. New York: Routledge.

Hulstijn, Jan. 2011. "Language Proficiency in Native and Nonnative Speakers: An Agenda for Research and Suggestions for Second-Language Assessment." *Language Assessment Quarterly* 8, no. 3: 229–49. http://dx.doi.org/10.1080/15434303.2011.565844.

———. 2012. "The Construct of Language Proficiency in the Study of Bilingualism from a Cognitive Perspective." *Bilingualism: Language and Cognition* 15, no. 2: 422–33. http://dx.doi.org/10.1017/S1366728911000678.

Kagan, Olga. 2005. "In Support of a Proficiency-Based Definition of Heritage Language Learners: The Case of Russian." *International Journal of Bilingual Education and Bilingualism* 8, no. 2–3: 213–221.

Kagan, Olga, and Maria Carreira. 2015. "Teaching Heritage Languages. Approaches and Strategies." ACTFL Webinar. January 28.

Maranville, Steven. 1992. "Entrepreneurship in the Business Curriculum." *Journal of Education for Business* 68, no. 1: 27–31. http://dx.doi.org/10.1080/08832323.1992.10117582.

Martínez, Glenn. 2010. "Medical Spanish for Heritage Learners: A Prescription to Improve the Health of Spanish-Speaking Communities." Cambridge Scholars Publishing in association with GSE Research. *Building Communities and Making Connections* 2, no. 15: 2–15. http://dx.doi.org/10.5848/CSP.2022.00001.

Nussbaum, Martha C. 2011. *Creating Capabilities: The Human Development Approach*. Cambridge, MA: Belknap Press of Harvard University Press. http://dx.doi.org/10.4159/harvard.9780674061200.

Parra, María Luisa. 2013. "Expanding Language and Cultural Competence in Advanced Heritage- and Foreign-Language Learners through Community Engagement and Work with the Arts." *Heritage Language Journal* 10, no. 2: 255–80. http://www.heritagelanguages.org/.

Polinsky, Maria, and Olga Kagan. 2007. "Heritage Languages: In the 'Wild' and in the Classroom." *Language and Linguistics Compass* 1, no. 5: 368–95. http://dx.doi.org/10.1111/j.1749-818X.2007.00022.x.

Potowski, Kim, ed. 2010. *Language Diversity in the USA*. New York: Cambridge University Press. http://dx.doi.org/10.1017/CBO9780511779855.

Ryan, Camille. 2013. "Language Use in the United States: 2011." American Community Language Survey Reports. Available at http://www.census.gov/prod/2013pubs/acs-22.pdf.

Schmidt, Richard. 1992. "Awareness and Second Language Acquisition." *Annual Review of Applied Linguistics* 13:206–26. http://dx.doi.org/10.1017/S0267190500002476.

Sen, Amartya. 1992. *Inequality Re-Examined*. Cambridge, MA: Harvard University Press.

———. 2000. *Development as Freedom*. New York: Anchor Books.

Siegel, Jeff. 2010. *Second Dialect Acquisition*. Cambridge: Cambridge University Press. http://dx.doi.org/10.1017/CBO9780511777820.

UCLA. 2001. *Heritage Language Research Priorities Conference Report*. Los Angeles: University of California, Los Angeles. Available: www.cal.org/heritage.

Valdes, Guadalupe. 1997. "The Teaching of Spanish to Bilingual Spanish-Speaking Students: Outstanding Issues and Unanswered Questions." In *La enseñanza del español a hispanohablantes: Praxis y teoría*, ed. M.C. Colombí y F.X. Alarcón, 8–44. Boston: Houghton Mifflin.

———. 2000. "Introduction." In *AATSP Professional Development Series Handbook for Teachers K–16: Spanish for Native Speakers*, 1–20. Fort Worth, TX: Harcourt.

———. 2001. "Heritage Language Students: Profiles and Possibilities." In *Heritage Languages in America: Preserving a National Resource*, ed. Joy Kreeft Peyton, Donald Ranard, and Scott McGinnis, 37–77. Washington, DC: Center for Applied Linguistics.

Van Deusen-Scholl, Nelleke. 2003. "Toward a Definition of Heritage Language: Sociopolitical and Pedagogical Considerations." *Journal of Language, Identity, and Education* 2, no. 3: 211–30. http://dx.doi.org/10.1207/S15327701JLIE0203_4.

Veltman, Calvin. 1983. *Language Shift in the United States*. Berlin: Mouton. http://dx.doi.org/10.1515/9783110824001.

Vygotsky, Lev. S. 1978. *Mind in Society: The Development of Higher Psychological Processes*. Cambridge, MA: Harvard University Press.

Wiley, Terrence. 2001. "On Defining Heritage Languages and Their Speakers." In *Heritage Languages in America: Preserving a National Resource*, ed. Joy Kreeft Peyton,

Donald Ranard, and Scott McGinnis, 29–36. Washington, DC: Center for Applied Linguistics.

Wiley, Terrence, Joy Kreeft Peyton, Donna Christian, Sarah K. Moore, and Na Liu, eds. 2014. *Handbook of Heritage, Community, and Native American Languages in the United States*. New York: Routledge.

Wolfram, Walt, and Natalie Schilling-Estes. 2006. *American English: Dialects and Variation*. 2nd ed. Malden, MA: Blackwell.

Wu, Ming-Hsuan, and Zhu-Min Chang. 2010. "Heritage Language Teaching and Learning through a Macro Approach." *Working Papers in Educational Linguistics* 25, no. 2: 23–33.

Part I

Foundations in Heritage Language Teaching

Essential Notions in Curricula, Teacher, and Program Development

1

Toward a Prototype Model of the Heritage Language Learner

Understanding Strengths and Needs

Eve Zyzik
UNIVERSITY OF CALIFORNIA, SANTA CRUZ

The difficulty of defining and characterizing the heritage speaker has been duly acknowledged in a wide range of scholarly publications with both theoretical and pedagogical motivations. This problem of definition is not unique to the heritage language (HL) context. In similar fashion, there continues to be debate about the criteria for defining the native speaker, with questions centering on whether a categorical distinction between the native speaker and the native user can be upheld (see Davies 2013). Establishing the criteria for group membership (e.g., being a native speaker of language X) is inherently problematic when there is variability within the group. Although we might be tempted to think of native speakers as constituting a homogeneous group—that is, as having the same mental grammar—research has begun to emphasize important differences among native speakers stemming from levels of formal education (see Dąbrowska 2012). In the HL bilingual context, the variability within the group is far greater than among monolingual native speakers (de Swart 2013; Rothman and Treffers-Daller 2014).

The goal of this chapter is to move beyond definitions in order to better understand the varied population of heritage speakers who, in the academic context, become HL learners. Traditionally, this variability has been presented on a bilingual continuum: monolinguals of language A and language B represent the two extremes, and HL learners are situated somewhere in between, depending on their relative strength (i.e., dominance) in both languages (Valdés 2001, 2005). An alternative way of understanding the diversity of HL learners is to situate the HL learner in a category that exhibits prototype effects. This view of categorization is well known in cognitive psychology (e.g., Rosch 1975) and is a fundamental tenet in cognitive linguistics (e.g., Taylor 2003). In the prototype model of categorization, a given category can have fuzzy boundaries and be internally graded, meaning that some members are more typical or central to the category than others. For example, it has been shown that "chair" and "sofa" are better representatives of the category "furniture" than are "telephone" or "lamp." Instead of defining a concept based on a set of discrete and necessary features, category membership is determined by approximation to the prototype. In the realm of linguistic description, Taylor (2015) suggests that the prototype model could be applied to elusive notions such as "native speaker" and "bilingual speaker." In fact, Escudero and Sharwood Smith (2001) developed a preliminary definition of "native speaker" along these lines by considering both prototypical and peripheral features. The prototype model holds promise for understanding the notion of HL learner as well. In such a model we dispense with comparing the HL learner to the monolingual speaker or to the second language (L2) learner; instead the HL learner is understood in relation to a central member of the category.

In constructing the prototype, a logical starting point is to examine the various attributes that have been proposed in existing definitions. My review of existing definitions in oft-cited publications, both classic and more recent (e.g., Benmamoun, Montrul, and Polinsky 2013; Polinsky 2015; Polinsky and Kagan 2007; Rothman and Treffers-Daller 2014; Valdés 2001; Van Deusen-Scholl 2003), reveals the following recurring attributes of HL learners:

- Early exposure to the heritage language in the home
- Proficiency in the heritage language
- Bilingual to some degree
- Dominant in a language other than the heritage language
- Ethnic/cultural connection to the heritage language

Among the aforementioned attributes, proficiency is particularly salient: it has been emphasized in all narrow definitions, thus excluding learners with a "heritage motivation" (Van Deusen-Scholl 2003, 222) but no functional ability in the language. Nevertheless, proficiency is by itself a poor predictor of group membership; there are many proficient speakers of a language who are not HL learners. In fact, L2 learners can match or surpass HL learners on standardized measures of proficiency (see discussion below). Thus, we need an attribute that can serve to differentiate HL learners from other types of proficient speakers. In this chapter, I outline a prototype model of the HL learner that includes the attribute of implicit knowledge. Implicit knowledge has received relatively little attention in the field of HL pedagogy but has become increasingly important in experimental research (e.g., Montrul et al. 2014). Understanding the HL learner from the perspective of implicit knowledge can also clarify why certain pedagogical methods and materials originally designed for the L2 classroom may not be easily transferable to the HL context.

CORE ISSUES: PROFICIENCY AND IMPLICIT KNOWLEDGE

Proficiency

Proficiency has figured prominently in descriptions of HL learners although the construct has been vaguely defined or simply assumed. Wu and Ortega (2013) explain that proficiency can be defined either broadly or narrowly. In the realm of standardized testing such as the ACTFL oral proficiency interview (OPI), proficiency is understood broadly as functional language ability, or "what individuals can do with language in terms of speaking, writing, listening, and reading in real-world situations in a spontaneous and non-rehearsed context" (ACTFL 2012, 3). In contrast, in research on L2 and HL acquisition, proficiency is generally defined in a narrow sense, that is, focusing on basic linguistic abilities (e.g., vocabulary and/or grammatical knowledge) rather than the full spectrum of communicative competence.

To complicate matters further, the ways in which proficiency has been measured for research purposes varies widely among studies and often differs from proficiency assessment for pedagogical purposes. For example, research on HL learners has used a variety of proficiency measures, including cloze tests (see Montrul and Foote 2014), speech rate (see Polinsky 2008), vocabulary knowledge (see Fairclough 2011; Polinsky 2006), elicited imitation (see Wu and Ortega 2013), and picture naming (see Montrul et al. 2014). In the pedagogical context, many studies report learners' self-assessments of proficiency, sometimes in combination with a test of oral proficiency such as the ACTFL OPI (see Kagan and Friedman 2003).

Although a theoretical discussion of proficiency is beyond the scope of this chapter (see Ilieva and Clark's chapter in this volume [2016]), there are recent definitions of this construct that are particularly appealing for understanding the nature of HL learners. Jan Hulstijn (2011, 2012, 2015) sets out to understand proficiency in both first language (L1) and L2 populations by drawing a distinction between basic-level cognition (BLC) and higher-level cognition (HLC). In Hulstijn's view, BLC is limited to listening and speaking (it does not comprise reading or writing) and subsumes all the high-frequency lexical items and frequent grammatical constructions that are used in routine, everyday conversations. More precisely, BLC consists of three components (Hulstijn 2011, 230):

1. The largely implicit, unconscious knowledge in the domains of phonetics, prosody, phonology, morphology, and syntax;
2. The largely explicit, conscious knowledge in the lexical domain (form–meaning mappings); and
3. The automaticity with which these types of knowledge can be processed.

In contrast, HLC is the extension of BLC: it includes low-frequency vocabulary, uncommon morphosyntax, grammatically (more) complex sentences, and it comprises written discourse. Hulstijn emphasizes that native speakers display large individual differences in HLC in accordance with their intellectual skills, education, professional careers, and leisure-time activities. In contrast, BLC is the language knowledge shared by all native speakers regardless of their educational backgrounds or cultural profiles. Hulstijn (2011) further argues many established proficiency scales (e.g., the Common European Framework of Reference, or CEFR) are, at the higher levels, inseparable from HLC. As a consequence, the higher levels of proficiency (B2, C1, and C2 on the CEFR scale) can only be attained by individuals with higher levels of education.

Hulstijn's (2011, 2012) discussion of proficiency does not make specific reference to HL learners although the applicability is rather straightforward: the prototypical HL learner's language proficiency is limited to BLC. It is precisely in this sense that HL learners *are* native speakers because BLC is what all native speakers have in common (see Rothman and Treffers-Daller 2014 for additional arguments in favor of considering HL learners as native speakers). If this is on the right track, we can predict that HL learners might be very similar to native speakers if tested with conceptually simple oral/listening tasks involving highly frequent linguistic units. Taking the comparison a step further, we might predict that HL learners' performance on a range of tasks will be comparable to native speakers who have limited formal education and do not use written language in their daily lives.[1] For most native speakers, however, BLC is only a part of their overall language proficiency (Hulstijn 2011) while for HL learners it is typically the only component.

Recent research on the ACTFL OPI supports this line of reasoning: higher-level ratings (e.g., Superior) are related to and perhaps contingent on formal education in the language of testing. Elvira Swender and colleagues (2014) analyzed the language samples of Russian and Spanish heritage speakers who took the OPI, finding similar trends in both groups. The speakers rated as Advanced could not reach the Superior level due to the limitations in the following areas: (a) inability to deal with the topic abstractly, support an opinion, and/or hypothesize; (b) lack of extended discourse; and (c) lack of precise vocabulary. Speaking about a topic from an abstract perspective posed a considerable challenge for many of the participants: "When prompted to speak about topics beyond self and their immediate environment, e.g., health policy, environmental issues, technology, or politics, the participants tended to revert to personal experiences" (437). Swender and colleagues also compared the participants' OPI ratings with individual characteristics such as language use at home and formal instruction in the heritage language. This analysis suggests a relationship between explicit/formal instruction in the heritage language at the college level, reading and writing in the heritage language, and higher levels of proficiency (see also Ilieva and Clark's chapter in this volume [2016]).

The results of Swender and colleagues (2014) can be understood in reference to HLC, a component of language proficiency that is developed primarily as a result of language use in academic and professional contexts (Hulstijn 2011). Consider the task of discussing issues (e.g., raising the federal minimum wage; building a desalination plant) from an abstract perspective, which is one of the hallmarks of Superior-level proficiency on the ACTFL scale. Dealing with such topics abstractly implies both being informed about the topic and being able to conceptualize the issues from a number of competing viewpoints—that is, understanding the opposing sides in a debate. Arguably, the ability to speak about issues abstractly is not only a matter of linguistic ability but also taps intellectual skills. Margaret Malone and colleagues (2003) underscore this point in their discussion of Superior-level proficiency: "Language alone is not sufficient to achieve a high level of proficiency; high-level speakers must also possess high-level academic skills typical of those of an educated person in the target culture" (4). Thus, although the OPI purports to measure functional language ability "regardless of where, when, or how the language was acquired" (ACTFL 2012, 3), an important caveat is in order: attaining a Superior rating is unlikely without some combination of formal education and literacy in the language of testing.

To summarize, the preceding discussion reveals that the speaker's academic background plays a nontrivial role in attaining higher-level proficiency. In practice, what this means is that HL learners and L2 learners can be matched in proficiency, giving the impression of comparable linguistic ability. In some cases, an L2 learner may even outperform a HL learner on a proficiency test that includes HLC tasks (e.g., discussing an issue from an abstract perspective). Hulstijn (2011) explains that L2 learners are capable of acquiring HLC in their second language just like native speakers (yet he questions whether L2 learners can ever fully acquire BLC in their second language). Although proficiency assessments are certainly useful and necessary in some contexts, they likely obscure important differences between the linguistic ability of HL learners and L2 learners.

Implicit and Explicit Knowledge

There is broad consensus that L1 acquisition is primarily an implicit process, meaning that children learn the structural properties of their native language without a conscious intention to learn them and without awareness of what they have acquired. The type of knowledge that underlies native speakers' ability to comprehend and produce language in spontaneous situations is considered implicit. Recall that Hulstijn (2011) makes reference to implicit knowledge in his definition of BLC. According to Rod Ellis (2005), implicit knowledge is procedural, unconscious, and involves automatic processing. Furthermore, implicit knowledge is verbalizable only under certain circumstances, that is, when it is made explicit. In other words, any attempt to verbalize what one knows implicitly will involve first forming an explicit representation of it. In contrast, explicit knowledge involves conscious awareness and controlled processing. Explicit knowledge is declarative in nature (i.e., composed of facts about the language) and is potentially verbalizable. Crucially, it is possible to verbalize one's conscious knowledge about language without the use of technical terms or metalanguage (e.g., verb, past tense). In other words, metalanguage is a secondary and nonessential component of explicit knowledge (Ellis 2004).

The dichotomy between implicit and explicit knowledge, as well as the question of an interface between these two types of knowledge, is a fundamental topic in the field of second language acquisition (see Ellis 2011; Rebuschat 2013). Surprisingly, little attention has been paid to HL learners in this context. The overarching goal of research on the linguistic competence of HL learners has been on documenting *what* HL learners know rather than *how* they know it. This latter question (how) has been largely overlooked, with the exception of a few studies that examine which type of knowledge—implicit and/or explicit—contributes to HL learners' performance on different types of tasks.

Melissa Bowles (2011) included HL learners of Spanish in her replication study of Ellis (2005), who had previously proposed different tasks for measuring implicit and explicit knowledge. Bowles compared the performance of HL learners, L2 learners, and native speakers on five tasks: an elicited imitation task, an oral narration, a timed grammaticality judgment task (GJT), an untimed GJT, and a test of metalinguistic knowledge. The comparison between the L2 learners and HL learners is especially revealing in that these two groups showed opposite patterns of performance on the five tasks. Specifically, the L2 group registered the highest scores on tests that were designed to tap explicit knowledge: the untimed GJT and the metalinguistic knowledge test. In contrast, the HL learners fared much better on tests that measured implicit knowledge (the oral narration, oral imitation, and timed GJT). The only test on which the HL learners showed a significant disadvantage vis-à-vis the L2 learners was the metalinguistic knowledge test. It should be noted that the metalinguistic knowledge test required participants to apply grammatical concepts such as finite verb, subject pronoun, auxiliary verb, and indefinite article. Evidently, this type of test proved difficult even for the native speakers, whose mean score (77 percent) was much lower than their scores on the remaining tasks (all above 95 percent).

That HL learners have limited metalinguistic knowledge regarding their heritage language should not be surprising. Nevertheless, Bowles (2011) highlights that, despite their relatively poor performance on the test of metalinguistic knowledge, HL learners were very successful at the oral narration task (mean score: above 95 percent). This outcome is consistent with the hypothesis that HL learners have primarily implicit knowledge of their HL, which has little or no relation to the specific type of explicit knowledge needed to recognize metalinguistic terminology. Additional evidence comes from a study by Maite Correa (2011), who compared HL learners and L2 learners of Spanish with respect to their metalinguistic knowledge and accuracy of use of the subjunctive.[2] The results indicate that, at all levels of instruction, HL learners outperform L2 learners in their accuracy of the subjunctive. The exact opposite pattern is observed for metalinguistic knowledge: L2 learners outperform HL learners at all levels. Moreover, there was a large and significant relationship between metalinguistic knowledge and accuracy of use of the subjunctive for the L2 learners. In contrast, for the HL learner groups, metalinguistic knowledge and subjunctive accuracy sometimes yielded a negative (nonsignificant) correlation.

Taken together, the studies by Bowles (2011) and Correa (2011) suggest that HL learners' knowledge is primarily implicit in nature, which is a consequence of having acquired the language naturalistically in early childhood. Having implicit knowledge gives HL learners certain advantages over L2 learners, which are maximized on oral/aural tasks as well as on tasks with an element of time pressure. For example, Silvina Montrul and colleagues (2014) demonstrated that HL learners of Spanish patterned differently from L2 learners on an implicit task that measured sensitivity to gender agreement violations. Although HL learners have advantages over L2 learners on implicit tasks, the opposite holds true on tasks that maximize explicit knowledge and metalinguistic awareness. These findings echo Montrul's (2009, 250) earlier statement that "early bilinguals [HL learners] appear to make substantially less use of explicit and metalinguistic knowledge than the adult L2 learners."

As a consequence, HL learners are at a disadvantage when exposed to materials that are intended to teach grammar to L2 learners, especially if such instruction relies heavily on students' metalinguistic awareness. Kim Potowski and colleagues (2009) compared HL learners and L2 learners who had been exposed to a pedagogical intervention of either traditional output-based instruction or processing instruction that targeted the Spanish past subjunctive. Both instructional treatments included a component with metalinguistic information about the target structure (i.e., how to form the past subjunctive, where to locate it in the sentence, and when to use it). Their findings indicate that the L2 learners outperformed the HL learners overall and, moreover, that only the L2 learners showed improvement in their grammaticality judgments. Thus, despite some modest improvement in the HL learner group after the instructional treatments, Potowski and colleagues suggest that HL learners may respond better to alternative methods that explicitly contrast competing forms.

More recently, Julio Torres (2013) investigated how HL learners and L2 learners respond to a task-based pedagogical intervention. The subjunctive in adjectival clauses was targeted through simple and complex tasks that engaged participants in explaining the behavior of students living in a university dorm. The task included images, written prompts, and corrective feedback but no metalinguistic information (unlike the study of Potowski et al. [2009]). The results of the study mirror those of Potowksi and colleagues in that L2 learners showed greater improvement, as measured by gain scores, than HLs overall. In addition, Torres documents that these two groups of learners approached the task in very different ways. The L2 learners were more focused on form and recognized that the task presented contrasting forms of the subjunctive and indicative. In contrast, the HL learners were oriented primarily to the content of the task; they were concerned with interpreting the meaning of the prompts and made no metalinguistic comments in the exit questionnaire. In short, it seems that HL learners processed the input provided by the task as authentic content rather than directing their attention to establishing new form–meaning connections.

To conclude, the existing research on the effects of grammatical instruction strongly suggests that the methods and materials originally designed for L2 learners are unlikely to provide the same kind of benefit to HL learners. This has to do with the nature of the grammatical activities themselves, which assume some experience with the study of language as a formal system. In other words, grammar activities designed for L2 learners draw heavily on explicit knowledge even in the absence of metalanguage. Classroom L2 learners are intimately familiar with exercises that ask them to fill in the blanks, transform sentences from one type to another, and replace underlined forms. Even if such mechanical activities are redesigned as meaningful or communicative (see VanPatten 1998), L2 learners are accustomed to completing them with the goal of applying previously learned vocabulary or grammar. This is perhaps why the L2 learners in Torres's (2013) study seemed predisposed to noticing differences in form (e.g., subjunctive versus indicative) in what was otherwise a communicative task. In contrast, HL learners who have primarily implicit knowledge will take a communicative task at face value, that is, as an opportunity to communicate a message using any combination of grammar and vocabulary they have at their disposal.

A PROTOTYPE MODEL OF THE HL LEARNER

Following the discussion of proficiency and implicit knowledge, we can revisit the attributes listed in the introduction in order to construct a prototype of the HL learner category. First, the attribute of proficiency is refined by limiting proficiency to what Hulstijn (2011) has labeled BLC. Second, we add the attribute of implicit knowledge to the prototype, which serves to differentiate HL learners from other types of proficient bilinguals. The remaining

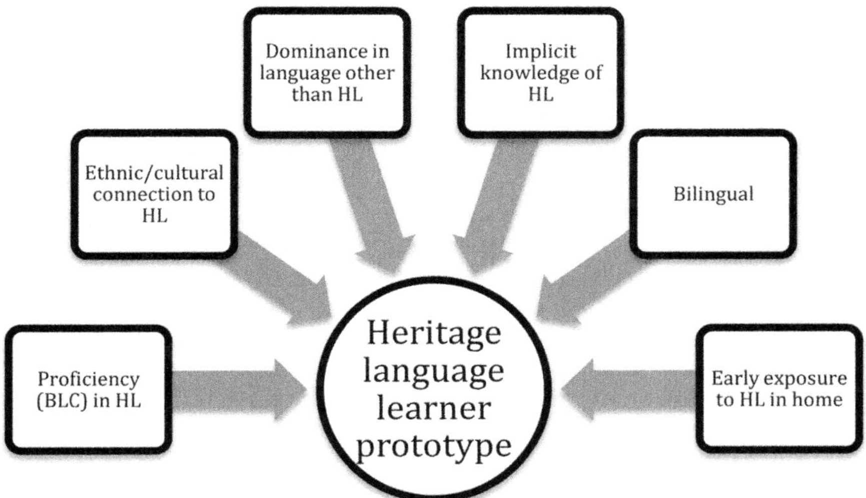

Figure 1.1. Prototype Model of Heritage Language Learner

attributes from previous scholarly work are included in the prototype, as shown in figure 1.1.

It should be noted that the individual attributes in figure 1.1 are scalar or gradient. Even those attributes that may seem categorical, such as early exposure to the heritage language in the home, are a matter of degree. For example, Tamar Gollan and colleagues (2015) recently demonstrated that language ability among young heritage speakers is positively correlated with the number of different speakers who regularly address them in the heritage language (also known as the "number-of-speakers effect"). Although early exposure to the heritage language could be framed as a dichotomous (yes/no) question, this would not capture the degree of exposure to the heritage language, which can be quantified with various metrics (e.g., number of hours the heritage language is spoken per week, percentage of time that adults in the home speak the heritage language). Likewise, language dominance is often stated in categorical terms (e.g., an individual is dominant in X language), but recent research emphasizes that dominance should be understood as a continuum (see Gertken, Amengual, and Birdsong 2014). For example, although an HL learner and an L2 learner may both be English dominant, the degree of English dominance may be greater for the L2 learner. This could be ascertained with a language-dominance questionnaire such as the Bilingual Language Profile (Birdsong et al. 2012), which measures dominance on four dimensions: language history, use, proficiency, and attitudes. Finally, what I have labeled as ethnic/cultural connection in figure 1.1 is actually a cluster of sociocultural variables that include attitudes, motivation, and social and ethnic identity. Research on the sociocultural dimensions of HL learning has emphasized that these attributes are not static or monolithic but rather emerge from interactions and social practice (see He 2006, 2010).

Let us consider examples of learners who are distant from the prototype. Beaudrie (2009b) describes a group of receptive bilinguals of Spanish who frequently overheard Spanish growing up but had relatively few opportunities to participate directly in conversations with Spanish-speaking relatives. These learners can produce sufficient language to engage in basic, everyday conversation (Novice–high level on ACTFL scale). Moreover, these learners express a significant cultural and personal connection to Spanish (90 percent of them agreed or strongly agreed that Spanish is an important part of who they are). The prototype model accommodates these receptive bilinguals but places them on the periphery. Even further removed from the prototype are the overhearers studied by Terry Kit-Fong Au and colleagues (2002); these are individuals who had minimal exposure to Spanish growing up and are currently "virtually monolingual in the majority language" (242). Another example of a learner who is far removed from the prototype is the fictional profile of "Robert" described by Erin Boon and Maria Polinsky (2014): Robert grew up in an English-speaking family in Atlanta but retains some of the Spanish he learned as a child from his nanny. Clearly, someone like Robert will have a lesser degree of personal and cultural connection to Spanish than a prototypical heritage speaker. Finally, we should mention the case of late arrivals such as "Luisa," who is described in María Carreira's 2004 work: Luisa was born in Argentina and arrived in the United States at age fourteen; she speaks only Spanish at home, reads and writes Spanish at grade level, and does not speak English well. Luisa is certainly a peripheral member of the heritage speaker category because she is described as Spanish dominant. Nevertheless, in the US university context, learners such as Luisa often enroll in courses for heritage language learners despite having a very different profile from the prototypical HL learner.

There are many advantages to the prototype model of categorization shown in figure 1.1. It shows that the HL learner, although difficult to define in terms of sufficient and necessary characteristics, can be understood as exhibiting a cluster of attributes. Crucially, an individual need not manifest each and every one of these attributes in order to belong to the category. However, an individual that displays all of the attributes in figure 1.1 is seen as the "best" example of the category. Collectively, these attributes serve to profile the prototypical heritage speaker and at the same time recognize that membership in the category is a matter of degree. Finally, some attributes might be viewed as more heavily weighted, meaning that their presence is a fairly reliable predictor of category membership. I have argued in this chapter that having fairly robust implicit knowledge (combined with minimal explicit knowledge) is a good diagnostic for HL learners because it distinguishes them from L2 learners.[3] Nevertheless, HL learners at the lower ends of the proficiency spectrum (e.g., receptive bilinguals) may also have limited implicit knowledge, as evidenced by lower accuracy and higher variability in their linguistic intuitions (see Sherkina-Lieber, Perez-Leroux, and Johns 2011). Again, these speakers would be situated on the outer edges of the HL learner category.

PRACTICAL CONSIDERATIONS AND EXAMPLES FOR THE CLASSROOM

Pedagogical Implications

There are two main pedagogical implications for HL learners stemming from the preceding discussion. The first is that materials designed originally for teaching grammar (syntax and morphology) to a population of L2 learners will have limited applicability to the HL classroom. This is because L2 materials usually capitalize on L2 learners' explicit knowledge of the language. When the same materials are used with HL learners, whose knowledge of the language is primarily implicit, the results are less than desirable. In the best-case scenario, HL learners simply do not benefit as much from these activities as a group of L2 learners would (see Potowski et al. 2009; Torres 2013). In the worst case, HL learners become confused by explicit grammatical explanations about aspects of the language they already know implicitly (see Beaudrie 2009a).

The second pedagogical implication is that L2 methods and materials targeting vocabulary will be readily transferrable to the HL context. This hypothesis stems from the nature of vocabulary knowledge, which is largely explicit. Hulstijn (2011) makes this point clearly in his definition of BLC, noting that proficiency includes the explicit knowledge of form–meaning mappings. Although some aspects of vocabulary representation are implicit (see Elgort and Warren 2014), Ewa Dąbrowska (2014) explains that knowledge of word meaning is clearly explicit: "native speakers not only know what words like *cat* or *sit* mean; they also know that they know and are able to provide a rough definition" (207). If vocabulary knowledge is explicit for all speakers (including HL learners), L2 vocabulary research can provide valuable direction for the HL context.

An immediate question that arises is why vocabulary should merit attention in the HL learner classroom. Most practitioners who work in the HL context will concur with Kagan and Friedman (2003) that HL learners have "an extensive everyday vocabulary" (536). Marta Fairclough (2011) demonstrated that a yes/no vocabulary test based on 5,000 high-frequency words proved too easy for most Spanish HL learners. The HL learners in the Fairclough study significantly outperformed L2 learners, recognizing nearly double the number of words (the mean for the HL learner group was 103.51 words, compared to 54.77 for the L2 learners). Fairclough concluded that most HL learners already have a highly developed receptive vocabulary at the 5,000-word level. Thus, both classroom-based observations and research identify vocabulary as one of HL learners' strengths.

Although having receptive knowledge of the core vocabulary (5,000 words) in any language will put HL learners at an immediate advantage over most L2 learners, it does not entail productive use of vocabulary beyond the mid-frequency range. Indeed, one of the recurring themes in the data presented by Swender and colleagues (2014) is that of the HL learners' limited vocabulary and, more specifically, the lack of precise vocabulary. Limited vocabulary was a major hurdle for speakers rated at the Intermediate level: all of them lacked the vocabulary to sustain conversations on topics beyond their everyday experience. At the Advanced-Low or Advanced-Mid level, limited vocabulary impeded the speakers' ability to handle topics abstractly (this was true for 77 percent of the Spanish HL learners). In practice, this means that HL learner courses should include systematic attention to vocabulary beyond the mid-frequency range—that is, vocabulary that HL learners are less likely to know.[4] In addition to simply learning more words (i.e., breadth of knowledge), vocabulary instruction tailored to HL learners should focus on improving depth of vocabulary knowledge. The ability to use a word productively involves many layers of knowledge beyond the primary form–meaning link. In what follows, I provide specific pedagogical suggestions for addressing lexical development in the HL learner classroom.

Examples for the Classroom

I. S. P. Nation (2001) provides a well-known framework for understanding the incremental nature of learning vocabulary in a second language, distinguishing between knowledge of word form, word meaning, and word use. These different dimensions of "knowing a word" also take into account the difference between receptive and productive knowledge. Many HL learners have partial knowledge of words, which means that they will not necessarily be able to use those words productively in the appropriate context. For example, consider the word *altivo* ("arrogant"): a HL learner might know this word has negative meaning but have no ability to use the word in a sentence. The focus of instruction should be on the meaning of the word in relation to other words the HL learner already knows (e.g., *orgulloso*, "proud") and also on collocations (e.g., *actitud altiva*, "arrogant attitude"). Another complementary approach is to draw the learner's attention to word parts (*alto*, "high" is the root) and highlight the relation to other, related words with the same root (e.g., *altanero*, "arrogant"). Teaching vocabulary for depth of knowledge means building on HL learners' strengths, specifically their knowledge of related (more generic or more frequent) words.

The approach described above should not be interpreted as simply recommending a good dictionary or thesaurus to HL learners. I am suggesting a much more comprehensive and systematic approach in order to develop the "expanded level of precise, sophisticated vocabulary" (439) mentioned by Swender and colleagues (2014). The target vocabulary may appear initially in written texts, but it cannot be assumed that learners will acquire these words incidentally. Although vocabulary acquisition does occur from reading, many L2 studies have shown that the "pick-up" rate of new words is relatively low and, more importantly, that incidental learning usually doesn't lead to productive mastery of the new words (see Schmitt 2008 for an overview). This calls for a combined approach of exposure through texts reinforced with intentional learning tasks, which I illustrate below with specific examples from the Spanish for Heritage Speakers (SPHS) program at the University of California, Santa Cruz.

In this SPHS program, which consists of a three-quarter sequence, HL learners read several authentic novels. One of the first novels is *Aura* by Carlos Fuentes (1962), which learners read online with computerized glosses for potentially difficult vocabulary words. For example, in the first chapter of *Aura*, the word *advertencia* ("warning") is glossed. Learners can (optionally) consult the gloss if they are unsure of the meanings of this word. In class, learners work in groups to answer comprehension questions based on what they have read. Crucially, some of the target words are used in the comprehension questions. For example, one question asks: *¿Qué advertencia hay en los números de los edificios?* ("What warning is on the numbers of the buildings?"). In this way, knowing the meaning of the target word (*advertencia*) is vital to answering the question; learners are encouraged to negotiate the meaning of words while working in groups. Finally, learners complete an individual homework assignment that requires them to write original sentences with fifteen of the target words. They receive feedback on their sentences, and if any of the words are used incorrectly, they are asked to rewrite those sentences. This type of activity requires productive knowledge of the vocabulary items and allows for critical follow-up in the case of false cognates (e.g., HL learners might use *advertencia* incorrectly to mean "advertisement").

To recap, consider the type of exposure that HL learners have to potentially new vocabulary items in this instructional sequence:

1. First exposure: Incidental through reading; target words are glossed.
2. Second exposure: Postreading task with vocabulary targeted in comprehension questions.
3. Third exposure: Write original sentences with target words, demonstrating productive knowledge.

The cycle ends with the provision of feedback, which constitutes a potential fourth exposure to the target word. This type of instructional sequence is a perfect example of how incidental and intentional vocabulary learning can work in sync, which is argued by some to be the most effective way of increasing the possibility that vocabulary be learned to a productive level (Schmitt 2008).

It should be mentioned that incidental exposure followed by explicit attention to vocabulary is not limited to reading but can also take place through listening exposure. For example, in an upper-division Spanish course,[5] HL learners read the story of the Mirabal sisters as told through the testimony of Dedé Mirabal (2009). While the reading is done outside of class, students listen to segments of the audiobook in class with the goal of focusing explicitly on difficult vocabulary. For example, students are given a list of twelve words or phrases to pay attention to as they listen. They mark the words as they hear them and jot down the context in which they occurred. Subsequently, the target words are discussed in small groups or with the entire class, clarifying definitions, providing synonyms, and making note of collocations. This type of listening activity can be done prior to the assigned reading, in which case it primes learners to notice the words while reading.

Another approach that holds promise for expanding the productive vocabulary of HL learners is by targeting derivative forms and word families. N. Schmitt and C. B. Zimmerman (2002) showed that English-language learners, even those enrolled in graduate-level courses, generally do not know all members of a word family (e.g., that knowledge of an adjective like "precise" does not imply productive knowledge of the noun "precision"). The same applies to HL learners, who may be familiar with one or two members of a word family without awareness of derived forms. In particular, pedagogical materials should emphasize creating abstract nouns from adjectives and verbs (e.g. *indignado—indignación*, "indignant—indignation"), a process known as nominalization. The importance of nominalization is that it permits the expression of abstract and complex concepts, which is a hallmark of academic language (Nagy and Townsend 2012). HL learners can expand their knowledge of word families by placing target words like *exigir* ("to demand"), *exigente* ("demanding"), and *exigencia* ("a demand") into the appropriate lexical category (verb, adjective, noun). This type of sorting activity encourages learners to see derivational morphology as a tool for creating new words and is a step toward developing metalinguistic awareness.

CONCLUDING REMARKS

This chapter developed a prototype model of the HL learner in order to better understand the traits that characterize this heterogeneous group of bilinguals. I examined the construct of proficiency since it figures so prominently in all narrow definitions, but I suggested that the particular component of proficiency that is relevant to understanding the HL learner is basic language cognition (Hulstijn 2011). In addition to proficiency, I argued for including implicit knowledge in the prototype because it is this attribute that serves to distinguish HL learners from other proficient bilinguals. The pedagogical implications presented in this chapter stem directly from the discussion of implicit and explicit knowledge. Specifically, I argued that L2-geared grammatical materials and methods, which presuppose explicit knowledge, should be applied with extreme caution or not at all to the HL classroom. In contrast, the observations from L2 vocabulary research are not subject to the same restriction because of the explicit nature of vocabulary knowledge. Specific examples of activities that promote both incidental and intentional vocabulary learning were presented.

Still unanswered is the pressing question of how to approach the teaching of grammar in the HL learner classroom. In other words, if we acknowledge that L2-designed methods and materials are unlikely to bring about positive results with HL learners, what are the alternatives? Although a full treatment of this complex question is not possible in this chapter, it seems clear that grammar itself must be conceptualized as a meaning-making tool for HL learners. On this view, grammar is harnessed as a resource for expressing a particular meaning rather than a collection of discrete forms or lists of rules. In practice, this conceptualization of grammar is compatible with a content-based approach in which the teacher's grammatical interventions respond to the meanings that HL learners are trying to express. For example, students might respond in writing to a prompt that relates directly to content they are studying in class (e.g., what would happen if the minimum wage were raised to $15/hour?). If HL learners struggle in formulating their responses because of difficulties with the conditional, this might be the opportune moment for a brief grammar lesson to highlight how this particular verb form can express outcomes and consequences.[6] Metalanguage could be kept to an absolute minimum (i.e., simply label the form) while drawing learners' attention to the equivalent construction in English, the dominant language for most HL learners. The key, however, is that this focus on form (Doughty and Williams 1998) stems from a communicative need and, thus, meaning is primary.

On the separate issue of building metalinguistic knowledge, this could be targeted through the route of the dominant language. For example, HL learners could be encouraged to take a course in English pedagogical grammar, which is generally a standard part of the curriculum at universities with a TESOL or applied linguistics program. The benefit of this approach is that metalinguistic ability would be targeted separately, that is, without the simultaneous pressure of working on their skills in the heritage language. As demonstrated in Correa (2011), HL learners' metalinguistic knowledge in English and in Spanish was highly correlated. Thus, we can hypothesize that strengthening their metalinguistic ability in English would yield positive effects for subsequent grammar instruction in the heritage language. At this point, however, it remains an empirical question and a potential area for future research.

In closing, the prototype model is one way of understanding the varied population of HL learners. It does not reduce the variation within the group, nor does it minimize the complexities surrounding the HL learner experience. As Peter de Swart (2013) eloquently states, "Each heritage speaker seems to tell his own story" (256). In the prototype model, HL learners are being examined in their own right, compared to the prototype rather than to the monolingual native speaker or the L2 learner.

NOTES

I am grateful to the following individuals who assisted me in the preparation of this chapter: Mark Amengual, who provided useful comments on an earlier draft of this chapter; María Victoria González-Pagani, who shared her materials from the Spanish for Heritage Speakers program at UC Santa Cruz, which she directs; and Julio Torres, who provided me with his latest manuscript. The comments of two anonymous reviewers were also very helpful in preparing the final version of the chapter.

1. This is an important weakness of many empirical studies that compare heritage speakers to a monolingual baseline group; often the monolinguals are highly educated native speakers who use the language in professional and/or academic settings.
2. Metalinguistic knowledge was tested in both English and Spanish by means of two tests: a test of terminology and a GJT. Accuracy of use of the subjunctive was tested with five different tasks, which were later combined to provide a composite score.
3. This does not imply that L2 learners do not have implicit knowledge; L2 learners, especially those at more advanced proficiency levels, undoubtedly have unconscious knowledge about their second language. However, for most L2 learners, this implicit knowledge exists in combination with highly developed explicit knowledge.
4. In vocabulary research, the first three thousand words are considered high frequency; the level between three thousand and nine thousand is mid-frequency; words beyond nine thousand comprise the low-frequency category (Schmitt and Schmitt, 2014).
5. The course being described here is Advanced Conversation and Composition, which is not part of the SPHS sequence, but the majority of students are HL learners.
6. I offer this particular example because it reflects one of the observations made by Swender and colleagues (2014) regarding the grammatical difficulties experienced

by some of the Spanish HL learner participants, namely, the use of the past subjunctive and conditional to speculate about outcomes and consequences.

REFERENCES

ACTFL. 2012. ACTFL Proficiency Guidelines. http://www.actfl.org/sites/default/files/pdfs/ACTFLProficiencyGuidelines2012_FINAL.pdf.

Au, Terry Kit-Fong, Leah Knightly, Sun-Ah Jun, and Janet Oh. 2002. "Overhearing a Language during Childhood." *Psychological Science* 13, no. 3: 238–43. http://dx.doi.org/10.1111/1467-9280.00444.

Beaudrie, Sara. 2009a. "Receptive Bilinguals' Language Development in the Classroom: The Differential Effects of Heritage versus Foreign Language Curriculum." In *Español en Estados Unidos y otros contextos de contacto: Sociolingüística, ideología y pedagogía*, ed. Manel Lacorte and Jennifer Leeman, 325–46. Madrid: Iberoamericana / Vervuert Verlag.

———. 2009b. "Spanish Receptive Bilinguals: Understanding the Cultural and Linguistic Profile of Learners from Three Different Generations." *Spanish in Context* 6, no. 1: 85–104. http://dx.doi.org/10.1075/sic.6.1.06bea.

Benmamoun, E., S. Montrul, and M. Polinsky. 2013. "Heritage Languages and Their Speakers: Opportunities and Challenges for Linguistics." *Theoretical Linguistics* 39: 129–181.

Birdsong, David, Libby Gertken, and Mark Amengual. 2012. "Bilingual Language Profile: An Easy-to-Use Instrument to Assess Bilingualism." COERLL, University of Texas at Austin. https://sites.la.utexas.edu/bilingual/.

Boon, Erin, and Maria Polinsky. 2014. "From Silence to Voice: Empowering Heritage Language Speakers in the 21st Century." *Dickens Quarterly* 31, no. 2: 113–26.

Bowles, Melissa. 2011. "Measuring Implicit and Explicit Linguistic Knowledge: What Can Heritage Language Learners Contribute?" *Studies in Second Language Acquisition* 33, no. 2: 247–71. http://dx.doi.org/10.1017/S0272263110000756.

Carreira, María. 2004. "Seeking Explanatory Adequacy: A Dual Approach to Understanding the Term 'Heritage Language Learner.'" *Heritage Language Journal* 2, no. 1: 1–25.

Correa, Maite. 2011. "Heritage Language Learners of Spanish: What Role Does Metalinguistic Knowledge Play in Their Acquisition of the Subjunctive?" In *Selected Proceedings of the 13th Hispanic Linguistics Symposium*, ed. Luis Ortiz-López, 128–38. Somerville, MA: Cascadilla Proceedings Project.

Dąbrowska, Ewa. 2012. "Different Speakers, Different Grammars: Individual Differences in Native Language Attainment." *Linguistic Approaches to Bilingualism* 2, no. 3: 219–53. http://dx.doi.org/10.1075/lab.2.3.01dab.

———. 2014. "Implicit Lexical Knowledge." *Linguistics* 52, no. 1: 205–23. http://dx.doi.org/10.1515/ling-2013-0060.

Davies, Alan. 2013. *Native Speakers and Native Users: Loss and Gain*. Cambridge: Cambridge University Press. http://dx.doi.org/10.1017/CBO9781139022316.

de Swart, Peter. 2013. "A Single (Case) for Heritage Speakers?" *Theoretical Linguistics* 39, no. 3–4: 251–58.

Doughty, Catherine, and Jessica Williams. 1998. "Pedagogical Choices in Focus on Form." In *Focus on Form in Classroom Second Language Acquisition*, ed. Catherine Doughty and Jessica Williams, 197–261. Cambridge: Cambridge University Press.

Elgort, Irina, and Paul Warren. 2014. "L2 Vocabulary Learning from Reading: Explicit and Tacit Lexical Knowledge and the Role of Learner and Item Variables." *Language Learning* 64, no. 2: 365–414. http://dx.doi.org/10.1111/lang.12052.

Ellis, Nick. 2011. "Implicit and Explicit SLA and Their Interface." In *Implicit and Explicit Language Learning: Conditions, Processes, and Knowledge in SLA and Bilingualism*, ed. Cristina Sanz and Ron Leow, 35–47. Washington, DC: Georgetown University Press.

Ellis, Rod. 2004. "The Definition and Measurement of L2 Explicit Knowledge." *Language Learning* 54, no. 2: 227–75. http://dx.doi.org/10.1111/j.1467-9922.2004.00255.x.

———. 2005. "Measuring Implicit and Explicit Knowledge of a Second Language: A Psychometric Study." *Studies in Second Language Acquisition* 27, no. 2: 141–72. http://dx.doi.org/10.1017/S0272263105050096.

Escudero, Paola, and Michael Sharwood Smith. 2001. "Reinventing the native speaker or 'What you never wanted to know about the native speaker so never dared to ask.'" In EUROSLA Yearbook, 1, 275–86. John Benjamins Publishing Company.

Fairclough, Marta. 2011. "Testing the Lexical Recognition Task with Spanish/English Bilinguals in the United States." *Language Testing* 28, no. 2: 273–97. http://dx.doi.org/10.1177/0265532210393151.

Fuentes, Carlos. 1962. *Aura*. Mexico: Ediciones Era.

Gertken, Libby, Mark Amengual, and David Birdsong. D. 2014. "Assessing Language Dominance with the Bilingual Language Profile." In *Measuring L2 Proficiency: Perspectives from SLA*, ed. Pascale Leclercq, Amanda Edmonds, and Heather Hilton, 208–25. Bristol, UK: Multilingual Matters.

Gollan, Tamar, Jennie Starr, and Victor Ferreira. 2015. "More Than Use It or Lose It: The Number-of-Speakers Effect on Heritage Language Proficiency." *Psychonomic Bulletin & Review* 22, no. 1: 147–55. http://dx.doi.org/10.3758/s13423-014-0649-7.

He, Agnes Weiyun. 2006. "Toward an Identity Theory of the Development of Chinese as a Heritage Language." *Heritage Language Journal* 4, no. 1: 1–28.

———. 2010. "The Heart of Heritage: Socio-Cultural Dimensions of Heritage Language Learning." *Annual Review of Applied Linguistics* 30:66–82. http://dx.doi.org/10.1017/S0267190510000073.

Hulstijn, Jan. 2011. "Language Proficiency in Native and Nonnative Speakers: An Agenda for Research and Suggestions for Second-Language Assessment." *Language Assessment Quarterly* 8, no. 3: 229–49. http://dx.doi.org/10.1080/15434303.2011.565844.

———. 2012. "The Construct of Language Proficiency in the Study of Bilingualism from a Cognitive Perspective." *Bilingualism: Language and Cognition* 15, no. 2: 422–33. http://dx.doi.org/10.1017/S1366728911000678.

———. 2015. *Language Proficiency in Native and Non-Native Speakers: Theory and Research*. Amsterdam, Philadelphia: John Benjamin. http://dx.doi.org/10.1075/lllt.41.

Ilieva, Gabriela, and Beth Clark-Gareca. 2016. "Heritage Language Learner Assessment: Towards Proficiency Standards." In *Innovative Strategies for Heritage Lan-*

guage Teaching: A Practical Guide for the Classroom, ed. Marta Fairclough and Sara M. Beaudrie, 214–36. Washington, DC: Georgetown University Press.
Kagan, Olga, and Debra Friedman. 2003. "Using the OPI to Place Heritage Speakers of Russian." *Foreign Language Annals* 36: 536–545.
Malone, Margaret, Benjamin Rifkin, Donna Christian, and Dora Johnson. 2003. "Attaining High Levels of Proficiency: Challenges for Language Education in the United States." In *Proceedings Conference on Global Challenges and US Higher Education.* http://ducis.jhfc.duke.edu/archives/globalchallenges/pdf/christian%20paper.pdf.
Mirabal, Dedé. 2009. *Vivas en su jardín*. New York: Vintage Español.
Montrul, Silvina. 2009. "Reexamining the Fundamental Difference Hypothesis." *Studies in Second Language Acquisition* 31, no. 2: 225–57. http://dx.doi.org/10.1017/S0272263109090299.
Montrul, Silvina, Justin Davidson, Israel De La Fuente, and Rebecca Foote. 2014. "Early Language Experience Facilitates the Processing of Gender Agreement in Spanish Heritage Speakers." *Bilingualism: Language and Cognition* 17, no. 1: 118–38. http://dx.doi.org/10.1017/S1366728913000114.
Montrul, Silvina, and Rebecca Foote. 2014. "Age of Acquisition Interactions in Bilingual Lexical Access: A Study of the Weaker Language of L2 Learners and Heritage Speakers." *International Journal of Bilingualism* 18, no. 3: 274–303. http://dx.doi.org/10.1177/1367006912443431.
Nagy, William, and Dianna Townsend. 2012. "Words as Tools: Learning Academic Vocabulary as Language Acquisition." *Reading Research Quarterly* 47, no. 1: 91–108. http://dx.doi.org/10.1002/RRQ.011.
Nation, I. S. P. 2001. *Learning Vocabulary in Another Language*. Cambridge: Cambridge University Press.
Polinsky, Maria. 2006. "Incomplete Acquisition: American Russian." *Journal of Slavic Linguistics* 14, no. 2: 191–262.
———. 2008. "Gender under Incomplete Acquisition: Heritage Speakers' Knowledge of Noun Categorization." *Heritage Language Journal* 6, no. 1: 40–71.
———. 2015. "When L1 Becomes an L3: Do Heritage Speakers Make Better L3 Learners?" *Bilingualism: Language and Cognition* 18, no. 2: 1–16. http://dx.doi.org/10.1017/S1366728913000667.
Polinsky, Maria, and Olga Kagan. 2007. "Heritage Languages: In the "Wild" and in the Classroom." *Language and Linguistics Compass* 1, no. 5: 368–95. http://dx.doi.org/10.1111/j.1749-818X.2007.00022.x.
Potowski, Kim, Jill Jegerski, and Kara Morgan-Short. 2009. "The Effects of Instruction on Linguistic Development in Spanish Heritage Language Speakers." *Language Learning* 59, no. 3: 537–79. http://dx.doi.org/10.1111/j.1467-9922.2009.00517.x.
Rebuschat, Patrick. 2013. "Measuring Implicit and Explicit Knowledge in Second Language Research." *Language Learning* 63, no. 3: 595–626. http://dx.doi.org/10.1111/lang.12010.
Rosch, Eleanor. 1975. "Cognitive Representations of Semantic Categories." *Journal of Experimental Psychology. General* 104, no. 3: 192–233. http://dx.doi.org/10.1037/0096-3445.104.3.192.
Rothman, Jason, and Jeanine Treffers-Daller. 2014. "A Prolegomenon to the Construct of the Native Speaker: Heritage Speaker Bilinguals Are Natives Too!" *Applied Linguistics* 35, no. 1: 93–8. http://dx.doi.org/10.1093/applin/amt049.

Schmitt, Norbert. 2008. "Review Article: Instructed Second Language Vocabulary Learning." *Language Teaching Research* 12, no. 3: 329–63. http://dx.doi.org/10.1177/1362168808089921.

Schmitt, Norbert, and Diane Schmitt. 2014. "A Reassessment of Frequency and Vocabulary Size in L2 Vocabulary Teaching." *Language Teaching* 47, no. 4: 484–503. http://dx.doi.org/10.1017/S0261444812000018.

Schmitt, N., and C. B. Zimmerman. 2002. "Derivative Word Forms: What Do Learners Know?" *TESOL Quarterly* 36, no. 2: 145–171.

Sherkina-Lieber, Marina, Ana Perez-Leroux, and Alana Johns. 2011. "Grammar without Speech Production: The Case of Labrador Inuttitut Heritage Receptive Bilinguals." *Bilingualism: Language and Cognition* 14, no. 3: 301–17. http://dx.doi.org/10.1017/S1366728910000210.

Swender, Elvira, Cynthia Martin, Mildren Rivera-Martínez, and Olga Kagan. 2014. "Exploring Oral Proficiency Profiles of Heritage Speakers of Russian and Spanish." *Foreign Language Annals* 47, no. 3: 423–46. http://dx.doi.org/10.1111/flan.12098.

Taylor, John. 2003. *Linguistic Categorization*. Oxford: Oxford University Press.

———. 2015. "Prototype Effects in Grammar." In *Handbook of Cognitive Linguistics*, ed. Ewa Dąbrowska and Dagmar Divjak, 562–79. Berlin: De Gruyter Mouton. http://dx.doi.org/10.1515/9783110292022-028.

Torres, Julio. 2013. "Heritage and Second Language Learners of Spanish: The Roles of Task Complexity and Inhibitory Control." PhD diss., Georgetown University.

Valdés, Guadalupe. 2001. "Heritage Language Students: Profiles and Possibilities." In *Heritage Languages in America: Preserving a National Resource*, ed. Joy Kreeft Peyton, Donald Ranard, and Scott McGinnis, 37–80. Washington, DC: Center for Applied Linguistics.

———. 2005. "Bilingualism, Heritage Language Learners, and SLA Research: Opportunities Lost or Seized?" *Modern Language Journal* 89, no. 3: 410–26. http://dx.doi.org/10.1111/j.1540-4781.2005.00314.x.

Van Deusen-Scholl, Nelleke. 2003. "Toward a Definition of Heritage Language: Sociopolitical and Pedagogical Considerations." *Journal of Language, Identity, and Education* 2, no. 3: 211–30. http://dx.doi.org/10.1207/S15327701JLIE0203_4.

VanPatten, Bill. 1998. "Perceptions of and Perspectives on the Term 'Communicative.'" *Hispania* 81, no. 4: 925–32. http://dx.doi.org/10.2307/345805.

Wu, Shu-Ling, and Lourdes Ortega. 2013. "Measuring Global Oral Proficiency in SLA Research: A New Elicited Imitation Test of L2 Chinese." *Foreign Language Annals* 46, no. 4: 680–704. http://dx.doi.org/10.1111/flan.12063.

2

Goals and Beyond in Heritage Language Education

From Competencies to Capabilities

Glenn Martínez
OHIO STATE UNIVERSITY

The escalating accountability framework in public education that began in the 1990s and flowered under the No Child Left Behind policies has exerted considerable pressures on educators to develop explicit performance standards and to consistently assess student progress toward them. In 1996, under the leadership of the American Council for the Teaching of Foreign Languages (ACTFL), the language teaching profession put forward a series of National Standards for Foreign Language Learning (NSFLL) known as the "Five Cs" (Phillips and Terry 1999). The standards were developed with the intent of serving learners from all backgrounds, including heritage learners (Valdés 2000). The varying needs of heritage language (HL) students and the widening imperatives facing HL educators, however, have made the implementation of NSFLL a slippery slope indeed. In tandem with—and, in some cases, in reaction to—the NSFLL, HL educators have proposed independent goals for HL education that reflect the social, cultural, and political struggles of HL students and the communities from which they hail (Beaudrie, Ducar, and Potowski 2014). Implicit in these goals is the view that language instruction is an optimal site to address broader academic and identity challenges that uniquely characterize HL students. At the same time, the goals conceptualize language instruction as a powerful engine for the improvement of HL communities. My purpose in this chapter is to unify these two facets of the HL goals based on current research on a wide spectrum of heritage languages in the United States.

In the first part of this chapter, I explore the differences between the NSFLL and the HL goals with a view toward an explicit identification of the salient issues that have incited educators to propose specific and independent goals for HL teaching. Further, I review the growing body of empirical research on the different goal areas from a variety of HL communities. This body of research, I argue, consistently points to the vital role of the community in HL education.

In the second part of the chapter, I propose a unified framework in which to couch the HL goals. The framework centers on the notion of "capabilities" as developed in the work of Amartya Sen and Martha Nussbaum (Sen 1992, 2000; Nussbaum 2011). The notion of "capabilities" differs significantly from the notion of "competency" that is embedded in the NSFLL. If competency refers to what a student is able to do, capability refers to what an individual is able to *do* and to *be* (Nussbaum 2011). Capabilities are created by a combination of personal abilities and the political, social, and economic environment (Sen 1992, 2000). Language teaching goals and standards have historically targeted specific individual competencies developed largely in the context of the classroom. Such goals inevitably constrain the potential of language instruction in addressing broader academic and social challenges faced in HL communities. HL education, however, aspires to a set of goals and standards that allow language instruction to unleash its full potential not only for student development but also for community advancement. The capabilities framework, I believe, imbues the HL goals with precisely this kind of potential.

In the third and final section of this chapter, I present a series of community-based pedagogical initiatives that reflect the capabilities approach. Through these examples, I demonstrate how a capabilities framework is operationalized in the day-to-day endeavors of HL practitioners in various regions of the country. At the same time, I show that the framework generates assets for HL communities as it facilitates the development of personal and professional commitments to community improvement among HL students.

THE PRESENT: CORE ISSUES AND TOPICS

The NSFLL were first articulated in 1999 and represented a consensus among language teaching professionals, educational administrators, and business leaders about the goals of foreign language learning. The NSFLL consist of five goal areas known as the "Five Cs" (see Phillips and Terry 1999 for a more comprehensive description of the NSFLL). The goals were proposed as interrelated facets, represented visually through interlocking circles, that together reflected the competencies expected of individual learners studying a foreign language.

In 2011 ACTFL commissioned a study of the impact of the NSFLL in the professional literature, in institutions, in teaching practice, and in teacher training and professional development (ACTFL 2011). While the report concluded that the NSFLL have impacted all areas of the language teaching profession, it also showed that important challenges to full implementation remain. The report states, for example, that "teachers have not embraced the Connections and Communities standards to the extent anticipated" (ACTFL

2011, 11). In fact, the Communication and Cultures standards remain the primary focus of the majority of the teachers surveyed. Further analysis on the impact of the NSFLL has shown that empirical studies of learner outcomes have been conducted only on the communication standard (Troyan 2012). Because of this gap in the research literature, we still do not know the impact of the remaining four C's on student learning. Notwithstanding the initial intent of the NSFLL to represent interlocking and equally important goal areas, in their operationalization in teaching and research, it has become evident that they have been prioritized with the Communication standard at the top of the list and the Communities standard at the bottom. Indeed, Judith Shrum and Eileen Glisan have gone so far as to refer to the Communities standard as "the lost C" (Shrum and Glisan 2010).

The deprioritization of the Communities standard is further complicated by internal tensions within the Communities standard itself. Jennifer Leeman (2011, 301) notes that the Communities standard may reveal an underlying commodification. She argues that local communities can be seen as simply a resource for language practice and that this conceptualization may mask the needs and aspirations of the communities themselves. She also critiques the standard's emphasis on "personal enjoyment and enrichment" as reinforcing a "one-way benefit" approach to community engagement.

The tendency toward commodification identified by Leeman can be seen as part of a more all-encompassing critique of the NSFLL that connects it to a culture of standardization (Train 2002, 2007). In this view, standardized and standardizing educational practices systematically disregard, and consequently devalue, the learner's personal, cultural, and community-based identities. In describing the effects of the culture of standardization in public schools in Texas, Angela Valenzuela (2005, 4) argued that the high-stakes testing embedded in the culture of standardization may "reduce children's worth to their test scores." The internal inconsistencies in the NSFLL together with their grounding in a culture of standardization have had an appreciable impact on their implementation within HL education specifically.

Early appraisals of the NSFLL within HL education revealed a high degree of optimism that standards-based education would significantly enhance the language teaching profession for traditional foreign language learners and for HL learners alike. In describing the crafting of the NSFLL, Guadalupe Valdés writes:

> What is especially important to those concerned about teaching Spanish to heritage learners is that the standards were written to take into consideration not only the needs of traditional foreign language learners but also the special strengths of home-background or heritage learners. . . . Each of the five goal areas and the standards themselves were carefully written so that they might be easily adaptable to a large number of very different settings involving students with diverse backgrounds in the target language (Valdés 2000, 13).

Ana Roca (2000) echoed Valdés's positive assessment of the NSFLL in her forecast of their potential impact on HL education. She argued that the application of the standards in Spanish HL instruction would "help teachers loosen the shackles of more rigid language teaching methodologies, reflecting different thinking on how languages are best learned and maintained" (106). John Webb and Barbara Miller (2000, 29), however, were a bit more cautious in their prognosis of the impact of the NSFLL in HL education: "Only implementation efforts will determine the degree to which the standards will be relevant to heritage learners."

Notwithstanding the optimism with which HL professionals welcomed the implementation of the NSFLL, its limitations in adequately covering the needs of HL learning were fairly quickly identified. Kim Potowski and Maria Carreira (2004) convincingly argue for the need to go beyond the NSFLL in HL education and teacher training. They argue that the NSFLL fails to align with the needs of HL students of Spanish because it does not address the student's affective, social, academic, and linguistic needs. For example, the NSFLL does not address the linguistic insecurities faced by Spanish HLs. It does not specifically address the complex sociolinguistic reality of Spanish in the United States. It does not signal the role of HL education in the development of general literacy skills, the transfer of literacy skills from English to Spanish, and the general academic skills needed to be successful in the US educational system. Finally, the NSFLL does not recognize the specific linguistic needs of HL students in developing a prestige variety of the language and in expanding bilingual range. The authors point to the National Council on the Teaching of English Standards as more appropriately fitted to the needs of HL learners.

Internal inconsistencies, the connection to the culture of standardization, and the misalignment of the NSFLL to the needs of HL students have led HL practitioners to opt for a separate set of goals for HL. The first four goals were proposed by Valdés in a seminal article in 1995. Valdés added two additional goals in a subsequent article, and the final goal was proposed in an article by Frances Aparicio (as cited in Beaudrie, Ducar, and Potowski 2014). The seven HL goals include

1. Maintenance of the heritage language
2. Acquisition of a prestige language variety
3. Expansion of bilingual range
4. Transfer of literacy skills
5. Acquisition of academic skills in the heritage language
6. Cultivation of positive attitudes toward the heritage language
7. Acquisition or development of cultural awareness

The HL goals differ significantly from the NSFLL in several ways. First, as noted by Potowski and Carreira (2004), they are well aligned to the specific needs of HL students. Second, whereas the NSFLL focus exclusively on the individual learner (at times at the expense of the community, as described in Leeman 2011), the HL goals aspire to address cultural and social issues beyond the individual learner. For example, the language-maintenance goal goes beyond the individual learner and is intended to impact the wider HL community. The goal of developing academic skills in the heritage language, furthermore, is responsive to the educational achievement gap in many HL communities and thus aspires to incite social change that goes beyond the individual learner. The cultivation of positive attitudes toward the heritage language and the development of cultural awareness are also community-oriented goals inasmuch as HL educators aspire to direct these attitudes to counteract the hegemony of English and its associated monolingual and monocultural policies in schools and in society at large. The HL goals have served the profession well in terms of curriculum development and in terms of the formulation of research questions that advance our understanding of HL acquisition and development. The implementation of an HL research agenda around the seven goal areas has revealed, furthermore, a profound embeddedness of the community in HL education.

In the goal area of language maintenance, for example, researchers have described the interaction between community assets such as community Spanish language programs, tutoring services, and religious education that interact with school-based HL programs (Carreira and Rodríguez 2011). Using an asset-based approach to evaluation (Lynch 2009), Carreira and Rodríguez argue that more support and engagement is needed from schools, universities, and local businesses for these efforts to thrive. A study of Punjabi maintenance in a Sikh community in Southern California, on the other hand, argues that community-based religious education converges on a view of HL maintenance as a moral obligation (Klein 2013). Klein argues that Punjabi HL education will need to draw on additional community resources in order to fully realize the potential of community-based religious education in Punjabi HL maintenance. Other researchers have demonstrated the substantial positive impact of academic–community collaboration in the documentation and revitalization of endangered languages when both entities agree upon mutually defined and mutually beneficial goals and objectives (Yamada 2007). Finally, research on Native American language revitalization has demonstrated that language instructional programs have the ability to transmit community-based values, recover traditions, and lead to positive behavior change while developing students' reasoning abilities and teaching solid academic content (Reyhner 2010).

In the goal area of acquisition of a prestige dialect, the HL goals have directed research questions leading to new knowledge of the instructional strategies that are most conducive to the use of prestige dialect forms (Fairclough 2005; Potowski and Parada 2010). Furthermore, the goal area has inspired a great deal of thinking and debate on the role of prestige and nonstandard dialects in instruction as well as the most effective ways to promote positive attitudes about the heritage language (Bernal-Enríquez and Hernández-Chávez 2003; Leeman 2005; Martínez 2003; Villa 1996, 2002). These debates have informed the approach to dialect acquisition in other heritage languages as well. A study of Chinese heritage learners from Cantonese backgrounds, for example, found that learners approach Mandarin instruction both as a way to connect to their heritage and as a way to claim their own part in the globalized Chinese community of the future (Wong and Xiao 2010). The authors propose that the teaching of Mandarin can become more welcoming of dialect learners by expanding the focus of Mandarin as a "bounded entity" to a focus of Mandarin as a link both to international Chinese networks and to their own home communities (see Fairclough, this volume [2016], for additional information on dialect acquisition and the expansion of HL learners' linguistic repertoire).

The goal area of the transfer of literacy skills has inspired research that raises questions about the situational factors that shape literacy practices. Martínez (2007), for example, studied subject pronoun expression among heritage learners in free writing and graded writing contexts. The findings revealed that students were more likely to express subject pronouns in graded writing contexts. The study concludes that a negative transfer from English exists where students are more likely to express subject pronouns in graded writing even though they would not express them in oral language or more informal (i.e., free) writing. Another study of Russian HL learners found that Russian HL writers tended to rely more on forms and structures with equivalents in English and to avoid unique Russian discourse features. The study also found a correlation between the HL learners' ability to write in Russian and their ability to write in English (Friedman and Kagan 2009). Both of these studies point to the need for a "multidimensional" model of literacy transfer (Martínez 2005) that recognizes and values the literacy practices of bilingual HL communities while developing advanced literacy skills in the heritage language.

The goal area of developing academic skills has also generated important research that suggests Spanish HL language instruction at the secondary level may be able to reverse the negative effect of the Latino achievement gap (Carreira 2007). Specifically, Carreira argues for an expanded role for Spanish HL teachers. These teachers can deliver content-based instruction and can serve as navigators for Spanish-speaking parents. Neriko Doerr and Kiri Lee (2009) conducted a study of perceptions of Japanese HL instruction among students, parents, and administrators. The study evaluated perceptions of weekend Japanese HL instruction using a program developed by the Japanese government (*kokugo*) and a program developed by teachers and administrators in the local Japanese community (*keishogo*). The perceptions of these different approaches held by students, parents, and administrators convincingly demonstrate that HL education is more than an effort to enhance awareness of one's heritage or to develop language proficiency. Instead, HL education is part of a larger "schooling process" that involves complex contestations around legitimate knowledge and how it is obtained. This study underscores the important role that HL education plays both in determining students' "future educational prospects" and in framing and legitimizing their "diasporic subjectivities" (Doerr and Lee 2009, 435–438). Both of these studies suggest that HL education has an important role to play in bridging mainstream schools and HL communities.

Another line of research connected to the HL goals centers on student perceptions and motivations in HL learning. This research has focused on the principal motivations for studying a heritage language among advanced learners, perceptions of the teaching of culture in the HL classroom, and the role of the community in motivating students to engage in HL pedagogy. Recent research clearly points to connection with the culture as the primary motivation for HL study. Xiaohong Wen (2011) found that self-concept, ethnic identity, and a desire to communicate with members of their community were fundamental motivational factors among students of Chinese as a heritage language. Soojin Han (2003) found that cultural motivation was more important than instrumental motivation among Korean HL students. Jin Sook Lee and Hae-Young Kim (2008) also studied Korean HLs and found that motivations were chiefly tied to issues of ethnic identity. Kimberly Noels (2005) found that German HL students were motivated primarily in order to be able to interact with their community. Roswita Dressler (2010), however, noted that many HL learners of German tend to demonstrate reluctance in self-identifying as such. She found that while some German HL students grounded their identification as HL speakers in expertise (German language proficiency), affiliation (citizenship in a German-speaking country), or inheritance (ancestral ties to a German-speaking country), others overlooked these same factors and shunned the HL label. Dressler explored this reluctance in depth and found that many "reluctant HLs" anchored their reluctance to self-include in the "positioning" assigned to them by others. Reluctant HLs discussed experiences where German teachers cast doubt on their identification as German HLs and experiences where others rejected their identification as Germans. Dressler argues that there is a need to counteract these experiences in the classroom and provide HL awareness among all learners. All of these studies suggest that the HL community plays an important role in HL student motivation. Dressler's study also suggests that HL education may also need to play a role in shaping and contesting community stereotypes. This reminds us of Agnes He's characterization of Chinese HL instruction as a conduit for both the *inheritance* of HL practices and the *transformation* of HL speech communities (He 2006).

In terms of culture instruction, Sara Beaudrie and colleagues (2009) found that Spanish HL students wanted cultural activities that would strengthen cultural ties with their home and community as opposed to increased exposure to films, literature, and other cultural products. Korean HL learners, on the other hand, are increasingly using social media and the Internet to gain access to the HL culture (Kim 2008). The evidence on student perceptions and motivations clearly points to a desire on the part of HL students to connect more directly and more deeply with local and transnational HL communities.

LOOKING INTO THE FUTURE

The HL goals described in the previous section and the research that they have spawned represent a clear departure from the NSFLL. While the NSFLL focuses on the competencies attained by the individual learner, the HL goals focus both on individual competencies and on community impact and inclusion. The research on HL maintenance, HL dialect acquisition, HL academic achievement, and HL attitudes and motivation reviewed in the previous section demonstrates the inter-animation of classrooms and communities in HL education. In this section, I will describe a theoretical framework that will unify these two important components of HL goals.

The core of the theoretical framework that I will describe is the distinction between competencies and capabilities. Competencies refer to what an individual can do. Competencies are viewed largely as context-independent skills that can be deployed at will. The NSFLL, for example, presents the goals of language education from the perspective of context-independent, voluntarily deployable competencies. Consider the subject positions and active verbs in the articulation of all of the standards: Standard 1.1 *Students engage* in conversations . . . , Standard 1.2 *Students understand* and interpret . . . , Standard 1.3 *Students present* information . . . , Standard 2.1 *Students demonstrate* an understanding . . . , and so on. The focus of the NSFLL is squarely on the "student" and on what the student does. Capabilities, on the other hand, refer to what an individual can do and what an individual can be. From a capabilities perspective, the issue is not only what a person can do but also the affordances that a person has to act and, through that action, to shape their environment. In applying the notion of capabilities to educational goals, we see how the competency perspective falls severely short of the goals for HL education. A capabilities approach to educational goals does not assume that competencies are context-independent and voluntarily deployable. Instead, it recognizes that competencies are shaped by the social, political, and economic environment in which they are enacted. The HL goals exemplify this approach inasmuch as they target the individual learner and her multiple, complex, and symbiotic connections to the HL community, as is clearly demonstrated in the research that has been conducted around them. The capabilities orientation, furthermore, imbues the HL goals with the dual purpose of both developing individual learners and impacting their communities. Consider, for example, that the goal areas of promoting language maintenance, improving academic skills, promoting positive attitudes, and enhancing cultural awareness all aim to impact both students and communities. Furthermore, a capabilities orientation that considers the needs and aspirations of both students and communities counteracts the tendencies toward commodification discussed by Leeman as a negative consequence of the Communities standard.

By theorizing HL goals as capabilities rather than competencies, however, we commit ourselves to a much broader agenda as HL educators. In fact, we assume responsibility not only for our students and what they learn but also for how competencies are actualized in local and transnational communities. We also assume greater responsibilities in partnering with HL communities and in drawing on their expertise in reaching our own goals. So, what might these new responsibilities entail with respect to the current HL goals?

In the goal area of language maintenance, we would need to go beyond the development of student attitudes and desires and include opportunities for students to participate in language maintenance and language revitalization activities in their own communities. In the goal area of acquisition of a prestige variety, we would seek not only to develop linguistic options and to make students conscious of that choice (Del Valle 2014; Leeman 2005; Martínez 2003; Villa 2002) but also to afford them opportunities to exercise that choice and observe its consequences in real interactions in the community. Glenn Martínez and Adam Schwartz (2012), for example, describe a project in which students are afforded the opportunity to see the high value of "low prestige" dialect variants in a service-learning assignment in public health. In the goal area of bilingual range, we would attempt not only to refine dexterity in moving back and forth between languages and sliding up and down the register scale but also to put this dexterity to work for the tangible benefit of community members who struggle to obtain access to social institutions such as schools, immigration enforcement agencies, and hospitals because they do not speak English. In the goal area of literacy skills, we would endeavor not only to expose students to multiple literacy practices and their associated perspectives but also to use these practices and perspectives in exercising civic responsibility within and on behalf of their communities. In the goal area of academic skills development, we would stress not only the development of techniques and behaviors to enhance the student's own academic success but also the sharing of this knowledge for the benefit of HL youth and their parents. In the goal area of positive attitudes, we would focus not only on the role of the classroom in developing positive attitudes but also on the agency exercised by students in promoting positive attitudes outside of the classroom. Finally, in the goal area of cross-cultural awareness, we would not only target knowledge and appreciation for cultural diversity within the global HL communities but would also strive to broker cultural differences within the community in order to promote greater tolerance and social justice.

It is evident from my conceptualization of a capabilities approach to HL goals that the achievement of these goals cannot occur in the classroom alone. I view community-based learning and teaching not as a tangential or supplementary activity to HL education; rather, I view it as a foundational activity that is essential to the achievement of its educational goals. In the next section, I discuss a variety of community-based learning and teaching projects that exemplify the capabilities approach that I have introduced in this chapter. Although these projects are mainly from the area of Spanish, based on the findings from research on diverse HLs, I believe they can be replicated in various HL communities.

PRACTICAL CONSIDERATIONS AND EXAMPLES

Over the past several years there has been a surge of HL and traditional foreign language programs with significant community service learning (CSL) components (Hellebrandt and Jorge 2013). Many of the programs that have been documented in the literature reveal the centrality of CSL in realizing the capabilities approach to HL goals, as discussed in the previous section. The sustained engagement with community stakeholders in these programs and the consistent integration of student learning outcomes and community benefits satisfy the imperatives discussed in the previous section. I highlight several particularly salient examples in this section and discuss how they meet the expanded responsibilities required by a capabilities approach to HL goals.

CSL in HL instruction dates back to the early twentieth century with the work of Leonard Covello in the Italian and Puerto Rican neighborhoods of New York City. Lisa Rabin (2011) presents a detailed analysis of Covello's effort over a forty-year period, pointing out the incontestable historical evidence that the opportunities to do community work in their own language helped HL learners to develop a civic identity that contrasted with the delinquent roles that were presupposed for them in society. The community work undertaken by the HL learners under Covello's direction included translation of vital information in housing, education, sanitation, and health for use by the HL community. This early example of CSL in HL education demonstrates the potential of language education to transform attitudes about the HL and its speakers. Rabin concludes by stating that "Covello's 40-year encouragement of student service and activism stood as a counterweight to the stereotyping of these youth in the larger culture" (2011, 348).

A more recent example of CSL interventions in the HL curriculum was developed at George Mason University in the suburbs of Washington, DC (Leeman, Rabin, and Román-Mendoza 2011a, 2011b). The project emerged in the context of a curricular reform effort directed at transforming the Spanish major at George Mason from a foreign language major into a US language major. These changes included injecting US-based content into the curriculum and abandoning the monolithic focus on literature that had been a signature of the old program. Emerging from these changes, there was a desire on the part of the students to put their learning into action and to move beyond the classroom walls. The CSL program was developed in response to this desire and consisted of transforming Spanish students into teacher activists in the community. It involved sending college Spanish students to a local elementary school to provide support for an after-school HL Spanish enrichment program. In this CSL experience, college-level HL students were encouraged to enter the community as experts in language and to participate directly in a language-maintenance project. Briefly stated, the project positioned HL students as language experts in the community, allowing them to exercise their "commitment to language rights" and to put their knowledge of language into action (Leeman, Rabin, and Román-Mendoza 2011b, 485). The results of the project demonstrated that students expanded their linguistic repertoires and developed critical language awareness, and they reported greater awareness of and pride in their linguistic knowledge and expertise. When the students were reinserted into the community as experts in language, they were afforded new and unique opportunities that benefited both themselves and the wider community.

María Parra (2013) describes the methodology and pedagogical practice of a CSL advanced Spanish course taught at Harvard University. The methodological approach for this course drew on service learning, multiliteracies, and critical border pedagogy. It explored the complexity of Latino history and experience in the United States, focusing on issues such as border crossings, cultural identity, the education of Latino children, and the future of the Latino community. The course also included a service component in a local organization that serves Latino communities. At the end of the course, students were required to complete an art project that included production of art object, a written essay, and a presentation of the project to the class. Among the many projects detailed in Parra's essay, several stand out as examples of capability-oriented activities. One student project consisted of a collage detailing her experience in a two-way bilingual school. The work in the school and the opportunity to reflect critically and creatively on the experience led her to develop a sense of profound hope for the Latino community. Another student showcased a painting representing intergenerational language loss within her own family. She concluded that the course impacted her profoundly and motivated her to continue studying Spanish. This CSL project also demonstrates the impact of injecting community-based experiences on a student's sense of belonging within the community.

Lisa Petrov (2013) reports on a CSL course for HL students offered at Dominican University in the suburbs of Chicago. The CSL component consisted of a minimum of fifteen service hours at a community organization. These experiences were then incorporated into the curriculum of the intermediate language course through reflection essays and class discussions. The author evaluated the class by using a survey and by analyzing students' final reflection essays. The results demonstrated that CSL was highly effective among HL students. Students overwhelmingly expressed that the CSL experience made them feel more connected to their community. These connections led to greater appreciation of the struggles faced in their community and by their family members. The author concluded that the CSL experience allowed students to recognize the role of the community in their own academic success and thus to develop a sense of communal achievement (Petrov 2013, 323). The emergence of communal success is an important outcome of CSL in this HL context. Petrov writes: "Individualism is generally understood to be an ideal of Anglo culture, a quintessentially American value, but it is not a Hispanic one, which more generally privileges the communal and familial" (2013, 323). The ability of CSL to recover community values in the face of more mainstream ideologies reflects the power of community participation in HL education.

A final example of the deployment of CSL in HL education that brings tangible benefits to both students and communities can be found in the Medical Spanish for Heritage Learners program founded at the University of Texas–Pan American (Martínez 2010). This program engaged pre-health students in CSL in local community health centers and provided them an opportunity to use their HL skills to improve health outcomes among non-English-speaking patients. The program was successful in developing intersectional identities that reflected both cultural heritage and professional training among these future Latino health professionals. A nursing student in the program commented on the impact of the program:

> Pues, me ha impactado porque ahora sé que soy como una persona bilingüe . . . ahora, pues uso más español y los términos médicos como por ejemplo con mi abuelita y con los doctores. Me ha hecho una persona más útil.
>
> It has really made an impact on me because now I know that I am like a bilingual person . . . I use Spanish more and also the medical vocabulary with my grandma and her doctors. It's made me a more useful person (Martínez 2011).

In this statement, the student reflected on how her exposure to the program and the community increased her use of Spanish and impacted her own identity in relation to those around her—it made her feel like a more "useful" person.

Each of these examples demonstrates how the achievement of HL goals is enhanced in partnership with HL communities. We see, for example, that Covello's CSL project led to improved attitudes about HL youth and challenged common stereotypes. Leeman and colleagues demonstrated significant gains in the goal area of expansion of bilingual range among HL college students and the goal area of promotion of academic skills among HL youth in the community. Parra showed that CSL enhances student commitment to language maintenance and to community advancement. Petrov's project contributed to the development of cultural awareness by allowing students to reframe their own academic experience within the context of the HL culture. Finally, Martínez's project demonstrated gains in the goal area of cultivation of positive attitudes by giving students opportunities to recognize the intersectionality of their professional aspirations and their HL community.

CONCLUDING REMARKS

In this chapter, I have analyzed the goals of HL education with an eye toward proposing a new theoretical framework that underscores the centrality of both classrooms and communities. I have reviewed the NSFLL and have shown how internal inconsistencies, misalignment with HL student needs, and their entrenchment in a culture of standardization have led to their rejection by many HL researchers and practitioners. I have also reviewed the current HL goals and demonstrated that empirical research around each of these goals consistently connects the HL learner with the HL community. In light of this insight, I have argued for a new theoretical framework that will bring together the individual competencies that we desire to attain and the community inclusion and impact that have been so salient in research on HL goals. The capabilities approach argues that the HL goals can best be articulated in terms of what HL students are able to do and be. The approach elevates the role of HL communities in achieving the goals of HL education and argues that community engagement is not a tangential or supplementary activity. Finally, I have reviewed several CSL programs, and I have shown how the capabilities approach sheds new light on their success.

The capabilities approach to HL goals nonetheless places significant responsibilities on the HL teaching profession. It forces us to come to terms with the fact that community involvement in HL education is not an option. Rather, it is an imperative that must be pursued. I am hopeful that a clear articulation of our goals and an accompanying theoretical framework to justify them will constitute a step forward in securing the institutional and community resources needed to successfully meet our goals.

REFERENCES

ACTFL Task Force on Decade of Standards Project. 2011. "*A Decade of Foreign Language Standardsl Influence, Impact, and Future Directions.*" http://actfl.org/files/public/national-standards-2011.pdf.

Beaudrie, Sara M., Cynthia Ducar, and Kimberly Potowski. 2014. *Heritage Language Teaching: Research and Practice*. New York: McGraw-Hill.

Beaudrie, Sara M., Cynthia Ducar, and Ana M. Relaño-Pastor. 2009. "Curricular Perspectives in the Heritage Language Context: Assessing Culture and Identity." *Language, Culture and Curriculum* 22, no. 2: 157–74. http://dx.doi.org/10.1080/07908310903067628.

Bernal-Enríquez, Ysaura, and Eduardo Hernández-Chávez. 2003. "La enseñanza del español en Nuevo México: ¿Revitalización o erradicación de la variedad chicana?" In *Mi lengua: Spanish as a Heritage Language in the United States*, ed. Ana Roca and M. Cecilia Colombi, 78–95. Washington, DC: Georgetown University Press.

Carreira, Maria. 2007. "Spanish for Native Speakers Matters: Narrowing the Latino Achievement Gap through Spanish Language Instruction." *Heritage Language Journal* 5, no. 1: 147–71. http://www.heritagelanguages.org/.

Carreira, Maria, and Rey Rodríguez. 2011. "Filling the Void: Community Spanish Language Programs in Los Angeles Serving to Preserve the Language." *Heritage Language Journal* 8, no. 2: 1–16.

Del Valle, José. 2014. "The Politics of Normativity and Globalization: Which Spanish in the Classroom." *Modern Language Journal* 98, no. 1: 358–72. http://dx.doi.org/10.1111/j.1540-4781.2014.12066.x.

Doerr, Neriko, and Kiri Lee. 2009. "Contesting Heritage: Language, Legitimacy, and Schooling at a Weekend Japanese-language School in the United States." *Language and Education* 23, no. 5: 425–41. http://dx.doi.org/10.1080/09500780802651706.

Dressler, Roswita. 2010. "'There Is No Space for Being German': Portraits of Willing and Reluctant Heritage Language Learners of German." *Heritage Languages Journal* 7, no. 2: 162–82. http://www.heritagelanguages.org/.

Fairclough, Marta. 2005. *Spanish and Heritage Language Education in the United States: Struggling with Hypotheticals*. Madrid, Frankfurt: Iberoamericana/Verveurt.

Fairclough, Marta. 2016. "Incorporating Additional Varieties to the Linguistic Repertoires of Heritage Language Learners: A Multidialectal Model." In *Innovative Strategies for Heritage Language Teaching: A Practical Guide for the Classroom*, ed. Marta Fairclough and Sara M. Beaudrie, 143–65. Washington, DC: Georgetown University Press.

Friedman, Debra, and Olga Kagan. 2009. "Academic Writing Proficiency of Russian Heritage Speakers: A Comparative Study." In *Heritage Language Education: A New Field Emerging*, ed. Donna E. Brinton, Olga Kagan, and Susan Bauckus, 181–98. New York: Routledge.

Han, Soojin. 2003. "Culture or Capital: What Motivates Heritage Language Achievement among Korean-American Youth." MA thesis, Stanford University, Stanford, CA.

He, Agnes W. 2006. "Toward an Identity Theory of the Development of Chinese as a Heritage Language." *Heritage Language Journal* 4, no. 1: 1–28. http://www.heritagelanguages.org/.

Hellebrandt, Josep, and Ethel Jorge. 2013. "The Scholarship of Community Engagement: Advancing Partnerships in Spanish and Portuguese." *Hispania* 96, no. 2: 203–14. http://dx.doi.org/10.1353/hpn.2013.0058.

Kim, Hae-Young. 2008. "Commentary." *Heritage Language Journal* 6, no. 2: 246–56. http://www.heritagelanguages.org/.

Klein, Wendy. 2013. "Speaking Punjabi(s): Heritage Language Socialization and Language Ideologies in a Sikh Education Program." *Heritage Language Journal* 10, no. 1: 36–50. http://www.heritagelanguages.org/.

Lee, Jin Sook, and Hae-Young Kim. 2008. "Heritage Language Learners' Attitudes, Motivations, and Instructional Needs: The Case of Postsecondary Korean Language Learners." In *Teaching Chinese, Japanese, and Korean Heritage Language Students: Curriculum Needs, Materials and Assessment*, ed. Kimi Kondo-Brown and J. D. Brown, 159–85. Mahwah, NJ: Lawrence Erlbaum.

Leeman, Jennifer. 2005. "Engaging Critical Pedagogy: Spanish for Native Speakers." *Foreign Language Annals* 38, no. 1: 35–45. http://dx.doi.org/10.1111/j.1944-9720.2005.tb02451.x.

———. 2011. "Standards, Commodification, and Critical Service Learning in Minority Language Communities." *Modern Language Journal* 95, no. 2: 300–303. http://dx.doi.org/10.1111/j.1540-4781.2011.01184.x.

Leeman, Jennifer, Lisa Rabin, and Esperanza Román-Mendoza. 2011a. "Critical Pedagogy beyond the Classroom Walls: Community Service-learning and Spanish Heritage Language Education." *Heritage Language Journal* 8, no. 3: 293–314. http://www.heritagelanguages.org/.

———. 2011b. "Identity and Activism in Heritage Language Education." *Modern Language Journal* 95, no. 4: 481–95. http://dx.doi.org/10.1111/j.1540-4781.2011.01237.x.

Lynch, Brian K. 2009. "Locating and Utilizing Heritage Language Resources in the Community: An Asset-Based Approach to Program Design and Evaluation." In *Heritage Language Education: A New Field Emerging*, ed. Donna E. Brinton, Olga Kagan, and Susan Bauckus, 321–36. New York: Routledge.

Martínez, Glenn. 2003. "Classroom Based Dialect Awareness in Heritage Language Instruction: A Critical Applied Linguistic Approach." *Heritage Language Journal* 1, no. 1: 44–57. http://www.heritagelanguages.org.

———. 2005. "Genres and Genre-Chains: Post-Process Perspectives on Heritage Language Writing." *Southwest Journal of Linguistics* 24:79–90.

———. 2007. "Writing Back and Forth: The Interplay of Form and Situation in Heritage Language Composition." *Language Teaching Research* 11, no. (1): 31–41. http://dx.doi.org/10.1177/1362168806072454.

———. 2010. "Medical Spanish for Heritage Learners: A Prescription to Improve the Health of Spanish-Speaking Communities." In *Building Communities and Making Connections*, ed. Susana Rivera-Mills and Juan A. Trujillo, 2–15. Newcastle Upon Tyne: Cambridge Scholars Publishing. http://dx.doi.org/10.5848/CSP.2022.00001.

———. 2011. "Language Barriers in Healthcare and Spanish Heritage Language Education: Language Assistance, Language Acceptance, and Language Affirmation." Paper delivered at the XXIII Conference on Spanish in the United States. University of California at Davis.

Martínez, Glenn, and Adam Schwartz. 2012. "Elevating 'Low' Language for High Stakes: A Case for Critical Community-based Learning in a Medical Spanish for

Heritage Learners Program." *Heritage Language Journal* 9, no. 2: 175–86. http://www.heritagelanguages.org/.

Noels, Kimberly. 2005. "Orientations to Learning German: Heritage Language Learning and Motivational Substrates." *Canadian Modern Language Review* 62, no. 2: 285–312. http://dx.doi.org/10.3138/cmlr.62.2.285.

Nussbaum, Martha C. 2011. *Creating Capabilities: The Human Development Approach*. Cambridge, MA: Belknap Press of Harvard University Press. http://dx.doi.org/10.4159/harvard.9780674061200.

Parra, María L. 2013. "Expanding Language and Cultural Competence in Advanced Heritage- and Foreign-Language Learners through Community Engagement and Work with the Arts." *Heritage Language Journal* 10, no. 2: 255–80. http://www.heritagelanguages.org/.

Petrov, Lisa Amor. 2013. "A Pilot Study of Service-Learning in a Spanish Heritage Speaker Course: Community Engagement, Identity, and Language in the Chicago Area." *Hispania* 96, no. 2: 310–27. http://dx.doi.org/10.1353/hpn.2013.0033.

Phillips, June K., and Robert M. Terry, eds. 1999. *Foreign Language Standards: Linking Research, Theories, and Practices*. Lincolnwood, IL: National Textbook Co.

Potowski, Kim, and Maria Carreira. 2004. "Teacher Development and the National Standards for Spanish as a Heritage Language." *Foreign Language Annals* 37, no. 3: 427–37. http://dx.doi.org/10.1111/j.1944-9720.2004.tb02700.x.

Potowski, K., and M. Parada. 2010. "An Online Placement Exam for Spanish Heritage Speakers and L2 Students." Presentation at the First International Conference on Heritage/Community Languages, UCLA, Los Angeles, California, February 19–21.

Rabin, Lisa. 2011. "Community Service and Activism in Heritage Languages, New York City, 1915–1956." *Foreign Language Annals* 44, no. 2: 338–52. http://dx.doi.org/10.1111/j.1944-9720.2011.01138.x.

Reyhner, Jon. 2010. "Indigenous Language Immersion Schools for Strong Indigenous Identities." *Heritage Language Journal* 7, no. 2: 299–313. http://www.heritagelanguages.org/.

Roca, Ana. 2000. "Heritage Learners of Spanish." In *AATSP Professional Development Series Handbook for Teachers K-16: Teaching Spanish with the Five C's*, ed. Gail Guntermann, 91–106. Boston: Thomson-Heinle.

———. 1992. *Inequality Re-examined*. Cambridge, MA: Harvard University Press.

Sen, Amartya. 2000. *Development as Freedom*. New York: Anchor Books.

Shrum, Judith, and Eileen Glisan. 2010. *Teacher's Handbook: Contextualized Language Instruction*. 4th ed. Boston: Heinle Cengage Learning.

Train, Robert. 2002. "The (Non)Native Standard Language in Foreign Language Education: A Critical Perspective." In *The Sociolinguistics of Foreign-Language Classrooms*, ed. Carl Blyth, 3–40. Boston: Heinle.

———. 2007. "Real Spanish: Historical Perspectives on the Ideological Construction of a (Foreign) Language." *Critical Inquiry in Language Studies* 4, no. 2–3: 207–35. http://dx.doi.org/10.1080/15427580701389672.

Troyan, Francis J. 2012. "Standards for Foreign Language Learning: Defining the Constructs and Researching Learner Outcomes." *Foreign Language Annals* 45, no. s1: s118–s40. http://dx.doi.org/10.1111/j.1944-9720.2012.01182.x.

Valdés, Guadalupe. 1995. "The Teaching of Minority Languages as Academic Subjects: Pedagogical and Theoretical Challenges." *Modern Language Journal* 79, no. 3: 299–328. http://dx.doi.org/10.1111/j.1540-4781.1995.tb01106.x.

———. 2000. "Introduction." In *AATSP Professional Development Series Handbook for Teachers K–16*, Vol. 1: *Spanish for Native Speakers*, 1–20. Fort Worth: Harcourt.

Valenzuela, Angela, ed. 2005. *Leaving Children Behind: How Texas-Style Accountability Fails Latino Youth*. Albany, NY: State University of New York Press.

Villa, Daniel. 1996. "Choosing a 'Standard' Variety of Spanish for the Instruction of Native Spanish Speakers in the US." *Foreign Language Annals* 29, no. 2: 191–200. http://dx.doi.org/10.1111/j.1944-9720.1996.tb02326.x.

———. 2002. "The Sanitizing of US Spanish in Academia." *Foreign Language Annals* 35, no. 2: 222–30. http://dx.doi.org/10.1111/j.1944-9720.2002.tb03156.x.

Webb, John, and Barbara Miller, eds. 2000. *Teaching Heritage Language Learners: Voices from the Classroom*. New York: ACTFL.

Wen, Xiaohong. 2011. "Chinese Language Learning Motivation: A Comparative Study of Heritage and Non-Heritage Learners." *Heritage Language Journal* 8, no. 3: 333–58. http://www.heritagelanguages.org/.

Wong, Ka F., and Yang Xiao. 2010. "Diversity and Difference: Identity Issues of Chinese Heritage Language Learners from Dialect Backgrounds." *Heritage Language Journal* 7, no. 2: 314–48. http://www.heritagelanguages.org/.

Yamada, Racquel M. 2007. "Collaborative Linguistic Fieldwork: Practical Application of the Empowerment Model." *Language Documentation and Conservation* 1, no. 2: 257–82.

3

Sociolinguistics for Heritage Language Educators and Students

A Model for Critical Translingual Competence

Jennifer Leeman and Ellen J. Serafini
George Mason University

The field of sociolinguistics—broadly defined as the study of social aspects of language as well as the interaction of language with sociocultural and political structures and phenomena—has much to offer to heritage language (HL) educators. For example, the study of language variation, contact, and change can provide insights on the formal features of HL students' language—such as the particular language varieties they speak or the ways English influences certain structures. Sociolinguistic research can also shed light on questions of ideology, identity, and language policy—such as how the view of the United States as a monolingual, English-speaking nation can influence language shift among HL speakers, or how multilingual students can use their linguistic knowledge to construct and perform a range of identities.

Until recently, recognition of the utility of sociolinguistics for HL education had tended to emphasize the importance of sociolinguistics for language instructors, with far less attention to how HL students might benefit from learning about sociolinguistics. In this chapter we argue that sociolinguistic topics should be included not only in teacher education and within the undergraduate major but also as content in HL education.[1] Our call for the incorporation of sociolinguistics reflects a critical approach to HL education, one that stresses the social, political, and ideological dimensions of language as well as the need for socially responsive pedagogies that incorporate students' experiences, promote equity both inside and outside the classroom, and foster student agency in making linguistic (and other) choices (Leeman 2014).

We begin with a discussion of the sociolinguistic issues of particular importance for HL educators and learners alike. This is followed by a critique of the conceptualization of sociolinguistic variation in "expansionist" models of HL education, which seek to promote HL students' acquisition of language varieties that are "appropriate" for formal settings. Next, we outline an alternative approach grounded in contemporary sociolinguistics and then analyze the Modern Language Association's (MLA) 2007 proposal to prioritize students' development of "transcultural and translingual competence." Rejecting both the notion that appropriateness and formality are sufficient to understand linguistic variation and the MLA's idea of delimitable "target languages" associated with distinct cultures or ways of understanding the world, we call for both second language (L2) and HL pedagogy to include fundamental sociolinguistic concepts and to explicitly recognize multilingual experiences and practices. Finally, we offer concrete curricular and classroom-level examples of pedagogical activities that are designed to promote HL students' critical translingual competence.

FUNDAMENTAL CONCEPTS IN SOCIOLINGUISTICS FOR HL EDUCATION

The Sociopolitical Context of HL Education in the United States

There is a long history of linguistic diversity in the United States, with numerous languages having been spoken by Native peoples, immigrants, enslaved peoples, and residents of conquered territories (Wiley 2005a), and before the late nineteenth century there was widespread acceptance and "tolerance" of multilingualism (Heath 1976; Pavlenko 2002). Since that time, languages other than English have come to be seen as a sign of potential disloyalty to the United States, a threat to English acquisition, and a marker of racial Otherness (Bonfiglio 2002; Leeman 2013; Schmidt 2002). This ideological climate, dominated by English monolingualism, constrains the implementational possibilities for language education (Hornberger 2002), and it has resulted in the predominance of the "language-as-problem" orientation in US language policy (Ruiz 1984) as well as the prevalence of English-only schooling for minority-language children, despite the documented benefits of providing education in children's home language(s) (e.g., Collier and Thomas 2013; Thomas and Collier 2002). Given the negative portrayal of minority languages as well as the lack of opportunities for children to develop literacy in their home language(s), it is not surprising that the United States continues to see high rates of linguistic assimilation, with the typical pattern consisting of some degree of bilingualism in the second generation and shift to English dominance or monolingualism by the third (Alba 2004; Rivera-Mills 2012).

These language policies and the ideologies that they embody shape students' linguistic and affective experiences with their heritage languages. Familiarity with the history of multilingualism in the United States as well as with patterns and causes of language shift is important not only for educators and policy; it can help HL students critically reflect on their own experiences, ideologies, and understanding of themselves as speakers of the heritage language.

Language Variation

As most people recognize, language varies from place to place, with speakers in different locales exhibiting phonological, lexical, syntactic, morphological, and pragmatic variation. For example, the French commonly spoken in Montreal, Canada, is different from that spoken in Abidjan, Ivory Coast; and the Spanish spoken in Tacna, Peru, is different from that spoken in Pucalpa, also in Peru. Such variation is particularly relevant in HL contexts because students' home varieties may differ from the one(s) spoken by the instructor or used in the classroom. The failure to recognize and legitimate students' home varieties can damage their self-esteem as well as their academic achievement and HL maintenance (Bartolomé and Macedo 1999; Carreira 2007; Hornberger 2005). For example, Doerr and Lee (2009) describe the marginalization experienced by a HL speaker of Osakan Japanese in a Japanese complementary school that privileged the Tokyo standard. The case of Chinese is particularly extreme, given that different "varieties" are actually mutually unintelligible and are considered by most linguists to be distinct languages. In the United States, many HL speakers of Chinese speak Cantonese whereas many Chinese-language pedagogical materials focus exclusively on Mandarin (Wu, Lee, and Leung 2014). As Wu and colleagues argue, this mismatch can negatively impact students' identities and investment in maintaining their HL language.

In addition to reflecting particular geographic regions, certain pronunciations, grammatical structures, or lexical items can index social class, educational attainment, or sexual identity. So too, particular linguistic features or practices may be linked to specific social networks or cliques (Eckert 2012; Mendoza-Denton 2008) or other communities of practice—groups of people who come together around a shared activity (Lave and Wenger 1998). HL students in the United States sometimes speak language varieties associated with rural communities of their, or their parents', home countries. Whereas early studies of social variation sought to identify differences in the ways these different groups of people used language, current understanding is that rather than *determining* language use, social identity is *constructed and performed through* language (Bucholtz and Hall 2005; Eckert 2012). For example, a study of HL speakers of Salvadoran and Honduran Spanish found that the pronoun "*vos*" (absent in many geographic varieties of Spanish, and associated with low socioeconomic status in some) was used to perform solidarity with Central American Spanish-speakers or to mark ethnic boundaries with those of other backgrounds (Rivera-Mills 2011).

Contextual variation, or differences in the ways people use language in different contexts or situations, is also intrinsic to language. For example, people tend to speak differently when relaxing with friends at a party, conducting a business meeting in an office, and praying in a house of worship. Although there is a great deal of terminological inconsistency in how scholars have categorized variation in language use, situationally defined varieties of language and specialized ways of speaking are often called "registers" (Lee 2001). The situational features that define registers encompass the activity with which it is associated, including the subject matter, the communicative mode (e.g., written or spoken), and the genre and rhetorical mode as well as the interactional roles and relationships among participants (Halliday and Hasan 1976). Registers include specialized ways of speaking associated not only with specific professions such as legalese or the language of business communication but also with social situations or specific activities, such as the language associated with skate-boarding (Matthiessen 1993). HL speakers are sometimes described as lacking the registers associated with academic or professional settings, although recent research by Sánchez-Muñoz (2010) has documented lexical variation in heritage languages in different social contexts.

Another approach to the variability of an individual's language use relies on the notion of style. William Labov's (1972) original discussions of sociolinguistic style suggested that an individual's attention to speech (which Labov linked with formality) was the primary determinate of an individual's language use in a given situation, but researchers now stress the social dimensions of style. Specific linguistic features are associated not only with the performance of particular identities but also with specific attitudes or orientations toward interlocutors or the topic at hand; linguistic styles and style-shifting can alternatively signal distance or intimacy with one's interlocutor, friendliness or indifference, and enthusiasm or skepticism regarding what is being said, among other stances (Coupland 2007; Eckert 2001; Johnstone 2009; Tannen 2005).

It is important to note that just as a person's membership in a particular social group does not directly correspond to speaking in a particular way, the contextual settings in which people find themselves do not *determine* how they speak. Rather, social and contextual variation reflects speakers' agency as they choose, sometimes unconsciously, among various alternatives in their linguistic repertoires in order to portray themselves in particular ways or to communicate particular interactional stances. Understanding social and contextual variation is particularly relevant for HL education in part because HL learners may use language to index hybrid social and cultural identities, a process that reflects belonging to and moving in and out of "simultaneously-existing multiple groups" (He 2006, 17). As such, HL languages serve a key sociocultural function (He 2010).

In addition to synchronic variation along the parameters of variation discussed above (geography, social group or identity, context), languages also exhibit diachronic, or temporal, variation. Understanding that language change is completely natural and that all living languages undergo change is important for HL speakers, as their home varieties may include innovative forms or structures associated with language contact (discussed below).

Language Attitudes and Ideologies

Regardless of the type of variation, a key tenet of sociolinguistics is that all language varieties are equally systematic, grammatical, and expressive. Nonetheless, people sometimes have strong convictions that certain language varieties are better or "more correct" than others. For example, many speakers of French (including many educators) perceive Parisian French as superior to the African and Caribbean varieties more commonly spoken by HL students in the United States. Such convictions are not based on objective linguistic criteria; instead, they are related to language ideologies—the often implicit beliefs and taken-for-granted notions regarding language, language varieties, and language practices. Language ideologies are intertwined with beliefs about other social and political categories (Woolard 1989; Woolard and Schieffelin 1994). For example, the preference for the Romance language varieties spoken in European capitals and the perception of such varieties as more "pure" and less "contaminated" by contact with other languages are linked to broader ideologies of nationalism, colonialism, modernity, and race. Similarly, subjective evaluations of social varieties, such as the speech of rural peasants or urban youth, often echo attitudes toward the social groups with which they are associated (Irvine and Gal 2000). For example, on the Southwest Texas border, Mariana Achugar and Silvia Pessoa (2009) found that while members of a bilingual academic community valued the use of Spanish and being bilingual, they were highly critical of the local variety, also known as Spanglish, Fronterizo, Border Spanish, or El Paso Spanish, which they associated with less educated speakers. Subjective evaluations of language varieties and practices can become so naturalized such that they seem like common sense, and speakers of disparaged varieties may share in the negative assessment of their own varieties.

Language ideologies are closely tied to social and political structures, and they tend to reflect the interests of dominant groups, with their power reinforced through their invisibility (Kroskrity 2004). This can be seen in the "standard language ideology," which holds that linguistic variation can and should be eliminated, and that everyone can and should speak a uniform standard variety (Lippi-Green 2012). In reality, because language is inherently variable, no one actually speaks standard languages, which exist only in grammar books and dictionaries (Penny 2000). Although this ideology portrays national standard varieties as neutral and equally accessible and available to all speakers, in fact it is the language of elites that is reified as the "universal" norm, while the varieties spoken by other groups are often labeled "nonstandard" and portrayed as ignorant, defective, or incorrect (Milroy and Milroy 1999; Woolard 2008). In addition to having a detrimental impact on the self-esteem, identity formation, HL maintenance, and academic achievement of HL students who do not speak the "standard" variety, these linguistic hierarchies curtail educational and professional opportunities for speakers of "nonstandard" varieties and thus propagate socioeconomic and political inequality (Fairclough 1995; Lippi-Green 2012; Milroy and Milroy 1999). For example, Arlene Dávila (2001) has documented the marginalization of US Latina/os within Spanish-language broadcasting in the United States based in part on the presumed "inauthenticity" of their Spanish. These ideologies about the relative value of different languages and language varieties are often reflected and reproduced in language teaching materials and practices (Leeman 2012).

Language Contact-Related Phenomena

Not surprisingly, HL students often exhibit linguistic manifestations of contact with English, including lexical borrowing (the incorporation in one language of a word from the other), calques (word-for-word translations or syntactic borrowings), and code-switching (the use of two languages during conversation). Another language contact phenomenon is grammatical convergence, in which bilinguals demonstrate increasing similarity of the grammatical or pragmatic systems of the two languages (Montrul 2004; Poplack 1997; Silva-Corvalán 1994).

While the linguistic features of language contact are often stigmatized as "deviant" or "impure," they are in fact quite natural. For example, numerous studies have shown that code-switching is systematic and rule-governed, just like other language practices. Rather than a hodgepodge or evidence of the inability to speak either language well, code-switching reflects sophisticated knowledge of both languages and of the ways in which they can be combined, and thus it can be considered a sign of proficient bilingualism (Carvalho 2012; Toribio 2001). In addition to showing that code-switching conforms to complex grammatical constraints, researchers have demonstrated that bilinguals shift between languages as a conversational strategy, such as to indicate a topic shift or to signal a change in stance (e.g., Gumperz 1982; Zentella 1997). Speakers choose among their languages or combine them in order to carry out various social functions such as marking identity and in-group membership (He 2006, 2010; Zentella 1997).

Recently researchers have suggested replacing the term "code-switching" with "translanguaging" in order to recognize that bilinguals perform these conversational and social functions by drawing on linguistic repertoires that encompass numerous varieties, registers, and styles distributed across languages (e.g., Canagarajah 2011; Creese and Blackledge 2010; García 2009; Wei 2011). By rejecting the notion of two monolithic and easily delimitable languages, translanguaging emphasizes the flexibility and richness of bilinguals' discursive practices and thus reflects current sociolinguistic understanding that "languages" are not clearly defined objects with clear boundaries and that the classification of different ways of speaking as belonging to distinct languages is influenced by social, political, and ideological factors (Makoni and Pennycook 2006), as is the denigration of language contact phenomena.

SOCIOLINGUISTICS AS CONTENT IN HL EDUCATION

Sociolinguistics in Expansion-Oriented Approaches to Heritage Language

Guadalupe Valdés's (1981) rejection of explicitly "eradicationist" approaches to HL instruction, which seek to replace students' "nonstandard" language varieties with a "standard" variety, and her call for educators to recognize the legitimacy of all language varieties was one of the first applications of sociolinguistic principles to HL education. Building on this early work, many models of HL education now stress the importance of appreciating and validating the language practices of students, their families, and their communities (e.g., Beaudrie, Ducar, and Potowski 2014; Potowski and Carreira 2004) with a focus on expanding students' linguistic repertoires to include additional registers as well as standard, prestige, or "global" varieties of the heritage language.[2] Some HL programs have also incorporated explicit sociolinguistic content within the curriculum, such as the Spanish HL program established by Sara Beaudrie at the University of Arizona (personal communication, 2015).

In many expansionist models, the discussion of sociolinguistic variation, and particularly contextual variation, centers on the notion of appropriateness (e.g., Beaudrie, Ducar, and Potowski 2014; González Pino and Pino 2000; Gutiérrez 1997). As a way to help students recognize and produce language that is "appropriate" in particular settings—and especially professional and academic settings—HL educators sometimes make analogies between language practices and clothing styles, comparing, for example, the use of "informal registers," local varieties, or code-switching in professional settings to wearing pajamas to work or a bathing suit to a wedding. According to this analogy, there is nothing inherently wrong with wearing pajamas or a bathing suit, which are acceptable at home and at the pool or the beach but inappropriate in the workplace or at a wedding because a formal context demands formal attire. Similarly, "nonstandard" language is said to be out of place in formal contexts.

One concern with these analogies and the appropriateness-based models they exemplify is that they represent social variation as if it were the same as contextual variation or registers, while also implying that variation is primarily a question of formality (Leeman 2005). So-called "nonstandard" linguistic forms (such as the English "ain't") are not simply less *formal* than the "standard" counterparts (i.e., "isn't"); they are stigmatized as incorrect, ignorant, or "uneducated." Framing prestigious or standard varieties as more appropriate for high-status contexts or activities downplays the social, economic, and ideological dimensions of language variation and erases the fact that the prescribed linguistic practices are those of powerful groups, thus legitimating their use as gate-keeping mechanisms for access to positions of social or economic power (Fairclough 1992; Leeman 2005). Further, appropriateness-based accounts ignore the interactional and rhetorical intent of the speaker and the possibility of using varieties, styles, and registers to carry out a broad range of conversational strategies and identity work. Thus, such approaches have been criticized both for misrepresenting variation and for legitimizing and reproducing linguistic and social inequalities (Alim 2010; Fairclough 1992).

Critical Language Awareness in Language Education

In contrast with models of education that socialize students into dominant social hierarchies and ideologies, "critical" approaches seek to engage students in examining and questioning taken-for-granted understandings of the world. Such approaches have their roots in both critical pedagogy and critical theory, both of which seek to uncover the often invisible ways in which inequality is reproduced and reinforced through ideology and culture as well as the liberatory possibilities of critical analysis. A key goal of critical pedagogy is to promote socially, politically, or educationally marginalized students' *conscientização*—or coming to critical consciousness, which is seen as the first step in improving their own conditions as well as developing a more just society (Freire 1970). Other key elements in critical pedagogy are the inclusion of students' experiences and knowledge in the curriculum and the promotion of student agency or purposeful engagement with the world.

Researchers and educators who advocate engaging students in the examination of how ideologies, politics, and social hierarchies are embodied, reproduced, and naturalized through language are often referred to as promoting students' "critical language awareness" (Fairclough 1995; Wallace 1999). Originally developed in first language (L1) educational contexts and subsequently applied to HL instruction, a central component of critical language awareness is the consideration of language variation and the mechanisms by which certain varieties are stigmatized and subordinated (Fairclough 1992). Critical language awareness differs from appropriateness-based accounts of language variation that accept and reinforce the status quo in that the goal is for students to actively engage in questioning dominant language ideologies (Alim 2010; Fairclough 1992). Further, the critical examination of taken-for-granted understandings about "good" and "bad" language is designed not only to promote understanding but also to foster student agency in resisting language-based discrimination (Leeman 2005).

Transcultural and Translingual Competence

A general suggestion to include sociolinguistics in L2 education can also be found in the MLA's 2007 *Foreign Language Report*, which aimed to revitalize the study of languages in higher education by realigning curriculum according to the changing needs and profiles of students (Pratt et al. 2008). The report's primary recommendation is to orient undergraduate majors toward students' achievement of "translingual and transcultural competence," defined in part as "the ability to operate between languages" and "to function as informed and capable interlocutors with educated native speakers in the target language" (MLA Ad Hoc Committee on Foreign Languages 2007, 4–5). To achieve this, the MLA recommends integrating the study of language and "content" and abandoning the almost exclusive focus on literary study in the upper levels. Suggested disciplinary content includes cultural studies, history, and politics, with sociolinguistics and bilingualism also mentioned, but specific details are not provided (Schechtman and Koser 2008; Wellmon 2008). Further, the majority of examples offered focus on trans*cultural* knowledge (e.g., in the analysis of cultural narratives in essays, poetry, political rhetoric, etc.) rather than unpacking trans*lingual* competence.

The MLA's definition of transcultural and translingual competence as the ability to operate between languages has been critiqued for reinforcing the notion of "the strict integrity of individual languages" (Kramsch 2014, 300). In addition, the goals of training students to "reflect on the world and themselves through the lens of another language and culture," to "comprehend speakers of the target language as members of foreign societies," and to "grasp themselves as Americans" (MLA Ad Hoc Committee on Foreign Languages 2007, 4–5) discursively exclude speakers of languages other than English as members of "American" society, thereby erasing the longstanding history of multilingualism in the United States and ignoring the presence of HL speakers in the classroom (Pomerantz and Schwartz 2011). Thus, even as the report appears to value linguistic diversity, like ACTFL's *Standards for Foreign Language Learning*, it continues to reproduce ideologies of monolingualism (see Leeman 2011). The report similarly portrays speakers of the "target language" as culturally and linguistically monolithic, and there is no indication that the revised curriculum recognizes the political aspects of language or language variation or that it seeks to engage students in questioning the status quo.

Sociolinguistics for Critical Translingual Competence

Our model for the incorporation of sociolinguistics builds on previous calls for critical language awareness in Spanish HL education (e.g., Martínez 2003; Leeman 2005; Leeman and Rabin 2007) while also incorporating some elements of the MLA proposal—in particular, the goal of fostering students' "ability to operate between languages" (MLA Ad Hoc Committee on Foreign Languages 2007, 4–5). However, we reject both the MLA's construction of students as monolingual English speakers and the notion that the goal is for students to acquire a delimitable "target language." Instead, we emphasize the importance of including considerations of variation and multilingualism (in the United States and abroad) as elements of a critical approach to language education, and we call for language education (including both L2 and HL education) to incorporate critical considerations of the sociopolitics of language and multilingualism in addition to discussions of aesthetic and cultural parameters.

In contrast with expansionist and appropriateness-based approaches to linguistic variation that focus primarily on acquiring the "standard" monolingual varieties, critical translingual competence goes beyond multiple dialect acquisition and entails exploration of the principles and social meaning of variation; the sociolinguistic functions of translanguaging practices, language attitudes, and ideologies; the relationship between language and identity; and the sociopolitics of language inside and outside the United States. The language curriculum must aim to develop the fundamental understanding that linguistic variation, including bilingual as well as nonstandard practices, constitutes a resource for carrying out a wide array of social and political functions and communicating a wide range of symbolic meanings. Rather than imposing any particular language variety (monolingual or otherwise), language education should seek to prepare students to understand variation and to interact with speakers of familiar and unfamiliar varieties and styles as well as to explore the political aspects of language while promoting students' critical consciousness of their own and others' experiences in order to foster their critical agency in making linguistic and other choices (Leeman 2005, 2014). The goal of including critical exploration of these sociolinguistic phenomena is not simply to promote students' understanding of the status quo but rather to enable students to challenge the status quo.

PROMOTING CRITICAL TRANSLINGUAL COMPETENCE: EXAMPLES FOR THE CLASSROOM

In this section, we provide concrete examples of how sociolinguistic content might be incorporated in language education to promote critical translingual competence. These pedagogical recommendations are informed by diverse methodological approaches and include activities centered on reading scholarly research, working with large scale survey data, collecting oral histories with family or community members, analyzing written and oral texts, and conducting community-based linguistic landscape research and analysis, to name a few. The sample activities provided here can be adapted according to the level of students' abilities and course content. While our focus in this chapter is on HL education, our proposal applies to both L2 and HL contexts.

Multilingualism

In addition to linguistic knowledge, developing critical translingual competence requires understanding how the heritage language (or second language) is situated in a broader sociolinguistic and sociopolitical context. As part of this objective, students should examine the history of multilingualism both in the United States and in countries where the heritage language is spoken, which can highlight the false rhetoric surrounding imagined notions of "one nation, one language." Further, studying the history of specific heritage languages in the United States is one way to include and validate HL students' experiences.

Resources for research on multilingualism in the United States include volumes such as Potowski (2010) and Wiley and colleagues (2014), which include chapters on the most commonly spoken languages in the United States, and survey data on the home use of minority languages as well as related data briefs, reports, and maps, which are available from the US Census Bureau's American Community Survey "Language Use" website.[3] Additional data, maps, and analyses are available via media outlets such as *Slate* (Blatt 2014) and the Pew Research Center's reports on Latina/o and Asian American communities.[4]

Students can carry out qualitative activities or research with their peers and families and in their local communities. For example, one approach to help students recognize and appreciate linguistic diversity as well as learn about community members' personal experiences of language discrimination, language maintenance or shift, and language-based identities is through oral history multimedia projects or digital storytelling. There are numerous free software programs that can be used for such projects, including Audacity, Apple iMovie, Microsoft Photo Story 3, and Windows Live Movie Maker. Students can conduct video or audio-recorded interviews with a family member, write a report, and create a final web-based project with recordings, photos, and other supplemental materials to share with peers, similar to what US high school students do in documenting the "linguistic life story" of a family elder as part of the SKILLS curriculum (Bucholtz et al. 2014, 151).[5]

In addition to observing, documenting, and analyzing spoken language, students can research the use of the heritage language in advertising, popular media, and the built environment (such as billboards and public signage). Students take on the role of language investigators (Sayer 2010) and analyze the kinds of information provided in different languages and how differences reflect their sociopolitical status.[6] In the case of Chinese, students might analyze the use of different writing systems in the linguistic landscape (i.e., traditional versus simplified characters) in order to see how different Chineses are used in local settings (Leung and Wu 2012). Students can also engage in critical analyses of how different languages and language varieties can be used to convey particular social meanings such as authenticity or exoticism (see Leeman and Modan 2009) or to reproduce negative stereotypes about speakers of minority languages, such as in the case of "Mock Spanish" in the United States (see Hill 2008). Such analyses should include media from abroad and linguistic landscape examples drawn from international research (see, for example, Gorter, Marten, and Van Mensel 2012; Shohamy, Ben-Rafael, and Barni 2010; or the journal *Linguistic Landscape*).

Several activities can also be designed to reveal monolingualism as a global exception. For example, students can collaborate in small groups to construct a multilingual world map representing the official, national, and spoken languages across different world areas using a site like Ethnologue .com, which offers statistics about the world's 7,106 living languages. Such an activity should promote discussion and problematization of definitions of "a language" and how languages are constructed and counted as well as critical analysis of the role of language in nationalism and the construction of the modern nation-state.

To further engage learners in understanding the political parameters and social impact of language policy, learners could research language-in-education policies where the heritage language is spoken abroad. For example, Spanish HL students can research the history of intercultural bilingual education initiatives in Latin America designed to combat linguistic and cultural subordination of speakers of indigenous languages like Quechua and Aymara (see López and Küper 1999) and can engage in a mock debate about the potential promise and limitations of its implementation. More broadly, students might examine UNESCO's Education for All by 2015 initiative and debate whether monolingual schooling violates the right of minority-language speakers to have equal access to quality education.[7]

Language Variation

In order to enable students to recognize variation as an inherent characteristic of language, students should study the ways languages vary across space, social groups or communities of practice, context, and time. Historical texts and corpora are useful for exploring the naturalness of language change (e.g., see the 100-million-word Spanish corpus or the International Corpus of Arabic[8]) and the linguistic consequences of language contact (see the World Loanword Database[9]). In conjunction with historical data, current examples of language variation can be drawn from both international and local sources such as linguistic landscape, social media, music and song lyrics, students' field notes or recordings of friends or family (with permission), and print, broadcast, and Internet media from the United States and abroad. For instance, HL speakers of Arabic should study not only the many contact situations of spoken language varieties in the Arab world but also the ethnic and sociopolitical tension surrounding such contact. One way for students to further explore this topic is to critically examine the choice of language variety in radio, television, and news broadcasting, along the lines of Mahmoud Al Batal's (2002) analysis of the mixing of the formal "standard" variety, fuṣḥā, and the Lebanese colloquial variety in forty local news broadcasts in Lebanon.

It is crucial that students also study contextual and stylistic variation, including socially indexed meanings, and the role of variation in identity performance and ascription. Film and TV clips can be used to explore how different languages and language varieties are used to portray characters in different ways (see Lippi-Green 2012 for discussion of the association of nonstandard varieties of English with villains in Disney movies; see Fuller 2012 regarding the linking of Spanish to traditional values; and see Bleichenbacher 2008 for a discussion of the discursive functions of multilingualism in Hollywood movies). Connections between identity construction and language variation could also be explored through playing audio snippets of a dialogue in a movie and asking students to interpret the characters' identities based solely on their speech. To expose and examine competing social meanings and norms regarding variation, students could administer surveys or conduct interviews regarding the attitudes held by family, peers, and community members toward different ways of performing speech acts in the heritage language (e.g., greetings, farewells, forms of address, thanking, making requests) in different situational contexts (e.g., home, school, work) (see Correa 2011; Martínez 2003; Rodríguez Pino and Villa 1994). Crucially, discussion must include a consideration of the social and power dynamics undergirding the results (Leeman 2005).

Discussions of social variation and identity should also include activities explicitly highlighting the role of speaker agency in choosing among different linguistic forms and styles. In this regard, movie clips can be used to show not only how certain varieties are associated with certain social groups or situations but also how characters style-shift between varieties in their linguistic repertoire in the construction and performance of identity (e.g., the *Key and Peele* series on Comedy Central). In order to explore this further, students could carry out analyses of how they use different languages and language varieties on a daily basis as well as how, when, and under what conditions they mix languages (MacGregor-Mendoza 1999). A key element of such activities is for students to analyze the various factors that shape their language choices and the (invisible) meanings conveyed by those choices, such as in the activity based on African American Vernacular English described by H. Samy Alim (2010).

Another activity that can be used to highlight both contextual variation and the agentive use of different styles to convey different social meanings involves asking students to brainstorm different HL expressions for a specific topic, for example, asking about someone's health in a range of settings, such as friendly conversation among friends and in a consultation with a doctor in a hospital setting (e.g., "How are you feeling?" versus "Tell me about your symptoms"). After discussing inherent differences between such settings, students can consider why a doctor might choose to use an "informal" style, such as to put a patient at ease or to establish rapport.

Multilingual Discourse

Together with the analysis of language variation described above, students should also analyze translanguaging or code-switching as a stylistic resource. In addition, they should examine how combining languages can serve as a discursive strategy to add emphasis, mitigate a request, or change topic. These functions can be studied through discourse analysis of multilingual data samples (drawn from sources such as those mentioned above), minimally identifying the interlocutor(s), conversational topic, or strategy being employed along with the linguistic and social context in which switches occur within and between sentences (Carvalho 2012; Creese and Blackledge 2010; Sayer 2008).

In order to grasp the rule-governed nature of code-switching, students can complete a pedagogical activity modeled on Almeida Jacqueline Toribio's (2002) research study in which participants read two fairy tales aloud and judged which one sounded better. One fairy tale conformed to structural code-switching constraints while the other violated them (such as by switching languages between an auxiliary and a main verb). Students could do the same and then try to derive patterns or constraints to account for the difference between "good" and "bad" switches. This can lead them to realize, in a bottom-up fashion, both that there are rules or patterns and that they already implicitly know them. Similar materials could easily be prepared in other languages.

Multilingual discourse in film, literature, and other resources from the United States and abroad (including conversations recorded by instructors or students) can also be used both to challenge hegemonic constructions of monolithic national standard languages and to foster awareness of translanguaging as a broader phenomenon. Jennifer Leeman and Lisa Rabin (2007) describe activities based on an early modern Latin American multilingual text (Guaman Poma's *Nueva corónica y buen gobierno*, 1615), which they used to promote recognition of Quechua/Spanish bilingualism as well as to engage students in critically analyzing ideologies and practices of literacy in colonial and postcolonial contexts.

Language Attitudes and Ideologies

After learning key sociolinguistic concepts, it is essential that students have the opportunity to apply them in the analysis of systems of values and beliefs about language, varieties of language, and specific language practices as well as the impact of such belief systems on language maintenance. One way to explore different language ideologies and their impact is by analyzing qualitative data provided in published studies. Depending on the course, students need not read the entire study. Instead, the instructor can extract the data for analysis and in-class discussion. For example, Mihyon Jeon (2008) and Sarah J. Shin (2005) provide ample quotes from different generations of Korean immigrants in both academic and community contexts that students can use to explore the role of language ideologies in the intergenerational transmission of heritage languages as well as the connection between language and identity.

To explore and expose attitudes toward different HL varieties, one technique is to use a matched-guise activity in which students listen to samples of speech and judge several personal attributes of speakers of different varieties of the heritage language. In a similar activity based on "perceptual dialectology" (Preston 1989), students ask friends and family to rank different national or regional varieties according to pleasantness and correctness and to provide descriptions of the speakers of those varieties. Responses are then tabulated and discussed in order to examine the connection between attitudes toward speakers and different varieties.

A course blog, wiki, or other online learning environment can also be used for students to explore ideologies surrounding language and ethnic identity. Blogs can be used to discuss examples of such ideologies in mainstream media. For example, HL students of Spanish might view "'Fake' Latinos," "a video-recorded debate on *HuffPost Live*, about whether the ability to speak Spanish is essential for "authentic" Latina/o identity. After watching the clip, students write a blog post about their own views and react to their peers' posts. As an in-class follow-up, the teacher might ask students to collectively identify and analyze recurring themes in the responses and to critically consider the source of negative opinions or evaluations.

As noted earlier, linguistic landscape studies can be used for analyses of the symbolic meanings of different languages. The analysis of multilingualism in international linguistic landscapes, such as Aneta Pavlenko's (2008) study on the visibility and everyday use of Ukrainian and Russian in Ukraine, can provide an excellent means to explore how language is tied to ideologies of nationalism. Depending on the class, instructors could assign the reading or simply use the images for class activities and discussion.

The pervasiveness of the standard language ideology can be explored with a simple Google-search activity in which students enter phrases like "Where is the best French spoken?" and then collaborate to identify the most commonly used words (e.g., "pure," "correct," "proper") and visually represent them in a word cloud using a program like Wordle.[10] Each group could then analyze the ideologies inherent in the question as well as in word clouds generated. HL educators might engage students in critical discussions about which varieties of the heritage language are represented in textbooks and other teaching materials and why that might be the case. As José Del Valle

(2014) notes, the choice of variety used in the classroom is less important than students' recognition that it involved a choice.

Finally, students should be given tools to grapple with the personal impact of language ideologies, such as through language shift within their family or personal experiences with linguistic discrimination. As mentioned previously, digital storytelling is one pedagogical technique that positions students as storytellers and cultural experts. Several recent HL service-learning projects have also sought to empower students as experts and activists combating linguistic discrimination in local communities (see Leeman, Rabin, and Román-Mendoza 2011; Lowther Pereira 2015; Martínez and Schwartz 2012).

CONCLUSION

In recent years, numerous factors have contributed to a growing interest in including sociolinguistics both in HL teacher preparation and within the language curriculum. These include recognition in the humanities and social sciences of the role of language in the construction of knowledge and social structures; greater attention to social aspects of language learning and education; and increased globalization and international migration as well as an increased emphasis on interdisciplinarity and practicality in postsecondary education (Kramsch 2014; MLA Ad Hoc Committee on Foreign Languages 2007). However, recent proposals to integrate sociolinguistic concepts into L2 and HL education have stopped short of using them as a foundation for building students' critical consciousness. On one hand, appropriateness-based approaches run the risk of misrepresenting linguistic variation and unquestioningly reproducing dominant linguistic and social hierarchies, while on the other hand, the MLA report downplays or ignores the presence of HL students and reinforces monolingualist ideologies.

In this chapter, we have presented an alternative critical model for how a broad range of sociolinguistic topics can be productively incorporated within the HL curriculum. Because we believe that L2 and HL education must take into account the broader sociolinguistic context in which the "target language," its speakers, and students are situated, we argue that sociolinguistics should play a fundamental role in curricular design and implementation. It must also be incorporated at the level of content within the curriculum as a way to help students develop critical language awareness, including an understanding of the social, cultural, and political aspects of language, language variation, and multilingualism.

In contrast with other proposals for including sociolinguistics in HL education, our critical approach seeks to use sociolinguistics to engage students in questioning the status quo. Rather than seeking to teach students how they should speak in various situations, our goals include fostering students' agency and their understanding of linguistic knowledge as a creative resource for performing identities, negotiating social relationships, and navigating political hierarchies. In line with critical pedagogical approaches, our proposed learner-centered objectives include achieving critical translingual competence and ensuring students' full participation in shaping and remaking the world in which they live.

NOTES

1. A full discussion of the competing definitions of "heritage language" is beyond the scope of this chapter, but see Hornberger and Wang (2008), Leeman (2015) and Van Deusen-Scholl (2003). In this chapter, we are referring primarily to "foreign" or additional language education designed for learners who have some home knowledge of that language. It should be noted that while heritage language education is a growing field within "foreign" language education, far too few HL speakers have access to such programs (Wiley 2005b).
2. Unfortunately, even when paying lip service to the equality of all varieties, teaching materials often continue to uphold European or "global" Spanish as the model and to disparage contact varieties (Ducar 2009; García 2009; Leeman and Martínez 2007; Lynch and Potowski 2014). There is a similar need for greater recognition of bilingual practices and regional varieties in the teaching of other HLs; as Jeffrey Bale (2010) notes, Arabic HL programs tend to focus exclusively on Modern Standard Arabic, while most Chinese textbooks were developed for either native speakers (e.g., in China or Taiwan) or foreign-language learners (e.g., in North America) and neither address HL learners' complex needs nor recognize different varieties of oral and written Chinese used by HL speakers.
3. "Language Use," US Census Bureau, Data Integration Division, https://www.census.gov/hhes/socdemo/language/data/acs/.
4. For the Pew Research Center reports, see http://www.pewhispanic.org/, and http://www.pewsocialtrends.org/asianamericans/.
5. For more digital storytelling applications in the classroom, see Vinogradova (2014a, 2014b) and the online *Foreign Language Technology Magazine* (FLTMAG).
6. See, for example, David Malinowski's (2013) course offered at UC-Berkeley, "Reading the Multilingual City: Chinese, Korean, and Japanese in Bay Area Linguistic Landscapes," and the photo-diary projects reported in Martínez (2014).
7. "Education for All," UNESCO, http://www.unesco.org/new/en/education/themes/leading-the-international-agenda/education-for-all/the-efa-movement/.
8. "International Corpus of Arabic," Ibrahim Shihata Arabic UNL Center, *Bibliotheca Alexandrina*, http://www.bibalex.org/unl/frontend/Project.aspx?id=9.
9. Martin Haspelmath and Uri Tadmor, eds., "World Loanword Database," Max Planck Institute for Evolutionary Anthropology, http://wold.clld.org.
10. Jonathan Feinberg, "Wordle," http://www.wordle.net/.

REFERENCES

Achugar, Mariana, and Silvia Pessoa. 2009. "Power and Place: Language Attitudes toward Spanish in a Bilingual Academic Community in Southwest Texas." *Spanish in Context* 6, no. 2: 199–223. http://dx.doi.org/10.1075/sic.6.2.03ach.

Al Batal, Mahmoud. 2002. "Identity and Language Tension in Lebanon: The Arabic of Local News at LBCI." In *Language Contact and Language Conflict in Arabic: Variations on a Sociolinguistic Theme*, ed. Aleya Rouchdy, 91–115. New York: Routledge.

Alba, Richard. 2004. *Language Assimilation Today: Bilingualism Persists More Than in the Past, but English Still Dominates*. Albany, NY: Lewis Mumford Center for Comparative Urban and Regional Research, University at Albany.

Alim, H. Samy. 2010. "Critical Language Awareness." In *Sociolinguistics and Language Education*, ed. Nancy Hornberger, 205–30. Tonawanda, NY: Multilingual Matters.

Bale, Jeffrey. 2010. "Arabic as a Heritage Language in the United States." *International Multilingual Research Journal* 4, no. 2: 125–51. http://dx.doi.org/10.1080/19313152.2010.499041.

Bartolomé, Lilia, and Donaldo Macedo. 1999. "(Mis)Educating Mexican Americans through Language." In *Sociopolitical Perspectives on Language Policy and Planning in the USA*, ed. Thom Huebner and Kathryn Davis, 223–41. Philadelphia: John Benjamins. http://dx.doi.org/10.1075/sibil.16.16bar.

Beaudrie, Sara, Cynthia Ducar, and Kim Potowski. 2014. "General Sociolinguistic Considerations." In *Heritage Language Teaching: Research and Practice*, ed. Sara Beaudrie, Cynthia Ducar, and Kim Potowski, 13–31. Boston: McGraw-Hill.

Blatt, Ben. 2014. "Tagalog in California, Cherokee in Arkansas: What Language Does Your State Speak?" *Slate*, May 13. http://www.slate.com/articles/arts/culturebox/2014/05/language_map_what_s_the_most_popular_language_in_your_state.html.

Bleichenbacher, Lukas. 2008. *Multilingualism in the Movies: Hollywood Characters and Their Language Choices*. Tübingen: Francke Verlag.

Bonfiglio, Paul Thomas. 2002. *Race and the Rise of Standard American*. Berlin: Mouton de Gruyter. http://dx.doi.org/10.1515/9783110851991.

Bucholtz, Mary, and Kira Hall. 2005. "Identity and Interaction: A Sociocultural Linguistic Approach." *Discourse Studies* 7, no. 4–5: 584–614.

Bucholtz, Mary, Audrey Lopez, Allina Mojarro, Elena Skapoulli, Chris VanderStouwe, and Shawn Warner-Garcia. 2014. "Sociolinguistic Justice in the Schools: Student Researchers as Linguistic Experts." *Language and Linguistics Compass* 8, no. 4: 144–57. http://dx.doi.org/10.1111/lnc3.12070.

Canagarajah, Suresh. 2011. "Codemeshing in Academic Writing: Identifying Teachable Strategies of Translanguaging." *Modern Language Journal* 95, no. 3: 401–17. http://dx.doi.org/10.1111/j.1540-4781.2011.01207.x.

Carreira, María. 2007. "Teaching Spanish in the US." In *Spanish in Contact: Policy, Social and Linguistic Inquiries*, ed. Kim Potowski and Richard Cameron, 61–79. Amsterdam: John Benjamins. http://dx.doi.org/10.1075/impact.22.07car.

Carvalho, Ana. 2012. "Code-Switching: From Theoretical to Pedagogical Considerations." In *Spanish as a Heritage Language in the United States*, ed. Sara M. Beaudrie and Marta Fairclough, 139–157. Washington, DC: Georgetown University Press.

Collier, Virginia P., and Wayne P. Thomas. 2013. *La educación de los estudiantes de inglés para un mundo en constante transformación*. Albuquerque, NM: DLENM Fuente Press.

Correa, Maite. 2011. "Advocating for Critical Pedagogical Approaches to Teaching Spanish as a Heritage Language: Some Considerations." *Foreign Language Annals* 44, no. 2: 308–20. http://dx.doi.org/10.1111/j.1944-9720.2011.01132.x.

Coupland, Nikolas. 2007. *Style: Language Variation and Identity*. Cambridge: Cambridge University Press. http://dx.doi.org/10.1017/CBO9780511755064.

Creese, Angela, and Adrian Blackledge. 2010. "Translanguaging in the Bilingual Classroom: A Pedagogy for Learning and Teaching?" *Modern Language Journal* 94, no. 1: 103–15. http://dx.doi.org/10.1111/j.1540-4781.2009.00986.x.

Dávila, Arlene. 2001. *Latinos, Inc.* Berkeley: University of California Press.

Del Valle, José. 2014. "The Politics of Normativity and Globalization: Which Spanish in the Classroom?" *Modern Language Journal* 98, no. 1: 358–72. http://dx.doi .org/10.1111/j.1540-4781.2014.12066.x.

Doerr, Neriko Musha, and Kiri Lee. 2009. "Contesting Heritage: Language, Legitimacy, and Schooling at a Weekend Japanese-Language School in the United States." *Language and Education: An International Journal* 23, no. 5: 425–41. http:// dx.doi.org/10.1080/09500780802651706.

Ducar, Cynthia. 2009. "The Sound of Silence: Spanish Heritage Textbooks' Treatment of Language Variation." In *Español en los Estados Unidos y en otros contextos: Cuestiones sociolingüísticas, políticas y pedagógicas*, ed. Jennifer Leeman and Manel Lacorte, 347–68. Madrid: Iberoamericana Editorial Vervuert.

Eckert, Penelope. 2001. "Style and Social Meaning." In *Style and Sociolinguistic Variation*, ed. Penelope Eckert and John R. Rickford, 119–26. Cambridge: Cambridge University Press.

———. 2012. "Three Waves of Variation Study: The Emergence of Meaning in the Study of Sociolinguistic Variation." *Annual Review of Anthropology* 41, no. 1: 87–100. http://dx.doi.org/10.1146/annurev-anthro-092611-145828.

Fairclough, Norman. 1992. *Critical Language Awareness*. London: Longman.

———. 1995. *Critical Discourse Analysis*. Boston: Addison-Wesley.

Freire, Paulo. 1970. *The Pedagogy of the Oppressed*. New York: Herder and Herder.

Fuller, Janet M. 2012. *Spanish Speakers in the USA*. Clevedon: Multilingual Matters.

García, Ofelia. 2009. *Bilingual Education in the 21st century: Global Perspectives*. Malden: Wiley–Blackwell.

González Pino, Barbara G., and Frank Pino. 2000. "Serving the Heritage Speaker across a Five-year Program." *ADFL Bulletin* 32:27–35.

Gorter, Durk, Heiko F. Marten, and Luk Van Mensel. 2012. *Minority Languages in the Linguistic Landscape*. Basingstoke, England: Palgrave Macmillan.

Gumperz, John J. 1982. *Language and Social Identity*. Cambridge: Cambridge University Press.

Gutiérrez, John. 1997. "Teaching Spanish as a Heritage Language: A Case for Language Awareness." *ADFL Bulletin* 29, no. 1: 33–36. http://dx.doi.org/10.1632 /adfl.29.1.33.

Halliday, Martin A. K., and Ruqaiya Hasan. 1976. *Cohesion in English*. London: Longman.

He, Agnes Weiyun. 2006. "Toward an Identity-based Model for the Development of Chinese as a Heritage Language." *Heritage Language Journal* 4, no. 1: 1–28.

———. 2010. "The Heart of Heritage: Sociocultural Dimensions of Heritage Language Learning." *Annual Review of Applied Linguistics* 30:66–82. http://dx.doi.org/10.1017/S0267190510000073.

Heath, Shirley Brice. 1976. "A National Language Academy: Debate in the New Nation." *International Journal of the Sociology of Language* 11:9–44.

Hill, Jane. H. 2008. *The Everyday Language of White Racism*. Chichester, UK: Wiley-Blackwell. http://dx.doi.org/10.1002/9781444304732.

Hornberger, Nancy. 2005. "Language and Education." In *Sociolinguistics and Language Teaching*, ed. Sandra L. McKay and Nancy H. Hornberger, 449–73. New York: Cambridge University Press.

———. 2002. "Multilingual Language Policies and the Continua of Biliteracy: An Ecological Approach." *Language Policy* 1, no. 1: 27–51. http://dx.doi.org/10.1023/A:1014548611951.

Hornberger, Nancy H., and Shuhan C. Wang. 2008. "Who Are Our Heritage Language Learners? Identity and Biliteracy in Heritage Language Education in the United States." In *Heritage Language Education: A New Field Emerging*, ed. Donna Brinton, Olga Kagan, and Susan Bauckus, 3–35. New York: Routledge.

Irvine, Judith T., and Susan Gal. 2000. "Language Ideology and Linguistic Differentiation." In *Regimes of Language: Ideologies, Politics, and Identities*, ed. Paul V. Kroskrity, 35–84. Santa Fe: School of American Research Press.

Jeon, Mihyon. 2008. "Korean Heritage Language Maintenance and Language Ideology." *Heritage Language Journal* 6, no. 2: 54–71.

Johnstone, Barbara. 2009. "Stance, Style, and the Linguistic Individual." In *Stance: Sociolinguistic Perspectives*, ed. Alexandra Jaffe, 29–52. Oxford: Oxford University Press. http://dx.doi.org/10.1093/acprof:oso/9780195331646.003.0002.

Kramsch, Claire. 2014. "Teaching Foreign Languages in an Era of Globalization: Introduction." *Modern Language Journal* 98, no. 1: 296–311. http://dx.doi.org/10.1111/j.1540-4781.2014.12057.x.

Kroskrity, Paul V. 2004. "Language Ideologies." In *Companion to Linguistic Anthropology*, ed. Alessandro Duranti, 496–517. Malden: Basil Blackwell.

Labov, William. 1972. *Sociolinguistic Patterns*. Philadelphia: University of Pennsylvania Press.

Lave, Jean, and Etienne Wenger. 1998. *Communities of Practice: Learning, Meaning, and Identity*. Cambridge: Cambridge University Press.

Lee, David YW. 2001. "Genres, Registers, Text Types, Domains and Styles: Clarifying the Concepts and Navigating a Path through the BNC Jungle." Language Learning and Technology 5, no. 3: 37–72. http://ro.uow.edu.au/artspapers/598/.

Leeman, Jennifer. 2005. "Engaging Critical Pedagogy: Spanish for Native Speakers." *Foreign Language Annals* 38, no. 1: 35–45. http://dx.doi.org/10.1111/j.1944-9720.2005.tb02451.x.

———. 2011. "Standards, Commodification, and Critical Service Learning in Minority Language Communities." *Modern Language Journal* 95, no. 2: 300–303. http://dx.doi.org/10.1111/j.1540-4781.2011.01184.x.

———. 2012. "Investigating Language Ideologies in Spanish as a Heritage Language." In *Spanish as a Heritage Language in the US: State of the Science*, edited by Sara Beaudrie and Marta Fairclough, 43–59. Washington, DC: Georgetown University Press.

———. 2013. "Categorizing Latinos in the History of the US Census: The Official Racialization of Spanish." In *A Political History of Spanish: The Making of a Language*, ed. José Del Valle, 305–24. Cambridge: Cambridge University Press. http://dx.doi.org/10.1017/CBO9780511794339.025.

———. 2014. "Critical Approaches to Teaching Spanish as a Local-foreign Language." In *The Handbook of Hispanic Applied Linguistics*, ed. Manel Lacorte, 275–92. New York: Routledge.

———. 2015. "Heritage Language Education and Identity in the United States." *Annual Review of Applied Linguistics* 35: 100–119.

Leeman, Jennifer, and Glenn Martínez. 2007. "From Identity to Commodity: Discourses of Spanish in Heritage Language Textbooks." *Critical Inquiry in Language Studies* 4, no. 1: 35–65. http://dx.doi.org/10.1080/15427580701340741.

Leeman, Jennifer, and Gabriella Modan. 2009. "Commodified Language in Chinatown: A Contextualized Approach to Linguistic Landscape." *Journal of Sociolinguistics* 13, no. 3: 332–62. http://dx.doi.org/10.1111/j.1467-9841.2009.00409.x.

Leeman, Jennifer, and Lisa Rabin. 2007. "Reading Language: Critical Perspectives for the Literature Classroom." *Hispania* 90, no. 2: 304–15.

Leeman, Jennifer, Lisa Rabin, and Esperanza Román-Mendoza. 2011. "Critical Pedagogy Beyond the Classroom Walls: Community Service-Learning and Spanish Heritage Language Education." *Heritage Language Journal* 8, no. 3: 1–21.

Leung, Genevieve Y., and Ming-Hsuan Wu. 2012. "Linguistic Landscape and Heritage Language Literacy Education: A Case Study of Linguistic Rescaling in Philadelphia Chinatown." *Written Language and Literacy* 15, no. 1: 114–40. http://dx.doi.org/10.1075/wll.15.1.06leu.

Lippi-Green, Rosina. 2012. *English with an Accent: Language, Ideology and Discrimination in the United States*. 2nd ed. London: Routledge.

López, Luis Enrique, and Wolgang Küper. 1999. "La educación intercultural bilingüe en América Latina: Balance y perspectivas." Revista Iberoamericana de Educación 20:17–85. http://www.rieoei.org/rie20a02.htm.

Lowther Pereira, Kelly. 2015. "Developing Critical Language Awareness via Service-Learning for Spanish Heritage Speakers." *Heritage Language Journal* 12, no. 2: 159–85.

Lynch, Andrew, and Kim Potowski. 2014. "La Valoración del Habla Bilingüe en Estados Unidos: Fundamentos Sociolingüísticos y Pedagógicos en Hablando Bien se Entiende la Gente." *Hispania* 97, no. 1: 32–46. http://dx.doi.org/10.1353/hpn.2014.0025.

MacGregor-Mendoza, Patricia L. 1999. "Looking at Life through Language." In *Language Alive in the Classroom*, ed. Rebecca S. Wheeler, 81–87. Westport, CT: Praeger.

Makoni, Sinfree, and Alastair Pennycook. 2006. "Disinventing and Reconstituting Languages." In *Disinventing and Reconstituting Languages*, ed. Sinfree Makoni and Alastair Pennycook, 1–41. Clevedon: Multilingual Matters.

Malinowski, David. 2013. "Reading the Multilingual City: Chinese, Korean, and Japanese in Bay Area Linguistic Landscapes." *Linguistic Landscape at UCBerkeley* (blog). April 24. http://ucblinguisticlandscape.edublogs.org/.

———. 2003. "Classroom Based Dialect Awareness in Heritage Language Instruction: A Critical Applied Linguistic Approach." *Heritage Language Journal* 1, no. 1: 1–14.

Martínez, Glenn. 2014. "Vital Signs: A Photovoice Assessment of the Linguistic Landscape in Spanish in Healthcare Facilities along the US–Mexico Border." *International Journal of Communication and Health* 4:16–24.

Martínez, Glenn, and Adam Schwartz. 2012. "Elevating "Low" Language for High Stakes: A Case for Critical, Community-Based Learning in a Medical Spanish for Heritage Learners Program." *Heritage Language Journal* 9, no. 2: 37–49.

Matthiessen, Christian M. I. M. 1993. "Register in the Round: Diversity in a Unified Theory of Register Analysis." In *Register Analysis: Theory and Practice*, ed. Mohsen Ghadessy, 221–92. London: Pinter.

Mendoza-Denton, Norma. 2008. *Homegirls: Language and Cultural Practice among Latina Youth Gangs*. Malden, MA: Blackwell. http://dx.doi.org/10.1002/9780470693728.

Milroy, James, and Lesley Milroy. 1999. *Authority in Language*. 3rd ed. London: Routledge.

MLA Ad Hoc Committee on Foreign Languages. 2007. Foreign Languages and Higher Education: New Structures for a Changed World. Retrieved from https://apps.mla.org/pdf/forlang_news_pdf.pdf.

Montrul, Silvina. 2004. "Subject and Object Expression in Spanish Heritage Speakers: A Case of Morphosyntactic Convergence." *Bilingualism: Language and Cognition* 7, no. 2: 125–42. http://dx.doi.org/10.1017/S1366728904001464.

Pavlenko, Aneta. 2002. "'We Have Room but for One Language Here': Language and National Identity at the Turn of the 20th Century." *Multilingua* 21:163–96.

———. 2008. "Linguistic Landscape of Kyiv, Ukraine: A Diachronic Study." In *Linguistic Landscape in the City*, ed. Elana Shohamy, Eliezer Ben-Rafael, and Monica Barni, 133–50. Bristol: Multilingual Matters.

Penny, Ralph. 2000. *Variation and Change in Spanish*. Cambridge: Cambridge University Press. http://dx.doi.org/10.1017/CBO9781139164566.

Pomerantz, Anne, and Adam Schwartz. 2011. "Border Talk: Narratives of Spanish Language Encounters in the United States." *Language and Intercultural Communication* 11 , no. 3: 176–96. http://dx.doi.org/10.1080/14708477.2010.550923.

Poplack, Shana. 1997. "The Sociolinguistic Dynamics of Apparent Convergence." In *Towards a Social Science of Language: Papers in Honor of William Labov*, ed. Gregory Guy, John Baugh, and Deborah Schiffrin, 285–309. Amsterdam: John Benjamins. http://dx.doi.org/10.1075/cilt.128.19pop.

Potowski, Kim, ed. 2010. *Language Diversity in the USA*. Cambridge: Cambridge University Press. http://dx.doi.org/10.1017/CBO9780511779855.

Potowski, Kim, and María Carreira. 2004. "Teacher Development and National Standards for Spanish as a Heritage Language." *Foreign Language Annals* 37, no. 3: 427–37. http://dx.doi.org/10.1111/j.1944-9720.2004.tb02700.x.

Pratt, Mary Louise, Michael Geisler, Claire Kramsch, Scott Mcginnis, Peter Patrikis, Karin Ryding, and Haun Saussy. 2008. "The Issue." *Modern Language Journal* 92, no. 2: 287–92. http://dx.doi.org/10.1111/j.1540-4781.2007.00719_2.x.

Preston, Dennis R. 1989. *Perceptual Dialectology: Nonlinguists' Views of Areal Linguistics. Dudecht*. Foris Publications. http://dx.doi.org/10.1515/9783110871913.

Rivera-Mills, Susana V. 2011. "Use of Voseo and Latino Identity: An Intergenerational Study of Hondurans and Salvadorans in the Western Region of the US." In *Selected Proceedings of the 13th Hispanic Linguistics Symposium*, ed. Luis A. Ortiz-López, 94–106. Somerville: Cascadilla Proceedings Project.

———. 2012. "Spanish Heritage Language Maintenance: Its Legacy and Its Future." In *Spanish as a Heritage Language in the United States: The State of the Field*, ed. Sara M. Beaudrie and Marta Fairclough, 21–42. Washington, DC: Georgetown University Press.

Rodríguez Pino, C., and Daniel Villa. 1994. "A Student-centered Spanish for Native Speakers Program: Theory, Curriculum and Outcome Assessment." In *Faces in a Crowd: Individual Learners in Multisection Programs*, ed. Carol Klee, 355–73. Boston: Heinle and Heinle.

Ruiz, Richard. 1984. "Orientations in Language Planning." *NABE Journal* 8:15–34.

Sánchez-Muñoz, Ana. 2010. "Different Words for Different Contexts: Intra-Speaker Variation in Spanish as a Heritage Language." In *Spanish of the Southwest: A Language in Transition*, ed. Susana Rivera-Mills and Daniel Villa, 337–52. Madrid: Iberoamericana.

Sayer, Peter. 2008. "Demystifying Language Mixing: Spanglish in School." *Journal of Latinos and Education* 7, no. 2: 94–112. http://dx.doi.org/10.1080/15348430701827030.

———. 2010. "Using the Linguistic Landscape as a Pedagogical Resource." *ELT Journal* 64, no. 2: 143–54. http://dx.doi.org/10.1093/elt/ccp051.

Schechtman, Robert R., and Julie Koser. 2008. "Foreign Languages and Higher Education: A Pragmatic Approach to Change." *Modern Language Journal* 92, no. 2: 309–12. http://dx.doi.org/10.1111/j.1540-4781.2007.00719_9.x.

Schmidt, Ronald Sr. 2002. "Racialization and Language Policy: The Case of the USA." *Multilingua* 21, no. 2–3: 141–62.

Shin, Sarah J. 2005. *Developing in Two Languages: Korean Children in America*. Clevedon, UK: Multilingual Matters.

Shohamy, Elana, Eliezer Ben-Rafael, and Monica Barni, eds. 2010. *Linguistic Landscape in the City*. Bristol: Multilingual Matters.

Silva-Corvalán, Carmen. 1994. *Language Contact and Change: Spanish in Los Angeles*. Los Angeles: Oxford University Press.

Tannen, Deborah. 2005. *Conversational Style: Analyzing Talk among Friends*. Oxford: Oxford University Press.

Thomas, Wayne P., and Virginia P. Collier. 2002. *A National Study of School Effectiveness for Language Minority Students' Long-term Academic Achievement*. Santa Cruz, CA: Center for Research on Education, Diversity and Excellence.

Toribio, Almeida Jacqueline. 2001. "On the Emergence of Bilingual Code-switching Competence." *Bilingualism: Language and Cognition* 4, no. 3: 203–31. http://dx.doi.org/10.1017/S1366728901000414.

———. 2002. "Spanish-English Code-Switching among US Latinos." *International Journal of the Sociology of Language* 158:89–119.

Valdés, Guadalupe. 1981. "Pedagogical Implications of Teaching Spanish to the Spanish-Speaking in the United States." In *Teaching Spanish to the Hispanic Bilingual*, ed. Guadalupe Valdés, Anthony G. Lozano, and Rodolfo García-Moya, 3–20. New York: Teacher's College.

Van Deusen-Scholl, Nelleke. 2003. "Toward a Definition of Heritage Language: Sociopolitical and Pedagogical Considerations." *Journal of Language, Identity, and Education* 2, no. 3: 211–30. http://dx.doi.org/10.1207/S15327701JLIE0203_4.

Vinogradova, Polina. 2014a. "Digital Stories in Heritage Language Education: Empowering Heritage Language Learners through a Pedagogy of Multiliteracies." In *Handbook of Heritage, Community and Native American Languages in the United States*, ed. Terrence G. Wiley, Joy Kreeft Peyton, Donna Christian, Sarah Catherine K. Moore, and Na Liu, 314–23. New York: Routledge. http://dx.doi.org/10.4324/9780203122419.ch29.

———. 2014b. "Digital Stories in a Language Classroom: Engaging Students through a Meaningful Multimodal Task." *The FLTMAG*, July 1. http://fltmag.com/digital-stories/.

Wallace, Catherine. 1999. "Critical Language Awareness: Key Principles for a Course in Critical Reading." *Language Awareness* 8 (2): 98–110. http://dx.doi.org/10.1080/09658419908667121.

Wei, Li. 2011. "Moment Analysis and Translanguaging Space: Discursive Construction of Identities by Multilingual Chinese Youth in Britain." *Journal of Pragmatics* 43, no. 5: 1222–35. http://dx.doi.org/10.1016/j.pragma.2010.07.035.

Wellmon, Chad. 2008. "Languages, Cultural Studies, and the Futures of Foreign Language Education." *Modern Language Journal* 92, no. 2: 292–5. http://dx.doi.org/10.1111/j.1540-4781.2007.00719_3.x.

Wiley, Terrence G. 2005a. *Literacy and Language Diversity in the United States*. 2nd ed. Washington, DC: Center for Applied Linguistics.

———. 2005b. "The Reemergence of Heritage and Community Language Policy in the US National Spotlight." *Modern Language Journal* 89, no. 4: 594–601.

Wiley, Terrence G., Joy Kreeft Peyton, Donna Christian, K. Moore Sarah Catherine, and Na Liu. 2014. *Handbook of Heritage, Community, and Native American Languages in the United States: Research, Policy, and Educational Practice*. New York: Routledge.

Woolard, Kathryn A. 1989. *Double Talk: Bilingualism and the Politics of Ethnicity in Catalonia*. Stanford, CA: Stanford University Press.

———. 2008. "Language and Identity Choice in Catalonia: The Interplay of Contrasting Ideologies of Linguistic Authority." In *Lengua, nación e identidad. La regulación del plurilingüismo en Espana y América Latina*, ed. Kirsten Süselbeck, Ulrike Mühlschlegel, and Peter Masson, 302–24. Berlin: Ibero-Amerikanisches Institut P.K.

Woolard, Kathryn A., and Bambi B. Schieffelin. 1994. "Language Ideology." *Annual Review of Anthropology* 23, no. 1: 55–82. http://dx.doi.org/10.1146/annurev.an.23.100194.000415.

Wu, Ming-Hsuan, Kathy Lee, and Genevieve Leung. 2014. "Heritage Language Education and Investment among Asian American Middle Schoolers: Insights from a Charter School." *Language and Education* 28, no. 1: 19–33. http://dx.doi.org/10.1080/09500782.2013.763818.

Zentella, Ana Celia. 1997. *Growing Up Bilingual: Puerto Rican Children in New York*. Malden, MA: Blackwell.

4

Building a Heritage Language Program

Guidelines for a Collaborative Approach

Sara M. Beaudrie
Arizona State University

Over the past two decades, heritage language (HL) learner programs have been steadily increasing in number and spreading across the United States. Although current federal and state education policies have substantially weakened or eliminated HL programs in the United States at the primary and secondary levels (Wright 2007), different kinds of innovative programs are emerging in various contexts, including communities, schools, and universities. All of these programs face a number of challenges in relation to student identification and recruitment, student placement, program building and promotion, curricular development, and funding and resources. Many programs never get started due to lack of support or adequate funding, whereas others receive initial support but cannot attract sufficient students to justify the expenditure over time. The aim of this chapter is to facilitate the task of building an HL program by providing teachers and administrators with practical guidelines for designing, developing, and evaluating an HL program to ensure that learners receive high-quality education that addresses their specific needs.

The chapter begins with an overview of different kinds of HL programs and continues with guidelines for language-program building in the HL context. Essential topics in this regard are program content and structure, language placement, student recruitment, and program promotion. Given that program evaluation is an invaluable tool to ensure curricular and instructional effectiveness and efficiency, the chapter also focuses on HL program evaluation options and appropriate evaluation methods. The resulting model represents a collaborative, integrative, and inclusive approach with an evaluation component as the recipe for success in establishing or expanding an HL program.

PROGRAMMATIC OPTIONS FOR HERITAGE LANGUAGE PROGRAMS

Various types of programs with a common goal of developing and maintaining heritage languages have emerged in recent years. These programs are commonly grouped into three types, based on the context where they are provided: (1) school-based programs; (2) higher-education programs; and (3) community-based programs. School-based programs are offered in primary and secondary schools and typically focus on commonly taught languages, such as Spanish or French, rather than languages not typically taught in schools, such as Japanese or Korean. The scope of these programs varies widely, from HL maintenance programs to immersion and two-way or dual-language programs (see Moore 2014). The Center for Applied Linguistics (CAL) school-based HL program database currently profiles 105 school-based programs addressing different heritage languages and distributed all around the United States.[1]

Higher-education programs are found in both public and private colleges and universities, with their locations being driven to a large extent by the US region and the size of the HL student population enrolled (Beaudrie 2011, 2012; Benmamoun and Kagan 2013). While at the secondary level the number of HL programs is still very low, at the university level the range of languages taught widens. Still, however, many HL learners must enroll in mixed heritage/foreign language classes for lack of specially designed heritage courses. The CAL higher-education HL program database currently lists fifty-three programs distributed all around the United States.

Community-based programs offer after-school, weekend, or summer-school instruction in the heritage language and are housed in nonprofit organizations, such as cultural, religious, or community centers (Liu and You 2014). Because the US educational system offers few options to develop bilingualism in different heritage languages, such programs have long existed to fill this void and help maintain immigrant languages and cultures. The CAL database lists 497 community-based programs in the United States, but this self-reported data greatly underestimates the number of programs. For example, the South Korean Embassy in the United States estimates that there are approximately 1,200 community schools teaching Korean, with a total student enrollment of around 60,000 (Lee and Shin 2008). According to Na Liu (2013), enrollments in community-based programs are increasing, due in part to English-speaking parents seeking to expose their children to languages like Chinese, even if this is not a heritage language for the family. Regardless of where they are located, all HL programs face many of the same challenges.[2] Although the discussion in the next section focuses on building an HL program in a higher-education setting, the principles are applicable to all three types of programs.

BUILDING AN HL PROGRAM

The task of building or redesigning an HL program is certainly challenging. This section reviews important considerations and suggestions about the process in hopes of facilitating what may seem like a daunting task. These ideas are organized in a series of sequential steps, but this should not be interpreted as marking a beginning and end to the process. Instead the process is cyclical, and it may be necessary to revisit the steps in light of new circumstances, such as a change in administration or policies. The following steps are detailed in the remainder of the chapter:

Steps in Building an HL Program

Step 1: Gathering information and building an argument for the creation of an HL program
Step 2: Gathering resources for program building
Step 3: Investing in teacher development in HL instruction
Step 4: Deciding on program structure and preliminary course content
Step 5: Identifying HL students
Step 6: Placing HL students in appropriate course levels
Step 7: Promoting the program and recruiting students
Step 8: Evaluating the program

Step 1: Gathering Information and Building an Argument for the Creation of an HL Program

The first step in building an HL program is to gather data to help build a strong case for why the new program (whether it be a single course or a course sequence) is beneficial and needed. Three types of evidence are useful for this purpose: research supporting the benefit of the program, comparisons with offerings at peer institutions, and learner input. For the first, it is important to focus on research that supports the value of HL education; the benefits of HL maintenance and bilingualism for society in general and for individual communities and families; and, when applicable, the reasons why it is necessary to create a separate track for HL learners within an existing foreign language program. Easy-to-read and accessible information on these topics is available from several sources, including the Heritage Briefs on the CAL website and several published books (e.g., Beaudrie et al. 2014; Peyton, Ranard, and McGinnis 2001; Roca and Colombi 2003; Webb and Miller 2000) and articles (e.g., Polinsky and Kagan 2007; Valdés 2001).[3]

In addition to research, exemplary HL programs offer good models of what a fully developed program would look like. Documenting program offerings at peer institutions or language centers may also help to justify an institution's new program. For example, if a peer institution already has an HL program, this fact provides a basis to argue that a given institution should have an HL program to remain competitive in meeting students' academic needs (or, in a community context, constituents' cultural, social, and continuing education needs). Alternatively, if peer institutions do not have an HL program, this can be cast as an opportunity for an institution to be innovative and distinguish itself.

Finally, it is crucial to collect data on the local population's desire for such a program. Doing so could be as easy as conducting a survey of HL learners currently enrolled in second/foreign language courses or interviewing community members in a local store or church about their interest in a program focused on HL development and maintenance. In this initial step, establishing collaborations and partnerships is a vital tool for building a strong case for the creation or redesign of the program.

Step 2: Gathering Resources for Program Building

Once the rationale for creating a program has been articulated and the need for the program documented, the next major stumbling block is typically a shortage of funding and other resources. In this case, it is important to think creatively, persevere, and identify all potentially available resources. There may be existing resources that can be adapted or recycled to serve the new program (e.g., existing websites, brochures). Perhaps students, community volunteers, or staff members have experience, talents, or knowledge that can be useful in the different steps of program building. Volunteers can help create email lists, design flyers, promote the program, host events, gather information, build a website, and so on. Grants, donors, or fundraising events can help garner resources and promote the program. As Elabbas Benmamoun and Olga Kagan (2013) point out, programs in the humanities typically do not have as broad fundraising networks as programs in the sciences do, but it is still essential to reach out to alumni and organizations to raise additional resources in order to build a successful HL program. Building a new program requires significant resources, work, and funds, so forming a team that can work collaboratively to secure adequate resources will greatly increase the chances of success.

Step 3: Investing in Teacher Development in Heritage Language Instruction

Few second language (L2) teacher preparation programs or graduate programs train future teachers to work with heritage learners. Unfortunately, as Kim Potowski and María Carreira (2004) note, a common false assumption is that teachers who have been trained in L2 acquisition and methodology will be competent HL teachers. As a consequence, teachers frequently find themselves at a loss working with HL learners; as Draper and Hicks (2000) point out, "the approaches that they have employed successfully for years with foreign language learners are no longer adequate or appropriate, and the resulting sense of frustration and inadequacy has become a part of their daily teaching experience" (19). It is therefore important that teachers placed in charge of HL courses are selected among the most accomplished and experienced instructors, who have received or are willing to receive additional training in HL education. Currently, there are free resources available through the National Heritage Language Resource Center, such as the online STARTALK modules and summer workshops. There are also special sessions for HL instruction in national conferences offered by organizations such as the American Council on the Teaching of Foreign Languages (ACTFL). For an overview of the key components needed in teacher development programs to prepare teachers to work with HL learners, see Manel Lacorte's chapter, this volume (2016), and Ana María Schwartz Caballero (2014).

Step 4: Deciding on Program Structure and Preliminary Course Content

A first step in deciding the program structure and course content is to identify the linguistic and cultural profiles of the students and community members who would benefit from and be interested in participating in the HL classes. Many educational institutions design the HL courses to mirror the foreign/L2 courses, offering either one HL course per semester of study (an exactly parallel sequence) or one intensive semester-long HL course per year of foreign/L2 study. Similarly, many community programs are able to divide their offerings by proficiency levels or age levels. The important factor to keep in mind is that the program structure must be tailored as closely as possible to the pedagogical needs of the local students. Designing only one course and placing every available student in it, regardless of their individual proficiency and needs, would likely compromise the quality and success of the program. Similarly, a group consisting of learners of widely different ages is likely to be very difficult to teach and to have limited success. Ultimately, the course sequence of the program needs to emerge from a careful consideration of the language proficiency levels and instructional needs of the target population in combination with program resources and limitations.

Thinking creatively about ways to build a new course on an existing foundation can often reveal unexpected solutions. Sara Beaudrie and colleagues (2014) provide an example of a university foreign/L2 program that initially did not seem to have a sufficient number of HL students to justify the creation of a separate course. On closer examination, however, they realized there were two HL students enrolled in each of the eight sections of an existing foreign/L2 course. Sixteen students are certainly enough to support modifying one section of this course to have an HL focus. Another creative solution is to offer an online course for heritage learners (see Florencia Henshaw, this volume [2016]). This avoids the scheduling conflicts that are likely to arise when a single classroom-based course is offered and some interested students are unable to fit it into their schedules.

To prevent student disengagement, the content of an HL course needs to be geared not only to learners' linguistic and pedagogical needs but also their interests and motivations for learning the HL. For example, an early study by Grace Feuerverger (1991) found that many students rejected HL courses because the courses were monotonous and did not include interesting curricular options for them. Increasingly, HL courses are incorporating rich cultural content in response to learners' desire to learn more about their cultural heritage and strengthen their sense of identity and community belonging. As Sandra Lee Wong (1988) argues, the role of HL programs is not solely to promote students' linguistic development but also to foster a sense of cultural and ethnic pride. Jin Sook Lee and Hae-Young Kim (2008) reported that Korean HL learners have a strong desire to connect with their Korean heritage and identity and suggested that Korean culture should constitute the main content for a Korean HL course. Similarly, Beaudrie and colleagues (2009) found that students' interest in their heritage culture, especially those aspects that strengthened their ties with their home and community, was so strong that it justified creation of an HL course with an exclusive focus on cultural content. Conducting a detailed survey or interview at the beginning of the course will help gather information about the learners' interests and preferences. Creating a program geared to promote student engagement is one of the key factors in ensuring the program's success and continued growth and expansion.

It is also important to build in enough flexibility so that both students and teachers can adjust the curriculum to address needs that arise as the class progresses. As Kimi Kondo-Brown (2010, 21) points out, "what makes HL curriculum development different from other curriculum is not the elements involved but rather the fact that the curriculum must be designed so specifically for the particular population of HL students." This means that the first step in designing the HL curriculum is to understand the learners' needs both in terms of their proficiency levels, academic goals, and literacy background and in terms of their motivations for and interests in taking the class. It is crucial to steer away from deficit-oriented proficiency assessments that focus exclusively on learners' "problems." Diagnostic assessment should identify strengths as well as weaknesses so that the course can emphasize strengths first and move into addressing weaknesses on the foundation of those strengths. Doing so helps overcome the linguistic insecurities many HL learners struggle with.

The last important consideration regarding course content is an appraisal of what can realistically be accomplished within a limited time frame. The HL field has espoused four major goals for HL education: maintenance of the heritage language, acquisition of a standard dialect, development of bilingualism, and development of literacy skills (see Valdés 1995, 2005; Martínez, this volume [2016]). The practical reality is that one or two HL courses cannot address all these goals fully. Thus, instead of focusing on specific topics, perhaps it would be more effective to teach learners the strategies they will need to become lifelong HL learners. What might such an approach look like? The first priority should be building learners' self-confidence in their linguistic abilities. Many students come to the classroom with poor linguistic self-esteem, either because they speak a language variety judged to be nonstandard or because they lack the fluency of a native speaker (Beaudrie and Ducar 2005; Gonzalez 2011). The first step toward HL development is giving learners sufficient confidence to begin using the language in the community and with family members. Next, students also need to develop strategies to support their own language development and maintenance independently as well as promote others'. In addition, in order to understand heritage language maintenance, they need to become aware of important sociolinguistic topics presented in Jennifer Leeman and Ellen Serafini's chapter in this volume (2016)—namely, the sociopolitical status of non-English languages in the United States, standard language ideologies, language discrimination, the relationship between language and identity, and cultural and ethnic pride.

In sum, making appropriate decisions regarding program structure and course content requires an integrated approach where students' voices are heard, instructors and administrators incorporate their valuable insights and expertise, and program resources and limitations are taken into account. In this process, flexibility is a key element in enabling an HL program to be inclusive of all learners and their diverse and changing needs while at the same time set realistic educational goals. Published research, as shown in this section, often includes recommendations for best practices to guide us toward the implementation of quality, research-based practices.

Step 5: Identifying HL Students

To be successful, an identification process needs to identify as many HL learners as possible, both quickly and accurately. The following three identification tools are common and have been proven effective: interviews, language-use surveys, and linguistic identifiers (Beaudrie et al. 2014). Interviews aim to determine whether the learner has had contact with the heritage language outside the classroom and has some degree of bilingualism. Relevant questions to ask are "What experiences have you had with X language?" and "Were you in contact with people who spoke X growing up?"

For a small program, interviewing all prospective learners is feasible. Some other HL programs use short language-use surveys to identify HL learners. Such a survey contains key questions regarding students' prior experiences with using the heritage language, in either yes/no or short-answer formats (Examples: "My parents spoke to me in the heritage language when I was growing up" [yes/no]; "I spoke the heritage language with my family or people in the community when I was a child" [yes/no]). Still other programs have opted to identify HL learners on the basis of their linguistic background, using linguistic identifiers. This approach uses a placement test containing language-based questions that only students who have had contact with the heritage language in their homes (rather than a classroom) would be expected to know (see Potowski et al. 2012). Examples are colloquialisms, idioms, and advanced structures.

Step 6: Placing HL Students in Appropriate Course Levels

Once learners qualify for the HL program, the next step is to determine what HL competencies they have and how well they match the expectations for each course. It is important to recognize that some students may not have the necessary proficiency to fit into the lowest-level HL course available, and others may have competencies that are too advanced for the highest-level course offering. This is one important reason, but not the only reason, to develop an effective placement test. A good placement exam increases the chances that students will be enrolled in classes with other learners of similar skill level—which in turn increases students' satisfaction with their learning experience and enhances the quality of the HL program. A good placement process also relieves teachers and administrators from the time-consuming and burdensome task of placing each student individually in the appropriate course (or of trying to assess students' language skills at the beginning of the course and then teaching to several levels simultaneously). In addition, asking all language learners to take a formal HL identification and placement test may identify a larger number of HL students than if students are asked to self-select as HL speakers. Finally, although this may seem labor intensive, developing an in-house test is likely to fit the needs of the local program and students better than borrowing an existing test. It is difficult to imagine that two HL programs could have such similar goals, course content, and student characteristics that they could share the same test and both obtain valid and reliable results.

For HL placement, most researchers strongly recommend that tests be locally designed in order to meet specific student and program needs (Beaudrie and Ducar 2012; Fairclough 2012; MacGregor-Mendoza 2012; Potowski et al. 2012). Each program has its own specific features designed to serve the unique characteristics of the local student population. In addition, there are very few commercially available HL placement exams (although for Russian, Kagan and Friedman [2003] demonstrated that oral proficiency interviews could potentially provide an accurate placement test). Given these circumstances, each HL program has little choice but to design its own language placement test. This task need not be as daunting as it may seem at first: it is possible to design a simple and effective placement exam with limited resources (Beaudrie and Ducar 2012). The first consideration is that certain types of tests may be more effective for beginning or for advanced learners. For example, Kondo-Brown (2004) suggested that the multiple-choice tests may effectively place low-proficiency HL learners, whereas a written essay may be more useful for highly proficient HL students.

Table 4.1 lists several exam options that can be used for placement purposes, along with their advantages and disadvantages. Clearly, many options

Table 4.1: Placement Test Options

Type of placement exam	Features	Advantages	Disadvantages
Oral interview	Face-to-face Requires administration and scoring expertise	Is personalized Provides opportunities for advising and mentoring	Provides no information on literacy skills Is time-consuming Scoring may be subjective
Written essay	May be paper-and-pencil or computerized Requires scoring expertise	Provides information on writing skills	Provides no information on other language skills
Multiple-choice exam with discrete items	May be paper-and-pencil or computerized Requires design expertise but minimal administration or scoring expertise	Is fast to administer Measures specific characteristics that help place a student	Requires some technical and statistical resources Provides limited information on proficiency
Proficiency test	May be paper-and-pencil or computerized Requires expertise in design, administration, and scoring	Provides good information on proficiency	Requires considerable technical and statistical resources

Source: Beaudrie, Ducar, and Potowski (2014).

are available, and each program needs to opt for the choice that best fits its needs and available expertise. Creation of a placement exam is best undertaken by a group of collaborators who can contribute in the different areas of expertise required for such a project. For more on language placement, see Ilieva and Clark-Gareca (this volume [2016]) and volume 12 of the *Heritage Language Journal* (a special issue on Spanish language placement).

Step 7: Promoting the Program and Recruiting Students

Creating a course and announcing it in a course catalog or community newsletter is certainly not enough to attract learners to a new HL course or existing HL program. As Carol Compton (2001) argues, raising public awareness is important in order for learners to take full advantage of the language-learning options available and for the general public to recognize and value the linguistic and cultural diversity that HL programs help preserve. Students need multiple chances to hear or read about the opportunity and advantages of taking a HL course. Among benefits to promote when contacting students are not only the opportunity to further develop HL skills but also to connect with other HL learners, to learn interesting content, and to prepare to use the heritage language in professional and academic contexts, which may facilitate career advancement. Engaging in program promotion and student recruitment is time-consuming and is most effective and impactful if everyone involved in the HL program contributes to the effort. Some activities that can be used to promote HL courses in a secondary or postsecondary setting are the following:

1. Send welcome letters or emails congratulating students who have qualified for the HL program and encouraging them to enroll in or find out more information about it.
2. Send frequent promotional letters or emails.
3. Visit classes that contain potential students and give a short presentation promoting the program.
4. Visit all second/foreign language courses to identify misplaced HL learners and encourage them to take HL courses.
5. Ask current students in enrolled in HL courses how they found out about the course and what or who helped them decide to enroll.
6. Visit events that attract potential students, such as language fairs or cultural events and festivals.
7. Create videos showcasing the HL program.
8. Talk to school or campus advisors to educate them about the value of encouraging students to continue learning their heritage language.
9. Engage in a program visibility and promotion campaign by conducting information sessions, events, and interviews with reporters for local media outlets.

10. Begin an HL program newsletter.
11. Use school or university resources to promote the program to students and community members.
12. Communicate frequently with other university units that can help recruit students, such as the admissions office and minority student affairs centers.
13. Create an HL program website (or web page on a community center site) containing information presented in a clear, concise, and engaging manner, and keep it updated so that students are motivated to contact you for more information.

In addition, finding a way to measure the effectiveness of the HL program promotion and student recruitment gives important guidance to stop ineffective activities and focus on those with broad impact.

Step 8: Evaluating the Program

Program evaluation is arguably the most important activity in the HL program building or redesign process. Defined as "the systematic collection of information about the activities, characteristics, and outcomes of programs to make judgments about the program, improve program effectiveness, and/or inform decisions about future programming" (Patton 1997, 23), language-program evaluation has long been recognized as yielding critical insights into language teaching and curricular practices (Norris 2009). Because of the lack of uniform standards for HL programs, frequent program evaluations are imperative to ensure program quality. In addition, because of the diversity of the HL population and their wide-ranging needs (see Zyzik, this volume [2016]), practices that work well in one setting or for a specific group of students are not guaranteed to be successful in a different context unless evaluation supports their effectiveness. Although program standards do not currently exist in HL education, it is useful to consult other types of programs standards such as the *Standards for Adult Education ESL Programs* (TESOL 2003) or the *CEA Standards for English Language Programs and Institutions* (CEA 2014).

A program evaluation can provide an in-depth, internal look at all aspects of a language program. In the case of an HL program, a comprehensive evaluation should include the following components:

1. An examination of the program mission and instructional objectives to verify their appropriateness for the current population of students and their alignment with the perspectives and needs of administrators, instructors, and students. The mission and objectives should also be compared to current recommendations in the academic literature to see if they merit revision based on new insights about effective administrative and curricular practices in HL

education. For example, many HL programs include literacy development as part of their instructional objectives, but few address development of learners' critical language awareness (as described in Leeman and Serafini, this volume [2016]). Instructional objectives should also be appropriately sequenced to provide an optimal distribution in the sequence of courses offered.

2. An analysis of the content and materials for each course to determine how well they fulfill the program mission and objectives and meet teachers' and students' expectations. The content and materials must be engaging and relevant to the current student population.

3. A careful inspection of the HL learner identification and placement procedures to make sure that the classes are maximally homogenous and that the official criteria for inclusion in the HL program are realized in practice.

4. An examination of the effectiveness of instruction to determine to what extent the current teaching methodologies are helping students reach the program's instructional goals and are based in research. Methodologies like macro-based approaches and differentiated instruction (see Carreira, this volume [2016]) as well as a sociolinguistically informed approach (see Beaudrie, Ducar, and Potowski 2014) should be mainstays in the classroom because they represent research-based best practices.

5. A scrutiny of current learner assessment methods to ensure they accurately reflect students' learning and proficiency levels and measure instructional goals (see Ilieva and Clark-Gareca, this volume [2016]).

6. A measurement of the health of the program in terms of student enrollment levels, instructor turnover, and instructor and student satisfaction levels.

Whether evaluation is internal, by instructors and administrators involved in the program, or is external, by an outside evaluator, the preceding list captures the main components of an HL program that should typically be examined. At the outset of each evaluation process, however, the areas to be examined should be revisited to determine if other aspects should be added.

The next important decision in program evaluation is the evaluation design and methods. Since the 1990s the most common approach to language-program evaluation has incorporated a combination of qualitative and quantitative methods (Ross 2009). The context adaptive model (Lynch 1996), for example, incorporates both quantitative and qualitative data in its methodology and is sensitive to the specific needs and goals of an individual language program. There has also been a parallel shift from exclusive reliance on program outcomes to an examination of both outcomes and processes. As Long (1984, 422) states, "using process and product evaluations in combination, one can then determine not only whether a program really works, or works better, but if so, why, and if not, why not." A focus on the process is critical to obtain rich information on what is actually going on in the classroom that has led the program to succeed or fail. This is also the preferred approach to facilitate curriculum improvement or development. Simultaneously, outcome evaluation is also important in order to determine whether the objectives of the HL program have been accomplished. A combined approach could make use of qualitative methods such as interviews or focus groups with all stakeholders and class observations. Possible quantitative methods include student questionnaires about their evaluation of the teacher and course, pre- and postcourse achievement tests, and standardized proficiency tests (see Ilieva and Clark-Gareca, this volume [2016]). The selection of methods depends primarily on the overall purposes of the evaluation. When the purpose is formative (to inform stakeholders on how well the program is working and its strengths and weaknesses), the emphasis will be on qualitative methods. When the purpose is summative (to inform stakeholders of program outcomes), the emphasis will be on quantitative methods (Ross 2009).

PRACTICAL EXAMPLES FROM CLASSROOMS AND PROGRAMS

In the final section of the chapter, I showcase a successful example of each program-building step:

Example of step 1: Heritage Language Initiative, Department of World Languages and Literatures, Portland State University (http://www.pdx.edu/wll/what-heritage-language-initiative): The department website articulates a rationale for why HL courses are important, describes their mission, and answers frequently asked questions about bilingualism, HL learners, and HL courses. This is a great example of building an argument for the creation of an HL program.

Example of step 2: The French Heritage Language Program (http://www.facecouncil.org/fhlp/): This program—created through partnerships with the French American Cultural Exchange Foundation and the French Embassy in the United States, with additional support from the Alfred and Jane Ross Foundation—offers a great example of gathering resources for program building. The program offers courses in ten high schools, one elementary school, and three community centers in New York City, along with programs in Florida, Maine, and Massachusetts; additional programs are scheduled to open in the near future. The main goal of the program is to support and enrich teaching about the French language and associated cultures among K–12 students and adults of francophone background, particularly new immigrants, in the United States.

Example of step 3: The easiest and most widely available training recourse for future or existing HL teachers is the online STARTALK module on Teaching Heritage Languages, designed by the National Heritage Language Resource Center (http://startalk.nhlrc.ucla.edu/startalk/startalk.aspx). The lessons are arranged in three parts: (1) Teaching heritage languages: Profiles and definitions; (2) Strategies for HL learners: Differentiated instruction; and (3) HL teaching: Language specific topics and approaches.

Example of step 4: Anne Fountain (2001) describes the development and structure of a culturally focused Spanish HL program in a small college setting with a growing Latino student population. This program focuses on making connections with the Hispanic community through an increase in the college library holdings of Spanish-language materials, trips to other Spanish-speaking communities in the United States, and internship opportunities with the local Spanish-speaking community. Fountain also describes how the college expanded its Latino activities and services and expanded its course offerings to meet the needs of the growing Latino population (e.g., Hispanic communities in the United States, cross-cultural seminar in Mexico, Hispanic practicum). This expansion of course offerings is a good example of step 3 in program building. For additional examples, see works by Christy Hargesheimer (2002) and Satoko Siegel (2004). Featured HL programs can be viewed in the Heritage Voice Collection from the Alliance for the Advancement of Heritage Languages.

Example of step 5: Several universities have implemented tools to distinguish L2 learners from HL learners, exemplifying step 4. Sara Beaudrie and Cynthia Ducar (2012) describe a successful identification survey. Potowski and colleagues (2012) provide an example of the incorporation of linguistic identifiers in a Spanish language placement exam.

Example of step 6: Excellent examples of step 5, HL student placement, can be found in volume 12 of the *Heritage Language Journal*.[4] Marta Fairclough (2006), Olga Kagan and Debra Friedman (2003), and Kimi Kondo-Brown (2004) also discuss placement-related issues.

Example of step 7: The Spanish HL program at the University of Arizona, directed by Sara Beaudrie from 2006 to 2014, engaged in almost all of the suggested activities in step 6 (student recruitment and program promotion). During this period, the program experienced tremendous expansion, growing from an annual enrollment of 587 students in 2007 to 1,234 in 2012 (110 percent growth).

Example of step 8: Although program evaluations are practically nonexistent for HL programs (see Elder 2005), examples of language-program evaluation from L2 education can illustrate the process. Tony Houston (2005) summarizes some good examples. WeiWei Yang (2009) provides an example of an internal evaluation, and Lorena Llosa and Julie Slayton (2009) give an example of an external evaluation.

CONCLUSION

As a relatively new field of research and area of instruction, HL education faces a very difficult endeavor of providing a growing population of HL learners with research-based, high-quality, and efficient instruction and programming. Although educators and administrators recognize the immense value of and pressing need to create specialized programs for HL learners, limitations in resources, funding, and expertise hinder the establishment or expansion of such programs. This chapter presents a model for program building or redesign that adopts a collaborative approach with participation by motivated students, instructors, community members, researchers, and administrators. This collaboration extends to all aspects and steps of the process and challenges interested parties to find creative opportunities, sources of strengths, and available resources. This model also integrates students' needs and interests with instructors' and administrators' perspectives, and uses insights from published research on HL language education in order to produce the desired outcome of a quality education program that the maintenance and development of minority languages truly deserves. Lastly, this program-building model recognizes the need for each unit to develop its own path toward self-improvement and to continually refine its programmatic and curricular practices through program evaluation. The ultimate goal is to build healthy, thriving HL programs that attract students seeking to cultivate their linguistic and cultural heritage and allow us to expand multilingualism in a predominantly monolingual society.

NOTES

1. This is a collection of program profiles gathered by the Alliance for the Advancement of Heritage Languages. Completion of a Heritage Language Program Profile is voluntary, so the number of programs is certainly underestimated (see http://www.cal.org/heritage/profiles/index.html).
2. The Alliance for the Advancement of Heritage Languages offers the "Heritage Voices Collection" to allow programs to share their experiences (http://www.cal.org/heritage/research/voices.html).
3. For the CAL website, see http://www.cal.org/resource-center/resource-archive/heritage-briefs.
4. The *Heritage Language Journal* is found at www.heritagelanguages.org.

REFERENCES

Beaudrie, Sara M. 2011. "Spanish Heritage Language Programs: A Snapshot of Current Programs in the Southwestern United States." *Foreign Language Annals* 44, no. 2: 321–37. http://dx.doi.org/10.1111/j.1944-9720.2011.01137.x.

———. 2012. "Research on University-based Spanish Heritage Language Programs in the United States: The Current State of Affairs." In *Spanish as a Heritage Language in the United States: The State of the Field*, ed. Sara M. Beaudrie and Marta Fairclough, 203–21. Washington, DC: Georgetown University Press.

Beaudrie, Sara, and Cynthia Ducar. 2005. "Beginning Level University Heritage Programs: Creating a Space for all Heritage Language Learners." *Heritage Language Journal* 3, no. 1: 1–26. www.heritagelanguages.org.

———. 2012. "Language Placement and Beyond: Guidelines for the Design and Implementation of a Computerized Spanish Heritage Language Exam." *Heritage Language Journal* 9, no. 1: 77–99. www.heritagelanguages.org.

Beaudrie, Sara, Cynthia Ducar, and Kim Potowski. 2014. *Heritage Language Teaching: Research and Practice*. New York: McGraw-Hill.

Beaudrie, Sara, Cynthia Ducar, and Ana Relaño-Pastor. 2009. "Curricular Perspectives in the Heritage Language Context: Assessing Culture and Identity." *Language, Culture and Curriculum* 22, no. 2: 157–74. http://dx.doi.org/10.1080/07908310903067628.

Benmamoun, Elabbas, and Olga Kagan. 2013. "The Administration of Heritage Language Programs: Challenges and Opportunities." *Heritage Language Journal* 10, no. 2: 281–93. www.heritagelanguages.org.

Carreira, María. 2016. "Supporting Heritage Language Learners through Macrobased Teaching." In *Innovative Strategies for Heritage Language Teaching: A Practical Guide for the Classroom*, ed. Marta Fairclough and Sara M. Beaudrie, 123–42. Washington, DC: Georgetown University Press.

Commission on English Language Program Accreditation (CEA). 2014. *CEA Standards for English Language Programs and Institutions.* http://cea-accredit.org/images/pdfs/2014-CEA-standards-jan.pdf

Compton, Carol. 2001. "Heritage Language Communities and Schools: Challenges and Recommendations." In *Heritage Languages in America: Preserving a National Resource*, ed. Joy Kreeft Peyton, Donald A. Ranard, and Scott McGinnis, 145–66. Washington, DC: Center for Applied Linguistics.

Draper, Jamie, and June Hicks. 2000. "Where We've Been; What We've Learned." In *Teaching Heritage Language Learners: Voices from the Classroom*, edited by J. Webb & B. Miller, 15–35. Yonkers, NY: American Council on the Teaching of Foreign Languages.

Elder, Catherine. 2005. "Evaluating the Effectiveness of Heritage Language Education: What Role for Testing?" *International Journal of Bilingual Education and Bilingualism* 8, no. 2–3: 196–212. http://dx.doi.org/10.1080/13670050508668607.

Fairclough, Marta. 2006. "Language Placement Exams for Heritage Speakers of Spanish: Learning from Students' Mistakes." *Foreign Language Annals* 39, no. 4: 595–604. http://dx.doi.org/10.1111/j.1944-9720.2006.tb02278.x.

———. 2012. "A Working Model for Assessing Spanish Heritage Language Learners' Language Proficiency through a Placement exam." *Heritage Language Journal* 9, no. 1: 121–38.

Feuerverger, Grace. 1991. "University Students' Perceptions of Heritage Language Learning and Ethnic Maintenance." *Canadian Modern Language Review / La revue Candienne des langues vivantes* 47, no. 4: 660–77.

Fountain, Anne. 2001. "Developing a Program for Spanish Heritage Learners in a Small College Setting." *ADFL Bulletin* 32, no. 2: 29–32. http://dx.doi.org/10.1632/adfl.32.2.29.

Gonzalez, Gwynne. 2011. "Spanish Heritage Language Maintenance: The Relationship between Language Use, Linguistic Insecurity, and Social Networks." PhD diss., University of Arizona.

Hargesheimer, Christy. 2002. "Spanish Language Instruction for Spanish Native Speakers: A Single Case Study of a Midwest High School Program." PhD diss., University of Nebraska.

Henshaw, Florencia. 2016. "Technology-Enhanced Heritage Language Instruction: Best Tools and Best Practices." In *Innovative Strategies for Heritage Language Teaching: A Practical Guide for the Classroom*, ed. Marta Fairclough and Sara M. Beaudrie, 237–54. Washington, DC: Georgetown University Press.

Houston, Tony. 2005. "Outcomes Assessment for Beginning and Intermediate Spanish: One Program's Process and Results." *Foreign Language Annals* 38, no. 3: 366–76. http://dx.doi.org/10.1111/j.1944-9720.2005.tb02223.x.

Ilieva, Gabriela, and Beth Clark-Gareca. 2016. "Heritage Language Learner Assessment: Towards Proficiency Standards." In *Innovative Strategies for Heritage Language Teaching: A Practical Guide for the Classroom*, ed. Marta Fairclough and Sara M. Beaudrie, 214–36. Washington, DC: Georgetown University Press.

Kagan, Olga, and Debra Friedman. 2003. "Using the OPI to Place Heritage Speakers of Russian." *Foreign Language Annals* 36, no. 4: 536–45. http://dx.doi.org/10.1111/j.1944-9720.2003.tb02143.x.

Kondo-Brown, Kimi. 2004. "Do Background Variables Predict Students' Scores on a Japanese Placement Test? Implications for Placing Heritage Language Learners." *Journal of the National Council of Less Commonly Taught Languages* 1:1–19.

———. 2010. "Curriculum Development for Advancing Heritage Language Competence: Recent Research, Current Practices, and a Future Agenda." *Annual Review of Applied Linguistics* 30:24–41. http://dx.doi.org/10.1017/S0267190510000012.

Lacorte, Manel. 2016. "Teacher Development in Heritage Language Education." In *Innovative Strategies for Heritage Language Teaching: A Practical Guide for the Classroom*, ed. Marta Fairclough and Sara M. Beaudrie, 99–119. Washington, DC: Georgetown University Press.

Lee, Jin Sook, and Sarah Shin. 2008. "Korean Heritage Language Education in the United States: The Current State, Opportunities, and Possibilities." *Heritage Language Journal* 6, no. 2: 153–72. www.heritagelanguages.org.

Lee, Jin Sook, and Hae-Young Kim. 2008. "Heritage Language Learners' Attitudes, Motivations, and Instructional Needs: The Case of Postsecondary Korean Language Learners." In *Teaching Chinese, Japanese, and Korean Heritage Language Students: Curriculum Needs, Materials, and Assessment*, ed. Kimi Kondo-Brown and James D. Brown, 159–85. New York: Routledge.

Leeman, Jennifer, and Ellen Serafini. 2016. "Sociolinguistics for Heritage Language Educators and Students: A Model for Critical Translingual Competence." In *Innovative Strategies for Heritage Language Teaching: A Practical Guide for the Classroom*, ed. Marta Fairclough and Sara M. Beaudrie, 56–79. Washington, DC: Georgetown University Press.

Liu, Na. 2013. "Program Quality of Heritage Language Programs." Paper delivered at the ACTFL Conference. Orlando, FL, November 22–24.

Liu, Na, and Byeong-Keun You. 2014. "Stakeholder Views of Community-based Heritage Language Programs: Chinese and Korean Cases." In *Handbook of Heritage, Community, and Native American Languages in the United States: Research, Policy, and Educational Practice*, ed. Terrence Wiley, Joy Kreeft Peyton, Donna Christian, Sarah Moore, and Na Liu, 333–340. New York: Routledge. http://dx.doi.org/10.4324/9780203122419.ch31.

Llosa, Lorena, and Julie Slayton. 2009. "Using Program Evaluation to Inform and Improve the Education of Young English Language Learners in US Schools." *Language Teaching Research* 13, no. 1: 35–54. http://dx.doi.org/10.1177/1362168808095522.

Long, Michael. 1984. "Process and Product in ESL Program Evaluation." *TESOL Quarterly* 18, no. 3: 409–25.
Lynch, Brian. 1996. *Language Program Evaluation Theory and Practice*. Cambridge: Cambridge University Press.
MacGregor-Mendoza, Patricia. 2012. "Spanish as a Heritage Language Assessment: Successes, Failures, Lessons Learned." *Heritage Language Journal* 9, no. 1: 1–26.
Martínez, Glenn. 2016. "Goals and Beyond in Heritage Language Education: From Competencies to Capabilities." In *Innovative Strategies for Heritage Language Teaching: A Practical Guide for the Classroom*, ed. Marta Fairclough and Sara M. Beaudrie, 39–55. Washington, DC: Georgetown University Press.
Moore, Sarah. 2014. "Program Models for Heritage Language Education." In *Handbook of Heritage, Community, and Native American Languages in the United States: Research, Policy, and Educational Practice*, ed. Terrence Wiley, Joy Kreeft Peyton, Donna Christian, Sarah Moore, and Na Liu, 341–48. New York: Routledge.
Norris, John. 2009. "Understanding and Improving Language Education through Program Evaluation: Introduction to the Special Issue." *Language Teaching Research* 13, no. 1: 7–13. http://dx.doi.org/10.1177/1362168808095520.
Patton, Michael. 1997. *Utilization-Focused Evaluation: The New Century Text*. Thousand Oaks, CA: Sage.
Peyton, Joy, Donna Ranard, and Scott McGinnis, eds. 2001. *Heritage Languages in America: Preserving a National Resource*. Washington, DC: Center for Applied Linguistics.
Polinsky, Maria, and Olga Kagan. 2007. "Heritage Languages: In the 'Wild' and in the Classroom." *Language and Linguistics Compass* 1, no. 5: 368–95. http://dx.doi.org/10.1111/j.1749-818X.2007.00022.x.
Potowski, Kim, and María Carreira. 2004. "Teacher Development and National Standards for Spanish as a Heritage Language." *Foreign Language Annals* 37, no. 3: 427–37. http://dx.doi.org/10.1111/j.1944-9720.2004.tb02700.x.
Potowski, Kim, MaryAnn Parada, and Kara Morgan-Short. 2012. "Developing an Online Placement Exam for Spanish Heritage Speakers and L2 Students." *Heritage Language Journal* 9, no. 1: 51–76.
Roca, Ana, and M. Cecilia Colombi, eds. 2003. *Mi lengua: Spanish as a Heritage Language in the United States*. Washington, DC: Georgetown University Press.
Ross, Steven. 2009. "Program Evaluation." In *The Handbook of Language Teaching*, ed. Michael Long and Catherine Doughty, 756–78. Oxford: Wiley-Blackwell. http://dx.doi.org/10.1002/9781444315783.ch39.
Schwartz Caballero, Ana María. 2014. "Preparing Teachers to Work with Heritage Language Learners." In *Handbook of Heritage, Community, and Native American Languages in the United States: Research, Policy, and Educational Practice*, ed. Terrence Wiley, Joy Kreeft Peyton, Donna Christian, Sarah Moore, and Na Liu, 359–69. New York: Routledge. http://dx.doi.org/10.4324/9780203122419.ch34.
Siegel, Satoko. 2004. "A Case Study of One Japanese Heritage Language Program in Arizona." *Bilingual Research Journal* 28, no. 1: 123–34. http://dx.doi.org/10.1080/15235882.2004.10162615.
Teachers of English to Speakers of Other Languages. 2003. *Standards for Adult Education ESL Programs*. Alexandria, VA: Teachers of English to Speakers of Other Languages.
Valdés, Guadalupe. 1995. "The Teaching of Minority Languages as Academic Subjects: Pedagogical and Theoretical Challenges." *Modern Language Journal* 79, no. 3: 299–328. http://dx.doi.org/10.1111/j.1540-4781.1995.tb01106.x.

———. 2001. "Heritage Language Students: Profiles and Possibilities." In *Heritage Languages in America: Preserving a National Resource*, ed. Joy Peyton, Donna Ranard, and Scott McGinnis, 37–80. Washington, DC: Center for Applied Linguistics.

———. 2005. "Bilingualism, Heritage Language Learners, and SLA Research: Opportunities Lost or Seized?" *Modern Language Journal* 89, no. 3: 410–26. http://dx.doi.org/10.1111/j.1540-4781.2005.00314.x.

Webb, John, and Barbara Miller. 2000. *Teaching Heritage Language Learners: Voices from the Classroom*. New York: American Council on the Teaching of Foreign Languages.

Wong, Sandra Lee. 1988. "The Language Situation of Chinese Americans." In *Language Diversity: Problem or Resource?* ed. Sandra Lee McKay and Sau-Ling Wong, 193–283. Boston, MA: Heinle and Heinle.

Wright, Wayne. 2007. "Heritage Language Programs in the Era of English-Only and No Child Left Behind." *Heritage Language Journal* 5, no. 1: 1–26.

Yang, WeiWei. 2009. "Evaluation of Teacher Induction Practices in a US University English Language Program: Towards Useful Evaluation." *Language Teaching Research* 13, no. 1: 77–98. http://dx.doi.org/10.1177/1362168808095524.

Zyzik, Eve. 2016. "Towards a Prototype Model of the Heritage Language Learner: Understanding Strengths and Needs." In *Innovative Strategies for Heritage Language Teaching: A Practical Guide for the Classroom*, ed. Marta Fairclough and Sara M. Beaudrie, 19–38. Washington, DC: Georgetown University Press.

5

Teacher Development in Heritage Language Education

Manel Lacorte
University of Maryland

Significant gains have been made in recent years in the professional development of both pre- and in-service instructors dealing with heritage language (HL) learners in regards to national initiatives supporting HL education and teacher education; the knowledge base and skills needed for teaching heritage languages; and the understanding of the institutional, curricular, and pedagogical contexts for HL learning and teaching (Schwartz Caballero 2014). These contexts include:

- Community-based schools or programs, which are often developed by community members—for example, families, churches, community organizations—rather than by public institutions. They tend to be quite diverse in terms of structure and organization, instructional methods, materials used, staff qualifications, funding sources, and so on. (Kelleher 2010).[1]
- K–12 education through immersion programs, two-way (dual) programs, courses for HL learners, or classes with HL learners within second language (L2) education programs (Wang and Green 2001).
- Higher education, with separate courses or programs for students with a background in the heritage language, or with L2 courses at a range of levels of proficiency that mix groups of L2 and HL students (Kono and McGinnis 2001).

This chapter presents several key components for teacher development programs, modules, or workshops that could be useful for instructors in any of the above settings. While we believe that the linguistic, cultural, and social diversity of HL learners distinctly distinguish HL and L2 education, this chapter draws upon concepts and tools from both fields. Most instructors working with HL learners teach HL and L2 courses or courses with a combination of HL and L2 students; therefore, instructors should be aware of substantial issues and developments in both fields and, more crucially, be able to adjust this knowledge to their immediate academic and professional realities (Lacorte 2014). Our position about teacher development is largely based on an ecological view of L2 and HL learning and teaching as activities inherently influenced by social, educational, cultural, economic, and political conditions (Hornberger and Wang 2008; Kramsch 2008). In other words, teachers should be seen as "a part of the larger system in which they shape and are shaped by various factors in the system" (Hornberger and Wang 2008, 6) not just as individuals with content and pedagogical knowledge, beliefs, and assumptions about the language(s) they teach.

The chapter begins with a discussion of current issues and topics in L2 education, L2 teacher preparation, and HL teacher education. Next we describe several components that should be taken into consideration for different types of professional activities, drawing upon relevant literature on professional development of HL practitioners (limited in comparison to other areas of analysis in the field), our ecological perspective about L2 and HL teaching and learning, and our own practical experience. Specifically, these seven components involve ideological, cultural, socioaffective, linguistic, curricular, pedagogical, and professional issues of interest for instructors working with HL learners in HL courses or courses with a combination of HL and L2 students. Our concluding remarks underline the need for further research and the significance of contextual factors for future valid models of HL teacher education that could adapt the previous components to various professional environments.

THE PRESENT: CORE ISSUES AND TOPICS

Current Trends in L2 Education

In recent years the field of second language acquisition (SLA) has moved from a cognitivist and a positivist perspective toward one that considers language as a social practice that is situated in historic, cultural, and sociopolitical conditions. At the theoretical level, this means allowing for a more thorough reflection on the connections between the learner's identity and the social situation in which the L2 is used as well as on the power relations that can influence the learner's access to the L2 speaking community (Kristjánsson 2013). It also involves placing less emphasis on attaining a "native-like competence" since one cannot be a native speaker of anything other than her first language; instead, the focus has shifted toward developing "L2 users," individuals who know and can use an L2 at any level by exploiting whatever linguistic resources they may have for a real-life purpose (Cook 2007). In the field of bilingualism, a related term to this view of language learning is "translanguaging," defined as the "multiple discursive practices in which bilinguals engage in order to make sense of their bilingual worlds" (García

2009, 45; for additional information on "translanguaging" see Leeman and Serafini, this volume [2016]).

At a curricular level, there is a rising interest in preparing L2 learners to participate in diverse discourse communities, both at home and in the target culture, whether it be with other L2 learners, L2 youth, or online communities (Lafford 2013). An approach founded on multiple literacies (see Samaniego and Warner's chapter on "Multiliteracies," this volume [2016]) encourages L2 learners to interpret, transform, and think critically about discourse through a variety of contexts and written, oral, and visual textual genres (Paesani et al. 2015), in contrast to the prominence of interactive, transactional oral language use and the somehow superficial treatment of cultural and textual content in communicative language teaching (Byrnes 2006). For some experts, the development of this approach might entail the reassessment of dominant frameworks, such as the American Council on the Teaching of Foreign Languages (ACTFL) Proficiency Guidelines for collegiate education, and the Standards for K–12 education; such a revision could allow for the development of coherent, comprehensive, and principled curricula that would eventually "affirm and realize a humanistically oriented approach to FL [foreign language] education" (Byrnes 2012, 1).

Current Trends in L2 Teacher Preparation

The last decades have also been decisive for language teacher education by contesting the traditional belief that teaching was simply an art and that teachers were born rather than made (Schulz 2000). L2 teacher education has gradually become a field for empirical research beyond essentially descriptive studies, and a number of studies, reports, and initiatives have created guidelines and standards that "are meant to represent professional consensus in the field of language teaching, add rigor to teacher preparation programs, including the admissions process, and provide consistency in the knowledge, skills, and dispositions of those entering the FL teaching profession" (Donato 2009, 267).

However, in line with the recent paradigm shift in SLA toward the social, some authors have pointed to a possible lack of sensitivity shown by strict guidelines and standards for teacher development in regards to the role of reflection and mediation in teaching; the diversity of languages to learner backgrounds, and learning/teaching conditions: "Teachers need to work with multiple languages in the classroom; they need to work both systematically and flexibly; they need to work with diverse learner perspectives, choices, and positions. In short, they need to be able to interpret their students' and their own teaching and learning practices in the context of diversity" (Scarino 2014, 394). Other issues affecting contemporary L2 teacher education are, first, the training of graduate teaching assistants (TA), which often is "not consistent with recent developments in the profession that have resulted in different priorities, objectives, and approaches" (Allen and Maxim 2013, xv). Second, faculty in L2 university departments commonly oriented toward literary or theoretical linguistics studies have given scarce interest to L2 teacher education (Allen and Negueruela-Azarola 2010). Furthermore, there appears to be a lack of communication between L2 departments and education programs concerning the preparation of future L2 teachers and professors (Pastor and Lacorte 2014). Among other suggestions to address these issues, Kate Paesani (2013, 77) argues for a literacy-based approach to L2 teacher development that would involve the development of teachers' ability to analyze, interpret, and adjust to diverse professional environments through the "implementation of more than one methods course; exploration of methods beyond CLT [communicative language teaching]; participation in curricular and pedagogical decision making; encouragement of reflective teaching; and development of pedagogical, content, and linguistic knowledge."

Knowledge Base and Skills in HL Teacher Professional Development

The greater awareness about the contextual factors described above for L2 education and L2 teacher education relates well to current language education for HL learners who may be immigrants born abroad; the first or second generation born in the United States; members of diverse language family settings; speakers of distinctive HL registers associated with family, social class, and levels of education; and proficient in certain linguistic abilities, sets of communicative strategies, or both. The significant progress made since the 1970s by researchers, practitioners, and institutions allows us to outline several dimensions that should be considered part of the knowledge base of instructors working with HL learners.[2] These areas include the following:

- Understanding of the historical, cultural, sociolinguistic, and academic backgrounds of HL learners as related to the immediate teaching environment.
- Awareness about the teacher's own background (e.g., country of origin, HL proficiency, teaching experience) and professional identity.
- Awareness about the distribution of language proficiency across modalities and skills among HL learners in connection with their cultural and sociolinguistic background.
- Knowledge about the nature of language proficiency assessment in order to interpret strengths and weaknesses derived from oral and written testing.
- Familiarity with issues of HL acquisition, especially those concerned with the integration of psycholinguistic and sociolinguistic factors.

- Familiarity with general approaches to teaching HL learners (e.g., differentiated instruction, language arts, and critical language pedagogy) (see chapters by Parra [2016] and Carreira [2016], this volume).
- Pedagogical strategies to encourage collaboration among HL and FL students with varying levels of proficiency in mixed classrooms.
- Classroom management strategies to address issues of intergroup and personal dynamics, motivations, and affective variables.
- Awareness of beliefs and attitudes regarding HL speakers and their language varieties.

In general, these areas of interest reflect important dimensions of the knowledge base of instructors working with HL learners. Specifically, instructors make pedagogical decisions based on an amalgamation of knowledge that includes linguistic, sociolinguistic and cultural content (content knowledge); teaching the content (pedagogical content knowledge); and connecting both content and teaching to the "life-worlds of teachers and the life-worlds of their students" (personal practical knowledge) (Scarino 2014, 396). On the other hand, Sara Beaudrie (2012a, 217) argues that more research is needed "to determine how these competencies are acquired and what should be the content of HL teacher development programs in order to ensure the development of these competencies." In connection with the above-mentioned relevance of contextual factors in SLA and L2 education, we would also argue that neither HL nor L2 teacher preparation programs have given enough attention to the interaction between teachers and the ideological, sociocultural, and institutional environments where they carry out their professional duties (contextual knowledge).

LOOKING TO THE FUTURE: KEY COMPONENTS FOR HERITAGE TEACHER DEVELOPMENT

The components described in this section review the current knowledge base of instructors working with HL learners in diverse contexts so that it can take into appropriate account contextual knowledge in L2/HL teaching; it may be applied and/or adjusted to a variety of professional development activities; and it could be used as a reference for future pedagogically based research on HL teacher education or well-grounded, dynamic, and responsive models of HL teacher development. Given space limitations, our considerations and illustrations for each component are certainly not exhaustive or described in any specific order of importance, but they are evidently interrelated. Readers should assess all or some of them according to their own knowledge and experience as instructors, teachers, educators, curriculum developers, language program directors, researchers, or administrators, among others.

Ideological Considerations

An increasing number of studies about teacher beliefs, language attitudes, and their impact on classroom practice have recently appeared in L2 education (e.g., Byrd et al. 2011; Kissau et al. 2012; Siskin 2008). Teacher beliefs refer to the values, goals, and assumptions that teachers have about the content and development of teaching. They develop gradually over time, have subjective and objective dimensions, and may originate from numerous sources, including but not limited to personality factors, their own experiences as language learners, their experiences with different types of teaching, their attitudes and assumptions toward the language(s) of instruction, and their attitudes toward specific individuals or groups learning the target language. The majority of teacher development programs and studies of teacher beliefs have viewed these features as mainly personal, therefore assuming that these beliefs "are supposed to be consistent, conscious, and [that] teachers should maintain fidelity to them across different situations" (Razfar 2012, 63). However, the concept of "teacher ideologies" connects beliefs about teaching with the social, cultural, and institutional environments in which the beliefs are enacted; therefore, it entails a much more dynamic relationship between local practices and broader historical and institutional practices, values, and interests (Kroskrity 2010).

Reflection on teacher ideologies as part of HL teacher development involves studying how linguistic diversity and instruction in languages other than English may generally be seen at the national level. For example, HL education has been described alternately as a form of economic capital in fields like communications, business, health, and public safety (Pomerantz 2002); as a likely national security tool (Edwards 2004); and even as a threat to the role of English as the exclusive linguistic marker of the country's identity and a sign of insufficient commitment to "American" values (Pavlenko 2002). Teacher ideologies also concern the notion of standard language ideologies—namely, "the idea that it is possible to eliminate variation within languages, the conviction that certain ways of speaking are 'correct' while others are 'wrong,' the acceptance of linguistic authority regarding correctness, and the conviction that the prestige of particular language forms or practices is related to their inherent worth, rather than society's attitudes towards the people who use them" (Milroy 2007, as cited in Leeman 2010, 313; for additional information on linguistic variation, see Fairclough, this volume [2016]). A third area of reflection has to do with institutional ideologies, especially the extent to which "departmental ideologies and practices interconnect with the broader social, political, and economic elements that are present in both the university and national contexts" (Valdés et al. 2003, 4). Not surprisingly, a final area of concern would be the way in which course goals, pedagogical materials, testing procedures, and group dynamics within the classroom may be affected by any of the above social, linguistic, and institutional aspects of teacher ideologies (see, e.g., Cho 2014; Lee and Bang 2011; Lee and Oxelson 2006).

Cultural Considerations

A significant first point of attention for this section involves the role that cultural affinity may play in the definition of a HL learner. In the main, the numerous definitions proposed so far have ranged from "narrow" to "broad" views of the concept (Polinsky and Kagan 2007). "Narrow" views define HL learners as individuals with an emotional attachment or family ties to the language and culture and varying grades of proficiency in the HL, while "broad" views of the concept include individuals who have been raised with a strong cultural connection to a concrete language but may not actually speak or understand the language at all (Fishman 2001; see also Zyzik, this volume [2016]).[3]

Culture is also one of the central factors behind HL learners' motivation to enroll in courses where they can learn more "about their cultural and linguistic roots and to strengthen their connections to their families and communities" (Kagan and Dillon 2009, 160). While the role of culture has usually been linked to an integrative notion of motivation—that is, a desire to associate with people who use the language—Cynthia Ducar (2012, 162) observes that it might be detrimental to completely disregard instrumental motivation, or an interest to learn the language because of "the practical value associated with L2 acquisition: increased job or business opportunities, passing a class, meeting a requirement, and so on."

A cultural dimension of particular interest for teacher education is the understanding of HL learners' funds of knowledge—"the historically accumulated and culturally developed bodies of knowledge and skills essential for household or individual functioning and wellbeing" (Moll et al. 1992, 134). Some examples include social or ceremonial activities, cultural identity and values, balance between work and family life, specific value assigned to certain professions, literacy practices, popular cultures, and so on. A variety of ethnographic field methods or techniques—for example, participant observation, open-ended interviewing strategies, case studies—intended to learn more about students' funds of knowledge may be implemented as training activities in courses, programs, or workshops for instructors working with HL learners (Hogg 2011). Instructors may be asked to research and document life in the HL community, conduct community ethnographies as an assignment, read texts or watch films dealing with issues affecting the HL community, attend talks or conversations with members of the HL community, or even identify their own funds of knowledge and reflect upon how they can influence the ways in which these funds may influence their perception of the HL community (see, e.g., Cho 2014; Lee and Bang 2011).

Socioaffective Considerations

As part of their professional development, instructors working with HL learners need to be aware of the strong, positive connection found by researchers between HL proficiency and maintenance with "identity development, higher self-esteem, confidence, self-determination, social interaction with peers, family relationships, second language development and academic achievement" (Lee and Suárez 2009, 157). Together with such understanding of the interaction between HL learners and their peers, family, and communal contexts, instructors working with HL learners should bear in mind that the language classroom is in itself a *practical community* where *all* participants share a degree of mutual compromise toward the learning experience and the community in itself; some common objectives and needs that can be shared even if they are understood differently; and a collective repertoire of practices, expressions, and symbols that evolve through a constant negotiation of pedagogical and social issues (Wenger 1998; Wright 2005). For example, Manel Lacorte and Evelyn Canabal (2005) observed several advanced L2 courses with HL and L2 learners in order to analyze the pedagogical interaction between teachers and students, the teachers' views of classroom environment (from "a space for open discussion" to "a teenage orchestra"), and what the teachers see as "desired" interaction (e.g., two-way communication in the L2 or a challenging conversation between all participants) versus what may actually happen in the classroom (e.g., common use of English among L2 and HL students, or "unequal" meeting points based on instructors' beliefs and experiences with either group of learners).

Teacher preparation activities in L2/HL education should consider that instructors' affective practices—the expression of feelings, moods, dispositions, and emotions—may entail a more complex dimension with HL learners. This is because these practices generally involve a cultural component (Atoofi 2013) in relation to the expectations that either the teacher or the students may have about the appropriate social and pedagogical management of the classroom; the degree to which the cultural and linguistic background of the instructor may affect these practices in the classroom; and the way in which the adjustment of affective behaviors among the participants may have a positive or negative impact on their overall motivation toward learning the HL or their (in)security and anxiety in the classroom. As an illustration of a possible teacher-training activity dealing with affective practices, Stephanie Alvarez (2013) presents her "*testimonio*" (autobiographical narrative) as a Latina transitioning from being an undergraduate student of Spanish to a junior faculty member in a university Spanish program. The way in which autobiographies may depict life stories, personal experiences, and perceptions makes them a valuable teacher education tool for exploring instructors' beliefs, personal knowledge, and changes in relation to the HL communities and cultures.[4]

Linguistic Considerations

The distribution of HL proficiency may differ substantially from the proficiency of L2 learners in terms of three categories. The first is related to language modalities, reading, writing, speaking, and listening. The second involves the genre of texts assigned on the basis of external criteria such as intended audience, purpose, and activity type. These include, for example, personal versus formal letters, student essays, business reports, legal documents, and so on. The third concerns language registers as defined in relation to their use in social situations. This involves teaching students to differentiate between the language appropriate for scientific, religious, political, academic, formal, and informal contexts, among others (see Zyzik's chapter, this volume [2016], for an in-depth discussion on HL proficiency). In this regard, instructors should be conscious about implicational hierarchies of linguistic knowledge that may allow them to make educated guesses about skills and knowledge brought by L2 learners to the classroom. Such practices may not work equally with HL learners who show great oral fluency in the language but partial or no academic background and, hence, limited knowledge of formal grammar structures (Potowski and Carreira 2004).

Familiarity with HL linguistic systems also means understanding the contrasts between first, second, and heritage language acquisition concerning grammatical areas (phonetics and phonology, vocabulary, morphology, syntax, pragmatics and discourse) and social areas (variability in dialects and registers, language contact, identity) (Lynch 2003; Montrul 2010; Fairclough, this volume [2016]). It is important as well that instructors are knowledgeable of their own ideological positions about these contrasts. Such awareness would imply an understanding of basic concepts in the fields of dialectology (phonological, lexical, and grammatical features that correspond to regional areas), sociolinguistics (language varieties used by a community due to certain social variables), and sociology of language (the ways in which social dynamics may be affected by individual and group language use). Furthermore, the instructor should become acquainted with relevant notions in bilingualism such as the aforementioned concepts of meaning-making practices, L2 user, translanguaging, code-switching, and so on. For example, Potowski (2002) describes a ninety-minute "Heritage Language Awareness" session for new TAs with three categories that could be easily adapted for other groups of instructors:

Language variation: Instructors should understand the concept of linguistic variation in the country/community. They need to be aware of the language varieties spoken in specific contexts and in bilingual contexts, be able to identify the majority language and its influence on the minority language thorough specific examples. Instructors should also have a clear notion of the type of HL variety/ies that should be taught in class. (Often, these notions can be elucidated by simply asking pertinent questions such as "If your country is bilingual, what is the majority language?" or "Can you think of any examples of the majority language influencing the minority language?")

Standard language ideologies: Instructors should work with their students to help them identify the standard variety of the heritage language by using text excerpts.

Language samples from HL learners: Instructors should become familiar with the writing of HL learners by analyzing several samples written by these students.

Curricular Considerations

In addition to previous remarks on instructors' knowledge and sensitivity toward the HL communities and cultures, we would first argue that instructors should make an effort to become more knowledgeable about the administrative practices of their institutions (Johnston and Janus 2003; Beaudrie, this volume [2016]). This could include, for example, an analysis of current or prospective HL learners' needs, curricular options for HL learners with diverse linguistic or cultural backgrounds, extra- or co-curricular activities carried out in HL communities, and the sequencing or articulation between courses intended for L2 students, HL students, or L2/HL students. Knowledge about administrative practices also involves a careful examination of pedagogical materials for courses designed specifically for HL learners or for L2/HL students. Such analysis should include not only customary textbook features—for example, objectives, scope and sequence, types of activities, teacher notes and other suggestions for instructors, supplementary materials, technological support—but also attention to underlying notions about individual or collective representations of HL communities, treatment of language variation, and discussion of cultural content, among others. We also suggest that the diverse cultural and linguistic backgrounds of HL learners require teacher preparation activities that allow instructors to become more familiar with current approaches to curriculum development—such as those based on the notion of multiple literacies described earlier in the chapter—and, at a more practical level, appropriate training for instructors to become conversant with different kinds of placement and assessment procedures—for example, oral presentations, written narratives, portfolios (see, e.g., Beaudrie 2012b; Beaudrie et al. 2014: 204–12; Moore et al. 2014; Ilieva and Clark-Gareca, this volume [2016]). Finally, community engagement, service-learning, experiential learning, and internships are some of the ways for HL learners to feel the need to use the HL outside the home and the classroom and to increase "students' civic agency, or ways they can develop as actors together with others, on the shared social world" (Rabin 2014, 178). While these initiatives are usually incorporated into specialized courses, it would also be beneficial for instructors to get training about strategies to include them as a component of regular language or culture courses (see, e.g., Lafford 2013; Lear and Abbott 2008; Martínez, this volume [2016]).

As Valdés (2001, 32–33) notes, it is important to discuss with each other details about possible challenges of instruction in various heritage languages. Even if we still do not know the answer or solution for these challenges, asking questions about them in a L2/HL teacher education context would, at the very least, entail an educator's interest in things that he could learn from the discussion. Guadalupe Valdés poses some questions that could be adapted as part of a teacher preparation activity: Is the HL commonly taught as an academic subject in schools or colleges in the community? What kinds of support are available to carry out such instruction and to plan pedagogical practices? Are pedagogical materials available? If instruction in the HL is already part of a curriculum, are HL learners well placed in existing language sequences? How well can students' strengths be developed by existing instruction? What are legitimate and valid language development goals for these students? Are school and college faculty interested in HL learners and willing to work closely with them? (Valdés 2001, 32–33).

Pedagogical Considerations

Teacher preparation for instructors working with HL learners should include information about the most common approaches to teaching HL learners to date:

The language arts: Instruction to support the development of general literacy skills in the heritage language; strategies to understand the core systems and structures of language (grammar, punctuation, spelling); and linguistic and academic skills to communicate in as many academic, social, and professional contexts as possible through the gradual command of registers and genres (Potowski and Carreira 2004).

Differentiated instruction: Strategies or classroom structures that support learning in classes with L2 learners and HL learners. This approach may result in modifications to the content or material, the dynamics of classroom activities, and the ways in which mastery of material is assessed (Carreira 2013). Differentiated instruction may also include a greater involvement by students in the design or implementation of the curriculum, the course goals, and the evaluation and grading procedures.

Critical language pedagogy: Practices and strategies to encourage the development of critical reflection and student agency—that is, their capacity to act upon their world and not only to know about it—in relation to the social and professional status of heritage languages outside the classroom, standard language ideologies, and linguistic and nonlinguistic resources for learners to become "critical social actors in whichever speech communities they choose to participate" (Leeman 2005, 26).

Instructors should also be trained in how to incorporate a variety of classroom strategies to adequately address HL learners' needs, such as the use of literature to both engage the students and draw attention to specific linguistic structures through meaningful activities; the use of various technological resources and electronic media as tools to facilitate differentiated instruction (see Henshaw's chapter, this volume [2016]); and the integration of nonstandard linguistic forms as part of the instruction (see also Fairclough, this volume [2016]). Consistent with the aforementioned ongoing innovations in SLA and L2/HL education, we would argue as well that teacher preparation programs should include activities focused on issues of identity and power relations in the language classroom, notions of translanguaging and L2/HL user, or participation in L2/HL communities through a range of oral, written, and visual means, among others.

The following questions posed by María Parra (2014) for TAs to explore previous experiences and beliefs regarding curricular and pedagogical matters could be modified to suit other teacher preparation settings:

Understanding and knowledge of HL learners: Who are they? Have you ever had HL learners in your classes? How would you define the term "heritage speaker"? What do you think are HL learners' motivations for enrolling in a formal language course?

Methods and approaches to teaching HL learners: How do we teach heritage languages? Have you ever taught a course designed particularly for HL learners? Mention three things that you think you need to do as a language teacher to create a productive and successful HL course.

Teaching goals: Organize in order of importance several statements about the place of grammar, registers of language, regional differences, literary texts, text genres, and textbook.

Mixed courses: Do you think HL learners can enrich the class if they are included in the general population of language learners? If so, how?

Affective factors: Two statements are provided about the relative importance of these factors, and TAs are asked to choose the one they agree more with.[5]

Challenges: What would you expect to be the biggest challenge of working with HL learners?

Professional Considerations

In general, instructors working with HL learners need to engage in a variety of professional development experiences that prepare them effectively: heritage methods courses; HL-related modules as part of L2-oriented methods courses; HL awareness workshops; faculty discussions and meetings focused on characteristics and needs of HL learners; attendance at or involvement in professional conferences; and regular review of free-access resources provided by a number of institutions and organizations (see note 2).

In line with current efforts in L2 teacher education, instructors working with HL learners should receive guidance about "reflective practices" (Naomi Geyer, quoted in Kagan and Dillon 2009, 157) in order to observe and assess students' performance in the classroom, ask the appropriate questions about the linguistic and social behavior observed in class, and design and evaluate activities that facilitate language and cultural development (Parra 2014). Reflective practices should be an essential component of language teacher courses and programs in L2 or general education units for both TAs and undergraduate students. As noted in our earlier discussion about teacher beliefs and ideologies, instructors' reflective practices should also address their own background as native or nonnative speakers of the languages that they teach; personal experience as language learners; experience with different kinds of teaching; attitudes or preferences concerning pedagogical or curricular options; views about communities where the heritage language is used, and so on. Moreover, reflective practices may be the foundation for a research component in teacher preparation programs or courses that, at the very least, should allow the adequate identification of specific classroom problems, the analysis of a range of solutions to the problem, and the implementation of suitable changes in discussion and collaboration with other colleagues, students, and administrators (Parra 2014; Potowski and Carreira 2004). Beyond the classroom space, it would also be relevant for instructors working with HL learners to have the opportunity to reflect on the support and resources provided by their own institutions for the teaching and learning of HLs at the community, curricular, pedagogical, and professional levels (Johnston and Janus 2003). Possible areas of reflection could include advocacy for HL learners or teachers, information about professional issues, options for cooperation and collaboration, or information about the use of technology. Adapted from a questionnaire prepared by Bill Johnston and Louis Janus (2003, 16–17) for instructors of less commonly taught languages, the following survey addresses four major areas:

Teaching situation: What language(s) do you teach? How many years of this language does your institution typically offer? What kind of students do you have to teach? Which course book or books do you use?

Professional background: What qualifications do you have? Are you a native speaker of the language(s) you teach?

Work situation: What position do you have? Is it permanent, annual, by semester? What is your official title? Are you full time or part time?

Professional development needs: Please check/rank the areas that you consider more related to professional development for teachers. Possible options include: language enhancement work, increased access to materials in the language you teach, opportunities for teacher research, workshops or course work on a variety of topics, opportunities for cooperation and collaboration with other colleagues.

CONCLUDING REMARKS

In contrast to other options mostly centered on certain populations—especially preservice teachers or TAs—this chapter has examined and illustrated a number of issues and topics applicable to professional development courses, programs, modules, or workshops for instructors working with HL learners in diverse educational environments. We have structured and described our considerations in relation to seven key components—ideological, cultural, socioaffective, linguistic, curricular, pedagogical, and professional—as an attempt to keep up with recent developments in SLA, L2/HL education, and L2/HL teacher preparation dealing with the growing significance of contextual factors at both theoretical and practical levels; the need to look beyond rigid professional standards or criteria in order to account for language diversity, individual or collective differences, and learning or teaching conditions; and the effort to enhance development for both pre- and in-service L2/HL educators regardless of their academic rank or position. Aware as we are of the need for further pedagogically based research on HL teacher education, we believe that an ecological perspective on the individual, educational, cultural, and sociopolitical circumstances of L2 and HL teaching and learning should constitute a crucial foundation for a comprehensive conception of the HL teacher knowledge base, and for well-grounded, dynamic, and responsive models of HL teacher development in the future.

NOTES

I am very grateful to Evelyn Canabal, Jason Bartles, Sara Beaudrie, Marta Fairclough, and the anonymous reviewers for their constructive comments on draft versions of this paper.

1. Peyton (2013) provides a wide overview of these programs in the United States as included in the Heritage Language Programs database of the Center for Applied Linguistics.

2. For further information about these dimensions, see Beaudrie 2012a; Beaudrie et al. 2014; Brinton et al. 2008; Carreira and Kagan 2011; Kagan and Dillon 2009; Potowski and Carreira 2004; Schwartz Caballero 2014; Wang and García 2002. More relevant materials can be found at the websites of the NABE Bilingual Multicultural Resource Center (http://www.nabe.org/ResourceCenter); the National Heritage Language Resource Center (http://www.nhlrc.ucla.edu/nhlrc); the Alliance for the Advancement of Heritage Languages (http://www.cal.org/heritage/); the National Capital Language Resource Center (http://nclrc.org/about_teaching/heritage_learners.html); the Center on Advanced Research on Language Acquisition (http://www.carla.umn.edu/); and the *Heritage Language Journal* (http://www.heritagelanguages.org/).
3. With a focus on "the language-teaching profession and the linguistic needs of learners," Beaudrie et al. (2014, 36) suggest a "quite broad" narrow definition of the term that would exclude only those learners without HL proficiency but not necessarily those with heritage motivation. See also Van Deusen-Scholl (2003), García (2005), García et al. (2013) and Wiley (2014) for discussions about challenges and alternatives to the term "heritage," seen by some authors as negative, offensive, or counterproductive.
4. Chang's *Autoethnography as Method* (2008) is a practical guide for autobiographical writing that includes theoretical information; methodological considerations; and particularly relevant, extensive appendices with exercises and examples of self-observational, self-reflective, and self-narrative data.
5. These statements are (1) Because heritage languages are a part of students' lives, it is important to take into account the role that affective factors (anxiety, emotional indicators, etc.) play in the learning process of the language; and (2) Because heritage languages are already a part of students' lives, it is not necessary to emphasize the affective component as part of the learning process (Parra 2014, 170).

REFERENCES

Allen, Heather W., and Hiram H. Maxim. 2013. "Introduction. Foreign Language Graduate Student Professional Development. Past, Present, and Future." In *Educating the Future Foreign Language Professoriate for the 21st Century*, ed. Heather W. Allen and Hiram H. Maxim, xv–xxv. Boston, MA: Cengage.

Allen, Heather W., and Eduardo Negueruela-Azarola. 2010. "The Professional Development of Future Professors of Foreign Languages: Looking Back, Looking Forward." *Modern Language Journal* 94, no. 3: 377–95. http://dx.doi.org/10.1111/j.1540-4781.2010.01056.x.

Alvarez, Stephanie. 2013. "Evaluating the Role of the Spanish Department in the Education of US Latin@ Students: *Un testimonio*." *Journal of Latinos and Education* 12, no. 2: 131–51. http://dx.doi.org/10.1080/15348431.2012.745405.

Atoofi, Saeid. 2013. "Classroom Has a Heart: Teachers and Students Affective Alignment in a Persian Heritage Language Classroom." *Linguistics and Education* 24, no. 2: 215–36. http://dx.doi.org/10.1016/j.linged.2012.11.010.

Beaudrie, Sara M. 2012a. "Research on University-based Spanish Heritage Language Programs in the United States." In *Spanish as a Heritage Language in the United*

States: The State of the Field, ed. Sara M. Beaudrie and Marta Fairclough, 203–21. Washington, DC: Georgetown University Press.

———, ed. 2012b. "Spanish Assessment." *Heritage Language Journal* [Special issue] 9, no. 1.

———. 2016. "Building a Heritage Language Program: Guidelines for a Collaborative Approach." In *Innovative Strategies for Heritage Language Teaching: A Practical Guide for the Classroom*, ed. Marta Fairclough and Sara M. Beaudrie, 80–98. Washington, DC: Georgetown University Press.

Beaudrie, Sara M., Cynthia Ducar, and Kim Potowski. 2014. *Heritage Language Teaching: Research and Practice*. New York: McGraw-Hill.

Brinton, Donna M., Olga Kagan, and Susan Bauckus, eds. 2008. *Heritage Language Education: A New Field Emerging*. New York: Routledge.

Byrd, David R., Anne Cummings Hlas, John Watzke, and María Fernanda Montes Valencia. 2011. "An Examination of Culture Knowledge: A Study of L2 Teachers' and Teacher Educators' Beliefs and Practices." *Foreign Language Annals* 44, no. 1: 4–39. http://dx.doi.org/10.1111/j.1944-9720.2011.01117.x.

Byrnes, Heidi. 2006. "Perspectives: Interrogating Communicative Competence as a Framework for Collegiate Foreign Language Study." *Modern Language Journal* 90, no. 2: 244–46. http://dx.doi.org/10.1111/j.1540-4781.2006.00395_1.x.

———. 2012. "Of Frameworks and the Goals of Collegiate Foreign Language Education: Critical Reflections." *Applied Linguistics Review* 3, no. 1: 1–24. http://dx.doi.org/10.1515/applirev-2012-0001.

Carreira, María. 2013. "Basic Principles for Teaching Mixed Classes." National Heritage Language Resource Center, http://ucla.in/1hy4zGZ.

———. 2016. "Supporting Heritage Language Learners through Macrobased Teaching: Foundational Principles and Implementation Strategies for HL and Mixed Classes." In *Innovative Strategies for Heritage Language Teaching: A Practical Guide for the Classroom*, ed. Marta Fairclough and Sara M. Beaudrie, 123–42. Washington, DC: Georgetown University Press.

Carreira, María, and Olga Kagan. 2011. "The Results of the National Heritage Language Survey: Implications for Teaching, Curriculum Design, and Professional Development." *Foreign Language Annals* 44, no. (1): 40–64.

Chang, Heewon. 2008. *Autoethnography as Method.* Walnut Creek, CA: Left Coast Press.

Cho, Hyesun. 2014. "It's Very Complicated': Exploring Heritage Language Identity with Heritage Language Teachers in a Teacher Preparation Program." *Language and Education* 28, no. 2: 181–95. http://dx.doi.org/10.1080/09500782.2013.804835.

Cook, Vivian. 2007. "The Goals of ELT: Reproducing Native-Speakers or Promoting Multi-Competence among Second Language Users?" In *Handbook of English Language Teaching*, ed. Jim Cummins and Chris Davison, 237–48. New York: Kluwer. http://dx.doi.org/10.1007/978-0-387-46301-8_18.

Donato, Richard. 2009. "Teacher Education in the Age of Standards of Professional Practice." *Modern Language Journal* 93, no. 2: 267–70. http://dx.doi.org/10.1111/j.1540-4781.2009.00860_3.x.

Ducar, Cynthia. 2012. "SHL Learners' Attitudes and Motivations: Reconciling Opposing Forces." In *Spanish as a Heritage Language in the United States: The State of the Field*, ed. Sara M. Beaudrie and Marta Fairclough, 161–78. Washington, DC: Georgetown University Press.

Edwards, J. David. 2004. "The Role of Languages in a Post-9/11 United States." *Modern Language Journal* 88, no. 2: 268–74.

Fairclough, Marta. 2016. "Incorporating Additional Varieties to the Linguistic Repertoires of Heritage Language Learners: A Multidialectal Model." In *Innovative Strategies for Heritage Language Teaching: A Practical Guide for the Classroom*, ed. Marta Fairclough and Sara M., Beaudrie, 143–65. Washington, DC: Georgetown University Press.

Fishman, Joshua. 2001. "300-Plus Years of Heritage Language Education in the United States." In *Heritage Languages in America: Preserving a National Resource*, ed. Joy Kreeft Peyton, Donald A. Ranard, and Scott McGinnis, 81–97. Washington, DC: Center for Applied Linguistics.

García, Ofelia. 2005. "Positioning Heritage Languages in the United States." *Modern Language Journal* 89, no. 4: 601–5.

———. 2009. *Bilingual Education in the 21st Century: A Global Perspective*. Malden, MA: Wiley-Blackwell.

García, Ofelia, Zeena Zakharia, and Bahar Otcu. 2013. Introduction to *Bilingual Community Education and Multilingualism: Beyond Heritage Languages in a Global City*, ed. Ofelia García, Zeena Zakharia, and Bahar Otcu, 3–42. Bristol: Multilingual Matters.

Henshaw, Florencia. 2016. "Technology-Enhanced Heritage Language Instruction: Best Tools and Best Practices." In *Innovative Strategies for Heritage Language Teaching: A Practical Guide for the Classroom*, ed. Marta Fairclough and Sara M. Beaudrie, 237–54. Washington, DC: Georgetown University Press.

Hogg, Linda. 2011. "Funds of Knowledge: An Investigation of Coherence within the Literature." *Teaching and Teacher Education* 27, no. 3: 666–77. http://dx.doi.org/10.1016/j.tate.2010.11.005.

Hornberger, Nancy H., and Shuhan C. Wang. 2008. "Who Are Our Heritage Language Learners? Identity and Biliteracy in Heritage Language Education in the United States." In *Heritage Language Education: A New Field Emerging*, ed. Donna M. Brinton, Olga Kagan, and Susan Bauckus, 3–38. New York: Routledge.

Ilieva, Gabriela, and Beth Clark-Gareca. 2016. "Heritage Language Learner Assessment: Towards Proficiency Standards." In *Innovative Strategies for Heritage Language Teaching: A Practical Guide for the Classroom*, ed. Marta Fairclough and Sara M. Beaudrie, 214–36. Washington, DC: Georgetown University Press.

Johnston, Bill, and Louis Janus. 2003. *Teacher Professional Development for the Less Commonly Taught Languages*. [Research report] Minneapolis: CARLA; http://www.carla.umn.edu/LCTL/resources/survey/surveyReport.pdf.

Kagan, Olga, and Kathleen Dillon. 2009. "The Professional Development of Teachers of Heritage Learners: A Matrix." In *Building Contexts, Making Connections: Selected Papers from the Fifth International Conference on Language Teacher Education*, ed. Mike Anderson and Anne Lazaraton, 155–75. Minneapolis: CARLA.

Kelleher, Ann. 2010. "What Is a Heritage Language Program?" *Heritage Briefs*. Center for Applied Linguistics. http://www.cal.org/heritage/pdfs/what-is-a-heritage-language-program.pdf.

Kissau, Scott P., Bob Algozzine, and Maria Yon. 2012. "Similar but Different: The Beliefs of Foreign Language Teachers." *Foreign Language Annals* 45, no. 4: 580–98. http://dx.doi.org/10.1111/j.1944-9720.2013.12001.x.

Kono, Nariyo, and Scott McGinnis. 2001. "Heritage Languages and Higher Education: Challenges, Issues, and Needs." In *Heritage Languages in America: Preserving a National Resource*, ed. Joy Kreeft Peyton, Donald A. Ranard, and Scott McGinnis, 197–206. Washington, DC: Center for Applied Linguistics.

Kramsch, Claire. 2008. "Ecological Perspectives on Foreign Language Education." *Language Teaching* 41, no. 3: 389–408. http://dx.doi.org/10.1017/S0261444808005065.

Kristjánsson, Carolyn. 2013. "Inside, Between and Beyond: Agency and Identity in Language Learning." In *Meaningful Action: Earl Stevick's Influence on Language Teaching*, ed. Jane Arnold and Tim Murphey, 11–28. Cambridge: Cambridge University Press.

Kroskrity, Paul V. 2010. "Language Ideologies: Evolving Perspectives." In *Handbook of Pragmatics Highlights: Society and Language Use*, ed. Jürgen Jaspers, Jan-Ola Östman, and Jef Verschueren, 192–211. Philadelphia: John Benjamins.

Lacorte, Manel. 2014. "Methodological Approaches and Realities." In *The Routledge Handbook of Hispanic Applied Linguistics*, ed. Manel Lacorte, 99–116. New York: Routledge.

Lacorte, Manel, and Evelyn Canabal. 2005. "Teacher Beliefs and Practices in Advanced Spanish Classrooms." *Heritage Language Journal* 3, no. 1: 83–107.

Lafford, Barbara. 2013. "The Next Frontier: A Research Agenda for Exploring Experiential Language Learning in International and Domestic Contexts." In *Selected Proceedings of the 16th Hispanic Linguistics Symposium*, ed. Jennifer Cabrelli Amaro, Gillian Lord, Ana de Prada Pérez, and Jessi Elana Aaron, 80–112. Somerville, MA: Cascadilla Proceedings Project.

Lear, Darcy W., and Annie R. Abbott. 2008. "Foreign Language Professional Standards and CSL: Achieving the 5 C's." *Michigan Journal of Community Service Learning* 14, no. 2: 76–86.

Lee, Jin Sook, and Eva Oxelson. 2006. "'It's Not My Job': K-12 Teacher Attitudes toward Students' Heritage Language Maintenance." *Bilingual Research Journal* 30, no. 2: 453–77. http://dx.doi.org/10.1080/15235882.2006.10162885.

Lee, Jin Sook, and Debra Suárez. 2009. "A Synthesis of the Roles of Heritage Languages in the Lives of Children of Immigrants: What Educators Need to Know." In *The Education of Language Minority Immigrants in the United States*, ed. Terrence G. Wiley, Jin Sook Lee, and Russell W. Rumberger, 136–71. Bristol, UK: Multilingual Matters.

Lee, Soyong, and Yoo-Seon Bang. 2011. "Listening to Teacher Lore: The Challenges and Resources of Korean Heritage Language Teachers." *Teaching and Teacher Education* 27, no. 2: 387–94. http://dx.doi.org/10.1016/j.tate.2010.09.008.

Leeman, Jennifer. 2005. "Engaging Critical Pedagogy: Spanish for Native Speakers." *Foreign Language Annals* 38, no. 1: 35–45 http://dx.doi.org/10.1111/j.1944-9720.2005.tb02451.x.

———. 2010. "The Sociopolitics of Heritage Language Education." In *Spanish of the US Southwest: A Language in Transition*, ed. Susana Rivera-Mills and Daniel Villa, 309–17. Madrid: Iberoamericana.

Leeman, Jennifer, and Ellen Serafini. 2016. "Sociolinguistics for Heritage Language Educators and Students: A Model for Critical Translingual Competence." In *Innovative Strategies for Heritage Language Teaching: A Practical Guide for the Classroom*, ed. Marta Fairclough and Sara M. Beaudrie, 56–79. Washington, DC: Georgetown University Press.

Lynch, Andrew. 2003. "The Relationship between Second and Heritage Language Acquisition: Notes on Research and Theory Building." *Heritage Language Journal* 1, no. 1: 26–34.

Martínez, Glenn. 2016. "Goals and Beyond in Heritage Language Education: From Competencies to Capabilities." In *Innovative Strategies for Heritage Language Teaching: A Practical Guide for the Classroom*, ed. Marta Fairclough and Sara M. Beaudrie, 39–55. Washington, DC: Georgetown University Press.

Milroy, James. 2007. "The Ideology of the Standard Language." In *Routledge Companion to Sociolinguistics*, ed. Carmen Mullany and Louise Stockwell Peter, 133–39. London: Routledge.

Moll, Luis C., Cathy Amanti, Deborah Neff, and Norma Gonzalez. 1992. "Funds of Knowledge for Teaching: Using a Qualitative Approach to Connect Homes and Classrooms." *Theory into Practice* 31, no. 2: 132–41. http://dx.doi.org/10.1080/00405849209543534.

Montrul, Silvina. 2010. "Current Issues in Heritage Language Acquisition." *Annual Review of Applied Linguistics* 30:3–23. http://dx.doi.org/10.1017/S0267190510000103.

Moore, M., J. Peyton, and K. Kim. 2014. "Assessment of Heritage Language Learners. Issues and Directions." In *Handbook of Heritage, Community, and Native American Languages in the United States*, ed. Terrence Wiley, Joy Kreeft Peyton, Donna Christian, Sarah K. Moore, and Na Liu, 349–58. New York: Routledge.

Paesani, Kate. 2013. "A Literacy-Based Approach to Foreign Language Teacher Development." In *Educating the Future Foreign Language Professiorate for the 21st Century*, ed. Heather W. Allen and Hiram H. Maxim, 60–81. Boston: Heinle Cengage.

Paesani, Kate, Heather W. Allen, and Beatrice Dupuy. 2015. *A Multiliteracies Framework for Collegiate Foreign Language Teaching*. Upper Saddle River, NJ: Pearson–Prentice Hall.

Parra, María L. 2014. "Exploring Individual Differences among Spanish Heritage Learners: Implications for TA Training and Program Development." In *Individual Differences, L2 Development and Language Program Administration: From Theory to Application*, ed. Cristina Sanz, Beatriz Lado, and Stacy Katz Bourns, 150–70. Boston: Cengage.

———. 2016. "Critical Approaches to Heritage Language Instruction: How to Foster Students' Critical Consciousness." In *Innovative Strategies for Heritage Language Teaching: A Practical Guide for the Classroom*, ed. Marta Fairclough and Sara M. Beaudrie, 166–90. Washington, DC: Georgetown University Press.

Pastor, Susana, and Manel Lacorte. 2014. "Teacher Education." In *The Routledge Handbook of Hispanic Applied Linguistics*, ed. Manel Lacorte, 117–33. New York: Routledge.

Pavlenko, Anita. 2002. "'We Have Room but for One Language Here': Language and National Identity at the Turn of the 20th Century." *Multilingua* 21, no. 2–3: 163–96.

Peyton, Joy K. 2013. "Community-Based Language Schools in the National Educational Landscape." Paper presented at the Community Language Schools Conference. Los Angeles, California, April 23.

Polinsky, Maria, and Olga Kagan. 2007. "Heritage Languages: In the 'Wild' and in the Classroom." *Language and Linguistics Compass* 1, no. 5: 368–95. http://dx.doi.org/10.1111/j.1749-818X.2007.00022.x.

Pomerantz, Anne. 2002. "Language Ideologies and the Production of Identities: Spanish as a Resource for Participation in a Multilingual Marketplace." *Multilingua* 21, no. 2–3: 275–302.

Potowski, Kim. 2002. "Educating University FL Teachers to Work with Heritage Spanish Speakers." In *Research and Practice in Language Teacher Education: Voices from the Field*, ed. Bill Johnston and Suzanne Irujo, 87–100. Minneapolis: CARLA.

Potowski, Kim, and María Carreira. 2004. "Teacher Development and National Standards for Spanish as a Heritage Language." *Foreign Language Annals* 37, no. 3: 427–37. http://dx.doi.org/10.1111/j.1944-9720.2004.tb02700.x.

Rabin, Lisa. 2014. "Service-Learning/*Aprendizaje-servicio* as a Global Practice in Spanish." In *The Routledge Handbook of Hispanic Applied Linguistics*, ed. Manel Lacorte, 168–83. New York: Routledge.

Razfar, Aria. 2012. "Narrating Beliefs: A Language Ideologies Approach to Teacher Beliefs." *Anthropology & Education Quarterly* 43, no. 1: 61–81. http://dx.doi.org/10.1111/j.1548-1492.2011.01157.x.

Samaniego, Malena, and Chantelle Warner. 2016. "Designing Meaning in Inherited Languages: A Multiliteracies Approach to HL Instruction." In *Innovative Strategies for Heritage Language Teaching: A Practical Guide for the Classroom*, ed. Marta Fairclough and Sara M. Beaudrie, 191–213. Washington, DC: Georgetown University Press.

Scarino, Angela. 2014. "Learning as Reciprocal, Interpretive, Meaning-making: A View from Collaborative Research into the Professional Learning of Teachers of Languages." *Modern Language Journal* 98, no. 1: 386–401. http://dx.doi.org/10.1111/j.1540-4781.2014.12068.x.

Schulz, Renate A. 2000. "Foreign Language Teacher Development: *MLJ* Perspectives 1916–1999." *Modern Language Journal* 84, no. 4: 495–522. http://dx.doi.org/10.1111/0026-7902.00084.

Schwartz Caballero, Ana María. 2014. "Preparing Teachers to Work with Heritage Language Learners." In *Handbook of Heritage, Community, and Native American Languages in the United States*, ed. Terrence Wiley, Joy Kreeft Peyton, Donna Christian, Sarah K. Moore, and Na Liu, 359–69. New York: Routledge.

Siskin, H. Jay, ed. 2008. *From Thought to Action: Exploring Beliefs and Outcomes in the Foreign Language Program*. Boston: Heinle and Heinle.

Valdés, Guadalupe. 2001. "Heritage Language Students: Profiles and Possibilities." In *Heritage Languages in America: Preserving a National Resource*, ed. Joy Kreeft Peyton, Donald A. Ranard, and Scott McGinnis, 37–80. Washington, DC: Center for Applied Linguistics.

Valdés, Guadalupe, Sonia V. González, Dania López García, and Patricio Márquez. 2003. "Language Ideology: The Case of Spanish in Departments of Foreign Languages." *Anthropology & Education Quarterly* 34, no. 1: 3–26. http://dx.doi.org/10.1525/aeq.2003.34.1.3.

Van Deusen-Scholl, Nelleke. 2003. "Toward a Definition of Heritage Language: Sociopolitical and Pedagogical considerations." *Journal of Language, Identity, and Education* 2, no. 3: 211–30. http://dx.doi.org/10.1207/S15327701JLIE0203_4.

Wang, Shuhan C., and María I. García. 2002. "Heritage Language Learners." http://www.ncssfl.org/papers/NCSSFLHLLs0902.pdf.

Wang, Shuhan C., and Nancy Green. 2001. "Heritage Language Students in the K-12 Education System." In *Heritage Languages in America: Preserving a National*

Resource, ed. Joy Kreeft Peyton, Donald A. Ranard, and Scott McGinnis, 167–96. Washington, DC: Center for Applied Linguistics.

Wenger, Etienne. 1998. *Communities of Practice: Learning, Meaning, and Identity*. Cambridge: Cambridge University Press. http://dx.doi.org/10.1017/CBO9780511803932.

Wiley, Terrence. 2014. "The Problem of Defining Heritage and Community Languages and their Speakers." In *Handbook of Heritage, Community, and Native American Languages in the United States*, ed. Terrence Wiley, Joy Kreeft Peyton, Donna Christian, Sarah K. Moore, and Na Liu, 19–28. New York: Routledge. http://dx.doi.org/10.4324/9780203122419.ch2.

Wright, Tony. 2005. *Classroom Management in Language Education*. London: Palgrave Macmillan. http://dx.doi.org/10.1057/9780230514188.

Zyzik, Eve. 2016. "Toward a Prototype Model of the Heritage Language Learner: Understanding Strengths and Needs." In *Innovative Approaches in Heritage Language Teaching: From Research to Practice*. Ed. Marta Fairclough and Sara M. Beaudrie, 19–38. Washington, DC: Georgetown University Press.

Part II

Strategies, Techniques, and Approaches in Heritage Language Teaching

6

Supporting Heritage Language Learners through Macrobased Teaching

Foundational Principles and Implementation Strategies for Heritage Language and Mixed Classes

Maria Carreira
National Heritage Language Resource Center, UCLA, California State University, Long Beach

This chapter discusses the use of macrobased (also known as top-down) approaches in heritage language (HL) teaching, focusing on foundational principles, classroom strategies, and issues of implementation. The chapter presents three college-level programs and a high school STARTALK program that instantiate best practices in macrobased teaching.[1] Particular attention is given to mixed classes (i.e., classes with HL learners and second language [L2] learners) because of the difficulties they present for instantiating these other best practices of HL teaching.

Macrobased approaches align well with HL teaching by virtue of their ability to attend to HL learners' linguistic and socioaffective needs. In the area of language, these learners can be characterized as having considerable functional abilities in the target language, particularly as it relates to the oral registers and everyday tasks. Attesting to the strength of those abilities, in a national survey of HL learners at the postsecondary level, 68 percent of respondents rated their listening skills as advanced or native-like and only 4 percent rated their listening skills in the low range. Similarly, 82 percent rated their speaking skills in the range of intermediate to native-like (Carreira and Kagan 2011).

In a seminal paper on HL teaching, Olga Kagan and Kathleen Dillon (2001, 512) argue that HL learners' functional abilities are best developed by macrobased teaching approaches, citing the following reasons: "Heritage learners have high aural proficiency; native-like pronunciation; vocabulary that is adequate for the needs of family and possibly community (e.g., shopping, making appointments, etc.). They also have some grammatical intuition that will function effectively if supported by declarative knowledge of grammar. . . . They need a macro, not micro, approach to grammar, paradigms of declensions and conjugations rather than one case at a time."

Macrobased approaches also support instruction that is responsive to HL learners' socioaffective needs. In this regard, research underscores the particular relevance of ethnic identity, which, according to Agnes He (2006, 7), is "the centerpiece rather than the background of HL development." Group membership is also of the essence, for the reasons put forward by Lucy Tse (2001, 60):

> While researchers have looked quite extensively at the language exposure we need to learn a new language, a second set of factors that are equally important has received far less attention. These factors relate to "group membership," or the allegiances we feel with particular language-speaking groups and the attitudes and feelings that flow from being associated with them. In other words, group membership is important because we tend to learn language better when we feel like a member of the group of people who speak that language.

As one Latino youth explains, the difficulties associated with finding identity and group membership loom large for HL learners, and, significantly for HL teaching, they provide a strong impetus for connecting with other HL learners.

> In high school I was one of very few Latinos. My friend and I were called the American kids. This was always funny to me because my Dad's family always told me I was American. In school I was labeled Mexican, but to the Mexicans, I am an American. I am part of each, but not fully accepted by either. It's this weird duality in which you are stuck in the middle. . . .You take pride in both cultures and learn to deal with the rejection. You may never be fully embraced by either side. That's why you seek out other people like yourself. Socializing with people who share a common experience helps you deal with this experience. (qtd. in Carreira and Beeman 2014, 88)

The kinds of practices associated with macrobased teaching—in particular, the strategic use of students' experiences and background knowledge—lend themselves to addressing the above concerns. More broadly, macrobased practices give a sense of personal relevance, immediacy, and authenticity to language learning that is difficult to achieve with microbased approaches. The next section offers a comparison of macro- and microbased approaches.

MACROBASED TEACHING: FOUNDATIONAL CONCEPTS

A defining feature of macrobased approaches is that they teach grammar and vocabulary as dictated by function or context. Accordingly, instruction proceeds from the general message or the big ideas in a text to the analysis of its linguistic building blocks. The inverse is true of microbased (bottom-up) approaches. Premised on the idea that understanding the components of a text is a prerequisite to grasping its overall meaning, microbased teaching relies on initial compartmentalization and decoding of the linguistic blocks of a message. Accordingly, instruction progresses from smaller, simpler units of knowledge to more complex ones—e.g., words → sentences → paragraphs → discourse. Table 6.1 summarizes key differences between the two approaches.

In foreign language classes, micro approaches are common at the earliest levels of instruction, where learners' proficiency is still limited and authentic materials are inaccessible without prior form-focused instruction. On the other hand, macro approaches are well suited to more advanced levels, where

Table 6.1: Macro versus Micro Approaches

Teaching domains	Macrobased approaches	Microbased approaches
Vocabulary and grammar	Age appropriate and integrated. Dictated by function and context.	Carefully controlled and selected. Isolated practice of different aspects of linguistic knowledge.
Reading	Fairly large and complex texts from the beginning. Unaltered authentic texts.	Small texts gradually increasing in volume and complexity. Altered texts to facilitate readability.
Writing	Longer texts from the beginning. Initial emphasis on the content, gradually building toward improving stylistics, grammar, spelling.	Sentence level gradually increasing to paragraph and then longer.
Speaking and listening	Full range of native input (movies, documentaries, lectures, news stories, plays) and output (discussions, conversations, monologues).	Initially restricted, gradually increasing in length and complexity. Initially restricted to dialogue.
Culture	Full range of topics, integrated.	Initially isolated and decontextualized.

Adapted from Wu and Chang (2010) and Kagan and Dillon (2001).

learners have the functional skills to engage in complex and authentic activities at the outset of instruction, with relatively little scaffolding. Activities associated with this approach tap into students' experiences and background knowledge, including topical knowledge, contextual or situational knowledge, and schemata knowledge, that is, understanding of the structure and relationship of events (Richards 1990).

Hui-Lung Chia (2001) singles out three techniques that prove particularly helpful for activating background knowledge. *Semantic mapping* involves making associations with a given topic. Students generate a list of words and then group them into categories. In the process, they identify the main ideas and labels (words) of the topic. *Generating questions* is frequently associated with reading and happens in three phases. At the prereading phase, the instructor introduces the topic of a reading and students work in groups to create a list of what they know and don't know about a topic. Representative items from each group are discussed by the class and written on the board. During the reading phase, students look for answers to their questions and verify the concepts that they thought they knew. At the postreading phase, students solidify their knowledge by producing something, such as a piece of writing or a presentation. *Previewing* involves using cues in a text such as the title, subheadings, and illustrations to make educated guesses about its content.

Macrobased teaching is closely associated with the "whole language" approach and top-down theories of processing. The whole language approach emphasizes having a print-rich classroom where learners are immersed in authentic texts and develop their reading skills through a variety of strategies, including skimming and scanning a reading, making inferences, and reacting personally to content (Heymsfeld 1989). These strategies contrast with those associated with phonics-first instruction, such as drills and the use of decodable texts, which are more common in microbased teaching.

Top-down theories of processing hold that processing is conceptually driven and perception is organized and shaped by experience, expectations, and context (Goldstein 2014). Examples of skills and activities associated with top-down processing are listed below:

Sample Top-Down Processing Skills (Richards 1990, 60)

- Use keywords to construct the schema of a discourse.
- Infer the role of the participants in a situation.
- Infer the topic of a discourse.
- Infer the outcome of an event.
- Infer missing details.
- Distinguish between literal and figurative meanings.
- Distinguish between facts and opinions.

Sample Activities Involving Top-Down Processing Skills (Richards 1990, 61–63)

- Guess what news headlines might refer to, then listen to or read the complete piece.
- Identify a picture from a description of it.
- Identify key ideas in a message.
- Listen to conversations containing small talk and recognize when the speaker is preparing to introduce a real topic.
- Read information about a topic; then listen to a talk on the topic and check whether the information was mentioned or not.
- Read one side of a telephone conversation and guess the other speakers' responses; then listen to the telephone conversation.

These examples are not intended to give the impression that macrobased approaches focus on message to the exclusion of form. To the contrary, like microbased approaches, macrobased approaches involve form-focused instruction. However, the two approaches diverge with regard to the role and timing of such instruction. In microbased teaching, form-focused instruction sustains and drives the progression to more complex uses of language. The opposite pattern holds with macrobased approaches; the use of form-focused instruction flows from activities that are discourse based, content based, task based, genre based, or experiential (Celce-Murcia and Olshtain 2000; Kagan and Dillon 2001). A brief overview of these approaches is provided in table 6.2.

The next section features two macrobased college programs that instantiate many of the principles and practices discussed in this section. A third example, a high school program for Chinese HL learners, is presented in a later discussion.

Best Practices in Macrobased Teaching

Glenn Martínez (2010) describes a program at the University of Texas–Pan American that instantiates best practices in macrobased teaching. Medical Spanish for Heritage Learners is a four-course sequence that focuses on content-based development of oral and literacy skills for health care professionals serving the US Latino community. The program uses genre-based teaching "as a means to ground the development of medical discourse in a variety of cultural and situational contexts" (Martínez 2010, 10). Particular diseases or health issues are examined in thematic units that integrate language development and the learning of medical concepts and issues surrounding the US Latino community. To that end, the thematic units use interrelated texts (through genre chaining) that progress from colloquial

Table 6.2: Overview of Approaches Compatible with Macrobased Teaching

Approaches	Basic tenets
Discourse-based teaching	"A general movement within language pedagogy which moves from focus on grammar to concern with discourse and also moves away from language analysis, as the goal of language teaching, to the goal of teaching language for communication" (Celce-Murcia and Olshtain 2000 5). In this approach "materials used in the learning/teaching process must allow the autonomous learner and the facilitating teacher to make choices, consider alternatives, and plan for specific needs" (Celce-Murcia and Olshtain 2000, 7).
Content-based teaching	"The concurrent teaching of academic subject matter and second language skills" (Brinton, Snow, and Wesche 1989, 2). Content-based teaching approaches "view the target language largely as the vehicle through which subject matter content is learned rather than as the immediate object of study" (Brinton, Snow, and Wesche 1989, 5).
Task-based teaching	An approach where pedagogical tasks involve "communicative language use in which the user's attention is focused on meaning rather than grammatical form" (Nunan 2004, 17)."A task is intended to result in language use that bears a resemblance, direct or indirect, to the way language is used in the real world" (Ellis 2003, 16).
Genre-based teaching	"A contextual framework for writing which foregrounds the meanings and text-types at stake in a situation. At their core, these methods offer writers an explicit understanding of how texts in target genres are structured and why they are written in the ways they are" (Hyland 2003, 26).
Experiential-based teaching	An approach that "takes the learners' immediate personal experience as the point of departure for the learning experience. This approach emphasizes the "transformation of knowledge within the learner rather than the transmission of knowledge from the teacher to the learner" (Nunan 2004, 12)."Experiential learning theory provides the philosophical view of learning as personal growth. The goal is to enable the learner to become increasingly self-directed and responsible for his or her own learning" (Kohonen 1992, 37).

discourse, to texts within the genre of popular scientific discourse, to scientific texts using technical terminology and the grammatical constructions of scientific discourse. As students progress through the units, they develop the linguistic and cultural resources to discuss these concepts in a variety of situational contexts. The experiential component of the program consists of field-based work available through the College of Medicine or the College of Nursing (see also Hechanova [2015] for a high school program on medical Spanish).

María Luisa Parra (2013) describes another macrobased program. Taught at Harvard University, SP59 is a fourth-year course designed for students with intermediate to high levels of proficiency (heritage and nonheritage). The course focuses on the experiences of Latinos in the United States, including immigration, identity, and language practices. Following a multiliteracy approach, students learn about these and other topics through a variety of genres (e.g., readings, film, music, and print art) in order to advance their language skills, their translinguistic and transcultural competency, their critical thinking skills, and their linguistic awareness.

SP59 also has a field trip and a guided visit to the university museum, where students focus on three works that speak to the immigrant experience from the perspective of Latin American and US Latino artists. Community ties are cultivated primarily by way of the service component, which places students in organizations that match their interests (e.g., adult literacy in Spanish, legal services, women's health, and civic engagement). As Parra (2013, 121) explains, such experience "brings students to a different level of understanding about the community and facilitates the advancement of transcultural knowledge" (see also Parra, this volume [2016]).

Both of these programs align well with the approaches described in table 6.2. In addition, they instantiate three principles of discourse-based teaching that are closely associated with macro approaches and that are particularly well suited to HL teaching. As explained by Marianne Celce-Murcia and Elite Olshtain (2000, 195), contextualization "refers to the need to present linguistic content within thematic and situational contexts that reflect the natural use of language." The second principle, authenticity, takes into account the type of language used in the classroom as well as the tasks employed in the learning process. Authentic classroom language is an "approximation of real speech that takes into account the learners' level of ability" (Celce-Murcia and Olshtain 2000, 195). Authentic tasks are "relevant and appropriate to the learning situation" (Celce-Murcia and Olshtain 2000, 196). Finally, integration refers to the consolidation of knowledge and skills. An integrated curriculum makes strategic use of learners' background knowledge and language skills.

Contextualization and authenticity are instantiated in both programs through the use of authentic texts and especially through experiential learning in organizations that serve the Latino community. Exemplifying an integrated approach, both programs build on learners' linguistic strengths and knowledge of the US Latino communities to further their learning objectives (see Martínez's [2016] and Parra's [2016] chapters, this volume).

The next section provides a blueprint for creating and implementing activities for HL learners that align with this general approach.

Principles and Strategies that Support Macrobased HL Teaching

From–To Principles

Five principles of HL teaching put forward by Olga Kagan (Kagan and Carreira 2015) provide a useful blueprint for creating macrobased curricula and activities that respond to HL learners' linguistic and affective needs. Designed to build on learners' global knowledge of their heritage language and culture as well as their functional skills, these principles are formulated in a "from–to" format, as listed below.

- Aural → Reading
- Spoken → Written
- Home-based register → General and academic registers
- Everyday, "real-life" activities → Classroom activities
- HL learners' motivations surrounding identity and group membership → Content

Regarding the first three points, Kagan's proposal is that HL teaching should make strategic use of HL learners' strengths to address gaps in their knowledge. Specifically, their listening and speaking skills should serve as the springboard for developing their reading and writing skills, respectively, and their home register should serve as a bridge to more formal registers. This approach is illustrated in Medical Spanish for Heritage Learners, where learners handle increasingly complex texts through genre chaining.

The premise of Kagan's fourth point is that authentic activities—the kind that form part of the everyday experiences of the community of speakers in the United States—should guide the design of classroom activities. This idea is consonant with Maria Carreira and Olga Kagan's (2011) community-based approach to HL teaching and is illustrated in the service component in SP59.

Lastly, the fifth principle holds that students' motivations and socioaffective needs should drive the content of instruction—for example, the readings, activities, and projects of HL teaching. This principle aligns with the concept of compelling input, as put forth by Krashen (2011, 1):

> To make sure that language acquirers pay attention to the input, it should be interesting. But interest may be not enough for optimal

language acquisition. It may be the case that input needs to be not just interesting but compelling. Compelling means that the input is so interesting you forget that it is in another language. It means you are in a state of "flow" (Csikszentmihalyi 1990). In flow, the concerns of everyday life and even the sense of self disappear—our sense of time is altered and nothing but the activity itself seems to matter.

Kagan's fifth principle maximizes the opportunity for creating compelling input by grounding HL teaching and learning in the socioaffective needs of learners and their reasons for studying their heritage language. Materials and activities that lend themselves to exploring issues of identity and that help learners wrestle with the challenges and rewards of straddling two cultures and languages might respond to such needs and motivations. In keeping with this approach, Ming-Hsuan Wu and Zhu-Min Chang (2010)'s high school STARTALK program for Chinese HL learners engaged students in debating such issues as what it means to be American, Chinese, or Chinese American as well as in discussing aspects of their lives that were not understood by their parents. The program used English texts written by Chinese American writers such as *The Accidental Asian* by Eric Liu and the edited book of stories by Asian American high school students, *Yell-Oh Girls*, to study Chinatowns and the experiences of Chinese immigrants to the United States. Students also explored their own immigration histories and shared them with the class (see also Carreira and Wijaya [2010] for an Indonesian macrobased HL curriculum).

Strategies That Support This Approach

To implement the "from–to" principles and, more generally, to engage in macrobased teaching, instructors must be able to gauge the suitability of different texts and scaffolding activities for a given level of instruction. Scaffolding refers to "a variety of instructional techniques used to move students progressively toward a stronger understanding and, ultimately, greater independence in the learning process" (Abbott 2014). Table 6.3, from Valdés (2003, 49), proves useful in this regard.

The chart in table 6.3 can help instructors implement the concept of genre chaining (Martínez 2010) and a multiliteracy approach (Parra 2013; also see Samaniego and Warner, this volume [2016]). For example, at the lower levels of instruction, learners may be asked to participate in a conversation and, moving up a level, write a personal letter related to the conversation. More advanced learners could listen to a TV drama based on a novel and subsequently read the actual novel, discuss it, and prepare a brief newspaper report summarizing its main points. Crucially, in both of these examples, instruction moves from the aural to the written registers, in keeping with Kagan's "from–to" principles.

Any move up the hierarchy of texts and registers requires scaffolding, but the bigger the jump, the more of it will be needed. This is not just because the higher registers are intrinsically more difficult to learn but also because they are less familiar in the target language to HL learners (as represented in the first column of table 6.3). It follows that a student who can comfortably read broad-audience magazine articles will need more scaffolding to work with an advanced college textbook than to work with a newspaper report.

It is important to remember that there is significant interlinguistic variation with regard to what HL learners can do in their heritage language. By way of illustration, figure 6.1 compares HL learners' self-reported aural proficiency scores, by language. Moreover, within a given language there is significant variation between HL learners. Effective HL teaching involves selecting texts types and using scaffolding activities that align with language-specific and class-specific realities.

The Sheltered Instruction Observation Protocol (SIOP) model (Echevarria and Graves 2007; Echevarria, Vogt, and Short 2013), developed

Table 6.3: Rank of Registers and HL Learners' Functional Differentiation for Different Text Types

Language(s) used	Language registers	Text types
English	High	Formal addresses to parliamentary bodies (scripted)
	Mid	Addresses to learned societies (scripted and unscripted)
		Legal documents
		Scholarly articles
		Formal academic lectures (scripted and unscripted)
		Committee and commission reports
		Advanced college textbooks
		Editorials
		Campaign speeches
Mainly English Some Spanish		TV news
		Business letters
		Newspaper reports
		Novels and short stories
English, Spanish, or both	Low	TV drama
		Broad-audience magazine articles
		Interviews
		Personal letters
		Private conversations

Adapted from Valdés (2003, 49).

Native-advanced **Intermediate** **Low**

Spanish Russian Persian Korean

Vietnamese

Mandarin and Cantonese

Tagalog

Figure 6.1. Aural Proficiency (Average of Listening and Speaking Scores)

with English-language learners in mind, offers a wide range of scaffolding strategies that prove useful with macrobased teaching. These include using preteaching vocabulary, breaking a task into smaller components with opportunities for intermittent feedback, using visual aids, modeling a skill, paraphrasing, summarizing information, and activating background knowledge. The last of these is closely associated with "semantic mapping" and "generating questions," as previously discussed. Celce-Murcia and Olshtain (2000) also recommend teaching learning strategies and incorporating activities that help learners become aware of differences between registers and language modes.

Valuable as they are for bridging learning gaps, scaffolding strategies have their limitations: some knowledge and skills will elude learners, even under optimal teaching conditions. Such knowledge can be said to lie outside of students' zone of proximal development (ZPD) (Vygotsky 1978). The ZPD is the "difference between what a child can do independently and what he or she is capable of doing with targeted assistance (scaffolding)" (Lui 2012, 2). Knowledge that is beyond the learners' ZPD will not likely be grasped, even with extensive scaffolding. This puts an upper limit on what can be accomplished through instruction at any given point in time. Returning to table 6.3 by way of example, this means that learners who find themselves at the low range of the scale will likely find the texts and registers at the top of the scale out of their reach, even with extensive scaffolding and help. Crucially, instruction is most effective when it is aimed at the ZPD. Missing that level, by aiming either too high or too low, reduces learning (Vygotsky 1978).

The ACTFL Proficiency Guidelines prove useful for conceptualizing learners' ZPD and aligning instruction accordingly. Maria Alexandra Elliot's (2008) study of writing by L2 learners exemplifies this approach. Finding that beginning Spanish college writers are able to progress from Novice-High to Intermediate-Low over the course of a semester, Elliot's study argues that this is consistent with them reaching their ZPD. Table 6.4 takes a similar approach to a study by Cynthia Martin and colleagues (2013), which sought to identify specific features that prevent Spanish and Russian HL speakers at the Intermediate and Advanced ACTFL OPI (oral proficiency interview) level from

Table 6.4: HL Learners' Skills and Knowledge Gaps in a Vygotskian Framework

I	II	III	IV
HL learners' ACTFL OPI level	HL learners' zone of independent developmental achievement	HL learners' zone of proximal development	Oral text types in learners' ZPD that they may produce with guided assistance
Intermediate	• Create with language, when talking about familiar topics • Produce language at the sentence level • Handle straight-forward survival situations	• Speak about topics beyond the auto-biographical • Produce text with connectors and organization • Control major time frames • Initiate Advanced-level tasks that involve past narrations and a situation with a complication	• Describe a current event following the format of a TV news report
Advanced	• Speak about topics of community, national, or inter-national interest • Communicate in paragraph-style oral discourse	• Discuss topics at an abstract level • Support an idea, or hypothesize • Sustain extended discourse • Use precise vocabulary	• Debate a current event topic or present a business proposal

receiving higher ratings. In column II are the functional skills associated with the Intermediate and Advanced levels of proficiency in the ACTFL OPI. These skills are depicted as being within HL learners' "zone of independent developmental achievement" (Vygotsky 1978, 90), which is to say, this is what learners can do on their own. Put differently, these constitute the "from" part of Kagan's principles. Column III lists the skills that, according to Cynthia Martin and colleagues (2013), prevent HL speakers from receiving higher ratings. These skills can be considered to be in HL learners' ZPD, which is to say, they are attainable with proper scaffolding and should be the goal of instruction. These constitute the "to" part of Kagan's principles. Finally, column IV associates HL learners' ZPD with texts from Valdés's hierarchy of text types.

In instantiating this approach, it is important to keep in mind that although HL learners can progress at a faster pace than L2 learners (Davidson and Lekic 2013), their linguistic development nevertheless requires significant investments of time. This is particularly true as it applies to literacy (Colombi and Harrington 2012) and, more generally, as it applies to proficiency beyond the Intermediate level (Clifford 2002). In particular, to reach Advanced-High and Superior, HL learners (and also L2 learners) need the kind of extensive, real-life exposure associated with study-abroad programs (Carreira 2012; Davidson and Lekic 2013).

With this overview of macrobased HL teaching complete, the next section examines the dynamics of macro- and microbased teaching in mixed classes.

MACRO AND MICRO APPROACHES IN MIXED CLASSES

Although the bulk of the literature on HL teaching focuses on HL classes, in actuality many HL learners study their heritage language in mixed classes (Beaudrie 2011, 2012; Carreira 2014). This fact underscores an undeniable reality surrounding the teaching of heritage languages: while having HL courses may be the prescribed course of action, various restrictions in practice may render such an option out of the question. Accordingly, it is important to develop protocols for addressing the needs of HL learners in mixed classes. Given the range and complexity of the issues, a complete treatment of this topic is beyond the scope of this chapter. The present discussion is thus narrowly circumscribed to a few points connected to macrobased approaches.

A good place to start this discussion is with the term "mixed classes," which is commonly used in reference to classes that enroll HL and L2 learners. Crucially, the term does not refer to classes that employ methods and materials designed specifically for teaching HL and L2 learners together. This distinction serves to highlight a significant shortcoming of mixed classes as they are currently conceived: they are a good fit for L2 learners but not for HL learners. Indeed, research suggests that for the most part, the instructional approaches, topics, and materials of such classes are indistinguishable from those of L2 classes (Carreira 2014). This means that mixed classes are a bad fit for HL learners in three particular ways: (1) with regard to their overall instructional approach, which, in keeping with L2 teaching practices, tends to be microbased, particularly at the lower levels of instruction; (2) with regard to social-cultural topics and issues of affect, which are geared toward students with no family connection to the target language; and (3) with regard to language topics, which are fine-tuned to the needs of L2 students. The present discussion will concern itself with the first point.[2]

Regarding instructional approaches, mixed classes present a perplexing challenge stemming from the fact that HL and L2 learners typically have divergent pathways to accessing authentic materials and form-focused instruction. As explained earlier, HL learners can and should engage with authentic materials from the start of instruction, following a macro approach. By contrast, L2 learners frequently need form-focused instruction before they can access authentic materials, which is to say, they need microbased instruction.

How can this fundamental difference between the two populations of learners be managed in mixed classes? A good place to start to examine this issue is with the goals of instruction, which, as previously noted, are generally the same for both populations of learners within a given unit and, more broadly, within a course and a program of study. Thus, although both learners have different entry points to and pathways through instruction, they have the same end point. This is depicted in the figure 6.2.

Putting the focus on the end point of instruction—that is, what all learners should know and be able to do with regard to a particular unit of instruction—brings to the fore an essential question: How can each population of learner meet these goals? Research indicates that both HL learners and L2 learners benefit from form-focused instruction and classroom interaction (Montrul and Bowles 2010; Potowski, Jegerski, and Morgan-Short 2009) and that they benefit from working together (Bowles 2011). However, given their different entry points to instruction, they need special preparation to be able to work together and derive benefit from different aspects of instruction.

In particular, to be able to work with authentic materials alongside HL learners, L2 learners need help with vocabulary and aspects of grammar as well as with cultural background knowledge. To be sure, HL learners may also need this type of scaffolding depending on their level of proficiency and the nature of the materials. However, they are not likely to need as much of it at the initial point of contact with such materials.

The opposite situation holds with form-focused activities: HL learners need more scaffolding than L2 learners. In particular, HL learners need to understand how form-focused activities relate to the authentic materials and tasks of instruction, and, more broadly, how they align with the larger learning objectives. They also need to be able to work with the relevant grammatical terminology and concepts. For example, when studying the past tense, HL learners need special instruction on key grammatical terms and concepts (e.g., conjugations, orthography, irregular forms) in order to participate in form-focused activities alongside L2 learners. Once again, this is not to say that L2 learners don't benefit from this type of scaffolding. They just don't need as much of it because they have more experience with formal instruction than HL learners.

In sum, teaching mixed classes involves balancing macro- and microbased teaching to facilitate collaborative learning among HL and L2 students and to make the activities and materials of instruction accessible and meaningful to both populations of learners. The final section of this chapter revisits some key strategies associated with macrobased instruction, with the goal of discussing issues of implementation.

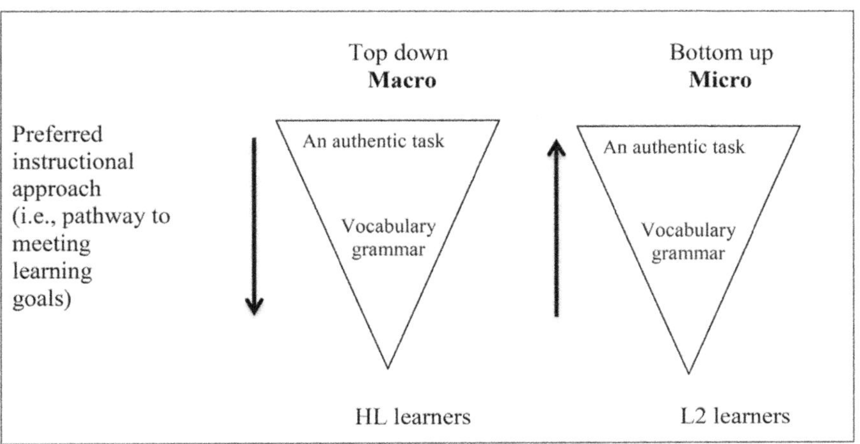

Figure 6.2. A Comparison of HL and L2 Learners' Learning Pathways

STRATEGIES THAT SUPPORT MACROBASED TEACHING AND LEARNING

Compared to micro approaches, macro approaches appear to take a more natural or organic approach to language learning by virtue of their initial focus on meaning and their use of authentic materials and tasks. This does not mean, however, that macrobased learning happens spontaneously. To the contrary, it requires careful planning and attention to issues of implementation. The strategies below undergird successful macrobased learning.

1. Break the task into small steps.
2. Provide clear and detailed directions for each step as well as for the task at large.
3. Provide opportunities to practice the various components and give feedback on the practice.
4. Model the different components of the task.
5. Monitor students' progress closely.

To illustrate the use of these strategies, I describe a macrobased project from my intermediate-level Spanish HL class at California State University, Long Beach. The project engages students in researching a topic in their field of study or intended profession and making a class presentation. In keeping with the first two strategies, the project is broken down into three steps, and the objectives, expectations, and grading criteria for each step are made explicit. At each step, students' work is carefully monitored and critical feedback is provided.

The first step involves extensive reading in Spanish. Over the course of three weeks, students research their selected topic and learn how to extract critical content and language from authentic materials. As they read, students take stock of what they know and don't know about their topic and select forty to fifty terms that they will need to learn in order to talk about their topic before the class. Students discuss their selection of terms with the instructor to ensure that it is customized to their needs.

The second step, which takes place over four weeks, involves preparing a glossary of these terms. This part of the project is grounded in corpus-driven learning, an approach "whereby learners observe grammar and vocabulary usages in concordance data, and then they discover and generalize findings about usage patterns and rules" (Liu and Jiang 2009, 62). Students use the Brigham Young University Corpus del Español (http://www.corpusdelespanol.org/x.asp) to prepare an entry for each term that includes its definition in Spanish, its English translation, three words with the same root, three authentic sentences that use the term, and five words that co-occur with the term (i.e., collocations). During the second week of this step, students submit one sample entry and receive corrective feedback. This serves to ensure that they are on the right track as they prepare the full glossary.

The final step involves making a ten-minute presentation using PowerPoint. The preparation takes place over three weeks, during which time students explore what is involved in making a good presentation and practice various elements of the process. In keeping with the fourth principle, they observe and discuss two presentations by the instructor modeling good and bad presentational techniques. They also practice their talk before a small group and receive peer feedback.

All told, the steps and principles outlined here make it possible for learners to work in their ZPD through instructional strategies that build on their functional skills, promote self-directed learning, and confirm understanding of and compliance with each step of the process.

SUMMARY AND CONCLUSIONS

Effective HL teaching is premised on the learners: their experiences, needs, and wants vis-à-vis the heritage language and culture. Macrobased approaches support this view of HL teaching by tapping into learners' background knowledge and functional skills and by providing a sense of personal relevance, immediacy, and authenticity from the very beginning of the instructional sequence.

Key concepts and principles that support macrobased teaching and various affiliated approaches (e.g., discourse, task, genre) include Kagan's "from–to" principles (Kagan and Carreira 2015), Valdés's (2003) hierarchy of registers for different text types, and the use of the ACTFL Proficiency Guidelines to identify learners' ZPD (Vygotsky 1978). Classroom strategies that help sequence, structure, and monitor the learning process are also essential.

These principles and strategies and, more broadly, macrobased teaching should apply across all instructional contexts involving HL learners, including mixed classes and customized options such as independent studies and service learning.

NOTES

1. STARTALK is a federal program that supports language education for students and professional development for teachers in K–16 in the critical languages, which include Arabic, Chinese, Dari, Hindi, Korean, Persian, Portuguese, Russian, Swahili, Turkish, and Urdu. For more information, see https://startalk.umd.edu.
2. For a discussion of the other points, readers should consult Carreira (2016).

REFERENCES

Abbott, S., ed. 2014. "Hidden Curriculum." In *The Glossary of Education Reform*. Portland, ME: Great Schools Partnership. Available at http://edglossary.org/hidden-curriculum.

Beaudrie, Sara M. 2011. "Spanish Heritage Language Programs: A Snapshot of Current Programs in the Southwestern United States." *Foreign Language Annals* 44, no. 2: 321–37. http://dx.doi.org/10.1111/j.1944-9720.2011.01137.x.

Beaudrie, Sara M. 2012. "Research on University-Based Spanish Heritage Language Programs in the United States: The Current State of Affairs." In *Spanish as a Heritage Language in the United States: The State of the Field*, ed. Sara M. Beaudrie and Marta Fairclough. Washington, DC: Georgetown University Press.

Bowles, Melissa. 2011. "Exploring the Role of Modality: Second-Language-Heritage Learner Interactions in the Spanish Language Classroom." *Heritage Language Journal* 8, no. 1: 30–65. www.heritagelanguages.org

Brinton, Donna, Margerite A. Snow, and Marjorie Bingham Wesche. 1989. *Content-Based Second Language Instruction*. Boston: Heinle and Heinle Publishers.

Carreira, Maria. 2012. "The Advanced Speaker: An Overview of the Issues in Heritage Language Teaching." White Paper. http://international.ucla.edu/media/files/CarreiraPositionPaperFinal.pdf

———. 2014. "Teaching Heritage Language Learners: A Study of Program Profiles, Practices, and Needs." In *Rethinking Heritage Language Education*, ed. Themistoklis Arovossitas and Peter Trifonas, 20–44. Cambridge: Cambridge University Press.

———. 2016. "A General Framework and Supporting Strategies for Teaching Mixed Classes." In *Advances in Spanish as a Heritage Language*, ed. Diego Pascual, 159–76. Studies in Bilingualism series. Amsterdam: John Benjamins.

Carreira, Maria, and Thomas Beeman. 2014. *Voces: Latino Students on Life in the United States*. Westport, CT: Praeger.

Carreira, Maria, and Olga Kagan. 2011. "The Results of the National Heritage Language Survey: Implications for Teaching, Curriculum Design, and Professional Development." *Foreign Language Annals* 44, no. 1: 40–64. http://dx.doi.org/10.1111/j.1944-9720.2010.01118.x.

Carreira, Maria, and Juliana Wijaya. 2010. "A Curriculum for Teaching Indonesian in Classes with Diverse Learners." *Journal of the National Council of Less Commonly Taught Languages* 8:169–94.

Celce-Murcia, Marianne, and Elite Olshtain. 2000. *Discourse and Context in Language Teaching: A Guide for Language Teachers*. New York, NY: Cambridge University Press.

Chia, Hui-Lung. 2001, "Reading Activities for Effective Top-Down Processing." *English Teaching Forum* 39, no. 1: 22–31.

Clifford, Ray. 2002. "Achievement, Performance, and Proficiency Testing." Paper presented at the Berkeley Language Center Colloquium on the Oral Proficiency Interview. University of California, Berkeley, February 22–23.

Colombi, Cecilia, and Joseph Harrington. 2012. "Advanced Biliteracy Development in Spanish as a Heritage Language." In *Spanish as a Heritage Language in the United States: The State of the Field*, ed. Sara M. Beaudrie and Marta Fairclough, 241–58. Washington, DC: Georgetown University Press.

Csikszentmihalyi, Mihaly. 1990. *Flow: The Psychology of Optimal Experience*. New York: Harper and Row.

Davidson, Dan, and Maria Lekic. 2013. "The Heritage and Non-Heritage Learner in the Overseas Immersion Context: Comparing Learning Outcomes and Target-Language Utilization in the Russian Flagship." *Heritage Language Journal* 10, no. 2: 226–52 www.heritagelanguages.org.

Echevarria, Jana, Mary Ellen Vogt, and Deborah Short. 2013. *Making Content Comprehensible for Elementary English Learners: The SIOP Model*. New York: Pearson Higher Education.

Echevarria, Jana, and Anne Wooding Graves. 2007. *Sheltered Content Instruction: Teaching English Language Learners with Diverse Abilities*. Boston: Pearson Allyn and Bacon.

Elliot, Maria Alexandra. 2008. "*Writing in Spanish as a Foreign Language at the Beginning College Level.*" PhD diss., University of North Carolina at Charlotte.

Ellis, Rod. 2003. *Task-Based Language Teaching and Learning*. Oxford: Oxford University Press.

Goldstein, E. Bruce. 2014. *Cognitive Psychology: Connecting Mind, Research and Everyday Experience*. Belmont, CA: Cengage Learning.

He, Agnes. 2006. "Toward an Identity Theory of the Development of Chinese as a Heritage Language." *Heritage Language Journal* 4, no. 1: 1–28. www.heritagelanguages.org

Hechanova, Maria. 2015. "Spanish for Future Medical Professionals." *Tucson News Now*, January 28. http://www.tucsonnewsnow.com/story/27961105/spanish-for-future-medical-professionals.

Heymsfeld, Carla R. 1989. "Filling the Hole in Whole Language." *Educational Leadership* 46, no. 6: 65–8.

Hyland, Ken. 2003. "Genre-Based Pedagogies: A Social Response to Process." *Journal of Second Language Writing* 12, no. 1: 17–29. http://dx.doi.org/10.1016/S1060-3743(02)00124-8.

Kagan, Olga, and Maria Carreira. 2015. "Teaching Heritage Languages. Approaches and Strategies." ACTFL Webinar. January 28.

Kagan, Olga, and Kathleen Dillon. 2001. "A New Perspective on Teaching Russian: Focus on the Heritage Learner." *Slavic and East European Journal* 45, no. 3: 507–18. http://dx.doi.org/10.2307/3086367.

Kohonen, Vijo. 1992. "Experiential Language Learning: Second Language Learning as Cooperative Learner Education." In *Collaborative Language Learning and Teaching*, ed. David Nunan, 14–39. Cambridge: Cambridge University Press.

Krashen, Stephen D. 2011. "The Compelling (Not Just Interesting) Input Hypothesis." *English Connection* (KOTESOL) 15, no. 3: 1.

Liu, Dilin, and Ping Jiang. 2009. "Using a Corpus-Based Lexicogrammatical Approach to Grammar Instruction in EFL and ESL Contexts." *Modern Language Journal* 93, no. 1: 61–78. http://dx.doi.org/10.1111/j.1540-4781.2009.00828.x.

Lui, Angela. 2012. "Teaching in the Zone. An Introduction to Working within the Zone of Proximal Development (ZPD) to Drive Effective Early Childhood Instruction." White Paper. Children's Progress. Norwich: TSO. http://www.childrensprogress.com/wp-content/uploads/2012/05/free-white-paper-vygotsky-zone-of-proximal-development-zpd-early-childhood.pdf.

Martin, Cynthia, Elvira Swender, and Mildred Rivera-Martinez. 2013. "Assessing the Oral Proficiency of Heritage Speakers According to the ACTFL Proficiency Guidelines 2012 – Speaking." *Heritage Language Journal* 10, no. 2: 211–25. www.heritagelanguages.org

Martínez, Glenn. 2010. "Medical Spanish for Heritage Learners: A Prescription to Improve the Health of Spanish-Speaking Communities." In *Building Communities and Making Connections*, ed. Susana Rivera-Mills and Juan Antonio Trujillo, 2–15. Newcastle upon Tyne, UK: Cambridge Scholars Publishing. http://dx.doi.org/10.5848/CSP.2022.00001.

———. 2016. "Goals and Beyond in Heritage Language Education: From Competencies to Capabilities." In *Innovative Strategies for Heritage Language Teaching: A Practical Guide for the Classroom*, ed. Marta Fairclough and Sara M. Beaudrie, 39–55. Washington, DC: Georgetown University Press.

Montrul, Silvina, and Melissa Bowles. 2010. "Is Grammar Instruction Beneficial for Heritage Language Learners? Dative Case Marking in Spanish." *Heritage Language Journal* 7, no. 1: 47–73. http://www.heritagelanguages.org/

Nunan, David. 2004. *Task-Based Language Teaching. A Comprehensively Revised Edition of Designing Task for the Communicative Classroom.* Cambridge: Cambridge University Press.

Parra, María Luisa. 2013. "Expanding Language and Cultural Competence in Advanced Heritage- and Foreign-language Learners through Community Engagement and Work with the Arts." *Heritage Language Journal* 10, no. 2: 252–80. http://www.heritagelanguages.org/

———. 2016. "Critical Approaches to Heritage Language Instruction: How to Foster Students' Critical Consciousness." In *Innovative Strategies for Heritage Language Teaching: A Practical Guide for the Classroom*, ed. Marta Fairclough and Sara M. Beaudrie, 166–90. Washington, DC: Georgetown University Press.

Potowski, Kim, Jill Jegerski, and Kara Morgan-Short. 2009. "The Effects of Instruction on Linguistic Development in Spanish Heritage Language Speakers." *Language Learning* 59, no. 3: 537–79. http://dx.doi.org/10.1111/j.1467-9922.2009.00517.x.

Richards, Jack C. 1990. *The Language Matrix.* Cambridge: Cambridge University Press. http://dx.doi.org/10.1017/CBO9780511667152.

Samaniego, Malena, and Chantelle Warner. 2016. "Designing Meaning in Inherited Languages: A Multiliteracies Approach to HL Instruction." In *Innovative Strategies for Heritage Language Teaching: A Practical Guide for the Classroom*, ed. Marta Fairclough and Sara M. Beaudrie, 191–213. Washington, DC: Georgetown University Press.

Tse, Lucy. 2001. *Why Don't They Learn English?* New York: Teachers College Press.

Valdés, Guadalupe. 2003. *Expanding Definitions of Giftedness: Young Interpreters of Immigrant Background.* Mahwah, NJ: Lawrence Erlbaum.

Vygotsky, Lev S. 1978. *Mind in Society: The Development of Higher Psychological Processes.* Cambridge, MA: Harvard University Press.

Wu, Ming-Hsuan, and Zhu-Min Chang. 2010. "Heritage Language Teaching and Learning through a Macro Approach." *Working Papers in Educational Linguistics* 25, no. 2: 23–33.

7

Incorporating Additional Varieties to the Linguistic Repertoires of Heritage Language Learners

A Multidialectal Model

Marta Fairclough
UNIVERSITY OF HOUSTON

In order to design effective instruction for heritage language (HL) learners, it is imperative to distinguish learners' proficiency levels and their linguistic needs. While those at the lower end of the language proficiency continuum usually present numerous linguistic gaps in the heritage language, as a large number of studies attest (e.g., Parodi 2008; Polinsky 2006), most HL learners master the language varieties typical of the speech community to which they belong. Many heritage languages in the United States are pluricentric, that is, there are multiple standards (e.g., Chinese, Spanish, Hindi, Arabic). Adding the broad range of linguistic proficiency in the heritage language that HL learners possess to this pluricentrism increases the amount of linguistic diversity.

These local varieties usually differ from the standard language, in part because HL speakers are usually exposed mainly to colloquial speech with their caregivers. Guadalupe Valdés (2005, 417) summarizes the differences as follows: (a) HL dialects converge through accommodation, (b) language change is induced by contact with the majority language, and (c) changes are present in the monolingual variety but accelerated due to linguistic contact. As Valdés (2007, 205) clearly posits,

> For the heritage speaker who has fully acquired a communal language that has undergone extensive changes through its contact with other varieties of the same language and with the dominant language, the instructional problem to be solved is quite different. If the goal is for such speakers to acquire the normative monolingual variety through

> formal instruction, what needs to be understood is the process of second dialect (D2) acquisition. . . . In this case, heritage speakers are involved in acquiring an additional variety of the same language. What they must learn is which features of the communal language do and do not correspond to the features of the normative monolingual varieties of the language.

The term "second dialect acquisition" typically refers to the acquisition of the standard variety of the majority language, with children typically attending school for many years in order to acquire the normative, or "standard," ways of speaking, reading, and writing (Nero 2006; Nero and Ahmad 2014). For linguists, the standard dialect is typically the normative monolingual variety, but it is also one dialect or variety out of many. Second dialect acquisition can, however, also take place in contact situations involving a minority language, as in the case of many heritage languages in the US context. Mariam Lam (2006) describes mismatches between the HL learners' home language and the standard dialect. For example, while heritage Vietnamese courses offered at universities in California teach standard Vietnamese, which is based on the northern dialect, the majority of Vietnamese speakers in the area communicate in the southern dialect of Vietnamese. A similar situation is present among Russian speakers in the United States. Most of them use the southern varieties of the language rather than standard Russian (Polinsky and Kagan 2007). The authors explain that it becomes more complicated with languages with differentiated registers such as Korean or Japanese, which vary according to social differences between interlocutors. Of the six registers in Korean, which present lexical and phonological variation, Korean HL speakers may be familiar with one or perhaps two of the most familial ones since the more formal ones are acquired through education. Kimi Kondo-Brown (2008, 21) also points at the many discrepancies between classroom Chinese and home varieties. For example, while Mandarin is the official language of the People's Republic of China and of the island of Taiwan, its status "as a common 'heritage' language for all ethnic Chinese is open to debate" (Wiley 2008, 96), especially considering the significant differences between the simplified characters of Mandarin and the more complex, traditional Taiwanese scripts. Another Chinese language, Cantonese, spoken in southern mainland China, shares a lot of vocabulary with Mandarin; yet, the two varieties are not mutually intelligible. The reality is that during school HL learners become immersed in the dominant language (English, in this case) and use it for most formal exchanges, while HL usage is limited to informal situations within the home and, in some cases, in the speech community, restricting their linguistic repertoire. Hence, they never acquire the normative variety of the heritage language, a process that is normally accomplished through years of formal schooling.

Overall, knowledge about how second dialects are acquired is limited. However, knowledge about second language acquisition (SLA) principles can contribute to an understanding of the learning process of other HL varieties. The mechanisms of SLA and second dialect acquisition (SDA) would normally be expected to be similar. If we consider the most basic processes in language acquisition, both SLA and SDA entail learning new lexical items for given referents or learning either adaptation or correspondence of phonological and grammatical rules between the two languages (L) or dialects (D) (Siegel 2010). However, there is an important difference: while SLA is always additive (L1 + L2), SDA can be subtractive (D2 replaces D1) or additive (D1 + D2). For the purposes of this chapter, the D1 constitutes the home variety an HL learner uses. The standard variety (i.e., the prescriptive hybrid form based on an ideal native speaker) or any other dialect of the language would be the D2.

When we add a second variety to the first, the result is bidialectalism (Kerswill 1994; Nero 2006; Porras 1997; Sánchez 1993). Just like learning another language, acquiring an additional language variety gives the language user more communicative options. Genevieve Escure (1997, 274) explains that bidialectalism consists of two overlapping but separate varieties and that teaching the prestigious varieties does not "seem to succeed in uprooting stigmatized varieties because such varieties preserve strong grassroots values." Shondel Nero (2006, 286) posits that "bidialectalism is both desirable and possible for students." There will be many contexts and situations where a standard dialect will be needed and others where the home variety will be indispensable. Glenn Martínez (2003) illustrates the importance of the additive process with some Spanish terms:

> If our students walk into the class saying *haiga* [D1 form] and walk out saying *haya* [D2 form], there has been, in my estimation, no value added. However, if they walk in saying *haiga* and walk out saying either *haya* or *haiga* and having the ability to defend their use of *haiga* if and when they see fit, then there has been value added. It is critical that we strive to allow students to develop this type of sociolinguistic sophistication in our endeavors as SHL [Spanish heritage language] educators. (10)

This chapter endorses SDA, an additive learning process, for the HL classroom. Learning more varieties of a language adds value in terms of expanding the sociolinguistic range by generating multiple, versatile repertoires and identities, and in terms of critically confronting the traditional (and still all too prevalent) monolingual bias of "subtractive schooling" (Valenzuela 1999) that only values the standard and therefore seeks to replace or subtract the student's local variety. After briefly reviewing the concepts of language, dialect, register, style, and genre (for a detailed explanation of these terms, see Leeman and Serafini's chapter in this volume [2016]), I compare the SLA and SDA processes and apply SDA principles in an attempt to better understand the addition of a language variety to the linguistic repertoire of HL students in academic settings. Given the paucity of research conducted on SDA in educational contexts (some recent studies are Clachar 2005; Fairclough 2005; Nero 2006), my goal is to try to shed some light on the basic acquisitional mechanisms and on some of the social and linguistic factors that contribute to the process. The second part of the chapter presents a pedagogical multidialectal model grounded on the notions of sociolinguistic variation and contrastive techniques, following a critical language awareness approach. The model includes concrete examples of how to apply SDA principles in the HL classroom.

LANGUAGE VARIETIES

Some Terminology Issues

Linguists consider "language" to be an abstract and inclusive term that refers to a collection of mutually intelligible dialects or varieties (Chambers and Trudgill 1998, 3). However, as Ronald Wardhaugh (1992, 24–38) clearly explains, in some cases the distinction between language and dialect can be difficult to determine. For example, spoken Cantonese and Mandarin are mutually unintelligible languages, but their speakers insist that they are dialects of Chinese. Carmen Silva-Corvalán (2001, 31) posits that nobody really speaks a language; we all speak a dialect of a language. Although Walt Wolfram and Natalie Schilling-Estes (2006, 2) consider "dialect" to be "a neutral label to refer to any variety of a language that is shared by a group of speakers," some associate the term "dialect" with "nonstandard" (Wardhaugh 1992, 25), so the word "variety" is often preferred and should be the term used in the HL classroom.

Languages may vary according to location, social group, and context or situation. The model in Figure 7.1 shows the different dimensions of a language variety.

Although this model might give the impression of a clear-cut typology of language varieties, the issue is a lot more complex, especially regarding stylistic variation. In practice and within the HL context, the outlined categories often seem to overlap and their definitions become somewhat fuzzy, making it difficult to distinguish among terms such as "academic/global/general/normative/monolingual variety" and "high register," "standard dialect" and "formal style." Wolfram and Schilling-Estes (2006, 267) find that when D1 speakers of African American Vernacular English shift from a casual to a formal register, it is sometimes difficult to decide whether the shift is a change of register/genre, a change of dialect, or both. In general terms, Jennifer Leeman and Ellen Serafini (this volume [2016]) underscore that "there is a great deal of terminological inconsistency in how scholars have categorized variation in language use" (see Leeman and Serafini's chapter, this volume, for more information about situationally defined language varieties).

temporal	→ diachronic, or historical, varieties
geographic	→ diatopic, or regional, varieties
social	→ diastratic varieties based on sociocultural variables (ethnicity, age, sex, etc.)
stylistic	→diaphasic varieties used in different communicative settings/situations • situation: formal or informal style • relationship between the participants: personal or impersonal style • purpose or function: high or low register • mode: written or oral discourse[a]
educational	→ standard or nonstandard variety[b]

Figure 7.1. Dimensions of a Language Variety

Source: Based on Silva-Corvalán (2001).

a. Silva-Corvalán (2001, 21) explains that the dichotomies used to classify diaphasic linguistic varieties are not mutually exclusive but often overlap.

b. The standard/nonstandard dichotomy extends well beyond the educational arena. For a broader perspective on standardization, see Armstrong and Mackenzie (2013).

The Standard Dialect

Within the educational context, when "academic register" or "formal styles" are discussed, they are usually associated with a standard variety. The division between standard and nonstandard varieties is not very clear either. Wolfram and Schilling-Estes (2006), for instance, describe two standards: A formal or prescriptive standard (usually in the form of written language and codified in grammar books) and an informal standard (used in speech) that exists on a continuum of standardness determined by a L listener. In figure 7.2, for example, speaker D produces more nonstandard forms than any of the other speakers.

Given the problematic issues that emerge when trying to classify and label linguistic varieties, especially the standard/nonstandard dichotomy that is the primary dimension in the educational context, Sara Beaudrie (2015, 3) argues for "the need to *deconstruct these artificial dichotomies* and use actual student language production as a starting point for deciding what to include in and exclude from our language teaching" in the HL classroom (my emphasis). The student's "voice" or "idiolect" should be the point of departure (D1) in expanding to another variety(ies), which usually include teaching the standard variety for use in formal styles, high registers, and so on.

A B C D

Standard ........I......I..............I............I.... Nonstandard

Figure 7.2. Degree of Informal Standardness

Source: Adapted from Wolfram and Schilling-Estes (2006, 11).

The Standard Variety in the HL Classroom

Silva-Corvalán (2001, 31) states that the so-called standard variety is merely a more widely socially accepted dialect of the language—not superior to other dialects, only different. However, since we live in what Harold Schiffman (1996) called "a linguistic culture" and James Milroy (2001) "standard language cultures," the average person believes that there are "correct" and "wrong" ways of speaking (and that the latter should be eliminated) based on societal attitudes toward a speech community. These attitudes lead to ideologies of language and education that shift the focus on individual attitudes to larger shared beliefs, values, and so on concerning language in education (Train 2003). They tend to reflect the dominant group's interests and have nothing to do with the inherent worth of a particular variety of a language (for further explanations of "standard language ideologies," see the chapters by Leeman and Serafini [2016] and Lacorte [2016] in this volume).

Teaching the standard, however, has been the focus of HL education since its early days, being one of the original objectives for HL programs proposed by Valdés in the 1990s (see Martínez, this volume [2016], for a list of goals) and one generally supported by the profession (e.g., Jo 2001; Kondo-Brown 2010; Rouchdy 2002; Valdés 2005, 2007, among many others). For instance, due to the multifaith, multinational, and multidialectal characteristics of Arabic, the standardized variety of the language serves as a source of identity and unity among Arab Americans (Bale 2010). Also, the highly heterogeneous linguistic background of Chinese HL learners (e.g., Mandarin versus non-Mandarin dialects) seems to be the reason why HL learners prefer to learn the traditional scripts of their regions of origin in the classroom instead of the simplified characters usually presented in class (Kondo-Brown 2010, 21).

In most HL classrooms, teaching varieties other than the standard is extremely challenging because materials and trained instructors are simply lacking, but multidialectism should be one of the main goals. As Stacey Katz (2003) posits in her study of Haitian immigrant Creole-speaking students in French classes, it is vital that everyone involved—from teachers to heritage and nonheritage students—understand the linguistic backgrounds of HL learners through critical language awareness. As previously noted,

HL learners rarely acquire the standard variety of the heritage language because they do not go through years of formal schooling in their home language. In reality, it is practically impossible to separate the linguistic from the ideological, affective, social, and political aspects of a language; and even though the advantages of the standard are generally framed in terms of "wider communication," the standard varieties versus variation / local varieties seems to rarely be about communication today. Nonetheless, one of the main objectives of HL education should be to expand the linguistic repertoire of the HL learner through the addition of other varieties, including the standard, by following a multidialectal model. Such knowledge would allow students to select the variety they consider best suited for a specific situation, audience, and purpose (Devereaux 2015). For students to have a linguistic repertoire (several languages, several varieties of the same language, or both) and, thus, agency to choose among various communication alternatives, language instructors need to offer them the tools to accomplish that. If students do not have those linguistic alternatives, which usually include proficiency in the prestige variety, their ability to make effective choices will be limited.

SECOND LANGUAGE VERSUS SECOND DIALECT ACQUISITION

Due to the many differences between second language (L2) and HL learners (see Zyzik's chapter, this volume [2016]), in most cases the former go through an SLA process while for the latter the process often entails the acquisition of a second dialect that seems to follow certain patterns regardless of the linguistic context (Escure 1997).[1] When HL learners are at the lowest end of the HL proficiency continuum (i.e., they hardly understand the heritage language and are considered more bicultural than bilingual) or when the two varieties are practically unintelligible (e.g., Chinese dialects), an SLA approach often makes more sense from a linguistic perspective. However, when the variety of the heritage language that the student brings to the classroom and the one taught in the program are mutually intelligible, an SDA process takes place. In SDA, students often use their knowledge of the home language when learning forms or rules in the new variety(ies). However, when HL learners are unaware of the differences between their variety and the target one(s), the process may be hindered.

Dialectal differences can be found mainly at the following linguistic levels: lexicon, morphosyntax, pragmatics, and pronunciation (including phonetic and phonological variables as well as suprasegmental features such as stress and pitch), which leads to a different "accent" (Siegel 2010, 7–11). Some researchers (e.g., Strevens 1985) separate "accent," which refers to phonological features, from other levels of a dialect. Rosina Lippi-Green (2012), among others, cautions us about the notion of "accent" (as well as other aspects of linguistic variation) and the way people are judged on the basis of how they speak by following a standard language ideology whose main goal is language subordination and assimilation to the linguistic and cultural norms of the norms of another, more powerful group (see Leeman and Serafini's chapter in this volume [2016], for additional information on "standard language ideology").

As noted earlier, SDA involves learning those features of the standard dialect that do not match the home variety the student knows. Although in some languages the linguistic distance between two varieties can be as broad as that between two different languages, the distance between the D1 and the D2 is usually small. Similarity between D1 and D2 has led to the popular consensus that SDA should be easier than SLA and, therefore, the process should be much faster. Despite this common belief, SDA in fact appears to be more difficult than SLA and to occur at a slower rate. In cases where the linguistic distance between the two varieties is small, it can become very difficult to notice pertinent differences and hence to attain the target forms (Albirini 2014; Clachar 2004, 2005; Fairclough 2005). Wolfram and Schilling-Estes (2006, 287), for instance, suggest, "When two systems are highly similar, with minor differences, it is sometimes difficult to keep the systems apart. . . . In some ways, it may be easier to work with language systems that are drastically different, since the temptation to merge the overlapping structures and ignore relatively minor differences is not as great." Richard Schmidt's noticing hypothesis (1990, 1992, 2001, 2010) from SLA supports these views. The hypothesis states that "input does not become intake for language learning unless it is noticed, that is, consciously registered" (Schmidt 2010, 721). When applied to SDA, the hypothesis would predict that due to the overlap or similarities between two language varieties, learners may not notice the differences between them and without noticing, the features may not be acquired.

Regarding the ease of SD versus SL acquisition, studies have shown different starting points (X) for each process (Belpoliti 2011; Fairclough 2005; Long 2007). Figure 7.3 shows that while L2 learners start learning a second language from scratch and have a long way to master it (Z), HL learners have different initial levels of proficiency in the HL, ranging from merely understanding the language to a high level of proficiency in the D1 (X_1, X_2, etc.).

The difficulty of acquisition depends on the student's starting point. At higher levels of language proficiency, the rate of acquisition slows down because the complexity and nuances of the target language increase considerably, as it is clearly depicted by the inverted pyramid (ACTFL 2012) (Figure 7.4).

The same principle seems to apply to both SLA and SDA students: The closer they are to the target, the slower the acquisition process becomes. The results from Marta Fairclough's (2005) study show that the HL group

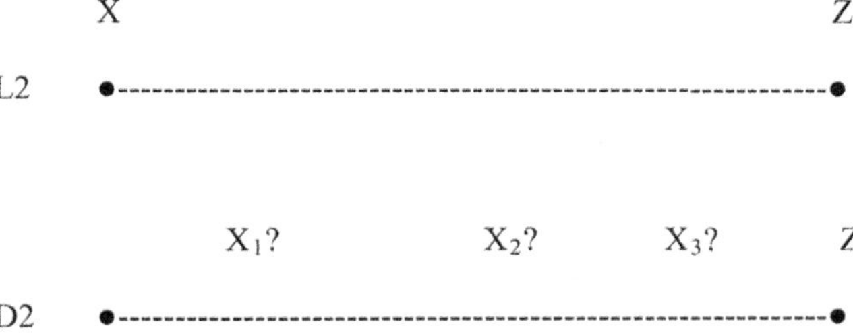

Figure 7.3. Different Starting Points for SLA and SDA

Adapted from Siegel (2010).

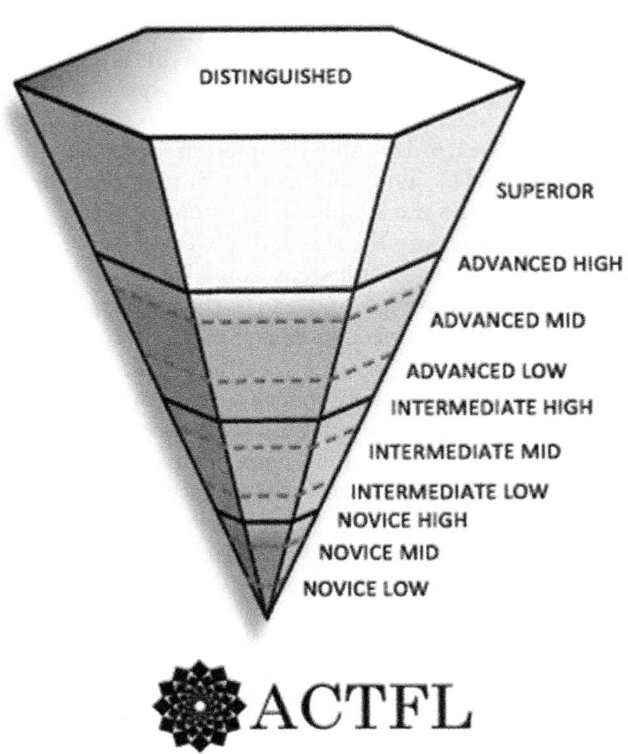

Figure 7.4. American Council on the Teaching of Foreign Languages: Proficiency Levels

produces a higher percentage of target-like forms both before and after instruction (46 percent to 62.5 percent), but the improvement is far more pronounced for the SL students, who start from zero and reach 35.2 percent. It is very likely that once the SL group reaches the same stage of acquisition as the HL group, that group's progress will slow down as well.

The Mechanisms of SDA

One of the best models to explain the basic mechanisms of SDA seems to be the acquisitional approach. Although, as previously indicated, it is practically impossible to isolate the linguistic from other aspects of the language (i.e., ideological, affective, social, and political) this approach focuses specifically on the learning process itself.[2] Following the acquisitional approach, for SDA to take place, there has to be

- *Lexical learning*: Learning (a) new words for the same referent (e.g., D1: *brecas* = "brakes," D2: *frenos* = "brakes"), or (b) different referents for a known word (e.g., semantic extension: D1: *carpeta* = "carpet"; D2: *carpeta* = "folder").
- *Rule learning*: Learning either adaptation or correspondence rules between D1 and D2. The rules can be (a) phonological rules (e.g., in US Spanish varieties the allophone [v] often appears as a variant of the phoneme /b/, whereas in the standard dialect they are pronounced the same); or (b) grammatical rules (e.g., some US Spanish speakers use the form "*fuera* + past participle" instead of the prescriptive "*hubiera* + past participle" for the pluperfect subjunctive; Gutiérrez 1997).[3]

The acquisition process of these mechanisms may be very complex. Jeff Siegel (2010, 74) warns us, "Although the D2 acquirers may have learned D2 lexical items and rules (explicit knowledge), *automaticity* (implicit linguistic competence) is not achieved by the majority, especially with phonological and morphological features." Just like in SLA, the degree of proficiency attained in additional language varieties may be affected by a number of social and individual factors as well as linguistic factors. Among the former, the following seem to affect the process:

- *Age of acquisition*: Those who begin learning the D2 before age thirteen have a higher chance of reaching native-like use of the D2.
- *Identity and social networks*: Identifying with the D2 group and maintaining social interaction through open networks with speakers of the D2 appear to promote SDA.
- *Motivation and attitudes*: Integrative as well as instrumental motivation can both contribute to the acquisition process. When the D2 is the

> standard dialect, acquiring it may be necessary for education or employment. Regarding attitudes, the more positively the D1 is regarded, the less likely the learner is to acquire and use the D2.[4]

HL learners usually acquire the minority language at home at an early age, usually as their first language, then they learn the majority language later, often at school (sequential bilinguals); others acquire both languages at the same time (simultaneous bilinguals). In some cases they may understand utterances addressed to them in the HL but consistently reply in the majority language for lack of expressive ability (receptive bilinguals); others may merely hear the language spoken around them (overhearers). Regardless of their level of experience with the HL in childhood, these learners still have certain advantages over late bilinguals who start studying the language later in life (Oh and Au 2005).

Being part of a community where the heritage language is spoken and traditions are maintained contributes to a feeling of belonging to the group, which in turn promotes the consolidation of an identity, especially when a child's social network includes peers from different contexts (school, family, church, work, etc.). These connections often help mitigate negative issues related to minority identity formation, such as lack of self-confidence, linguistic insecurity, and anxiety. It is essential for family members, community members, and especially teachers to express positive attitudes toward the heritage language in order to reduce that insecurity by validating the home variety and fostering a positive attitude toward it in the individual child (Borland 2005; Lee 2013; Potowski 2012).

Regarding motivation, a large study conducted by Maria Carreira and Olga Kagan (2011) showed that HL learners are interested in learning their heritage language for career opportunities as well as for strengthened sociocultural connections. The maintenance of tight connections with family and community, identity consolidation, and positive attitudes toward the home variety jointly motivate HL students to preserve the home language they acquired during their early years and to expand their proficiency in the heritage language through additive bi/multidialectalism.

Vis-à-vis the linguistic factors that affect the process of acquiring a second variety, all forms do not have the same level of difficulty. Citing R. Vousten (1995) and Jack K. Chambers (1998), Kathy Rys (2007, 93) states that "some dialect features are more complex than others . . . and are therefore more difficult to acquire by (second) dialect learners."[5] She argues that "predictability" indicates how much a learner can foresee the D2 form based on his knowledge of the D1. Vousten (1995) argues that a dialect feature is more complex if there is not a one-to-one relationship between two dialectal varieties—that is, if there is a many-to-one or one-to-many, or even a many-to-many, relationship between the two. In SDA, a one-to-one relationship between varieties would facilitate acquisition because one element in the D1 corresponds to another in the D2. All the other types of relationships would present additional complexity, making the acquisition process a lot harder. Rys and Dries Bonte (2006) assume that the formation of "correspondence rules" is the basic learning strategy of D2 learners (204).

Although there are many aspects of ideological, affective, and social nature that play a significant role in learning other language varieties, the following linguistic factors appear to contribute to SDA (Auer, Barden, and Grosskopf 1998; Kerswill and Williams 2002; Rys 2007; Rys and Bonte 2006; Siegel 2010; Vousten 1995):

- *Linguistic level* (lexical, phonological, morphological, etc.): For older students, it appears to be easier to acquire lexical and morphological forms than phonological ones in the D2.
- *Salience*, or the characteristic of being easily noticeable (Trudgill 1986; e.g., stigmatized forms; perceptual prominence): Salient features seem to be more easily acquired because they are noticeable (Schmidt's noticing hypothesis). For Peter Trudgill (1986, 11), "salience" is associated with "awareness." He stated that "in contact with speakers of other language varieties, speakers modify those features of their own varieties of which they are most aware."
- *Comprehensibility*: D2 forms are sometimes used in situations where a D1 form obstructs communication.
- *Type of word*: Open-class words (i.e., nouns, verbs, and adjectives) with heavy semantic content seem to be incorporated into the D2 more often than closed-class words (e.g., pronouns, prepositions) that are dependent on grammar.

All these linguistic factors need to be taken into account when teaching a D2 in the classroom, from clearly explaining correspondence rules to making students aware of the differences between the varieties and concentrating on the linguistic levels and types of words/forms that constitute the biggest challenges.

A MULTIDIALECTAL MODEL FOR THE HL CLASSROOM: FROM THEORY TO PRACTICE

In this section I present the main components that contribute to acquiring additional language varieties in the HL classroom: the sociolinguistic component and contrastive techniques. They are followed by some concrete examples of how to incorporate them in the teaching of a D2. The pedagogical suggestions follow an "awareness approach" for SDA (e.g., James and Garrett 1991; Nero and Ahmad 2014; Siegel 1999; Wolfram 1999) with a "critical" component that accepts the value of teaching a standard variety when it is taught from a perspective that critically analyzes and challenges language policies and ideologies that exclude certain varieties from the classroom. Critical pedagogy raises students' awareness of the relationship between language and power within the dominant society and offers them some agency in their learning (e.g., Clark et al. 1990, 1991; Fairclough 1989, 1992; Leeman 2005; Martínez 2003; for a detailed explanation of "critical language awareness" as applied to HL education, see Leeman and Serafini, this volume [2016]). Given space limitations, I will not delve into advanced literacy issues such as the development of academic discourse through constructs such as grammatical metaphor, nominalization, lexical density, and clause-combining strategies (for comprehensive discussions on the subject, see, e.g., Schleppegrell and Colombi 2002; Valdés and Geoffrion-Vinci 1998).

The Sociolinguistic Component

In this component, students learn about linguistic variation and different language varieties from sociopolitical, ideological, and historical perspectives. The variety the student brings to the classroom is viewed as an asset to the process of learning additional varieties. Students share their knowledge with instructors and peers, and the students' varieties are used as the basis for learning the standard dialect as well as expanding their knowledge of other varieties. This knowledge allows them to better understand and deconstruct certain beliefs and practices that most people take for granted, such as the superiority of the standard dialect over other varieties. In the HL classroom as well as in L2 teaching, in addition to teaching the simplified and hybrid standard variety of the language that is the norm in most language programs, "instruction should gradually move from awareness of linguistic variation to productive use of alternative dialects, and from a focus on local varieties, registers, and styles to other varieties, registers, and styles of Spanish around the world" (Gutiérrez and Fairclough 2006, 184). Given that in the United States linguistic interactions in the heritage language will most likely occur between two HL speakers, knowledge of more than one language variety would be extremely useful. It would be unfair to deny any language learner—whether a native speaker, HL learner, or L2 student—professional opportunities in government, business, media, health care, and other fields that require not only bilingual but bi- or multidialectal speakers.

Understanding linguistic variation as well as language ideologies from a critical perspective should be part of language courses as early as the beginning levels. In order to accomplish this goal, sociolinguistic information should be included in instructional materials. Gradually HL learners will become aware of other varieties and cultures by becoming familiar with basic sociolinguistic concepts and how they apply to everyday situations. In addition, HL learners should have opportunities to interact with HL speakers in the community as well as activities that allow them to put into practice the new variety(ies) they are learning.

In HL classes, students can role-play (with different types of interlocutors, using different varieties), conduct service-learning and internships in the community to appreciate the real value of linguistic diversity (see Martínez's [2016] and Parra's [2016] chapters, this volume), and read literary texts written in different varieties in the heritage language or publications in the emerging genre of literary code-mixing that include a variety of pertinent cultural issues. Shondel Nero and Dohra Ahmad (2014, 13–15), for example, suggest teaching vernacular literature in the classroom to strengthen language awareness, appreciate diversity, develop critical language awareness, foster critical thinking by engaging students in complex topics and challenge "standard language ideology."

Another option would be to complete class projects on cultural topics related to the heritage language. Marta Fairclough and Flavia Belpoliti (2016) propose inquiry-based cultural projects to develop proficiency in the heritage language. Different levels of HL learners can become familiar with the HL culture by collecting data using a variety of tools (surveys, interviews, the Internet, etc.) to conduct research through scaffolding projects that expand from the immediate context to the broader community. For these projects, students often use their own language variety for interview purposes whereas the final oral and written products may be a mixture of both dialects since students are expected to use the standard dialect in their work but they quote language from the interviews. This type of activity contributes to enhance critical language awareness since students are participants in a project that expects multidialectal competence.

Contrastive Techniques

Contrasts help students learn about the rule-governed nature and linguistic characteristics of their own variety and see how it differs from the varieties of other students and from the standard. Schmidt's noticing hypothesis supports use of contrastive techniques. If they do not notice the differences between the D1 and other dialects, learners will fail to acquire them. Carl James called contrastive techniques "interfacing"—that is, "juxtaposing or confronting D1 and D2 and helping the learner to notice the differences between them, sometimes subtle and sometimes gross. It is a modern development of contrastive analysis . . . which is now done *by the learner* himself rather than by the teacher" (James 1996, 255, my emphasis). So how can instruction focus on highlighting the differences between and separating the varieties? Use of the students' home language is essential for comparing and especially contrasting forms that diverge across varieties. To make specific forms more salient, one can draw students' attention to specific features through critical language awareness to help them notice them. Once students notice the differences, it becomes easier to separate the forms and acquire new ones.

One way to help students notice the differences is through translation from English into the heritage language. Students with different varieties will in many cases offer diverse choices of words or phrases in their translations, offering a perfect opportunity to discuss—in the heritage language, in English, or both—pertinent sociolinguistic information about the forms they suggest. This type of activity empowers learners as sources of knowledge while the instructor acts as a facilitator as she validates linguistic variation. A point of caution: Translations need to be purposeful, contextualized, and meaningful (e.g., translation of a medical brochure for a local clinic where most patients belong to the minority group).

Translation activities from the D1 to the D2 and vice versa are also extremely useful for identifying differences and acquiring additional forms. While HL learners are usually asked to translate from a local or colloquial variety into the standard dialect (Leeman 2005), it is important to do bidirectional translations to underscore the value of all varieties. Regarding lexical learning, for example, HL students enrolled in language courses for specific professions (e.g., medical Spanish—see Martínez, this volume [2016]) need to be familiar with both standard and colloquial forms of expressions normally used at the doctor's office. Rosario Casillas at the University of Texas at El Paso teaches medical professionals both varieties so they can communicate effectively with their patients (personal communication). The following is a sample of phrases students practice in class by creating dialogues simulating office visits. One student plays the patient role (often using colloquial forms from the list in the D1) and the other acts as the physician (using medical terminology in the D2):

Fever = D2 (doctor): *fiebre*; D1 (patient): *calentura* or simply "temperature"
Bruises = D2 (doctor): *hematomas*; D1 (patient): *morados, moretones, cardenales, derrames*
Croup = D2 (doctor): *laringo traqueítis*; D1 (patient): *tengo tos de perro* or *tos de foca*
Wheezing = D2 (doctor): *sibilancias;* D1 (patient): *me pilla el pecho* or *tengo silbido en los pulmones*
Itching = D2 (doctor): *comezón*; D1 (patient): *picazón*, or *rasquiña*
Pregnant = D2 (doctor): *embarazada*; D1 (patient): *estoy en cinta, estoy en estado*, or *estoy preñada*
Abdominal pain = D2: *dolor en el abdomen*; D1 (patient): *me duele la panza, me duele la barriga*, or *me duele el vientre*

An example of rule learning would be Spanish HL learners who use a one-person second-person singular pronoun system (informal *tú* only) rather than the *tú/usted* ("you" informal/formal) dichotomy, even though the formal *usted* is very likely to be part of their receptive abilities. Since the correspondence rule in the standard dialect is not one-to-one (i.e., second-person singular = *tú*) but one-to-many (two, in this case; second-person singular = *tú* or *usted*), it is often very difficult for these students to make the correct distinction and use the corresponding verb form and pronouns in all cases. In addition, since usage of the one-person system in this case (D1) does not obstruct communication, D2 forms will be more difficult to acquire.

To put these concepts into practice in a first-year intensive Spanish class for HL learners, a classroom lesson began with a discussion of when and with whom students used *tú/usted*, as well as the pragmatic differences between the two pronouns; then the corresponding verb and pronoun forms were contrasted. About half of the HL students in the class were second-, third-, or later-generation Mexican, whereas the rest hailed from other Spanish-speaking heritage countries, so a lot of variation was apparent according to country of origin. Students were then asked to draft a list of twenty biographical questions for an interview with a family member or family friend who was born in a Spanish-speaking country. Students could address the interviewee formally or informally, depending on the form they considered more appropriate. Not only were subject–verb agreement problems evident (a), but there was also a lot of inconsistency in pronoun choice across the sequence of questions prepared for a single interviewee (b and c):[6]

a. ¿Que **sientes usted** de peligro en México?
"What do you (formal) feel (informal) is dangerous in Mexico?"

b. ¿**Tu** papá es de México o de aquí? Followed by ¿Qué parte de México son **sus** padres?
"Your (informal) dad is from Mexico or from here?" followed by "What part of Mexico are your (formal) parents?"

c. ¿**Tú** es muy religioso?
"You (informal) are very religious?"

¿Qué religión **practica**?
"What religion do you practice (formal)?"

¿**Sus** padres enseñan a ser religioso?
"Your (formal) parents teach to be religious?"

To master cases of rule learning such as this one, students need to practice a lot of role-playing in class. Translation activities from English to the heritage language, set in informal situations (e.g., a conversation between friends) versus formal ones are also very helpful because students have to not only decide which pronoun to use but also to conjugate the verbs and translate the pronouns accordingly.

As previously stated, Wolfram and Schilling-Estes (2006, 318–20) caution us that when two systems are very similar, a lot of monitoring is required to notice and acquire the differences, so a lot of practice may be needed to add new varieties to an existing one. Students whose D1 starting point is close to the target also have difficulty acquiring certain forms because the linguistic nuances at high levels of proficiency tend to slow down the acquisition rate. There may also be resistance due to personal and social identity issues; therefore, it is very important to have classroom discussions about the value of both the home varieties and the standard and to underscore the utility of both.

CONCLUDING REMARKS

This chapter offers a glimpse at some ways to successfully incorporate additional varieties into an individual's linguistic repertoire through a multidialectal model. A review of some key concepts related to linguistic variation was followed by a brief description of certain key social and linguistic factors that seem to contribute to the acquisition of a second dialect. The importance of following a critical awareness approach to language learning in the HL classroom was underscored because this enables both teachers and students to understand linguistic variation. From a critical perspective, two main components emerged as foundations of a model for acquiring additional language varieties: a sociolinguistic approach and strong contrastive techniques with a language awareness component (i.e., noticing forms to become aware of the differences between the varieties) are both essential to achieve success in the HL classroom.

Our HL learners should not only be proficient in English and the standard variety of their home language. They should be multidialectal speakers, able to communicate using the local or regional varieties of the heritage language so that they can communicate with speakers of the language in other parts of the world and with other HL speakers in the United States. Sociolinguistic knowledge is fundamental to achieving this goal.

It cannot be denied that the goal of most HL classes at academic institutions is acquisition of the idealized language variety labeled "the standard" (which can hide under different labels such as academic or high register, prestigious or general variety, formal style, etc.). HL learners have not usually been provided with comprehensive schooling in the heritage language, yet many practitioners in the field of HL education often expect them to master both written and oral standard discourses over a brief period of time even though research shows that SDA does not appear to be easier or faster than SLA.

The world is built on variation and diversity. Bearing in mind Richard Ruiz's (1988) model of language-as-problem/as-right/as-resource, sociolinguistic variation should not be seen as a "problem" but as a "resource" (Nero 2006; Train 2003). Restricting instruction to the standard model of language, based on a generic/ideal "native" speaker, only limits students' options. To succeed in today's globalized society, they need to recognize and respect linguistic differences through critical language awareness and by incorporating additional language varieties to their repertoire. It is up to the professionals in the field to guide them. The multidialectal model presented in this chapter could be the way to accomplish such an endeavor.

NOTES

1. Escure (1997), for instance, compared SDA to SLA in two distinct sociolinguistic situations. The researcher conducted discourse-level studies on a complex linguistic variable: topic marking phenomena (i.e., strategies, topic-comment structures) in several communities in both creole (Belize) and non-creole (China) contexts. In both cases the focus was the acquisition of the standard: Standard English in the former (among speakers of an English-based creole) and standard Mandarin in the latter (for speakers of other varieties of Chinese). The results of the study show that SDA acquisition processes in both contexts follow similar patterns.
2. Accommodation theory, from social psychology, has usually been used as a theoretical framework for the acquisition of other varieties. "Long-term accommodation" could also explain SDA.
3. The examples are from Spanish.
4. For examples of these factors from a large number of studies mainly in naturalistic contexts, see Siegel (2010).
5. Rys (2007) studied the acquisition of a vernacular variety by speakers whose home language was standard Dutch.
6. Students' spellings are also retained in these examples.

REFERENCES

ACTFL. 2012. Proficiency Guidelines, http://www.actfl.org/publications/guidelines-and-manuals/actfl-proficiency-guidelines-2012

Albirini, Abdulkafi. 2014. "The Role of the Colloquial Varieties in the Acquisition of the Standard Variety: The Case of Arabic Heritage Speakers." *Foreign Language Annals* 47, no. 3: 447–63. http://dx.doi.org/10.1111/flan.12087.

Armstrong, Nigel, and Ian E. Mackenzie. 2013. *Standardization, Ideology and Linguistics*. London: Palgrave Macmillan.

Auer, Peter, Birgit Barden, and Beate Grosskopf. 1998. "Subjective and Objective Parameters Determining "Salience" in Long-term Dialect Accommodation." *Journal of Sociolinguistics* 2 (2): 163–87. http://dx.doi.org/10.1111/1467-9481.00039.

Bale, Jeffrey. 2010. "Arabic as a Heritage Language in the United States." *International Multilingual Research Journal* 4, no. 2: 125–51. http://dx.doi.org/10.1080/19313152.2010.499041.

Beaudrie, Sara. 2015. "Approaches to Language Variation: Goals and Objectives of the Spanish Heritage Language Syllabus." *Heritage Language Journal* 12, no. 1: 1–21.

Belpoliti, Flavia. 2011. "Los Conectores Consecutivos en el Español de Herencia de Houston: un Estudio de los Efectos de la Instrucción Formal." PhD diss., University of Houston.

Borland, Helen. 2005. "Heritage Languages and Community Identity Building: The Case of a Language of Lesser Status." *International Journal of Bilingual Education and Bilingualism* 8, no. 2–3: 109–23. http://dx.doi.org/10.1080/13670050508668600.

Carreira, Maria, and Olga Kagan. 2011. "The Results of the National Heritage Language Survey: Implications for Teaching, Curriculum Design, and Professional Development." *Foreign Language Annals* 44, no. 1: 40–64. http://dx.doi.org/10.1111/j.1944-9720.2010.01118.x.

Chambers, Jack K. 1998. "Dialect Acquisition." In *The Sociolinguistics Reader*. Vol. 1, *Multilingualism and Variation*, ed. Peter Trudgill and Jenny Cheshire, 145–78. London: Edward Arnold. Originally published in *Language* 68, no. 4 (1992): 673–705.

Chambers, Jack K., and Peter Trudgill. 1998. *Dialectology*. 2nd ed. New York: Cambridge University Press. http://dx.doi.org/10.1017/CBO9780511805103.

Clachar, Arlene. 2004. "The Construction of Creole-Speaking Students' Linguistic Profile and Contradictions in ESL Literacy Programs." *TESOL Quarterly* 38, no. 1: 153–65. http://dx.doi.org/10.2307/3588267.

———. 2005. "Creole English Speakers' Treatment of Tense-Aspect Morphology in English Interlanguage Written Discourse." *Language Learning* 55, no. 2: 275–334. http://dx.doi.org/10.1111/j.0023-8333.2005.00305.x.

Clark, Romy, Norman Fairclough, Roz Ivanic, and Marilyn Martin-Jones. 1990. "Critical Language Awareness. Part I: A Critical Review of Three Current Approaches to Language Awareness." *Language and Education* 4, no. 4: 249–60. http://dx.doi.org/10.1080/09500789009541291.

Clark, Romy, Norman Fairclough, Roz Ivanic, and Marilyn Martin-Jones. 1991. "Critical Language Awareness. Part II: Towards Critical Alternatives." *Language and Education* 5, no. 1: 41–54. http://dx.doi.org/10.1080/09500789109541298.

Devereaux, Michelle D. 2015. *Teaching about Dialect Variations and Language in Secondary English Classrooms: Power, Prestige, and Prejudice*. New York: Routledge.

Escure, Genevieve. 1997. *Creole and Dialect Continua: Standard Acquisition Processes in Belize and China (PRC)*. Amsterdam: John Benjamins. http://dx.doi.org/10.1075/cll.18.

Fairclough, Marta. 2005. *Spanish and Heritage Language Education in the United States: Struggling with Hypotheticals*. Madrid, Frankfurt: Iberoamericana Libros and Vervuert.

Fairclough, Marta, and Flavia Belpoliti. (2016). "Inquiry-Based Projects: Understanding Culture through Research in the Spanish Heritage Language Classroom." *Hispania*, June.

Fairclough, Norman. 1989. *Language and Power*. London: Longman.

Fairclough, Norman, ed. 1992. *Critical Language Awareness*. London, New York: Longman.

Gutiérrez, Manuel J. 1997. "Discurso irreal de pasado en el español de Houston: la disputa continúa." *Bulletin of Hispanic Studies* 74, no. 3: 257–69. http://dx.doi.org/10.1080/000749097760121962.

Gutiérrez, Manuel, and Marta Fairclough. 2006. "Incorporating Linguistic Variation into the Classroom." In *The Art of Teaching Spanish: Second Language Acquisition, from Research to Praxis*, ed. M. Rafael Salaberry and Barbara Lafford, 173–92. Washington, DC: Georgetown University Press.

James, Carl. 1996. "Mother Tongue Use in Bilingual/Bidialectal Education: Implications for Bruneian Dwibahasa." *Journal of Multilingual and Multicultural Development* 17, no. 2–4: 248–57. http://dx.doi.org/10.1080/01434639608666277.

James, Carl, and Peter Garrett, eds. 1991. *Language Awareness in the Classroom*. London: Longman.

Jo, Hye-Young. 2001. "'Heritage' Language Learning and Ethnic Identity: Korean Americans' Struggle with Language Authorities." *Language, Culture and Curriculum* 14, no. 1: 26–41. http://dx.doi.org/10.1080/07908310108666610.

Katz, Stacey. 2003. "Near-Native Speakers in the Foreign-Language Classroom: The Case of Haitian Immigrant Students." In *The Sociolinguistics of Foreign-Language Classrooms: Contributions of the Native, the Near-Native, and the Non-Native Speaker*, ed. Carl Blyth, 131–55. Boston: Heinle.

Kerswill, Paul. 1994. *Dialects Converging: Rural Speech in Urban Norway*. Oxford: Clarendon Press.

Kerswill, Paul, and Ann Williams. 2002. "'Salience' as an Explanatory Factor in Language Change: Evidence from Dialect Levelling in Urban England." In *Language Change: The Interplay of Internal, External and Extra-linguistic Factors*, ed. Mari C. Jones and Edith Esch, 81–110. The Hague: Mouton de Gruyter. http://dx.doi.org/10.1515/9783110892598.81.

Kondo-Brown, Kimi. 2008. "Issues and Future Agendas for Teaching Chinese, Japanese, and Korean Heritage Students." In *Teaching Chinese, Japanese, and Korean Heritage Language Students: Curriculum Needs, Materials, and Assessment*, ed. Kimi Kondo-Brown and J. D. Brown, 17–43. Mahwah, NJ: Laurence Erlbaum.

———. 2010. "Curriculum Development for Advancing Heritage Language Competence: Recent Research, Current Practices, and a Future Agenda." *Annual Review of Applied Linguistics* 30:24–41. http://dx.doi.org/10.1017/S0267190510000012.

Lacorte, Manel. 2016. "Teacher Development in Heritage Language Education." In *Innovative Strategies for Heritage Language Teaching: A Practical Guide for the Classroom*, ed. Marta Fairclough and Sara M. Beaudrie. Washington, DC: Georgetown University Press.

Lam, Mariam B. 2006. "The Cultural Politics of Vietnamese Language Pedagogy." *Journal of Southeast Asian Language Teaching* 12, no. 2: 2–19.

Lee, Boh Young. 2013. "Heritage Language Maintenance and Cultural Identity Formation: The Case of Korean Immigrant Parents and Their Children in the USA." *Early Child Development and Care* 183, no. 11: 1576–88. http://dx.doi.org/10.1080/03004430.2012.741125.

Leeman, Jennifer. 2005. "Engaging Critical Pedagogy: Spanish for Native Speakers." *Foreign Language Annals* 38, no. 1: 35–45. http://dx.doi.org/10.1111/j.1944-9720.2005.tb02451.x.

Leeman, Jennifer, and Ellen Serafini. 2016. "Sociolinguistics for Heritage Language Educators and Students: A Model for Critical Translingual Competence." In *Innovative Strategies for Heritage Language Teaching: A Practical Guide for the Classroom*, ed. Marta Fairclough and Sara M. Beaudrie, 56–79. Washington, DC: Georgetown University Press.

Lippi-Green, Rosina. 2012. *English with an Accent: Language, Ideology, and Discrimination in the United States*. 2nd ed. New York: Routledge.

Long, Michael H. 2007. *Problems in SLA*. New York, London: Erlbaum.

Martínez, Glenn. 2003. "Classroom Based Dialect Awareness: A Critical Applied Linguistic Approach." *Heritage Language Journal* 1, no. 1: 44–57. www.heritagelanguages.org.

———. 2016. "Goals and Beyond in Heritage Language Education: From Competencies to Capabilities." In *Innovative Strategies for Heritage Language Teaching: A Practical Guide for the Classroom*, ed. Marta Fairclough and Sara M. Beaudrie, 39–55. Washington, DC: Georgetown University Press.

Milroy, James. 2001. "Language Ideologies and the Consequences of Standardization." *Journal of Sociolinguistics* 5, no. 4: 530–55. http://dx.doi.org/10.1111/1467-9481.00163.

Nero, Shondel J., ed. 2006. *Dialects, Englishes, Creoles, and Education*. Mahwah, NJ: Lawrence Erlbaum.

Nero, Shondel J., and Dohra Ahmad. 2014. *Vernaculars in the Classroom: Paradoxes, Pedagogies, Possibilities*. New York: Routledge.

Oh, Janet, and Terry Kir-Fon Au. 2005. "Learning Spanish as a Heritage Language: The Role of Sociocultural Background Variables." *Language, Culture and Curriculum* 18, no. 3: 229–41. http://dx.doi.org/10.1080/07908310508668744.

Parodi, Claudia. 2008. "Stigmatized Spanish Inside the Classroom and Out: A Model of Language Teaching to Heritage Speakers." In *Heritage Language Education: A New Field Emerging*, ed. Donna M. Brinton, Olga Kagan, and Susan Bauckus, 199–214. New York: Routledge.

Parra, María Luisa. 2016. "Critical Approaches to Heritage Language Instruction: How to Foster Students' Critical Consciousness." In *Innovative Strategies for Heritage Language Teaching: A Practical Guide for the Classroom*, ed. Marta Fairclough and Sara M. Beaudrie, 166–90. Washington, DC: Georgetown University Press.

Polinsky, Maria. 2006. "Incomplete Acquisition: American Russian." *Journal of Slavic Linguistics* 14:161–219.

Polinsky, Maria, and Olga Kagan. 2007. "Heritage Languages: In the 'Wild' and in the Classroom." *Language and Linguistics Compass* 1, no. 5: 368–95. http://dx.doi.org/10.1111/j.1749-818X.2007.00022.x.

Porras, Jorge E. 1997. "Uso local y uso estándard: Un enfoque bidialectal a la enseñanza del español para nativos." In *La enseñanza del español a hispanohablantes: Praxis y teoría*, ed. M. Cecilia Colombi and Francisco X. Alarcón, 190–97. Boston: Houghton Mifflin.

Potowski, Kim. 2012. "Identity and Heritage Learners: Moving beyond Essentializations." In *Spanish as a Heritage Language in the United States: The State of the Field*, ed. Sara M. Beaudrie and Marta Fairclough, 179–99. Washington, DC: Georgetown University Press.

Rouchdy, Aleya. 2002. "Language Conflict and Identity: Arabic in the American Diaspora." In *Language Contact and Language Conflict in Arabic: Variations on a Sociolinguistic Theme*, ed. Aleya Rouchdy, 133–48. London: Routledge/Curzon.

Ruiz, Richard. 1988. "Orientations in Language Planning." *In Language Diversity, Problem or Resource? A Social and Educational Perspective on Language Minorities in the United States*, ed. Sandra L. McKay and Sau-Ling C. Wong, 1–25. New York: Newbury House.

Rys, Kathy. 2007. "Dialect as Second Language: Linguistic and Non-linguistic Factors in Secondary Dialect Acquisition by Children and Adolescents." PhD diss., Ghent University.

Rys, Kathy, and Dries Bonte. 2006. "The Role of Linguistic Factors in the Process of Second Dialect Acquisition." In *Language Variation: European Perspectives*, ed. Frans Hinskens, 201–15. Amsterdam: John Benjamins. http://dx.doi.org/10.1075/silv.1.13rys.

Sánchez, Rosaura. 1993. "Language Variation in the Spanish of the Southwest." In *Language and Culture in Learning: Teaching Spanish to Native Speakers of Spanish*, ed. Barbara J. Merino, Enrique T. Trueba, and Fabián A. Samaniego, 75–81. London: Falmer Press.

Schiffman, Harold F. 1996. *Linguistic Culture and Language Policy*. London: Routledge. http://dx.doi.org.10.4324/9780203021569.

Schleppegrell, Mary, and M. Cecilia Colombi, eds. 2002. *Developing Advanced Literacy in First and Second Languages: Meaning with Power*. Mahwah, NJ: Erlbaum.

Schmidt, Richard. 1990. "The Role of Consciousness in Second Language Learning." *Applied Linguistics* 11, no. 2: 129–58. http://dx.doi.org/10.1093/applin/11.2.129.

———. 1992. "Awareness and Second Language Acquisition." *Annual Review of Applied Linguistics* 13:206–26. http://dx.doi.org/10.1017/S0267190500002476.

———. 2001. "Attention." In *Cognition and Second Language Instruction*, ed. Peter Robinson, 3–32. Cambridge: Cambridge University Press. http://dx.doi.org/10.1017/CBO9781139524780.003.

———. 2010. "Attention, Awareness, and Individual Differences in Language Learning." In *Proceedings of CLaSIC 2010*, Singapore, December 2–4, ed. W. M. Chan, S. Chi, K. N. Cin, J. Istanto, M. Nagami, J. W. Sew, T. Suthiwan, and I. Walker, 721–37. Singapore: National University of Singapore, Centre for Language Studies.

Siegel, Jeff. 1999. "Stigmatized and Standardized Varieties in the Classroom: Interference or Separation?" *TESOL Quarterly* 33, no. 4: 701–28. http://dx.doi.org/10.2307/3587883.

———. 2010. *Second Dialect Acquisition*. Cambridge: Cambridge University Press. http://dx.doi.org/10.1017/CBO9780511777820.

Silva-Corvalán, Carmen. 2001. *Sociolingüística y pragmática del español*. Washington, DC: Georgetown University Press.

Strevens, Peter. 1985. "Standards and the Standard Language." *English Today* 1, no. 2: 5–7. http://dx.doi.org/10.1017/S0266078400000055.

Train, Robert W. 2003. "The (Non)native Standard Language in Foreign Language Education: A Critical Perspective." In *The Sociolinguistics of Foreign Language Classrooms: Contributions of the Native, the Near-native and the Non-native Speaker*, ed. Carl Blyth, 3–39. Boston: Heinle.

Trudgill, Peter. 1986. *Dialects in Contact*. Oxford: Blackwell.

Valdés, Guadalupe. 2005. "Bilingualism, Heritage Language Learners, and SLA Research: Opportunities Lost or Seized?" *Modern Language Journal* 89, no. 3: 410–26. http://dx.doi.org/10.1111/j.1540-4781.2005.00314.x.

———. 2007. "Making Connections: Second Language Acquisition Research and Heritage Language Teaching." In *The Art of Teaching Spanish: Second Language Acquisition, from Research to Praxis*, ed. Rafael Salaberry and Barbara Lafford, 193–212. Washington, DC: Georgetown University Press.

Valdés, Guadalupe, and Michelle Geoffrion-Vinci. 1998. "Chicano Spanish: The Problem of the "Underdeveloped" Code in Bilingual Repertoires." *Modern Language Journal* 82:473–501.

Valenzuela, Angela. 1999. *Subtractive Schooling: US-Mexican Youth and the Politics of Caring*. Albany: State University of New York Press.

Vousten, R. 1995. "Dialect als tweede taal: Linguïstische en extra-linguïstische aspecten van de verwerving van een Noordlimburgs dialect door standaardtalige jongeren." PhD diss., University of Nijmegen.

Wardhaugh, Ronald. 1992. *An Introduction to Sociolinguistics*. Cambridge, MA: Blackwell.

Wiley, Terrence. G. (2008). "Chinese "Dialect" Speakers as Heritage Language Learners: A Case Study." In *Heritage Language Education: A New Field Emerging*, ed. Donna M. Brinton, Olga Kagan, and Susan Bauckus, 91–106. New York: Routledge.

Wolfram, Walt. 1999. "Repercussion for the Oakland Ebonics Controversy: The Critical Role of Dialect Awareness Programs." In *Making the Connection: Language and Academic Achievement among African American Students*, ed. Carol Tempe Adger, Donna Christian, and Orlando Taylor, 61–80. Washington, DC: Center for Applied Linguistics.

Wolfram, Walt, and Natalie Schilling-Estes. 2006. *American English: Dialects and Variation*. 2nd ed. Malden, MA: Blackwell.

Zyzik, Eve. 2016. "Towards a Prototype Model of the Heritage Language Learner: Understanding Strengths and Needs." In *Innovative Strategies for Heritage Language Teaching: A Practical Guide for the Classroom*, ed. Marta Fairclough and Sara M. Beaudrie, 19–38. Washington, DC: Georgetown University Press.

8

Critical Approaches to Heritage Language Instruction

How to Foster Students' Critical Consciousness

María Luisa Parra
Harvard University

As heritage language (HL) programs expand throughout the United States, and as teachers become aware of the inherent diversity among HL learners in our classrooms, important questions about our role as teachers emerge: What are our goals in the classroom? Are they exclusively linguistic? Are we aware of and sensitive to our students' own needs and goals for studying heritage languages? What are the meaning and contributions of the study of heritage languages to the broader context of student's education? What kinds of connections and relations do we seek to establish with our students?

The answers to these questions used to reflect a traditional and prescriptive framework that emphasized a narrow understanding of the teaching of heritage languages: the teaching of standard and prestigious variants of the heritage language. However, the goals of our profession are shifting as educators become aware of the complex sociocultural and political circumstances under which many heritage learners have grown up, as children of immigration. Many heritage learners bring into the classroom important feelings of stigmatization about the way they speak, which challenge not only the use of their languages but also their sense of identity in relation to the American and country-of-origin mainstream cultures. This broader consideration of the intricacies of HL students' identities are bringing new understandings of the impact and significance of our work as teachers of heritage languages. The purposes of our profession comprise engaging students in deep reflections to raise their critical awareness around important and sensitive issues such as language ideologies and the power structures that have shaped students' beliefs about their own languages, cultures, and identities. The ultimate goal of teaching heritage languages is to empower students' ethnolinguistic identity as part of their lives in the United States and as part of their global citizenship.

This new reading of our endeavor has led educators to search for more socially responsive frameworks. In this chapter, I elaborate on the relevance of the critical pedagogy tenets developed by the Brazilian pedagogue Paulo Freire for the teaching of heritage languages. The chapter has three main parts. In the first part, I present an overview of some of the main theoretical and pedagogical underpinnings of critical pedagogy (Freire 2005). In the second part, the body of the chapter, I elaborate on how critical pedagogy tenets can enhance HL curriculum and pedagogical practices. I give practical considerations on how to use critical pedagogy within three frameworks that are currently used in heritage languages to foster students' language and cultural awareness: Sociolinguistics (Leeman and Serafini, this volume [2016]; Leeman 2005; Martínez 2003; Villa 2002), multiliteracies (NLG 1996; Unsworth 2001), and service learning (Bringle and Clayton 2012; Clayton, Bringle, and Hatcher 2013; Leeman, Rabin, and Román-Mendoza 2011; Parra 2013; Rabin and Leeman 2015). The combination of critical pedagogy and these frameworks can greatly help to develop a more inclusive and socially responsive teaching environment with the fundamental goal of supporting students' progress in their use of their heritage language as a vehicle to become agents of social change. In the last part of the chapter, I reflect on some of the main challenges of creating a critical teaching-learning environment. For the critical approach to result in engaging and effective practice, teachers need to be aware of their own linguistic, social, and cultural biases toward their students as well as the resistances that some students might bring into the classroom. I conclude by concurring with Henry Giroux and Peter McLaren (1986), who proposed that teachers should embrace a role of "transformative intellectuals" to bring into the classroom a mutual process of critical consciousness (Freire 2005).

CRITICAL PEDAGOGY TENETS

Critical pedagogy and its main goal, critical consciousness, were first proposed by the Brazilian educator Paulo Freire in his 1968 seminal and profound book *Pedagogy of the Oppressed*. Freire developed his method as a result of his work with impoverished and illiterate people in Brazil. He was deeply concerned about the clenched dynamics between the oppressed and the oppressor, and how the oppressed—even when yearning for freedom—would fail to engage in effective practices and actions that would lead to social change.

Freire proposed that the first step to social change is the recognition of our own position within the oppressed/oppressor dialectic while at the same time part of a system of societal hegemonies. Freire hoped that individuals would engage in critical self-reflection to understand their own biases, assumptions, and values that would allow them to change their perception of themselves and of others, and to recognize the conditions of injustice that surround them. In Freire's words, critical consciousness is the "process in which [men and women], not as recipients but as knowing subjects, achieve a deepening awareness both of the sociocultural reality that shapes their lives and of their capacity to transform that reality" (Freire 1970, 452).

Freire suggested that the raising of critical consciousness, *conscientização*, is rooted in dialogue and in its "essence," the word: "to speak a true word is to transform the world" (Freire 2005, 87). Therefore, for Freire, words and dialogue are the first steps for taking action toward changing social dynamics based on the powerful oppressed/oppressor dialectic. However, it is crucial for teachers to note that Freire's "dialogue" is not a mere conversation or technique; on the contrary, as he explained,

> dialogue characterizes an epistemological relationship . . . a way of knowing and should never be viewed as a mere tactic to involve students in a particular task. We have to make this point very clear. I engage in dialogue not necessarily because I like the other person. I engage in dialogue because I recognize the social and not merely the individualistic character of the process of knowing. In this sense, dialogue presents itself as an indispensable component of the process of both learning and knowing. (Freire and Macedo 1995, 379)

This notion of dialogue represents the core of the critical pedagogy: dialogue as a social action. Dialogue, the praxis, means to engage in a cycle of reflection: starting with an "epistemological curiosity" about a subject—for example, in the case of heritage learners, the student's linguistic and cultural background and lived experience—framed by a theory to critically analyze such experiences. The key to this critical analysis is to conceptualize language—that is, students' heritage languages—as a form of social practice. In other words, any language's main goal is for communication with others. This communication, however, encodes societal power relations among different groups (what is called "ideology"). Societal hierarchies are constructed through what is said; how the message is said, by whom, and to whom; and where the message is delivered. We find these hierarchies, for instance, between parents and children, teachers and students, men and women, minority groups and mainstream. Sociocultural and political values about ourselves and the groups we belong to are transmitted through these messages. The goal of a teacher working within a critical framework is to provide students with analytic tools to identify the power relations encoded in the messages we receive. It is only until we critically analyze these messages and become aware of their content and the ideologies they entail (and our part in perpetuating them) that we can access a different level of understanding that can lead to actively changing the social messages that have shaped our identities.[1]

This pedagogical tenet geared to develop students' critical awareness and to empower their voices has been embraced by some educators in the United States who have looked for alternative models of education beyond what Freire called "banking model of education," a teacher-centered classroom where teachers are conceived as providers of information and students are conceived as mere and passive recipients (Freire 2005).[2] Critical pedagogy has been particularly meaningful for minority children and youth attending the American educational system, as it presents an alternative for immigrant voices to be heard and taken into account as a contribution to the overall classroom learning experience (see Kelly 2012; Kersten 2006 for projects that work with critical pedagogy in diverse classrooms at the elementary and middle school levels in the United States; and see Lopez 2011 for such projects in Canada).

For immigrant youth, like many of our heritage students, critical pedagogy can be even more powerful as a tool for analyzing and becoming aware of the hegemonic discourses that have shaped their lived experiences and use of their heritage languages. They are at a stage in life where reframing their ethnolinguistic identities is a crucial endeavor.[3]

We can take as an example of the significance of this critical consciousness the reflections that Donaldo Macedo, one of Freire's closest collaborators in the United States, shares with the reader in the introduction to the thirtieth anniversary edition of *Pedagogy of the Oppressed.* Macedo recalls the impact Freire's ideas had on his own life as a young Cape Verdean man:

> Reading *Pedagogy of the Oppressed* also gave me the inner strength to begin the arduous process of transcending a colonial existence that is almost culturally schizophrenic: being present and yet not visible, being visible and yet not present. It is a condition that I painfully experienced in the United States, constantly juggling the power asymmetry of the two worlds, two cultures, and two languages. (Macedo, in Freire 2005, 11)

Macedo's words are a reminder of the colonialism and power asymmetry most children of immigrants face growing up in this country.

By embracing a critical pedagogy approach, teachers of heritage languages can empower and raise students' awareness on two fronts: first, the way in which their lived experience and heritage language relate to the mainstream culture of the United States; and, second, the way in which the students' own heritage dialect relates to the standard or prestigious version of the heritage language, which in many cases is the result of a deep history of colonization back in their countries of origin.

It is through the epistemological curiosity about the use of the heritage language in these two social contexts—the United States and the students' countries of origin—in combination with the principles of inquiring and dialogue of critical pedagogy that teachers can open the path for heritage learners to reflect on issues related to their heritage language and their experiences of immigration, power relations, inequality, oppression, and discrimination encoded in mainstream public discourse in the United States and in the students' countries of origin (see, for example, Aparicio 1997; Correa 2011; Ducar 2008; Leeman 2005; Leeman and Rabin 2007; Martínez and Schwartz 2012, for critical analysis of these issues in relation to Spanish heritage learners). The ultimate goal is for students to embrace their own language and use it to develop their social consciousness and voice, to become agents of constructive action toward positive change in their communities and beyond.

CRITICAL PEDAGOGY AND THE TEACHING OF HERITAGE LANGUAGES

Integrating a critical pedagogy approach to the teaching of heritage languages starts with a curiosity and interest on the teacher's part to know who his students are and what they are interested in learning. In general, teachers decide the curriculum and tend to follow the topics and structure of textbooks. However, it is also beneficial to gather information about students' interests to guide the selection of possible topics and materials to work with beyond the textbook. As research has shown, students' interest and motivation can fluctuate within the length of one course if expectations are not met (Yanguas 2013). When possible, students applying for an HL course could fill out a course application form with questions about students' family and linguistic background, topics of interests, and topics of language they want to learn. This form can give key information about students' needs, strengths, and goals that teachers should take into account as they design their syllabus. This form can also provide interesting information about what students think is relevant to learn in a heritage language: Do they give importance to traditional topics such as spelling, grammar rules, and accent marks, or to how to speak and write "correctly"? Do they struggle to find a topic they want to learn about? Do they want to learn about certain aspects of their cultures in relation to the United States? In my experience, any information students write in these forms shines light into their system of beliefs about what is important to learn about the heritage language. It can give teachers a baseline to build on conversations through critical lenses: Why do students think these topics are important? Where do they learn these assumptions? Who sets these standards?

As suggested by many authors in the field of HL and foreign language learning, class materials should be meaningful and include topics that speak to students' interests and lived experiences. At the same time, although materials are very important, what matters most is what we actually do with them. Critical pedagogy requires, for example, going beyond the traditional reading comprehension exercises. Teachers need to guide students in becoming aware of given assumptions when interpreting any kind of text (and even the same notion of "text" and "literacy," as I will present later on). Teachers need to encourage epistemological curiosity and provide the theoretical basis so students can succeed in reaching new levels of understanding through a critical dialogue, respect for, and trust in the whole group.[4]

In what follows, I present practical suggestions about how to integrate critical pedagogy tenets with three commonly used frameworks in HL teaching: sociolinguistics, multiliteracies, and service learning. The main goal of this combination is to develop critical language and cultural awareness as well as a sense of social commitment and agency in HL students.

Sociolinguistics and Critical Language Awareness

As Jennifer Leeman and Ellen Serafini (in this volume [2016]) remind us, sociolinguistics has much to offer to the teaching of heritage languages and second language learning (McKay and Hornberger 1996; Moreno-Fernández 1994; Preston and Bayley 2000). It provides us with an overview not only of languages but of the relationships between the different participants within any linguistic exchange, highlighting the social, cultural, and political dimensions of language. Teachers of heritage languages can use sociolinguistics to frame students' critical thinking and critical language awareness around topics of language variation, multilingualism, and identity (Fairclough 1995; Leeman and Serafini, this volume [2016]; Leeman, Rabin, and Román-Mendoza 2011; Urciuoli 2008).

In the next paragraphs, I present three suggestions for integrating critical pedagogy principles with three relevant sociolinguistic topics for the HL classroom: (a) the relationship between heritage languages and English; (b) the relationship between heritage languages and the HL variant of prestige, and (c) the dynamics of heritage languages in the classroom. The suggestions I provide also highlight the fact that the inclusion in the curriculum of the sociocultural and political dimensions of heritage languages presents yet another advantage for our students: it brings the possibility to work from an interdisciplinary perspective where sociology, history, anthropology, immigration studies, social and cultural psychology, education, theories of identity, and the arts (literature and visual arts, as we will see later in the chapter) can only enrich our classroom discussions, dialogues, and students' perspectives.

Heritage Languages and English

A first approach to the study of the social, cultural, and political dimensions of heritage languages can be done through a historical analysis of the linguistic history of the United States. American history and sociolinguistics can be a powerful combination to analyze: on the one hand, the many Native American languages that have been part of what the United States is today and, on the other hand, the impact of the different immigration waves of the twentieth century in the linguistic landscape of the United States (see Potowski 2010 for an overview of the linguistic diversity in the United States).

A closer look into the patterns of how languages are maintained and lost in the United States (Alba 2004; Fishman 1991; Rumbaut and Massey 2013) allows the possibility of discussing important and well-known topics for HL learners. For instance, an analysis of the different social scenarios where children grow up bilingual (Skutnabb-Kangas 2007) would allow students to discuss the pressures for assimilation and the academic demands in English that many of them underwent growing up, the tensions between home and school they lived through, and the impact these tensions had on their HL development.

The topic of languages in the context of immigration opens up two other paths for critical dialogue with students: first, the history of bilingual education in the United States and the impact of English-language policies in students' educational opportunities (see Crawford 1998; Nieto 2009); second, the range of "functional proficiencies" (Valdés 2005) that HL speakers bring into our classroom as a result of their own individual immigration circumstances and home–school relation. Guadalupe Valdés (1997, 30) defines this range as "the continuum of linguistic abilities and communicative strategies that [HL learners] may access in one or the other of two languages at a specific moment." Such a range includes grammatical and textual competencies as well as illocutionary and sociolinguistic competencies (Bachman 1990), all of which are in continuous interaction (Valdés 1997).

From a sociolinguistic perspective, this range of proficiencies is a rich subject of knowledge. For example, the study of the bilingual range can engage students in productive and meaningful dialogues about languages in contact, code-switching (see Carvalho 2012 for a review of theoretical and pedagogical approaches in the HL classroom, and Leeman and Serafini, in this volume [2016]), translanguaging (García and Li 2014),[5] and the performativity of multicultural identities through bilingualism (see Leeman and Serafini, in this volume [2016]; Block 2007; Potowski 2012; Zentella 1997) as common and meaningful practices within their communities. At the same time, a critical approach on these topics would let students pose fundamental questions about the relation between these linguistic behaviors and their identity formation process. At the same time, combining sociolinguistic knowledge with a critical perspective would lead students to question such notions as "native speaker," "balanced bilingual," "speaking well," and "speaking bad" constructed on theoretical suppositions instead of on the realities of the speakers of multilingual communities (Romaine 1995).

If teachers want to include a broader interdisciplinary perspective into their class discussion, they could incorporate, for example, academic readings and short stories about immigrant children at school. Important critical analysis can be made as HL students might identify with stories that portray immigrant children or youth struggling to adapt and succeed in school as they are discriminated against because of their culture and language abilities.[6] Building on previous discussions about bilingual proficiencies, teachers can organize discussions around two opposite theoretical approaches within which to frame the stories and bilingual practices they portray. One of these approaches is the deficit approach, which interprets students' bilingual range (under this perspective mainly understood as code-switching) as a result of lacking proficiency in both English and the heritage language. This conception has even more detrimental consequences as many times the supposed language deficiency is paired with a lack of cognitive abilities. Teachers can discuss the fact that this kind of approach entails a normative perspective on languages—and many times a form of discrimination—and disregards possibilities for understanding the bilingual abilities of immigrant children within a comprehensive perspective of communication. On the contrary, an interdisciplinary approach that includes sociolinguistics, anthropological, and "anthropolitical" linguistics (Zentella 1997) as well as social and cultural psychology approaches to bilingualism (Romaine 1995) would consider the bilingual range of immigrant children not only as a *result* of the sociocultural and political circumstances that the student grew up in but also as an expression of giftedness (Valdés 2005) and as a "vital resource" for the students' process of negotiating and performing their social identities (Leeman, Rabin, and Román-Mendoza 2011).

In sum, the purpose of analyzing the relation between the heritage languages and mainstream English is to raise students' awareness toward the realization that language hierarchies, linguistic subordination, and the racialization of speakers in the United States are instantiated in social and institutional norms regarding the "correct" way of speaking and the "appropriate" language to use (Leeman 2005; Martínez 2003; Villa 2002).

Heritage Languages and Standard Language Prestige

Unfortunately, teachers and heritage students need to be aware of the fact that language hierarchies, linguistic subordination, and the racialization of speakers happen not just in the United States. In any given society, different variants of the language coexist, some having more social prestige and value than others. Therefore, heritage students' own language variants are also part of social hierarchies, subordination, and markers of social class back in their countries of origin.

Since many HL learners have internalized negative messages about their own language variant, the goal is to help students become aware of these messages and validate their own ways of speaking. A critical sociolinguistic approach to problematize and question such notions as the "correct" way of speaking, "standard" and "prestigious" variants could have a significant positive impact on students' confidence, self-esteem, and sense of identity. In this regard, teachers can promote reflections about two main aspects of the heritage language: HL variation (between different countries and regions within the same country) and the language ideologies that support some variants of the heritage language as more prestigious than others.

Taking language variation by region or comparing rural with urban varieties can also lead teachers to include discussions about how languages change over time. Many linguistic forms that we consider archaic today were actually widely used in earlier times by mainstream speakers of the community. However, over time, new words emerge and old forms fall into disuse. Speakers who lack access to formal education tend to keep the old forms that they learned from their parents and grandparents. This can present an opportunity to organize sociolinguistic research projects. Students can identify specific linguistic features from different regions of their countries or from the communities they (or their parents) grew up in and compare them with current forms to learn about how languages change (for more extensive project ideas on this topic, see Carreira 2000; Leeman and Serafini, this volume [2016]). This exercise can provide students with a new understanding of language variation as associated with historical changes, social hierarchies, and educational opportunities but *always* as a valuable vehicle of communication for the corresponding community.

These reflections can help teachers introduce the topic of language ideologies. Building on the understanding that there are no languages "better" than others, teachers can analyze the criterion of "correctness" and "prestige" from a critical perspective to show that the prestige and correctness we associate with specific variants reflect (or are a symptom of) the hierarchical relationship between speakers in any given society. Through this hierarchy, the mainstream determines the value and prestige of one variant over others (Bourdieu 1991). In the light of this new understanding, the idea of "standard variant" can be challenged as a construct based on mainstream ideologues (Fairclough 1995; Rodríguez Pino and Villa 1994; Villa 1996).

Critical Language Awareness in the Classroom

Because of the diverse backgrounds of heritage learners, it is likely that we would have a significant mix of HL variants in classroom. This diversity is often seen as a challenge for finding pedagogical practices that fit the needs of all students. Many times teachers think that the best way to deal with this situation is to follow a version of the banking model where they lecture and test so students learn grammar rules. However, a critical pedagogy approach can turn diversity into a rich source of knowledge and discussion. As I have discussed already, teachers can use the grammatical or lexical variations of the heritage language to problematize notions of language prestige/standard as well as to enlarge students' vocabulary (Martínez 2003). Different accents can also be a central topic for critical discussion. In her work with Latino students, for example, Bonnie Urciuoli (2008) has identified how accents play a role in setting up hierarchies among college students, where Caribbean Spanish accents tend to be perceived as less prestigious than other variants of Spanish. This hierarchy is also predominant between teacher and students, where both assume that the teacher speaks the variant with more prestige.

However, encouraging students to reflect on the aforementioned social dimensions of language can pose important challenges to teachers of heritage languages. It questions what has been understood to be the traditional goal of the profession: to "teach" students to speak and write "correctly." As discussed above, this conception of speaking "well" is rooted in dominant ideologies of language and social prestige within which many teachers have been raised and trained. Many teachers, claiming to know the "right way" of speaking the language, do not question themselves when using a framework of correction with their students, thus perpetuating power relations that harm students' self-esteem and interests in the learning process (Potowski 2001, 2002).[7]

As an alternative to the correctness criteria, some scholars have proposed that teachers of heritage languages should teach students not what is "correct" but what is "appropriate" for informal and formal contexts. However, for other researchers, this criterion of "appropriateness" shrouds yet another form of "correctness" (for a review of this issue, see Leeman and Serafini, this volume [2016]). Associating the "appropriate" forms with specific contexts (i.e., standard variation with formal contexts and nonstandard with informal contexts) is to say that there are "correct" forms for formal contexts, whereas informal forms would be stigmatized in the same context.

What is important is that teachers emphasize that different communicative situations require specific language features or registers.[8] Different situations might require the use of the oral or written modalities, specific vocabulary about the subject matter, different genres, and linguistic features related to the nature of the interactions between participants in that specific context (Schiffrin 2001; Van Dijk 2001). Thus, the task of HL teachers is not "eradicating" students' variants (Valdés 1981), correcting errors, or teaching students a narrow definition of "appropriateness" (close to that of "correctness"). Teachers need to broaden students' linguistic repertoires and expand students' understanding of the different communicative and social functions of the language in different social contexts, including the academic one (Achugar and Colombi 2008; Colombi 1994, 2003).

Multiliteracies and Critical Cultural Awareness

Teachers embracing a critical framework learn a new discourse that encourages students to problematize important assumptions they have about the use of their heritage language and its social and cultural meanings. One of the main goals within this framework is to enhance students' voices, as Giroux (1991, 249) proposes, "not merely as an opportunity to speak, but to engage critically with the ideology and substance of speech, writing, and other forms of cultural production." This section provides teachers with concrete suggestions to expand the scope of materials to build on critical reflections beyond the traditional written, through "other forms of cultural production" or what is known as "mutiliteracies" (New London Group 1996), the myriad ways and mediums of communication that exist beyond written texts.[9] HL learners are daily exposed to ideologies and misrepresentations of their language and culture through texts but mainly through mass media and the messages they find within the public spaces they inhabit. Therefore, it is important to critically consider these mediums and its content as we aim to empower students' sense of cultural identity. In what follows, I present some examples of three topics related to heritage cultures that can be critically analyzed through different literacies or mediums of communication to develop critical cultural awareness: cultural images and stereotypes, heritage language use in the media and public spaces, and cultural richness.

Cultural Images and Stereotypes

Extrapolating from functional approaches to language, some authors have developed a functional "visual grammar" that recognizes that images, like language, are not only representations of a material reality but they also represent interpersonal interactions of social reality (such as relations between viewers and what is viewed) (see Unsworth 2001 for a review of this topic). This work acknowledges that images are part of coherent textual compositions, to be understood as a product of a given ideology with specific purposes.

There is probably no better place to see and to understand the power of images than the mass media advertisement campaigns, movies, TV shows, and videos. These media provide teachers of heritage languages with plenty of opportunities to work on the central topic of cultural stereotypes. Derogatory and controversial images about physical characteristics, cultural practices, and accents of different ethnic groups abound in the media. A critical perspective will guide students through an analysis and discussion about ethnic stereotypes related to bodies, sexuality, identities, family values, accents, and the representations of "the good" and "the bad" in advertisements, TV shows, and movies.

Teachers can guide discussions around how mass media images contribute to the construction of the heritage community's identity: Why are these representations successful or not? What kind of models are they providing to younger generations? Do these representations match what they know about their communities? What can they do to raise awareness of these stereotypes in their communities? For teachers of heritage languages, these reflections can be fruitful for discussing how students' sense of identity has been shaped by these public messages and negative "social mirroring."[10]

Heritage Language Use in the Media

Another source for critical reflection on cultural stereotypes is the analysis of the heritage language(s) within mainstream movies or advertisement. Urciuoli (1996), for example, has analyzed how stereotypes and racist messages about Latinos are reinforced when the use of Spanish is presented as the marked option, while the use of English—along with notions of whiteness—is presented as "the unmarked, normal, and natural order in the United States" (Zentella 2003, 51). Furthermore, Jane Hill's (1993) work has analyzed how these stereotypes are reinforced even when an Anglo-American uses the heritage language (in the case of Hill's research, also Spanish) resulting in what she calls "Mock Spanish" (e.g., phrases like, *no problemo, mañana, Ah-dee-os, macho man*; *hasta la vista*, with the aspiration of the "h").

The relationship between the heritage language—and bilingualism in general—and notions of US citizenship and nationalism can also be discussed through the analysis of the comments that social media users post under any given article or video online regarding the use of a specific heritage language or in regard to the possibility of the United States becoming a multilingual country. Take as an example the controversial video that Coca-Cola made for the Super Bowl in 2014. The video presented images of people from different ethnic groups playing, eating, sharing with family members, and singing the song "America, the Beautiful." Interestingly enough, the patriotic song is sung in some of the languages spoken today in the United States. The video sparked a wide range of responses, from positive attitudes toward multiculturalism to hateful comments against immigration and multilingualism. This video, along with the posts, can serve as a rich text to discuss notions of attitudes toward multilingualism, ethnicities, national identity, and monolingualism, among other topics.[11]

Heritage Language Use in Public Spaces

Another setting where students can analyze critically the relationship between English and the heritage language is in the public space they inhabit. Some authors have become interested in analyzing how language(s) are used in public spaces. The study of linguistic landscapes is a newly developing field which, following the definition given by Rodrigue Landry and Richard Bourhis (1997, 25), includes "the language of public road signs, advertising billboards, street names, place names, commercial shop signs, and public signs on government buildings combined to form the linguistic landscape of a given territory, region, or urban agglomeration." Questions that can lead to critical reflections are: In which public spaces is the heritage language part of the linguistic landscape? Schools? Hospitals? Restaurants? What is the meaning of this linguistic presence or absence? Are English and the heritage language used together? And if they are used together in print, are the letter fonts the same size? And what about the use of English in their communities of origin? Answering these questions can also lead to discussions about cultural (ex)changes in the United States and countries of origin and the relation between the heritage language and English in the economic and global setting.

Cultural Richness

Different from mass media and linguistic landscapes, working with the arts provides unique opportunities for heritage learners to become aware of the richness of their own culture and celebrate it. Visual arts, music, and folk art are powerful multimodal texts that can engage students in rich discussions and critical analysis around the various layers of social and cultural meanings that converge in a work of art. Music can be used, for example, to analyze the different influences that emerge from old music traditions. (For instance, Latin American music has multiple rhythm influences: African, Arabic, Spanish, Indigenous, even German!) At the same time, some of those influences have had a fundamental role in the history of the United States' music tradition.[12] Lyrics are also a productive source for analyzing, for instance, cultural values around love, male and female representations, national identity, or matters of social justice.

Teachers can use art from students' countries of origin (and their communities in the United States) to discuss the various facets of students' identities: cultural representations, the relation between such representations and the students' experiences in the United States, the community's imaginary in the context of immigration, and the relationship between art and identity. Working with art is also a great opportunity for students to connect with their creative side (which is not very honored in academic settings) providing them with opportunities to focus on a process of meaning-making at a different level from traditional written assignments. I use art making, for example, as a final project in heritage and second language (L2) advanced classes (Parra 2013). I ask students to create an art object that reflects what they learned about themselves and their language throughout the course. The art object can be anything, but students need to explain in a written essay what the object is and what ideas or concepts learned in the class are represented or symbolized by the object. Students have made posters, collages, PowerPoints, poems, black-out poetry, spoken word, short stories, photo albums, drawings, videos, and beautiful paintings that reflect their awareness about language ideologies, the richness of linguistic variation, myths about language and Spanglish, the role of their families in the maintenance of Spanish language and culture, and the integration of their languages with their identities. At the end of the course, students present their projects to the whole group. The art making and the sharing of it with a whole group is a process where students "redesign" (New London Group 1996) their identities in relation to their heritage language. The consistent result, in the case of my students, has been the conviction that their heritage language and culture matter and that they wish to continue their study and pass their knowledge to future generations.

In sum, working with multiliteracies provides teachers and students with an important advantage: it expands the range of genres that can be included in class, giving students and teachers a broader choice of possibilities for exercising their critical thinking and raising their critical cultural awareness.

Service Learning

Within the critical pedagogy framework, the results of the reflections that students and teachers have in the classroom don't mean much if they are not translated into action. A powerful opportunity for this translation to take place is in the incorporation of a community service–learning component in the HL curriculum. Service learning aligns with main critical pedagogy tenets that state that the most local and immediate experiences should become the material of learning (Freire 2005).

Community service learning has been proposed as a main venue to engage HL and L2 students in meaningful experiences that foster language learning and community understanding (Hellebrandt and Varona 1999; Lear and Abbot 2008; Parra 2013; Thompson 2013; Wurr and Hellebrandt 2007). It is considered an effective pedagogical resource that provides HL and L2 students with experiences and tools that broaden their education goals and deepens their capacity to reflect about themselves and others (Parra 2013).

Service learning is particularly effective for heritage students as a way to foster the epistemological curiosity and critical analysis of their own communities and the power structures that shape them (Leeman 2005; Martínez and Schwartz 2012; Samaniego and Pino 2000; Parra 2013; Trujillo 2009). Other advantages of service learning for HL learners are fostering students' development of identities as "legitimate" as opposed to deficient (Leeman, Rabin, and Román-Mendoza 2011, 1) and providing students with "a level of motivation and investment in language learning that would be difficult to achieve in a classroom setting alone" (Martínez and Schwartz 2012, 46).

It is central to emphasize that a successful service-learning experience is not just "a form of volunteerism and it is not the addition of service activities to otherwise unchanged learning activities" (Clayton, Bringle, and Hatcher 2013, 7). It is also not a form of "charity." In order to become a meaningful learning and life experience, the service-learning component has to be aligned with topics discussed in the classroom, and this alignment needs to provide students with the tools "to understand the structural underpinnings of the social problems [students] seek to address" (Rabin and Leeman 2015, 130).[13] Therefore, it is crucial to "[design] an intentional [and meaningful] curriculum and activities grounded in well-articulated goals for both learning in the classroom and in the community in order to achieve a high-quality service learning" (Clayton, Bringle, and Hatcher 2013, 7).

Meaningful topics that teachers can include and explore in the HL classroom that will also be relevant in the community include the immigration debate and reform; access to education and social mobility; access to health services; health education; bilingual education; parents' and teachers' attitudes toward bilingualism; and language use and identity.[14]

A critical pedagogy framework is fundamental for a successful integration of curriculum and service learning. A critical analysis of both curriculum materials and students' own experiences with the community will bring in the possibility of integrating theory and practice, one of the most valuable outcomes of this pedagogical model (Parra, Liander, and Muñoz 2011; Thomsen 2006). When discussed from a critical perspective, students' connections between theory and practice will provide, in turn, meaningful materials for achieving new levels of self-understanding and involvement with the community.

The alignment between curriculum materials and service learning is then facilitated when the organizations or agencies where students are placed work on similar issues to those of the heritage class curriculum, for instance, immigration, working status, translation, inequality, education, bilingual practices, identity, and health and leaderships, among other important issues.

Because the thread that ties together classwork and community experience is the heritage language (Parra 2013), activities in the heritage language can help to integrate both the classroom discussion and the community work, including the following:

- Journal entries linking the student's personal history with his experience in the community;
- Observations about the use of the HL, its variants, and its relation with English;
- Small research projects about relevant topics for the community (research on demographics, needs, and strengths of members of the community by age);
- Essays in which students reflect about the connections between an issue studied in class (e.g., labor conditions for immigrant workers) and the situation of these workers in the community they work in;

- Presentations to the class about the work being done in the community; and
- Work with art that integrates what students have learned about themselves through the class discussions and the work with the community (see, for example, Parra 2013).

In this setting, the teacher's role becomes that of a guide and discussion leader. Among the tasks a teacher should prepare for when integrating a service-learning component in the HL class are: to provide meaningful materials related to students' communities; to elicit questions (epistemological curiosity) from students about relevant topics for the community; to help students generate hypotheses and possible answers based on their volunteer experience and academic readings; to provide students with a format (e.g., a journal) to collect reflections on specific categories (language use, interactions with community members, interactions with organization staff or administration); and to organize class sessions where students bring their reflections and engage in a process of group critical dialogue. Through this dialogue, teachers and students inform and transform the academic experience. Students need, however, to feel that the classroom is a "safe space" (Correa 2011; Ducar 2008) where knowledge is shared and constructed (Rodríguez Pino, and Villa 1994) without the risk of being judged or undermined.

Finally, incorporating a community service–learning component into heritage classes benefits not just the group and organizations. It can contribute in important ways to "model scholarly practices for others; and contribute to a campus culture of inquiry related to teaching and learning" (Clayton, Bringle, and Hatcher 2013, 4). Including a service-learning component in heritage classes should emphasizes collaboration between the university and the community partners where, as proposed by Jennifer Leeman and colleagues (2011), both contribute political and intellectual resources and work democratically toward social change.

Logistics and Challenges of Service Learning

Although work with the community is a powerful appeal for HL classes, the logistics for a successful experience can be especially challenging. It requires time and extra work. It can be particularly difficult for courses with various sections. Finding organizations and placing students is laborious and sometimes requires several attempts. However, students are often involved in school or university initiatives or volunteer opportunities that already reach out to the community.[15] For large courses, the work within these initiatives could be an option to integrate the service-learning component into the HL class. As with any other class material, it is important to remember that what matters is what teachers and students do with—how they problematize and critically analyze and discuss—the experiences with the community that students bring in into the classroom.

The partnerships between the teacher and the community organization or agency need to be built on a reciprocal basis "that engage[s] students, faculty/staff, and community members to achieve academic, civic, and personal learning objectives as well as to advance public purpose" (Bringle and Clayton 2012, 105). Teachers (or language program directors) need to establish continuous communication with the organization administration to build trust and generate stable opportunities for collaboration. Stable communication is also needed to ensure that students and organization are both meeting the course goals and expectations.[16] It is important to note that getting students to become familiar with the organization's administrative structure is also a topic for critical analysis: Who are the directors of the organization? Are they members of the community or members of the mainstream culture? How do staff relate to each other? Are there any conflicts between leadership and staff? What do these relations say about the community and its relation with the mainstream?

This communication, however, is not always fluid as staff and administrators in many of these organizations tend to rotate or move to other similar organizations. Students can also find it very challenging to fit an extra activity into their busy extracurricular schedule. Other students have to work to support their studies or families. In this regard, teachers need to assess how much time students can devote to service learning without interfering with their activities but without sacrificing the learning experience.[17] For students who work, their employer could be a way to cover this requirement. These students would bring firsthand, powerful experiences to analyze key issues of inequality and social mobility. These experiences might be enlightening to those students who are devoted only to their studies.

CONCLUSIONS

In this chapter I have discussed the main tenets of the critical pedagogy framework and its relevance for the HL classroom. Working within this framework brings possibilities for building an inclusive learning environment, rich analysis, and deep discussions to empower HL learners sense of social agency.

There are important challenges to consider when integrating this perspective into our practices. A main challenge is students' own beliefs about what the HL classes are about. Even when teachers work outside normative frameworks, students want to be "corrected" and learn to speak "well."

Diversity in the classroom is also a challenge since HL learners are diverse not only linguistically but also socially and racially. Because of their different life experiences, students can bring into the classroom feelings of hierarchy coming from their culture of origin about race and social class. Teachers would need to be aware of these differences and the possible tensions and resistances they can create in the classroom. In this regard, teachers' "metalanguage" (Unsworth 2001) about the subject of study or discussion is of particular importance to scaffold critical language and cultural awareness as well as a respectful learning environment. This level of metacommunication is central "so that the teacher and students can identify, talk about, and learn the various elements that contribute to particular meanings in communication" (Kern 2004, 4). Metalanguage provides the basis for a critical discussion where "learners can gain the necessary personal and theoretical distance from what they have learned, constructively critique, account for its cultural location, creatively extend and apply it, and eventually innovate on their own, within old communities and in new ones" (New London Group 1996, 87).

Finally, from a critical pedagogy point of view, HL teachers who want to develop students' social consciousness and voice so they can become agents and leaders (Martínez 2012) of action toward constructive change (Freire 2005) should embrace the role of what Giroux and McLaren (1986, 215) call "transformative intellectuals":

> By the term "transformative intellectual," we refer to one who exercises forms of intellectual and pedagogical practice which attempt to insert teaching and learning directly into the political sphere by arguing that schooling represents both a struggle for meaning and a struggle over power relations. We are also referring to one whose intellectual practices are necessarily grounded in forms of moral and ethical discourse exhibiting a preferential concern for the suffering and struggles of the disadvantaged and oppressed. . . . Teachers who assume the role of transformative intellectuals treat students as critical agents, question how knowledge is produced and distributed, utilize dialogue, and make knowledge meaningful, critical, and ultimately emancipatory.

Embracing the possibility of becoming "transformative intellectuals" is not trivial, and it comes with great responsibility and commitment to our work and our students. Above all, it means that we teachers need to embark on a process of deep critical reflection of our assumptions about the language we teach, the goals of our work, and the relationships we want to develop with our students as well as our contribution to the field and the institutions we work for.

A critical perspective about our own work will lead us to the conclusion that the quality of our teaching depends on our capacity to listen carefully to our students' goals, needs, strengths, and expectations. They will engage in meaningful learning as long as we show them that we can engage in meaningful listening and collaboration with them. Following Freire's advice: Critical consciousness and liberation are not a gift, not a self-achievement, but a mutual process (Freire 2005).

NOTES

1. Teachers can refer to the seminal work of Fairclough (1995) on critical discourse analysis and identity.
2. Freire's seminal work was first published in English in 1971. It first caught the attention of educators in the United States in relation to the education of illiterate adults in Latin America. However, it soon became central for many educators deeply concerned with traditional education practices and policies that privileged knowledge of facts, efficiency, accountability, and standardized testing (what Freire called "the banking model of education") leaving little room, if any, to the teaching and nurturing of critical awareness, civic engagement, and social transformation in students attending the American school system. In 1986, in their article "Teacher Education and the Politics of Engagement: The Case for Democratic Schooling," Henry Giroux and Peter McLaren put to the foreground the profound crisis that the educational system and teacher training in the United states suffered at the time. Unfortunately, educational policies like No Child Left Behind have reinforced the banking model of education that still prevails today in most of the US schools.
3. For Michael Silverstein (2003, 532), ethnolinguistic identity emerges "where people ascribe a certain primordiality to language and a certain consequentiality to language difference. They consider it for one or another cultural reason to be a guide to socially meaningful differences among people and to people's socially effective membership in groups."
4. The class dynamics can benefit from including common pedagogical practices like collaborative small group activities, individual independent work, and common whole-class tasks to enhance discussion possibilities. At times the teacher will be a facilitator and guide or a coresearcher (Unsworth 2001, 20).
5. Ofelia García and Wei Li define translanguaging as "the simultaneous process of continuous becoming ourselves and of our language practices, as we interact and make meaning in the world" (García and Li 2014, 8).
6. Examples of these stories in Spanish include *Cajas de Cartón* by Francisco Jiménez, *La casa en Mango Street* by Sandra Cisneros, *Cuando era puertorriqueña* by Esmeralda Santiago, *The Wondrous Life of Oscar Wao* by Junot Díaz.
7. See Potowski 2001, 2002; and Potowski and Carreira 2004 for a teachers' training proposal outside the frame of correction.
8. A detailed description of the definition and scope of this framework as well as practical ideas to apply it in the HL classroom can be found in Samaniego and Warner, this volume (2016).
9. Analyzing videos, posts, and blogs on the Internet is part of what some authors call today "cyberliteracy." There are many current debates about the impact of new information technologies and computer mediation communications on the way we live and construct our daily life and social interactions.

10. This term was coined by the child psychoanalyst D. W. Winnicott, and refers to the child's sense of self that is shaped by the reflections mirrored back to her by significant others.
11. An example of these reflections online can be found in Steve Leveen, "America the Biligingually Beautiful," *Huffington Post*, March 4, 2014, http://www.huffingtonpost.com/steve-leveen/america-the-bilingually-b_b_4853762.html.
12. PBS produced the wonderful documentary *Latin Music USA*. The full show can be watched at http://www.pbs.org/wgbh/latinmusicusa/.
13. Some examples of courses for heritage Spanish that have aligned the curriculum with service learning are Abbott and Lear (2010), around critically oriented perspectives on gender, immigration, and Latino culture; Parra (2013), on topics on the Latino experience in the United States; Rabin and Leeman (2015), on Latin American and Latino literature and notions of nationalism; and Martínez and Schwartz (2012), on Spanish for the medical profession.
14. A form asking students about their previous community service experiences and interests can provide valuable information for the future placement of the students in the different partner organizations. Some students would like to work in organizations dealing with topics they already have experience with while others might want to engage in new experiences. Knowing students' previous experience with community service can also be informative in terms of how much guidance the students would need to start their work at the given organization.
15. Universities usually have various mentorship or tutoring programs with local schools. Work on Sunday schools could also be an interesting possibility. Students would see firsthand how these schools work, what makes them effective and what dynamics take away the motivation from some students. Many of them can contribute with their own experiences in these schools.
16. To ensure that students and organization meet each other's expectations and comply with the course goals, teachers can design a "contract" where the program coordinator of the organization and the students agree on the schedule (dates for beginning and ending of the work as well as the times for the week) and the type of activities the student will be participating in.
17. In my experience (Parra 2013), four hours a week is a good amount of time. It is not overwhelming for students, and it can be covered in one shift. Sometimes these slots of time can be covered in one afternoon or two. It mostly depends on coordinating students' schedules with the organization's needs. Although teachers should select organizations within an acceptable distance from their schools, time for transportation is also a factor to consider, as it could take a significant amount of time to get to some of those organizations by public transportation.

REFERENCES

Abbott, Annie, and Darcy Lear. 2010. "The Connections Goal Area in Spanish Community Service-Learning: Possibilities and Limitations." *Foreign Language Annals* 43, no. 2: 231–45.

Achugar, Mariana, and M. Cecilia Colombi. 2008. "Systemic Functional Linguistic Explorations into the Longitudinal Study of Advanced Capacities." In *The*

Longitudinal Study of Advanced L2 Capacities, ed. Lourdes Ortega and Heidi Byrnes, 36–57. New York: Routledge.

Alba, Richard. 2004. *Language Assimilation Today. Bilingualism Persist More than in the Past, but English Still Dominates*. Working paper, Center for Comparative Immigration Studies, UC San Diego. http://escholarship.org/uc/item/0j5865nk.

Aparicio, Francis R. 1997. "La enseñanza del español para hispanohablantes y la pedagogía multicultural." In *La enseñanza del español a hispanohablantes*, ed. M. Cecilia Colombi and Francisco X. Alarcón, 222–32. Boston: Houghton Mifflin.

Bachman, Lyle F. 1990. *Fundamental Considerations in Language Testing*. Oxford: Oxford University Press.

Block, David. 2007. "The Rise of Identity in SLA Research, Post Firth and Wagner (1997)." *Modern Language Journal* 91, no. 1: 863–76. http://dx.doi.org/10.1111/j.1540-4781.2007.00674.x.

Bourdieu, Pierre. 1991. *Language and Symbolic Power*. Boston: Harvard University Press.

Bringle, Robert G., and Patti H. Clayton. 2012. "Civic Education Through Service Learning: What, How, and Why?" In *Higher Education and Civic Engagement: Comparative Perspectives*, ed. Lorraine McIlraith, Ann Lyons, and Ronaldo Munck, 101–24. New York: Palgrave Macmillan. http://dx.doi.org/10.1057/9781137074829.0013.

Carreira, María. 2000. "Validating and Promoting Spanish in the United States: Lessons from Linguistic Science." *Bilingual Research Journal* 24, no. 4: 423–42. http://dx.doi.org/10.1080/15235882.2000.10162776.

Carvalho, Ana M. 2012. "Code-Switching: From Theoretical to Pedagogical Considerations." In *Spanish as a Heritage Language in the United States: The State of the Field*, ed. Sara M. Beaudrie and Marta Fairclough, 139–57. Washington, DC: Georgetown University Press.

Clayton, Patti H., Robert G. Bringle, and Julie A. Hatcher, eds. 2013. *Research on Service Learning. Conceptual Frameworks and Assessment. Volume 2A: Students and Faculty. IUPUI Series on Service Learning Research*. Sterling, VA: Stylus Publishing.

Colombi, M. Cecilia. 1994. "Perfil del discurso escrito en textos hispanohablantes: Teoría y práctica." In *La enseñanza del español a hispanohablantes*, ed. M. Cecilia Colombi and Francisco X. Alarcón, 175–89. Boston: Houghton Mifflin.

———. 2003. "Un enfoque functional para la enseñanza del ensayo expositivo." In *Mi lengua: Spanish as a Heritage Language in the United States*, ed. Ana Roca and M. Cecilia Colombi, 78–95. Washington, DC: Georgetown University Press.

Correa, Maite. 2011. "Advocating for Critical Pedagogical Approaches to Teaching Spanish as a Heritage Language: Some Considerations." *Foreign Language Annals* 44, no. 2: 308–20. http://dx.doi.org/10.1111/j.1944-9720.2011.01132.x.

Crawford, John. 1998. *Bilingual Education: History, Politics, Theory, and Practice*. Trenton, NJ: Crane.

Ducar, Cynthia M. 2008. "Student Voices: The Missing Link in the Spanish Heritage Language Debate." *Foreign Language Annals* 41, no. 3: 415–33. http://dx.doi.org/10.1111/j.1944-9720.2008.tb03305.x.

Fairclough, Norman. 1995. *Critical Discourse Analysis: The Critical Study of Language*. London: Longman.

Fishman, Joshua. 1991. *Reversing Language Shift: Theoretical and Empirical Foundations of Assistance to Threatened Languages*. Clevedon, UK: Multilingual Matters.

Freire, Paulo. 1970. "Cultural Action and Conscientization." *Harvard Educational Review* 40, no. 3: 452–77. http://dx.doi.org/10.17763/haer.40.3.h76250x720j43175.

———. 2005. *Pedagogy of the Oppressed.* 30th anniversary edition; trans. Myra Bergman Ramos. New York: Continuum. http://www.msu.ac.zw/elearning/material/1335344125freire_pedagogy_of_the_oppresed.pdf.

Freire, Paulo, and Donaldo Macedo. 1995. "A Dialogue: Culture, Language, and Race." *Harvard Educational Review* 65, no. 3: 377–403. http://dx.doi.org/10.17763/haer.65.3.12g1923330p1xhj8.

García, Ofelia, and Wei Li. 2014. *Translanguaging: Language, Bilingualism and Education.* Palgrave Mcmillan.

Giroux, Henry A. 1991. "Postmodernism as Border Pedagogy." In *Postmodernism, Feminism, and Cultural Politics: Redrawing Educational Boundaries*, ed. Henry A. Giroux, 217–56 Albany: State University of New York Press.

Giroux, Henry, and Peter McLaren. 1986. "Teacher Education and the Politics of Engagement. The Case for Democratic Schooling." *Harvard Educational Review* 56, no. 3: 213–39. http://dx.doi.org/10.17763/haer.56.3.trr1473235232320.

Hellebrandt, Josef, and Lucía T. Varona, eds. 1999. *Construyendo puentes: Concepts and Models for Service-Learning in Spanish.* AAHE's Series on Service-Learning in the Disciplines 13. Washington, DC: American Association for Higher Education.

Hill, Jane. 1993. "Hasta la vista, Baby: Anglo Spanish in the American Southwest." *Critique of Anthropology* 13, no. 2: 145–76. http://dx.doi.org/10.1177/0308275X9301300203.

Kelly, Courtney. 2012. "A Critical Pedagogy of Cafeterias and Communities: The Power of Multiple Voices in Diverse Settings." *Middle Grades Research Journal* 6, no. 2: 97–111.

Kern, Richard. 2004. "Literacy and Advanced Foreign Language Learning: Rethinking the Curriculum." In *Advanced Foreign Language Learning: A Challenge to College Programs*, ed. Heide Byrnes and Hiram H. Maxim, 2–18. Boston: Heinle.

Kersten, Jodene M. 2006. "Why's Everyone White? Moving toward Critical Pedagogy in an Elementary Classroom." *Journal of Urban Learning, Teaching, and Research* 2:35–44.

Landry, Rodrigue, and Richard Y. Bourhis. 1997. "Linguistic Landscape and Ethnolinguistic vitality: An Empirical Study." *Journal of Language and Social Psychology* 16, no. 1: 23–49. http://dx.doi.org/10.1177/0261927X970161002.

Lear, Darcy W., and Annie R. Abbot. 2008. "Foreign Language Professional Standards and CSL: Achieving the 5 C's." *Michigan Journal of Community Service Learning* 14, no. 2. http://www.freepatentsonline.com/article/Michigan-Journal-Community-Service-Learning/187695577.html.

Leeman, Jennifer. 2005. "Engaging Critical Pedagogy: Spanish for Native Speakers." *Foreign Language Annals* 38, no. 1: 35–45. http://dx.doi.org/10.1111/j.1944-9720.2005.tb02451.x.

Leeman, Jennifer and Lisa Rabin. 2007. "Reading language: Critical perspectives for the literature classroom." *Hispania* 90, no. 2: 304–15.

Leeman, Jennifer, Lisa Rabin, and Esperanza Román-Mendoza. 2011. "Critical Pedagogy beyond the Classroom Walls: Community Service-Learning and Spanish Heritage Language Education," *Heritage Language Journal* 8, no. 3: 293–314. http://www.heritagelanguages.org.

Leeman, Jennifer, and Ellen Serafini. 2016. "Sociolinguistics for Heritage Language Educators and Students: A Model for Critical Translingual Competence." In *Innovative Strategies for Heritage Language Teaching: A Practical Guide for the Classroom*, ed. Marta Fairclough and Sara M. Beaudrie, 56–79. Washington, DC: Georgetown University Press.

Lopez, Ann E. 2011. "Culturally Relevant Pedagogy and Critical Literacy in Diverse English Classrooms: A Case Study of a Secondary English Teacher's Activism and Agency." *English Teaching* 10, no. 4: 75–93.

Martínez, Glenn. 2003. "Classroom Based Dialect Awareness in Heritage Language Instruction: A Critical Applied Linguistic Approach." *Heritage Language Journal* 1, no. 1: 44–57. http://www.heritagelanguages.org.

———. 2012. "Policy and Planning Research for Spanish as a Heritage Language. From Language Rights to Linguistic Resource." In *Spanish as a Heritage Language in the United States: The State of the Field*, ed. Sara M. Beaudrie and Marta Fairclough, 61–77. Washington, DC: Georgetown University Press.

Martínez, Glenn, and Adam Schwartz. 2012. "Elevating "Low" Language for High Sakes: A Case for Critical, Community-Based Learning in a Medical Spanish for Heritage Learners Program." *Heritage Language Journal* 9, no. 2: 175–86. http://www.heritagelanguages.org

McKay, Sandra L., and Nancy Hornberger. 1996. *Sociolinguistics and Language Teaching*. Cambridge: Cambridge University Press.

Moreno-Fernández, Francisco. 1994. "Aportes de la sociolingüística a la enseñanza de lenguas." Revista de estudios de adquisición de la lengua española 1:107–35.

New London Group. 1996. "A Pedagogy of Multiliteracies: Designing Social Futures." *Harvard Educational Review* 66, no. 1: 60–93. http://dx.doi.org/10.17763/haer.66.1.17370n67v22j160u.

Nieto, David. 2009. "A Brief History of Bilingual Education in the United States." *Perspectives on Urban Education* 6, no. 1: 61–72.

Parra, María Luisa. 2013. "Expanding Language and Cultural Competence in Advanced Heritage- and Foreign-Language Learners through Community Engagement and Work with the Arts." *Heritage Language Journal* 10, no. 2: 115–42.

Parra, María Luisa, Johanna Liander, and Carmen Muñoz. 2011. "Spanish in the Community: An Inter-Active Language Course." Paper delivered at the ACTFL Conference, Denver, CO, November 18–20.

Potowski, Kim. 2001. "Educating University Foreign Language Teachers to Work with Heritage Spanish Speakers." In *Research and Practice in Language Teacher Education: Voices from the Field.* Selected Papers from the First International Conference on Language Teacher Education, ed. Bill Johnston and Suzanne Irujo, 87–100. Minneapolis: University of Minnesota, Center for Advanced Research in Language Acquisition.

———. 2002. "Experiences of Spanish Heritage Speakers in University Foreign Language Courses and Implications for Teacher Training." *ADFL Bulletin* 33:35–42. http://dx.doi.org/10.1632/adfl.33.3.35.

———, ed. 2010. *Language Diversity in the US*. Cambridge: Cambridge University Press. http://dx.doi.org/10.1017/CBO9780511779855.

———. 2012. "Identity and Heritage Learners: Moving beyond Essentializations." In *Spanish as a Heritage Language in the United States: The State of the Field*, ed. Sara M. Beaudrie and Marta Fairclough, 179–199. Washington, DC: Georgetown University Press.

Potowski, Kim, and María Carreira. 2004. "Teacher Development and National Standards for Spanish as a Heritage Language." *Foreign Language Annals* 37, no. 3: 427–37. http://dx.doi.org/10.1111/j.1944-9720.2004.tb02700.x.

Preston, Dennis, and Robert Bayley, eds. 2000. *Second Language Acquisition and Language Variation*. Amsterdam: John Benjamins.

Rabin, Lisa, and Jennifer Leeman. 2015. "Critical Service-Learning and Literary Study in Spanish." In *Service Learning and Literary Studies in English*, ed. L. Grobman and R. Rosenberg, 128–37. New York: Modern Language Association.

Rodríguez Pino, Cecilia, and Daniel Villa. 1994. "A Student-Centered Spanish for Native Speakers Program: Theory, Curriculum and Outcome Assessment." In *Faces in a Crowd: Individual Learners in Multisection Programs*, ed. Carol Klee, 355–73. American Association of University Supervisors and Coordinators and Directors of Foreign Language Programs Issues in Language Program Direction. Boston: Heinle and Heinle.

Romaine, Suzanne. 1995. *Bilingualism*. Malden, MA: Wiley-Blackwell.

Rumbaut, Rubén, and Douglas Massey. 2013. "Immigration and Language Diversity in the United States." *Daedalus* 142, no. 3: 141–54. http://dx.doi.org/10.1162/DAED_a_00224.

Samaniego, Fabián, and Cecilia Pino. 2000. "Frequently Asked Questions about SNS Programs." In *ATTSP Professional Development Series Handbook for Teachers K-16*, vol. 1, *Spanish for Native Speakers*, ed. American Association of Teachers of Spanish and Portuguese, 29–63. Fort Worth, TX: Hartcourt College.

Samaniego, Malena, and Chantelle Warner. 2016. "Designing Meaning in Inherited Languages: A Multiliteracies Approach to HL Instruction." In *Innovative Strategies for Heritage Language Teaching: A Practical Guide for the Classroom*, ed. Marta Fairclough and Sara M. Beaudrie, 166–90. Washington, DC: Georgetown University Press.

Schiffrin, Deborah. 2001. "Discourse Markers: Language, Meaning and Context." In *The Handbook of Discourse Analysis*, ed. Deborah Schiffrin, Deborah Tannen, and Heidi E. Hamilton, 54–75. Malden, MA: Blackwell.

Silverstein, Michael. 2003. "The Whens and Wheres—as Well as Hows—of Ethnolinguistic Recognition." *Public Culture* 15, no. 3: 531–58. http://dx.doi.org/10.1215/08992363-15-3-531.

Skutnabb-Kangas, Tove. 2007. *Bilingualism or Not: The Education of Minorities*. 1984. Reprint, Clevedon, Avon: Multilingual Matters.

Thompson, Gregory L. 2013. *Intersection of Service and Learning. Research and Practice in the Second Language Classroom*. Charlotte, NC: Information Age Publishing.

Thomsen, Katherine. 2006. *Service-Learning in Grades K–8: Experiential Learning That Builds Character and Motivation*. Thousand Oaks, CA: Corwin Press.

Trujillo, Juan A. 2009. "Con todos: Using Learning Communities to Promote Intellectual and Social Engagement in the Spanish Curriculum." In *Español en estados unidos y otros contextos de contacto: Sociolingüística, ideología y pedagogía*, ed. Manel Lacorte and Jennifer Leeman, 369–95. Madrid: Iberoamericana.

Unsworth, Len. 2001. *Teaching Multiliteracies across the Curriculum. Changing Contexts of Text and Image in Classroom Practice*. Buckingham, UK: Open University Press.

Urciuoli, Bonnie. 1996. *Exposing Prejudice: Puerto Rican Experiences of Race, Class, and Language in the US*. Boulder, CO: Westview.

———. 2008. "Whose Spanish? The Tension between Linguistic Correctness and Cultural Identity." In *Bilingualism and Identity: Spanish at the Crossroads with other Languages*, ed. Mercedes Niño-Murcia and Jason Rothman, 257–77. Amsterdam: John Benjamins. http://dx.doi.org/10.1075/sibil.37.16urc.

Valdés, Guadalupe.1981. "Pedagogical Implications of Teaching Spanish to the Spanish-Speaking in the United States." In *Teaching Spanish to the Hispanic bilingual: Issues, Aims, and Methods*, ed. Guadalupe Valdés, Anthony G. Lozano, and Rodolfo García-Moya, 3–20. New York: Teachers College Press.

———. 1997. "The Teaching of Spanish to Bilingual Spanish-Speaking Students: Outstanding Issues and Unanswered Questions." In *La enseñanza del español a eispanohablantes: Praxis y teoría*, ed. M. Cecilia Colombi and Francisco X. Alarcón, 8–44. Boston: Houghton Mifflin.

———. 2005. "Bilingualism, Heritage Language Learners, and SLA Research: Opportunities Lost or Seized?" *Modern Language Journal* 89, no. 3: 410–26. http://dx.doi.org/10.1111/j.1540-4781.2005.00314.x.

Van Dijk, Teun A. 2001. "Critical Discourse Analysis." In *The Handbook of Discourse Analysis*, ed. Deborah Schiffrin, Deborah Tannen, and Heidi E. Hamilton, 352–71. Malden, MA: Blackwell.

Villa, Daniel J. 1996. "Choosing a 'Standard' Variety of Spanish for the Instruction of Native Spanish Speakers in the US." *Foreign Language Annals* 29, no. 2: 191–200. http://dx.doi.org/10.1111/j.1944-9720.1996.tb02326.x.

———. 2002. "The Sanitizing of US Spanish in Academia." *Foreign Language Annals* 35, no. 2: 222–30. http://dx.doi.org/10.1111/j.1944-9720.2002.tb03156.x.

Wurr, Adrian J., and Josep Hellebrandt, eds. 2007. *Learning the Language of Global Citizenship: Service-Learning in Applied Linguistics*. Bolton, MA: Anker.

Yanguas, Íñigo. 2013. "Hispanic Heritage Language Learners in the Spanish classroom: A Semester-long Investigation of Their Attitudes and Motivation." In *Individual Differences, L2 Development, and Language Program Administration: From Theory to Application*, ed. Cristina Sanz and Beatriz Lado, 71–89. Boston: Cengage Learning.

Zentella, Ana Celia. 1997. *Growing up Bilingual: Puerto Rican Children in New York*. Malden, MA: Wiley-Blackwell.

———. 2003. ""José can you see": Latin@ Responses to Racist Discourse." In *Bilingual Games*, ed. Doris Sommer, 51–68. New York: Palgrave Macmillan.

9

Designing Meaning in Inherited Languages

A Multiliteracies Approach to HL Instruction

Malena Samaniego and Chantelle Warner
Universidad Austral de Chile and University of Arizona

Writing instruction and, in particular, the development of academic literacy have in many ways defined the field of heritage language (HL) pedagogy. The focus on academic, written discourse has been motivated by the social reality that, for many speakers, the use of the heritage language is largely restricted to conversational, informal settings in home and local communities, often as a result of monolingual educational policies (Chevalier 2004; Kono and McGinnis 2001; Shin 2005, 13; Yi 2008). Because the programmatic argument for offering special tracks or courses for heritage learners is grounded in the recognition that these individuals are typically more linguistically fluent and more familiar with sociocultural contexts than their second language (L2) peers (e.g., Cummins 2005; Leeman 2005; Villa 2002), it is their lack of advanced literacy skills that these curricula then seek to address (e.g., Chevalier 2004; Colombi, Pellettieri, and Rodríguez 2007). Indeed, it is this "deficit" that typically distinguishes a "heritage" language speaker from a first language (L1) speaker or a bilingual. Over the last decade, however, numerous scholars have cautioned that an exclusive focus on academic and professional registers of the public sphere may erode HL speakers' pride in their own vernacular uses of the heritage language and the specific sociocultural heritage that these index (Bernal-Henríquez and Hernández-Chávez 2003; Correa 2011; Hidalgo 1997, 1993; Leeman 2010, 2005; Martínez 2003; Villa 2002, 1996). An important challenge for HL teaching is therefore to enable learners to develop those "secondary discourse" genres (Gee 2002) learned in the educational system and practiced in more formal encounters without inadvertently devaluing or degrading nonstandard and vernacular varieties (Leeman 2005; Train 2007, 2002; Yi 2008).

As the deficit model has been questioned and critiqued, teachers and scholars have moved away from a linear view of literacy, which posits an idealized, educated native speaker as the desired end point, and toward an understanding of advanced literacy development as the expansion of learners' resources for making meaning. Within this expanded view of literacy, challenge of biliterate education is thus how to expand learners' communicative and expressive potential, not how to evolve their abilities into something widely recognized as "advanced." This requires a framework for literacy that embraces the multiplicity and polysemy of language use rather than conceiving of communication as the manifest singularity of expression and intent.

In this chapter we explore the potential of the multiliteracies framework, as it has been conceptualized in education and more recently in foreign language teaching and learning, for expanding the notion of literacy as it is operationalized in HL pedagogy. Following a brief review of the state and stakes of literacy instruction in HL education, we discuss contemporary frameworks within educational linguistics and L2 teaching and learning for understanding and teaching literature as multiple and manifold. We then conclude in the final section with a practical example and recommendations for what a pedagogy of multiliteracies might look like in the HL classroom (see also Parra, this volume [2016], for practical ideas of the multiliteracies framework in the classroom).

LITERACY INSTRUCTION IN THE HL CLASSROOM

Pedagogical imperatives to grant heritage learners access to more formal, typically written registers and the so-called genres of power and prestige (see Cope and Kalantzis, 1993) have often been cited as central objectives of HL education (Kono and McGinnis 2001; Valdés 1995; Valdés and Teschner 2003). Following a general tendency in L2 education (e.g., Hyland 2004), HL writing instruction has moved toward a "process" orientation (Raimes 1991, 1992; Zamel 1982, 1987) and even more recently toward what has been described as a "postprocess" or "genre" approach (Atkinson 2003; Matsuda 2003). As the name implies, process-oriented approaches shift the focus from the product—the written document—to the writer's expressiveness and the act of composition, through brainstorming, drafting, and feedback cycles. "Postprocess" approaches maintain the focus on process writing while also reattributing value to linguistic and formal awareness (within HL scholarship, see Colombi 2002, 84–85; Colombi, Pelletieri, and Rodriguez 2007; Martínez 2005, 81; Schwarz 2003). A large number of postprocess approaches posit genre as a central category for understanding the relationships between forms and functions; deliberate and guided attention to the patterns exhibited in particular genres and the linguistic, textual, and cultural conventions governing them are viewed as means of fostering and accelerating advanced literacy.

By complementing students' expressiveness with language awareness, a "postprocess" focus on genre may empower heritage learners to critically and creatively maneuver between various vernacular and academic genres (Colombi 2003, 2002, 2009); however, the implementation of this approach within HL teaching has not been without problems. Glenn Martínez (2005) notes, for example, that many HL pedagogy scholars who have embraced genre approaches have adopted a somewhat restrictive view of genre, which emphasizes professional and academic discourse.

In genre-based curricula for Spanish HL teaching (Colombi, Pellettieri, and Rodríguez 2007) and research (Chevalier 2004; Colombi 2009), genres are believed to be "key descriptors of advanced language capacities, that is, of language capacities that enable their users to function in a range of social circumstances, including most particularly the academy, professional, and public life" (Colombi 2009, 48). From this emerges a limited canon of genres that find their place in HL textbooks and curricula, including most prominently the essay, the opinion letter, the report, and the occasional inclusion of literary narrative (Colombi, Pellettieri, and Rodríguez 2007; Potowski 2011).

The experiences of immigration and frequent social subordination of HL populations of the Western hemisphere are largely linguistic (Lippi-Green 2012; Martínez 2006; Urciuoli 1996). HL communities are frequently burdened with strong linguistic stigma under the pressure of dominant monolingual and standard language ideologies. HL maintenance, bilingual practices, and local dialectal varieties are often portrayed as unpatriotic, uneducated, or "othered" (Hsu, Pang, and Haagdorens 2012; Leeman 2005; Leeman and Martínez 2007). By emphasizing the canonical genres described above, L2 and HL pedagogies tacitly assume the inherent value of standard varieties and are thus also complicit in perceptions that the languages of HL speakers, their families, and their communities are less valuable and deviant (García 1993; Leeman 2005; Train 2007; Valdés 1989; Villa 2002).

At the same time, in many L2 and HL curricula, literacy development is treated as a unidirectional progression from primary to the secondary genres. This risks creating a sense that linguistic development is a move away from oral language and toward academic registers, which in turn reproduces a dichotomy between speech and literacy found in many curricula and textbooks (Kern 2000).[1] Moreover, the emphasis on one end of the continuum—namely, academic genres—easily leads to essentializing views of literacy, which understand genres as more or less rigid sets of features and organizational structures, functionally coupled to particular contexts. For example, the use of nominalization—the transformation of a verb, an adjective, or an adverb into a noun phrase, for example, "the destruction of the city" for "the army destroyed the city" or "the city was destroyed"—becomes emblematic for academic writing, without considering the varied ways in which it functions as a semiotic means of concealing subjective viewpoints and creating a formal distance between author and reader (see, e.g., Halliday and Matthiesen 2004).

When genres are reified in this way, learners are not made aware of how stylistic and linguistic choices vary and what effects that might have on less structurally tangible elements of literacy such as tone, perspective, and voice (Matsuda 2001; Matsuda and Tardy 2007, 2008). They are also not encouraged to ponder how these choices are influenced by complex and emergent relationships of power, identity, and investment. What is missing is an understanding of literacy as dynamic and interactive processes of socially situated meaning making. This is the conceptual core of the multiliteracies approaches, which we outline in the following section. Our contention is that such an approach could help HL instructors and curriculum designers to integrate form, meaning, and context in the ways envisioned in postprocess approaches while also embracing the inherent complexity of language use.

MULTILITERACIES

The term "multiliteracies" was first coined by the New London Group (NLG), a collective of ten education scholars from Australia, Europe, and the United States who came together in the mid-1990s to try to redefine literacy. They were frustrated with traditional education's failure to account for the rapid changes in literacy caused by globalization, new technologies, and the increasing social and cultural diversity of local communities (NLG 1996, 63). The plural form of the term denotes both the variability and the contingency of communication in contemporary globalized societies, which are characterized by the use of new technologies and multimodal text production as well as shifting notions of discourse community and literacy practices.

A number of scholars of foreign language education have taken up the challenges posed by the NLG in their own teaching contexts (e.g., Byrnes 2005; Byrnes and Sprang 2004; Byrnes, Crane, Maxim, and Sprang 2006; Byrnes, Maxim, and Norris 2010; Kern 2000; Kramsch 2011, 2006; Swaffar and Arens 2005). Within L2 educational discussions more specifically, multiliteracies approaches are often touted as a way of creating vertical articulation across curricula that have been traditionally bifurcated into the language classes at the lower levels and the content courses at the upper division by bringing language and culture together at every level (Byrnes 2001; Kern 2000). In one of the seminal works on literacy and foreign language teaching, Richard Kern (2000, 16) offers the following working definition:

> Literacy is the use of socially, historically, and culturally situated practices of creating and interpreting meaning through texts. It entails at

> least a tacit awareness of the relationships between textual conventions and their contexts of use and, ideally, the ability to reflect critically on those relationships. Because it is purpose sensitive, literacy is dynamic—not static—and variable across and within discourse communities and cultures. It draws on a wide range of cognitive abilities, on knowledge of written and spoken language, on knowledge of genres, and on cultural knowledge.

Kern concludes that literacy must necessarily be understood as part of communication, given that we communicate through, in, about, and under the influence of texts. He identifies seven principles of literacy that ought to be integrated at every level of L2 curricula: language use, collaboration, conventions, cultural knowledge, problem solving, reflection and self-reflection, and interpretation.

Of particular importance to pedagogical implementations of multiliteracies frameworks in L2 education are three guiding notions that can aid in the developing awareness of these relationships: genres as sites of socially situated linguistic practices; the understanding of communication as "design"; and the centrality of critical awareness. In the following subsections, we discuss each of these in brief.

The Pedagogical Role of Genres and the Genre Continuum

As recognizable and sanctioned ways of getting things done with language within a particular discursive community (Martin 1985, 248; Halliday and Hasan 1989; Hyland 2007), genres link language and cultures; that is, they link the linguistic (and other semiotic) choices manifest in texts with particular contexts and conventions for their use. Genre-based pedagogies of multiliteracies in collegiate L2 education (e.g., Byrnes et al. 2006; Byrnes, Maxim, and Norris 2010; Crane 2006; Maxim 2009; Maxim et al. 2013) have tended to use the predictable structures of genres to link particular forms of expression to specific purposes, domains of interaction, and social identities. In conceiving curricula, genres are often distributed along a continuum ranging from what James Gee (2002) described as "primary discourses," ways of speaking, behaving, thinking, and using objects typical of the private domains of the home, to "secondary discourses," those more commonly encountered in the public sphere (see table 9.1). While one end of the continuum includes genres such as personal stories and informal letters, the other is populated by various forms of writing commonly marked as academic (Crane 2006; Maxim 2009). Advanced literacies—which include but are not limited to academic literacy—can and should be developed through carefully constructed encounters with texts across the genre continuum.[2]

Table 9.1: Examples of Genres on the Primary–Secondary Discourse Continuum

Primary discourse	"Blurred" discourses	Secondary discourses
casual conversation	personal ads	housing or traveling ads
picture stories	information enquiry	memos, minutes of a meeting, formal emails
cartoon strips	short descriptive texts	brochures, pamphlets, flyers
groceries lists	autobiographical accounts	users' manuals
personal narratives	recipes	invitations, thank-you notes
short personal notes	directions, short instructions	announcements, public notices
text messages	songs	business/formal letters
personal emails	poems	news reports
journal entries	rhymes	editorials
		film/book/video game reviews
		political speech
		essays, position papers, academic articles

Adapted from Byrnes, Crane, Maxim, and Sprang (2006, 94).

In his model of heritage literacy education, Martínez (2005) draws from Norman Fairclough's work in critical discourse analysis in order to suggest an alternative definition of genres as "socially available resource[s]," which are not fixed ways of realizing given social events but can be drawn upon in "complex and creative ways" (Fairclough 2003, 69; cited in Martínez 2005, 83). Challenging HL scholars and teachers to recognize the hybridity and mobility of HL communities across languages, dialects, cultures, *and* genres, Martínez argues: "We need a theory that considers how genres are disembedded and recontextualized in the life of the heritage language community; how professional discursive practices are transformed into HOMELY ones and how homely discursive practices are recast as professional ones in the lived experience of multicultural interaction and interchange" (Martínez 2005, 83, emphasis in the original). Martínez's characterization of biliterate education shares with multiliteracies approaches a sense of genre as social practice.

To develop a sense of genres as socially situated linguistic practice, learners must have opportunities not only to master the forms typical to particular genres but also to see how variable and even vulnerable genres often are in social practice. This requires more than a familiarity with the schemas and structures typical in dominant genres; curricula must also encourage critical awareness of how one takes up space in the social world through language, the social constraints at play, and the potential for transgressive and oppositional practices (even and especially in conjunction with academic writing) (see Nolden and Kramsch 1996). For example, how are childhood genres of the home (stories, folktales, songs, etc.) recontextualized when they become the object of a scholarly research paper? What is the lived experience of bringing ways of speaking encountered in the HL classroom back into the home?

Designing Meaning

Another key notion in multiliteracies frameworks that is closely linked to the creative dimension of meaning making is that of design. The design metaphor is offered as an alternative to predominant metaphors in second language acquisition and language pedagogy fields, which cast communication as the "transfer" of ready-made meanings that have been "packaged" in words through a "conduit" (Kern 2000, 47; Reddy 1979). The word design purposefully denotes both a noun and verb, a relatively stable object and a dynamic process. The NLG (1996, 74–77) describes three interrelated elements of meaning design: (1) *available designs*, the existing linguistic, cultural, and multimodal (visual, auditory, spatial, gestural) resources for meaning collectively making up a given culture's semiotic conventions and symbolic associations; (2) *designing*, the creative and transformative process of using and rearranging or combining available designs to establish certain meanings; and (3) *the redesigned*, the result of repurposing and recontextualizing existing designs (NLG 1996, 75). These three notions aid us in understanding language use as a dynamic and agentive process crucially marked by the tension between old and new (NLG 1996, 74). It is important to emphasize that these three elements are present in any and all instances of language use, which are always both derivative and unique.

In writing an op-ed for the local newspaper in Spanish on the value of HL teaching in the United States, for example, many available designs come to play at once. The learner might bring to the classroom a familiarity with newspaper genres in English and an awareness that public writing of this type requires a certain level of formality in syntax and lexical choices. At home or in the classroom, she may have also encountered examples of formal writing in Spanish or related genres such as TV news reports. In addition, the writer of this op-ed in the heritage language may have her own personal experiences with bilingual practices at home, at school, and in other spaces. She will likely also be familiar with other related discourses, for example, grand narratives of the United States as a land of immigrants and of socioeconomic opportunities or public policy debates around bilingual education, immigration reform, and multilingualism. The HL teacher could provide additional examples of op-eds in Spanish from a variety of newspapers. As she begins composing her own text, she will adopt, rearticulate, and remix these available designs in order to design her op-ed piece. The result is, as the NLG emphasizes, never simply a reproduction of available designs. Even the most generically normative op-ed language in the composition of this imagined heritage speaker takes on new meanings, that is, is redesigned within the uniquely positioned product that is the learners' homework assignment.

The "hybridity of discursive events" that are characteristic of heritage speakers' literacy practices and in which genres become "disembedded and recontextualized" (i.e., redesigned) (Martínez 2005, 83; see also Haneda and Monobe 2009, Spicer-Escalante 2005) increase the complexity of meaning design and push back on any static rules that we might ascribe to genres. To put it another way, heritage speakers draw from diverse sets of available designs as they engage in inherently translingual practices of meaning design. Language learners, including heritage learners, do not merely acquire genres that are out there in the world but redesign them through individual instantiations of meaning making. For this reason, an emphasis on form needs to be complemented by a full awareness of "the context of learners' active, imaginative, and critical involvement with their own and others' texts" (Kern 2000, 40).

THE RELEVANCE OF THE CRITICAL COMPONENT

Because meaning making is construed as creative and agentive acts of design in particular social moments, rather than as the recourse to static rules, it is inherently an interpretative and critical activity. Rather than relegating interpretation to particular stages or courses in a curriculum, multiliteracies frameworks emphasize that every act of communication requires interpretation (Kern 2000, 45). Language use involves problem solving in ways that go beyond functional goals of "getting one's meaning across"; it also involves the recognition and critical evaluation of relationships—between words and worlds, between individuals, and among stylistic and linguistic features in a text. Every choice of text design represents particular stagings of the world, positionings and beliefs, reconstructed by the reader or writer through experience, associations, and analysis. For these reasons, the multiliteracies approach necessarily integrates critical thinking at every level of instruction.

Scholarship in HL teaching and learning has more or less since its inception been concerned with the sociopolitical circumstances of learners (Fishman 2001; Valdés 1980; Van Deusen-Scholl 2003) and in this regard has maintained a steadier commitment to critical pedagogy than some other areas of language education (see Leeman and Serafini's chapter, in this volume [2016], on sociolinguistics in HL instruction; and Parra's chapter [2016] about critical pedagogy). The prizing of sociopolitical interest in heritage curricula is motivated by a critical pedagogical commitment to honor practices and stories from subaltern or minority groups within a society (Correa 2011; Faltis 1990; Leeman 2005); a multiliteracies approach can help teachers and learners to more deliberately connect these counternarratives to choices of meaning design.

In addition, in assuming collective identities for their students, teachers and curriculum designers with critical pedagogical approaches might risk limiting the scope of what might be relevant to learners (see Hislope 2003, 2–3; Jia 2009, 73). Without diminishing the value of developing heritage learners' sense of themselves as authentic and legitimate speakers of their "inherited" languages and cultures, HL curricula can acknowledge that students might also benefit from exploring how sociopolitical issues unfold in less familiar communities and settings. Multiliteracies approaches were born in part out of sensitivity to the multiplicity of rhetorical and biographical experiences that learners were bringing to the classroom. This attention to multilingualism and multiculturalism might push us to question the social and linguistic homogeneity of many L1 and L2 classrooms as well, but it is particularly relevant to the situation of heritage learners, who in some cases find themselves most "at home" in translingual and transgeneric practices (see Hashimoto and Lee 2011; Martínez 2005, 2006; Spicer-Escalante 2005, 2006). By integrating critical awareness with design, multiliteracies pedagogies promote learners' (re)construction of their hybrid or multiple identities in and across multiple genres.

IMPLEMENTING A MULTILITERACIES APPROACH IN THE HL CURRICULUM

With the pedagogical goal of realizing discourse from texts in all of their complexity and cognizant of the principles discussed in detail in the preceding sections, literacy scholars since the NLG have conceptualized four distinct but complementary curricular components, stances that can be taken up regarding a text or task, which can guide pedagogical practice. In the terms of the NLG (1996, 83–88) these are

- *Situated practice*, the immersion of learners in language use;
- *Overt instruction*, direct assistance in conceptualizing and understanding aspects of meaning design;
- *Critical framing*, conscious reflection on the available designs and their effects; and
- *Transformed practice*, opportunities to design, redesign, and reshape texts (see also Kern 2000, 135).

Although these four components are often interconnected and overlapping, the decision of which to emphasize at any given moment is an important part of instructional design. They are also importantly not conceived as part of a clear, linear sequence but can be combined in various ways to

Table 9.2: The Curricular Components of a Pedagogy of Multiliteracies

Curricular Component	Pedagogical Angle	Subcategories
Situated Practice	Experiencing	Experiencing the known
		Experiencing the new
Overt Instruction	Conceptualizing	Conceptualizing by naming
		Conceptualizing by theorizing
Critical Framing	Analyzing	Analyzing functionally
		Analyzing critically
Transformed Practice	Applying	Applying appropriately
		Applying creatively

structure and scaffold a lesson or activity. For these reasons, two members of the original NLG, Mary Kalantzis and Bill Cope (2008, 205), have proposed that these four components should rather be theorized as pedagogical "angles" that can be taken up by teachers and learners when working with texts in an educational context. As alternatives to the original components, they have suggested four active verbs that are intended to describe the most salient angle in any given pedagogical activity: "experiencing," "conceptualizing," "analyzing," and "applying" (Cope and Kalantzis 2000; Kalantzis and Cope 2008). They further divide each of these angles into two subcategories (experiencing *the known* and *the new*; conceptualizing *by naming* and *theorizing*; analyzing *functionally* and *critically*; and applying *appropriately* and *creatively*), which together reflect the movements between the conventionalized (available designs) and the creative or the new (redesigning) inherent in any act of communication.[3] Table 9.2 provides a quick overview of the curricular components from the NLG and the corresponding pedagogical angles.

Cope and Kalantzis (2000) freely admit that these four teaching foci are already present in many educational theories and practices, but they also note that they have not always been given equal importance at any given historical moment, and the relationship between them is often unclear. By naming and conceptualizing these pedagogical activities, their model helps educators to make purposeful decisions about which angle to adopt at which moment and to what ends.

In what follows, we present a sample lesson that demonstrates how these angles can be integrated into pedagogical presence. For the sake of brevity, the sample text we have chosen is a Spanish language television advertisement produced for an Argentine audience. The relative shortness of the text itself and its semiotic richness will enable us to illustrate key terms and concepts from this chapter in brief. The classroom context we have in mind is an intermediate/advanced Spanish HL class in the United States. We wish to emphasize, however, that these curricular angles are meant to be generally applicable to a variety of contexts of literacy and language teaching. We have chosen to work with television advertisements, which are easily available using the Internet, and to anchor our lesson in linguistic concepts, the imperative and the indicative, which are likely to appear in multiple teaching contexts and across various language families. Advertisements also combine linguistic with other semiotic modes and cultural expectations (here, regarding parent–children relationships), which enables us to bring to the fore work on the multiplicity of modes as well as on critical framing and the articulation of grammatical available designs with functional and social meaning making.

The TV advertisement chosen for this sample lesson was part of a promotional ad campaign for the multinational cellphone corporation Nokia, which ran in Argentina leading up to Father's Day a couple of years ago.[4] The initial short scene, shot in a realist style, takes place in a master bedroom at night and features the interaction of two young boys who wake their mother abruptly to inform her that they—and not she—will be the ones choosing their father's gift this year. In a kind but firm tone, the children insist that her misguided attempt from the previous Father's Day—a set of scented candles—might be fine for her own father, but they know better what their own dad wants. The humor of the interaction arises from the role reversal brought about by the distinctly grownup language use, which stands in contrast to the two small, pajama-clad boys at the edge of the bed.

The parodic juxtaposition of the physical appearance of the young boys and their adult discourse makes this advertisement well suited for a lesson highlighting the use of imperative and indicative forms for the establishment of authority. The creative combination of cinematography common to feature films with traditional TV ad production styles can be used to make students aware of genre mixing and the semiotic power of visual designs in combination with linguistic ones. In addition, the presence of dialectal suprasegmental features in the language of the ad related to the use of imperatives in Argentine Spanish makes it possible to integrate awareness of sociolinguistic variation with likely more accessible multimodal designs.[5] The TV advertisement, a genre that often makes use of comedic and sentimental effects in order to garner the attention and emotional investment of viewers, couches the interpersonal functions of the forms in larger sociocultural discourses of father–son relationships, gift-giving rituals, and even late capitalist advertising practices.

Assuming a group of learners for whom the indicative and imperative forms are not wholly new linguistic concepts, the first step of a multiliteracies lesson might emphasize "experiencing" the text. Students could initially view without sound just the first approximately thirty-five seconds of the ad, in which the mother and children interact. The silent viewing will allow students to speculate and "analyze functionally" what is going on in the scene: who are the participants, what are they talking about, and what might be their relationship? Students could also speculate about the genre type. In the subsequent in-class discussion, possible genres and the "clues" from the clip—that is, the stylistic and filmic features that seem to index one genre or another—could be mapped by the instructor or small groups of students onto the board or another space. The act of classifying genre features moves students gradually from "experiencing" to "conceptualizing," as they draw from their previous experiences of advertisements and other related filmic genres in order to name and describe the clip.

In a second viewing, the last ten seconds or so of the ad are revealed. Information about the Nokia phones appears in yellow print on a predominantly red screen with a square at the top right showing the father gleefully trying out his new phone. This use of visual designs—the noticing of which is facilitated by the silent viewing strategy—differs clearly from the filmic composition of the first part. As students watch the advertisement in its entirety, its generic identity becomes apparent, giving students an opportunity to reconsider their initial impressions.

After responding to these initial viewings, at which time the more macrostructural relations between participants potentially identifying the text type are addressed, students might be asked to focus on the more discrete linguistic features and their role in the design of meaning. During this third viewing, sound could be added back in and students could check their hypotheses about the relationships between individuals in the clip by looking at the language to decide whether it does or does not substantiate their answers. Alternatively, students with less experience with the language could be given examples of authoritative language (forms of address, the indicative, the imperative) and asked to identify and analyze similar expressions in the film.

Students could now begin to focus more attention on "analyzing functionally" the use of imperatives and other accompanying structures to express authority and create hierarchical relations between participants. Through this process, the relationship between formally unrelated but functionally interconnected features can be made more salient for students, for example, by showing them that in the presence of imperatives (such as *regaláselas al abuelo* [give them as a gift to grandpa] or *descansá* [rest well]), indicative forms (such as in *Este año, el regalo del día del padre lo pensamos nosotros* [This year, *we* will take care of the gift for Father's Day]) also signify command and authority. In addition to analyzing the imperative in terms of its function, distinguishing that verb form from the indicative mode, and reviewing their distinct conjugation while attentive to their interaction to make specific meanings, students will be also "conceptualizing by naming." The emphasis of pedagogies of multiliteracies on relationships is realized as the imperative is discussed in conjunction with other structures in the text, namely non-imperative forms. To further develop a functional perspective on forms, instructors could rely on students to find further examples of adult and child language, which they may organize into a matrix as they are assisted in describing the structures used in them. At this time, it may be pertinent to address the use of the Argentine dialectal variety in the stressing and morphology of imperatives. After the difference is pointed out, a discussion may be encouraged on the social value of this regional variety, and how this may compare with other dialects connoting other social identities beyond nation or region, and why (see Martínez [2016]; Leeman and Serafini [2016] for information on linguistic varieties and sociolinguistics in the HL classroom).

Relationships between the intent of the text (reflected in the genre) and the interpersonal meanings studied earlier (the challenge of parental authority) could now be addressed through the "critical focus" question (Kern 2000, 156): How does the challenge of authority in parental relationships contribute to the intents of the text? The use of parody as a creative resource may come up, by which instruction would be moving from "analyzing functionally" to "analyzing critically." Here students might also consider the role of the parody brought about through the role reversal in marketing a product, namely a cell phone plan to families on Father's Day.

In a final phase of critical analysis, students could consider critical focus questions that would help them to link the meanings around a "challenge of authority as parody" to the larger values and discourses in which the ad is used and consumed: Would the challenge of parental authority as it is performed in this ad work in communities with other values about parental relationships? Why or why not? What specific communities are you thinking of? What other ways of challenging authority would work there? How is this reflected in the linguistic choices made? The nature of the parental, including father–son, relationships implied and legitimized in this ad can also be interrogated and elicited by requesting students to write reactions to the ad impersonating members of their families or communities with a more traditional outlook on social issues of this kind. Alternatively, similar ads or other texts set in alternative sociocultural contexts may also be explored.[6]

Finally, learners can creatively and appropriately apply their knowledge and awareness of how authority is designed by creating a skit in which intergenerational authority is challenged. It is important that instructors provide ongoing intermediary prompts that remind students of the available designs they have encountered and that scaffold their design choices. For example, in a first phase, students could outline the scene setting or stage directions including the broader sociocultural context of the event (e.g., the geographical and social context and the identities of the participants); then the dialogue can be composed; finally a written or oral reflection on their narratives gives the learners space to combine the act of communication with careful reflection (see table 9.3) (see Kern 2000; Maxim 2009; Paesani, Allen, and Dupuy 2015; and Swaffar 2004, for further examples of activities).

Table 9.3: Summary of Activities Organized by Pedagogical Components

	Situated practice	Overt instruction	Critical framing	Transformed practice
First viewing of the first "filmic" part of the ad (silent)	experiencing the new (in contrast to the known)			
Speculating about the participants and their relationships			analyzing functionally	
Describing stylistic and filmic features		conceptualizing by naming		
Genre mapping		conceptualizing by theorizing		
Second silent viewing including the first and second part of the ad	experiencing the known			
Reconsidering the genre map		conceptualizing by theorizing		
Third viewing (with sound), describing linguistic forms: address, the indicative, the imperative		conceptualizing by naming		
Speculating about the relationships between the participants based on linguistic choices			analyzing critically	
"Critical focus" questions			analyzing critically	
Creating a matrix with other examples of adult/child language		conceptualizing by naming		
Interrogating parent-child relations in the film			analyzing critically	
Writing reactions to the ad from the perspectives of family and community members				applying appropriately / creatively
Composing a skit, in which intergenerational authority is challenged				applying appropriately / creatively

Note: The processes of design knowledge are indicated within the body of the table.

CHALLENGES AND PRACTICAL RECOMMENDATIONS

As can be seen in the activity proposed above, to adopt a multiliteracies approach suggests an attitudinal or perspectival shift in the classroom rather than a prescribed chronology of methodological steps or set of materials. The shift operates on the curricular level in the choice of texts and tasks, which will present learners with multiple resources—linguistic as well as other modalities—and will enable them to design meaning in creative and critical ways. A multiliteracies approach also allows teachers to recognize their own assumptions and blind spots as socially situated both in the teaching traditions and the larger sociocultural contexts in which they are inculcated so that they might take note of moments of friction, tension, and transgression as they arise in their classrooms.[7]

While authentic texts are certainly privileged in much of the scholarship in this area (Allen and Paesani 2010, 129), the HL textbook—which is arguably the most authentic genre in the classroom—can itself be the object of analysis and critical reflection as a cultural artifact with underlying assumptions, value, and relevance. Analyzing and conceptualizing the textbook or existing materials can also help alleviate the pressure to find a semester's worth of new readings while also denaturalizing the design choices and effects that went into a hybrid text, which assumes the students one of its primary audience (together with teachers and administrators).

When shifting perspectives in teaching, it is important to take small steps. With this in mind, we offer three principles for teachers interested in beginning to adopt a multiliteracies approach to HL and literacy teaching based on their existing curricula.

- *Available curricular components*: Identify which of the four curricular components laid out by the NLG (1996) are most and least addressed in current curricula and how to better articulate the connections between them—for example, by more systematically connecting the functional and critical analysis of text contents (critical framing) with the analysis and conceptualization of specific design choices (overt teaching). The curricular components can also help to identify opportunities for pedagogical sequencing in a lesson or across a unit. For example, what might be the implications of beginning a lesson with students' experience of a text versus starting with a prereading activity emphasizing genre recognition? By emphasizing design, educators can also, for example, shift the focus in transformed practice activities from adequately and appropriately applying genre norms to creativity.
- *Available texts*: The materials featured in a textbook can provide a starting point or even the backbone to a multiliteracies curriculum. Looking at the textbook, which genres are well represented and which are missing? Does the textbook focus on only one end of

the genre continuum? If so, what related genres could be included in order to draw connections across genre chains (Martínez 2005)? For example, multiple literary or written personal narratives could be supplemented with an orally performed narrative in a political public talk and a more spontaneous oral narrative from a video blog. Curriculum designers should also consider the extent to which the examples provide models for the kinds of genres students will be expected to create. A film can provide content for a scholarly essay, but it doesn't enable students to notice different design choices and how they might play out in that more academic genre. The shift to available designs rather than abstracted notions of content also means a move away from standard comprehension questions and a heightened focus on response and effect.

- *Available designs*: The grammatical foci in the textbook can often be an initial source of ideas when considering which designs to highlight; however, a multiliteracies approach pushes educators to go beyond the focus on form to focus on how meanings are designed through forms. This moves the study of grammatical forms from *what* a given structure looks like to *why* it is being used in a given context and *how* (that is, to what effect). For example, students might not only notice the use of nominalization in academic writing but also contemplate the objectifying effects of its use. Students should also be encouraged to ask how multiple designs—linguistic and otherwise—combine to shape particular meanings in a given text or genre.

FINAL REMARKS

In this chapter we have outlined a multiliteracies approach for HL teaching, which encourages teachers and learners to reflect on acts of communication as purposefully designed choices that are meaningful in particular sociocultural circumstances. Through these choices, we have argued, speakers create and in many cases recreate relationships between text components, participants, and their words and the world. We have also presented an illustration of how this model can be implemented in teaching with a mind toward angles—experiencing, conceptualizing, analyzing, and applying.

By laying bare the multiple layers of meaning at play in an act of communication, a multiliteracies approach presumes that the contexts of texts and text interpretation importantly include individual values and discourses. Encouraging and welcoming students' individual interpretations and fostering their awareness of the experiences and identities that shape their responses is of crucial importance. The movement between the sociocultural context and stylistic design, between norms and deviations, positions the multiliteracies approach to address key concerns of HL educators, including the need to prepare learners to engage with so-called genres of power while also fostering their self-possession and awareness of all of the discursive and cultural experience that they bring to the design of meaning in the languages that they have inherited.

NOTES

1. As one of the few HL teaching textbooks conceptualized along a genreapproach, Colombi and colleagues' 2007 *Palabra abierta* is interesting in this regard, in that the texts that stand in for stylistically oral, narrative language and that are contrasted with impersonal, formal academic writing are short stories—mixed genres that in some sense question the linearity of literacy development and point instead to ways in which expert writers play with the registers, styles, and modalities that we construe as oral and literate.
2. For further models proposed for individual courses within foreign language instruction, see Allen (2009), Allen and Paesani (2010), Michelson and Dupuy (2014), and Swaffar (2004). For an example of a complete language program that has been designed along a genre-based multiliteracies approach, see the Georgetown German Studies curriculum described in Byrnes and Sprang (2004).
3. See also these authors' website on a pedagogy of multiliteracies: http://newlearningonline.com. Even though it is mostly geared toward elementary education, it is rich in activities and outlines of the several elements of the multiliteracies framework, especially under the tabs "Multiliteracies" and "Learning by Design."
4. The Nokia ad was last retrieved on June 27, 2014, from https://www.youtube.com/watch?v=dzMIm90d3JI.
5. Argentine and Uruguayan Spanish stress the final syllable of imperatives in the second person singular (*regalá*, *descansá*), instead of the second to last syllable in Mexican and other Spanishes in Latin American (*regala*, *descansa*).
6. A potential expansion on aspects related to the social values projected in the ad about the place of children in parental relationships and distinct realizations of the TV genre ad can be further discussed using another ad for the Best Buy company also involving gift giving among parents and children. This ad was last retrieved on June 27, 2014, from https://www.youtube.com/watch?v=BuOGaYwfUDk.
7. It is worth noting that teachers' lack of preparation to appropriate and embrace the new views of language, literacy, and language learning entailed in pedagogies of multiliteracies has been identified as an important challenge for its implementation in collegiate foreign language teaching (Allen and Dupuy 2013; Allen and Paesani, 2010; Dupuy and Allen, 2012). Individual and departmental buy-in may be further restricted by the strong predominance of the communicative language teaching approach and the extent to which it may contradict some of the precepts embraced by the multiliteracies approach. (For these contradictions, see Kramsch 2006; Swaffar 2006; Byrnes 2006; Levine 2014). These challenges are likely to also apply to the HL context.

REFERENCES

Allen, Heather. 2009. "A Literacy-Based Approach to the Advanced French Writing Course." *French Review (Deddington)* 83, no. 2: 368–85.

Allen, Heather, and Beatrice Dupuy. 2013. "Evolving Notions of Literacy-Based Teaching: A Case Study of Graduate Student Instructors." In *Educating the Future Foreign Language Professoriate for the 21st Century*, ed. Heather Allen and Hiram Maxim, 171–91. Boston: Heinle Cengage Learning.

Allen, Heather, and Kate Paesani. 2010. "Exploring the Feasibility of a Pedagogy of Multiliteracies in Introductory Foreign Language Courses." *L2 Journal* 2, no. 1: 119–42.

Atkinson, Dwight. 2003. "L2 Writing in the Post-Process Era." *Journal of Second Language Writing* 12, no. 1: 3–15. http://dx.doi.org/10.1016/S1060-3743(02)00123-6.

Bernal-Henríquez, Ysaura, and Eduardo Hernández-Chávez. 2003. "La enseñanza del español en Nuevo México: ¿Revitalización o erradicación de la variedad chicana?" In *Mi lengua: Spanish as a Heritage Language in the United States*, ed. Ana Roca and M. Cecilia Colombi, 78–95. Washington, DC: Georgetown University Press.

Byrnes, Heidi. 2001. "Reconsidering Graduate Students' Education as Teachers: "It Takes a Department!" *Modern Language Journal* 85, no. 4: 512–30. http://dx.doi.org/10.1111/0026-7902.00123.

———. 2005. "Literacy as a Framework for Advanced Language Acquisition." *ADFL Bulletin* 37, no. 1: 11–5. http://dx.doi.org/10.1632/adfl.37.1.11.

———. 2006. "Perspectives: Interrogating Communicative Competence as a Framework for Collegiate Foreign Language Study." *Modern Language Journal* 90, no. 2: 244–46. http://dx.doi.org/10.1111/j.1540-4781.2006.00395_1.x.

Byrnes, Heidi, Cori Crane, Hiram H. Maxim, and Katherine A. Sprang. 2006. "Taking Text to Task: Issues and Choices in Curriculum Construction." *International Journal of Applied Linguistics* 152:85–110. http://dx.doi.org/10.2143/ITL.152.0.2017864.

Byrnes, Heidi, Hiram Maxim, and John Norris. 2010. *Realizing Advanced Foreign Language Writing Development in Collegiate Education: Curricular Design, Pedagogy, Assessment*. Hoboken, NJ: Wiley-Blackwell.

Byrnes, Heidi, and Katherine A. Sprang. 2004. "Fostering Advanced L2 Literacy: A Genre-Based, Cognitive Approach." In *Advanced Foreign Language Learning: A Challenge to College Programs*, ed. H. Byrnes and H. Maxim, 47–85. Boston: Heinle Thomson.

Chevalier, Joan. 2004. "Heritage Language Literacy: Theory and Practice." *Heritage Language Journal* 2, no. 1: 1–19.

Colombi, M. Cecilia. 2002. "Academic Language Development in Latino Students' Writing in Spanish." In *Developing Advanced Literacy in First and Second Languages: Meaning with Power*, ed. Mary Schleppegrell and M. Cecilia Colombi, 67–86. Mahwah, NJ: Lawrence Erlbaum.

———. 2003. "Un enfoque funcional para la enseñanza del ensayo expositivo." In *Mi lengua: Spanish as a Heritage Language in the United States*, ed. Ana Roca and M. Cecilia Colombi, 78–95. Washington, DC: Georgetown University Press.

———. 2009. "A Systemic Functional Approach to Teaching Spanish for Heritage Speakers in the United States." *Linguistics and Education* 20, no. 1: 39–49. http://dx.doi.org/10.1016/j.linged.2009.01.004.

Colombi, M. Cecilia, Jill Pellettieri, and María Isabel Rodríguez. 2007. *Palabra abierta*. 2nd ed. Boston: Houghton Mifflin.
Cope, Bill, and Mary Kalantzis. 1993. "The Power of Literacy and the Literacy of Power." In *The Powers of Literacy: A Genre Approach to Teaching Writing*, ed. Bill Cope and Mary Kalantzis, 63–89. Pittsburgh: University of Pittsburgh Press.
———. 2000. *Multiliteracies Literacy Learning and the Design of Social Futures*. London: Routledge.
Correa, Maite. 2011. "Advocating for Critical Pedagogical Approaches for Teaching Spanish as a Heritage Language: Some Considerations." *Foreign Language Annals* 44, no. 2: 308–20. http://dx.doi.org/10.1111/j.1944-9720.2011.01132.x.
Crane, Cori. 2006. "Modelling a Genre-Based Foreign Language Curriculum: Staging Advanced Learning." In *Advanced Language Learning: The Contribution of Halliday and Vygotsky*, ed. Heidi Byrnes, 227–45. London: Continuum.
Cummins, Jim. 2005. "A Proposal for Action: Strategies for Recognizing Heritage Language Competence as a Learning Resource within the Mainstream Classroom." *Modern Language Journal* 89:585–92.
Dupuy, Beatrice, and Heather Allen. 2012. "Appropriating Conceptual and Pedagogical Tools of Literacy: A Qualitative Study of Two Novice Foreign Language Teaching Assistants." In *Working Theories for Teaching Assistant and International Teaching Assistant Development*, ed. Greta Gorsuch, 275–315. Stillwater, OK: New Forums Press.
Fairclough, Norman. 2003. *Analyzing Discourse: Textual Analysis for Social Research*. New York: Routledge.
Faltis, Christian. 1990. "Spanish for Native Speakers: Freirian and Vygotskian Perspectives." *Foreign Language Annals* 23, no. 2: 117–25. http://dx.doi.org/10.1111/j.1944-9720.1990.tb00349.x.
Fishman, Joshua. 2001. "300-Plus Years of Heritage Language Education in the United States." In *Heritage Languages in America: Preserving a National Resource*, ed. Joy Kreeft Peyton, Donald A. Ranard, and Scott McGinnis, 81–98. Washington, DC: Center for Applied Linguistics.
García, Ofelia. 1993. "From Goya Portraits to Goya Beans: Elite Traditions and Popular Streams in U.S Spanish Language Policy." *Southwest Journal of Linguistics* 12:69–86.
Gee, James Paul. 2002. "Literacies, Identities and Discourses." In *Developing Advanced Literacy in First and Second Languages: Meaning with Power*, ed. Mary Schleppegrell and Cecilia Colombi, 159–76. Mahwah, New Jersey: Lawrence Erlbaum.
Halliday, M. A. K., and Ruqaiya Hasan. 1989. *Language, Context, and Text: Aspects of Language in a Social-Semiotic Perspective*. Oxford: Oxford University Press.
Halliday, M. A. K., and Christian Matthiesen. 2004. *An Introduction to Functional Grammar*, 3rd. ed. New York: Routledge.
Haneda, Mari, and Gumiko Monobe. 2009. "Bilingual and Biliteracy Practices: Japanese Adolescents Living in the United States." *Journal of Asian Pacific Communication* 19, no. 1: 7–29. http://dx.doi.org/10.1075/japc.19.1.02han.
Hashimoto, Kumi, and Jin-Sook Lee. 2011. "Heritage-Language Literacy Practices: A Case Study of Three Japanese American Families." *Bilingual Research Journal* 34, no. 2: 161–84. http://dx.doi.org/10.1080/15235882.2011.597821.
Hidalgo, Margarita. 1993. "The Teaching of Spanish to Bilingual Spanish-Speakers: A 'Problem' of Inequality." In *Language and Culture in Learning: Teaching Spanish to*

Native Speakers of Spanish, ed. Barbara J. Merino, Henry T. Trueba, and Fabián A. Samaniego, 82–93. London: Falmer.

Hidalgo, Margarita. 1997. "Criterios normativos e ideología lingüística: aceptación y rechazo del español de los Estados Unidos." In *La enseñanza del español a hispanohablantes: praxis y teoría*, ed. M. Cecilia Colombi and Francisco X. Alarcón, 109–20. Boston: Houghton Mifflin.

Hislope, Kristi. 2003. "A Reading Study of Spanish Heritage Speakers." *Reading Matrix: An International Online Journal* 3, no. 2: 1–20.

Hsu, Hsiu-Pei, Ching Lin Pang, and Wim Haagdorens. 2012. "Writing as Cultural Practice: Case Study of a Chinese Heritage School in Belgium." *Procedia: Social and Behavioral Sciences* 47:1592–96. http://dx.doi.org/10.1016/j.sbspro.2012.06.868.

Hyland, Ken. 2004. *Second Language Writing*. Cambridge: Cambridge University Press.

———. 2007. "Genre Pedagogy: Language, Literacy and L2 Writing Instruction." *Journal of Second Language Writing* 16, no. 3: 148–64. http://dx.doi.org/10.1016/j.jslw.2007.07.005.

Jia, Li. 2009. "Contrasting Models in Literacy Practice among Heritage Language Learners of Mandarin." *Journal of Asian Pacific Communication* 19, no. 1: 56–75. http://dx.doi.org/10.1075/japc.19.1.04jia.

Kalantzis, Mary, and Bill Cope. 2008. "Language Education and Multiliteracies." In *Encyclopedia of Language and Education*, ed. Nancy H. Hornberger, 195–211. New York: Springer. http://dx.doi.org/10.1007/978-0-387-30424-3_15.

Kern, Richard. 2000. *Literacy and Language Teaching*. Oxford: Oxford University Press.

Kono, Nariyo, and Scott McGinnis. 2001. "Heritage Languages and Higher Education: Challenges, Issues and Needs." In *Heritage Languages in America: Preserving a National Resource*, ed. Joyce Kreeft Peyton, Donald Ranard, and Scott McGinnis, 197–206. Washington, DC: Center for Applied Linguistics.

Kramsch, Claire. 2006. "From Communicative Competence to Symbolic Competence." *Modern Language Journal* 90, no. 2: 249–52. http://dx.doi.org/10.1111/j.1540-4781.2006.00395_3.x.

———. 2011. "The Symbolic Dimensions of the Intercultural." *Language Teaching Research* 44, no. 3: 354–67. http://dx.doi.org/10.1017/S0261444810000431.

Leeman, Jenifer. 2005. "Engaging Critical Pedagogy: Spanish for Native Speakers." *Foreign Language Annals* 38, no. 1: 35–45. http://dx.doi.org/10.1111/j.1944-9720.2005.tb02451.x.

———. 2010. "The Sociopolitics of Heritage Language Education." In *Spanish of the US Southwest: A Language in Transition*, ed. Susana Rivera-Mills and Daniel Villa, 309–18. Madrid: Iberoamericana.

Leeman, Jennifer, and Glenn Martínez. 2007. "From Identity to Commodity: Ideologies of Spanish in Heritage Language Textbooks." *Critical Inquiry in Language Studies* 4, no. 1: 35–65. http://dx.doi.org/10.1080/15427580701340741.

Leeman, Jennifer, and Ellen Serafini. 2016. "Sociolinguistics for Heritage Language Educators and Students: A Model for Critical Translingual Competence." In *Innovative Strategies for Heritage Language Teaching: A Practical Guide for the Classroom*, ed. Marta Fairclough and Sara M. Beaudrie, 56–79. Washington, DC: Georgetown University Press.

Levine, Glenn S. 2014. "From Performance to Multilingual Being in Foreign Language Pedagogy: Lessons from L2 Students Abroad." *Critical Multilingualism Studies* 2, no. 1: 74–105.

Lippi-Green, Rosina. 2012. *English with an Accent: Language, Ideology, and Discrimination in the United States*. New York: Routledge.
Martin, James R. 1985. "Process and Text: Two Aspects of Semiosis." In *Systemic Perspectives on Discourse*, Vol 1: *Selected Theoretical Papers from the 9th International Systemic Workshop*, ed. James D. Benson and William S. Greaves, 248–74. Norwood, NJ: Ablex.
Martínez, Glenn. 2003. "Classroom Based Dialect Awareness in Heritage Language Instruction: A Critical Applied Linguistic Approach." *Heritage Language Journal* 1:1–14.
———. 2005. "Genres and Genre Chains: Post-process Perspectives on HL Writing." *Southwest Journal of Linguistics* 24, no. 1–2: 79–90.
———. 2006. *Mexican Americans and Language: Del dicho al hecho*. Tucson: University of Arizona Press.
———. 2016. "Goals and Beyond in Heritage Language Education: From Competencies to Capabilities." In *Innovative Strategies for Heritage Language Teaching: A Practical Guide for the Classroom*, ed. Marta Fairclough and Sara M. Beaudrie, 39–55. Washington, DC: Georgetown University Press.
Matsuda, Paul K. 2001. "Voice in Japanese Written Discourse: Implications for Second Language Writing." *Journal of Second Language Writing* 10, no. 1–2: 35–53. http://dx.doi.org/10.1016/S1060-3743(00)00036-9.
———. 2003. "Process and Post-Process: A Discursive History." *Journal of Second Language Writing* 12, no. 1: 65–83. http://dx.doi.org/10.1016/S1060-3743(02)00127-3.
Matsuda, Paul Kei, and Christine Tardy. 2007. "Voice in Academic Writing: The Rhetorical Construction of Author Identity in Blind Manuscript Review." *English for Specific Purposes* 26, no. 2: 235–49. http://dx.doi.org/10.1016/j.esp.2006.10.001.
———. 2008. "Continuing the Conversation on Voice in Academic Writing." *English for Specific Purposes* 27, no. 1: 100–105. http://dx.doi.org/10.1016/j.esp.2007.04.002.
Maxim, Hiram. 2009. "Developing Formal Language Abilities along a Genre-based Continuum." In *Conceptions of L2 Grammar: Theoretical Approaches and their Application in the L2 Classroom, AAUSC Volume on Issues in Language Program Direction*, ed. Johanna Watzinger-Tharp and Stacey Katz, 172–88. Boston: Heinle.
Maxim, Hiram, Peter Höyng, Marianne Lancaster, Caroline Schaumann, and Maximilian Aue. 2013. "Overcoming Curricular Bifurcation: A Departmental Approach to Curriculum Reform." *Die Unterrichtspraxis / Teaching German* 46, no. 1: 1–26. http://dx.doi.org/10.1111/tger.10126.
Michelson, Kristen, and Beatrice Dupuy. 2014. "Multi-Storied Lives: Global Simulation as an Approach to Developing Multiliteracies in an Intermediate French Course." *Journal of Linguistics and Language Teaching* 6:21–49.
New London Group (NLG). 1996. "A Pedagogy of Multiliteracies: Designing Social Futures." *Harvard Educational Review* 66 (1): 60–93. http://dx.doi.org/10.17763/haer.66.1.17370n67v22j160u.
Nolden, Thomas, and Claire J. Kramsch. 1996. "Foreign Language Literacy as Oppositional Practice." In *Germanics under Construction: Intercultural and Interdisciplinary Prospects*, ed. Jörg Roche and Thomas Salumets, 61–76. Munich: Judicium.
Paesani, Kate, Heather Allen, and Beatrice Dupuy. 2015. *A Multiliteracies Framework for Collegiate Foreign Language Teaching*. Upper Saddle River, NJ: Prentice Hall.
Parra, María Luisa. 2016. "Critical Approaches to Heritage Language Instruction: How to Foster Students' Critical Consciousness." In *Innovative Strategies for*

Heritage Language Teaching: A Practical Guide for the Classroom, ed. Marta Fairclough and Sara M. Beaudrie, 166–90. Washington, DC: Georgetown University Press.
Potowski, Kim. 2011. *Conversaciones escritas: Lectura y redacción en contexto*. Hoboken, NJ: Wiley.
Raimes, Ann. 1991. "Out of the Woods: Emerging Traditions in the Teaching of Writing." *TESOL Quarterly* 19:529–34.
———. 1992. *Exploring through Writing: A Process Approach to ESL Composition*. 2nd ed. Boston: Allyn and Bacon.
Reddy, Michael. 1979. "The Conduit Metaphor." In *Metaphor and Thought*, ed. Andrew Ortony, 284–324. Cambridge: Cambridge University Press.
Schwartz, Ana María. 2003. "¡No me suena! Heritage Spanish Speakers' Writing Strategies." In *Mi Lengua: Spanish as a Heritage Language in the United States: Research and Practice*, ed. Ana Roca and M. Cecilia Colombi, 235–56. Washington, DC: Georgetown University Press.
Shin, Sarah J. 2005. *Developing in Two Languages: Korean Children in America*. Clevedon, UK: Multilingual Matters.
Spicer-Escalante, María Luisa. 2005. "Writing in Two Languages/Living in Two Worlds: Rhetorical Analysis of Mexican-American Written Discourse." In *Latino Language and Literacy in Ethnolinguistic Chicago*, ed. Marcia Farr, 217–44. London: Lawrence Erlbaum.
———. 2006. "The Use of Verbal Forms in the Spanish and English Writing Discourse of Spanish Heritage Speakers in the United States: A Contrastive Linguistic Analysis." *Río Bravo: A Journal of Borderlands* 2, no. 1: 13–24.
Swaffar, Janet. 2004. "A Template for Advanced Learner Tasks: Staging Genre Reading and Cultural Literacy through the Précis." In *Advanced Foreign Language Learning: A Challenge to College Programs: Issues in Language Program Direction*, ed. Heidi Byrnes and Hiram Maxim, 19–45. Boston: Heinle.
———. 2006. "Terminology and Its Discontents: Some Caveats about Communicative Competence." *Modern Language Journal* 90, no. 2: 246–49. http://dx.doi.org/10.1111/j.1540-4781.2006.00395_2.x.
Swaffar, Janet, and Katherine Arens. 2005. *Remapping the Foreign Language Curriculum: A Multi-Literacies Approach*. New York: Modern Language Association.
Train, Robert. 2002. "Foreign Language Standards, Standard Language and the Culture of Standardization: Some Implications for Foreign Language and Heritage Language Education." Paper delivered at the Language Consortium Conference on Language Learning and Teaching: Theoretical and Pedagogical Perspectives, Irvine, CA, May 8–9
———. 2007. "'Real Spanish': Historical Perspectives on the Ideological Construction of a (Foreign) Language." *Critical Inquiry in Language Studies* 4, no. 2–3: 207–35. http://dx.doi.org/10.1080/15427580701389672.
Urciuoli, Bonnie. 1996. *Exposing Prejudice: Puerto Rican Experiences of Language, Race, and Class*. Boulder, CO: Westview Press.
Valdés, Guadalupe. 1980. "Teaching Ethnic Languages in the United States: Implications for Curriculum and Faculty Development." *ADFL Bulletin* 11 , no. 3: 31–35. http://dx.doi.org/10.1632/adfl.11.3.31.
———. 1989. "Teaching Spanish to Hispanic Bilinguals: A Look at Oral Proficiency Testing and the Proficiency Movement." *Hispania* 72, no. 2: 392–401. http://dx.doi.org/10.2307/343163.

———. 1995. "The Teaching of Minority Languages as Academic Subjects: Pedagogical and Theoretical Challenges." *Modern Language Journal* 79, no. 3: 299–328. http://dx.doi.org/10.1111/j.1540-4781.1995.tb01106.x.

Valdés, Guadalupe, and Richard V. Teschner. 2003. *Español escrito: curso para hispanohablantes bilingües*. Upper Saddle River, NJ: Prentice Hall.

Van Deusen-Scholl, Nelleke. 2003. "Toward a Definition of Heritage Language: Sociopolitical and Pedagogical Considerations." *Journal of Language, Identity, and Education* 2, no. 3: 211–30. http://dx.doi.org/10.1207/S15327701JLIE0203_4.

Villa, Daniel. 1996. "Choosing a 'Standard' Variety of Spanish for the Instruction of Native Spanish Speakers in the US." *Foreign Language Annals* 29, no. 2: 191–200. http://dx.doi.org/10.1111/j.1944-9720.1996.tb02326.x.

———. 2002. "The Sanitizing of US Spanish in Academia." *Foreign Language Annals* 35, no. 2: 222–30. http://dx.doi.org/10.1111/j.1944-9720.2002.tb03156.x.

Yi, Youngjoo. 2008. "Voluntary Writing in the Heritage Language: A Study of Biliterate Korean-Heritage Adolescents in the US." *Heritage Language Journal* 6, no. 2: 72–93.

Zamel, Vivian. 1982. "Writing: The Process of Discovering Meaning." *TESOL Quarterly* 16, no. 2: 195–209. http://dx.doi.org/10.2307/3586792.

———. 1987. "Recent Research on Writing Pedagogy." *TESOL Quarterly* 21, no. 4: 697–715. http://dx.doi.org/10.2307/3586990.

10

Heritage Language Learner Assessment

Toward Proficiency Standards

Gabriela Nik. Ilieva and Beth Clark-Gareca
NEW YORK UNIVERSITY AND COLUMBIA UNIVERSITY

Over the last few decades, heritage language (HL) learners have taken a more prominent role in foreign language classrooms than ever before (Beaudrie 2011). With the number of HL learners on the rise, diverse language programs that specifically target a variety of students have become more and more critical (Beaudrie and Ducar 2012; Beaudrie and Fairclough 2012). This change in demographics has challenged professionals in the language education field to find new ways to meet the needs of this increasingly mixed-ability student body in language classrooms (Llosa 2014). Recognizing that the linguistic skill set that HL learners bring to the classroom is quite different from that of foreign language (FL) learners functions as a first step toward determining appropriate instruction and assessment for HL learners (Fairclough 2012a). However, there is a distinct lack of empirical studies and assessment tools related to the assessment of HL learners to guide this process (Fairclough 2012b; MacGregor-Mendoza 2012). Although many practitioners have voiced a need for distinct criteria to chart the proficiency and progress of HL learners, clear and careful articulation of these differences has been elusive thus far, resulting in the evaluation of HL learners' language skills being largely unchartered.

One cause for this difficulty in assessing HL learners rests with the tests themselves. An important component in any FL program is the use of reliable and valid assessments to monitor student achievement and guide future instruction and learning (Bachman and Palmer 1996, 2010; Brown, 2014). Many different kinds of tests have been researched in the field of foreign language—oral proficiency tests, grammar tests, computer-based tests; however, for results to be meaningful for subsequent decision making about diagnosis or placement, any test must be specifically created for a predetermined, designated group of test takers (Bachman and Palmer 1996, 2010). In most instances, language tests are designed with the needs of FL learners in mind; however, HL learners, their particular learning profiles overlooked, are usually subject to the same placement and proficiency criteria as their FL learner classmates. In the field of FL education, a backward design framework recommends that lesson objectives be designed in tandem with assessments in order to adequately measure what learners know. But if these objectives are not differentiated for the particular needs of HL learners, the meaningfulness of the assessments and the resulting scores may have serious limitations when making educational decisions for HL learners.

Many studies have examined the differences between HL learners and FL learners in terms of instruction (Beaudrie and Ducar 2005; Fairclough 2012a; Ilieva 2008, 2012; Kagan 2005; Kondo-Brown 2005). It is true that HL learners have been found to have some similar traits with FL learners (see Zyzik, this volume [2016]), especially at higher proficiency levels (Lynch 2008), although these determinations tend to lack specificity that could meaningfully guide instruction. Oral skills—for example, phonology or fluency—have been hailed as a strength of many HL learners' language production (Fairclough 2012a); however, other heritage literacy skills can lag behind insofar as these proficiencies are not well captured in available language assessments. Certainly the overall learning profile of the HL learner is quite different from that of the FL learner (Kagan and Dillon 2001, 2006; Kondo-Brown 2005), and these differences need to be examined systematically to improve assessment as a tool to measure students' linguistic proficiency as well as to guide effective classroom learning.

But to what extent are the tests available in FL classrooms appropriate and fair for measuring HL learners' proficiency? This question was posed more than a decade ago (Elder 2000) and continues to be a matter of discussion today. In a recent update, the ACTFL performance descriptors for language learners focused attention on specific changes that have transpired in classrooms since the earlier version released in 1998. This update included references to online, hybrid, and project-based learning scenarios (ACTFL 2012a, 3), but the growing numbers of HL learners and the unique linguistic features that characterize their language production were not sufficiently reflected in these new considerations. In addition to ACTFL, several other language proficiency scales, frameworks, and standards have been used in the assessment of HL learners (e.g., Foreign Service Institute rating scale, Common European Framework of Reference for Languages, the World-Readiness Standards for Learning Languages); yet there are no current models specifically created for HL learners that can adequately describe their abilities at a given level of proficiency (see Martínez, this volume [2016], for additional information on the ACTFL standards). If HL learners and FL learners represent intrinsically different populations of learners, then suggesting that the same scale can be used to evaluate both groups is problematic and will likely introduce validity concerns when attributing meaning to scores.

The goal of this chapter is, first, to offer an overview of assessment, including related definitions, theoretical concepts, assessment use, and implementation in educational contexts for HL learners. Second, a review of specific assessment types is extended, which explores how HL learners' language abilities have been assessed using the current measures available. The section initially examines the overall efficacy of proficiency tests, followed by diagnostic and placement tests when assessing FL learners and HL learners and the meaningfulness of their scores. In addition, the need for specific assessment proficiency models, including performance descriptors and guidelines specific to HL learners, is demonstrated in an effort to better meet the goals of this growing population of students. Next, innovative testing measures are presented through a discussion of multimeasure tests as alternatives to traditional testing with some examples from programs geared toward HL learners. Finally, we offer an organically integrated assessment model as a means by which to measure the proficiency levels of HL learners and their varied language abilities more completely across multiple modalities and modes of communication.

CONCEPTUAL FRAMEWORK FOR LANGUAGE ASSESSMENT

Creating a conceptual understanding of tests, their qualities, and consequences helps to frame our analysis of the specific assessment contexts in world language classrooms. Through this lens, we consider the ways that FL learners' and HL learners' language proficiency levels have traditionally been assessed, and we highlight some fundamental differences in these groups of students. In addition, we bring to light some successful practices as well as essential concerns about test-based decision making.

Lyle Bachman and Adrian Palmer (2010, 20) define language assessment as a process of collecting information on test takers' ability to determine what they know in a particular domain of language learning. This collected information is then evaluated by test administrators or teachers through a process of making value judgments and decisions (Bachman and Palmer 2010, 21). For example, if a program wants to assess students' writing ability, a writing test would be administered to those students and scored based on established criteria. Then results would be calculated and would form the basis for decision making about test takers' admission, placement, promotion, or retention within language courses. These decisions cause both intended and unintended consequences for the varied stakeholders, including programs, institutions, and individuals (Bachman and Palmer 2010). The intended consequences of tests are almost always beneficial in that a test will document learning, measure what test takers know and do not know, and provide opportunities for understanding their strengths and weaknesses. However, unintended consequences can also ensue in the form of unfounded decisions that are made based on test scores, for example, students being placed in the wrong level or mismatched instruction-to-student proficiency level.

Assessment selection and implementation in a classroom must be guided by the idea that there is no single, perfect test for any given purpose. Tests themselves cannot be considered good or bad; rather, the ways in which tests are used, for what purpose, for which audience, and to what end are the criteria upon which to determine if a test is suitable in a given context (Bachman and Palmer 2010).

Assessment decisions are often categorized as being summative or formative. Summative decisions are usually connected to student performance at the end of a unit or course, and may involve determinations related to "passing students to the next course of study, or requiring them to repeat a course" (Bachman and Palmer 2010, 197). Standardized tests, in the form of placement and achievement tests, are typically characterized as summative, in that student learning from the test is not a goal. Summative tests are usually intended to assess mastery of concepts and typically have high-stakes implications, either positive or negative, for the test taker. On the other hand, formative decisions are "intended to help students guide their own subsequent learning, or for helping teachers modify their teaching methods and materials so as to make them more appropriate" (Bachman and Palmer 2010, 197). These lower-stakes assessments are directed more toward informing future learning than evaluating skills at a given moment (Brookhart 2007; Stiggins 2007). Formative assessment is typically managed locally, and scores are not likely to be heavily consequential; rather, they provide information on learning that can be invested by both teacher and student into the next day's lesson.

Finally, keeping in mind the goals of this chapter, reliability and validity are regarded as essential considerations in the assessment process. Reliability refers to consistency of measurement, that is, a test taker's likelihood to score similarly on the same test across testing situations and contexts. Reliability is a necessary quality of meaningful language tests since, with too much inconsistency or error in measurement, the yielded results will not reflect the test taker's true abilities and will lead to faulty decisions in terms of diagnosis or placement. Validity refers to whether a test is actually measuring what we hope it is measuring or whether the interpretations made based on test scores are truly justified (Bachman and Palmer 1996). To preserve the validity of a test, Bachman and Palmer (1996, 18) have outlined several qualities of usefulness, including that a test must be developed with a particular group of test takers in mind. Designing assessments for a particular population may present quite a challenge since creating tests and quizzes from scratch can be a time-consuming endeavor that naturally affects the practicality of administration (Brown and Abeywickrama 2010). Nonetheless, if a group of students is being tested using measures that were designed for an essentially different group, the interpretations and inferences that can be made based on scores will be limited. Furthermore, if an assessment's use cannot be sufficiently justified in a particular context or with a particular population, then it should not be used (Alderson, Brunfaut, and Harding 2015; Bachman and Palmer 2010; Brown and Abeywickrama 2010) because of concerns about the validity of the subsequent inferences that will be made.

In other words, reliability and validity in assessment are directly related to the testing of a specific student population, and since the HL learner field is at an emerging stage, clearly the assessment of the HL learners is still being explored. Because of the insufficiency of examples of tests created exclusively for this group of learners and a general lack of HL learner–specific testing guidelines, accurate and specific measurement of HL learner language proficiency is an area that requires more discussion and research.

TYPES OF TESTS BASED ON USE

Proficiency Tests

Oral proficiency assessment is particularly important in the education of HL learners because of its emphasis not only in education but also in other public sectors such as business, nongovernmental organizations, health care, banking, and government. The fact that oral skills are the main focus of many HL learner examinations is understandable. It derives directly from the HL learners' history of language acquisition. Because HL learners start acquiring language through aural interaction at home or among a community of speakers in naturalistic settings, their linguistic knowledge is generally implicit and intuitive. Migration circumstances, age, intensity and volume of exposure, the family's or individual's commitment to preserve the language, motivation to use the language, attitudes, academic and personal interests, and many other variables determine the linguistic abilities of these learners (Lacorte and Canabal 2002; Potowski 2010; also see Zyzik, this volume [2016] for more information about HL learner profiles and type of knowledge). Many studies have shown that, despite their strengths in oral language, HL learners do not always develop extensive literacy, grammatical accuracy, and other language modalities (Fairclough Belpoliti, and Bermejo 2010; Potowski and Carreira 2004; Valdés 2006).

The ACTFL oral proficiency interview (OPI) is often conducted in formal learning environments to assess oral proficiency. A standardized procedure for global assessment of functional speaking ability, an OPI is conducted in a face-to-face, video, or telephonic interaction. During an interview process between an examiner and a test taker, an ACTFL-certified examiner attempts to discover a speaker's proficiency level by establishing a baseline (referred to as the "floor") as a starting point for the interview. By moving into increasingly difficult topics of conversation and structures by which to discuss them (referred to as "spiraling up"), the examiner tests and probes a test taker's abilities by uncovering linguistic areas in which complete mastery has not yet been attained (referred to as "breakdown"). At this point the examiner notes the student's upper range of linguistic ability (referred to as the "ceiling") and then concludes the interview (ACTFL 2012b; Swender and Vicars 2012). It is a criterion-referenced evaluation, and rating procedures are based on the ACTFL Proficiency Guidelines (ACTFL 2012c), which describe five major levels—Novice, Intermediate, Advanced, Superior, and Distinguished—each with a low, mid, and high sublevel, except in the case of the highest level (for detailed information, consult Swender and Vicars 2012).

Although measures like the OPI may be used within college programs to assess FL proficiency, the standardization of determining oral language ability differs widely from institution to institution. At times, students' language levels are established through an informal conversation with a proficient interlocutor. At other times, the ACTFL OPI or an OPI-like interview may be administered, which in many cases, for practical reasons, are conducted by informally trained, uncertified teachers. The fact that high-stakes decisions are made based on variably rated tests raises a reliability concern in the consistency of scores. For scores to be reliable, raters must receive consistent training so they can agree on an interpretation of the scale (called "norming") and eventually arrive at a score that can be justified according to established benchmarks. In the absence of rater training, scores tend to have characteristics of individual rater interpretation. This process almost always results in bias, which, if not held in check, may lead to an inaccurate understanding of a student's proficiency.

To gain insight into differences in rating practices between HL learners and FL learners, a study, supported by STARTALK was conducted as part of the annual Hindi and Urdu ACTFL OPI training at New York University.[1] For this study, data were collected through audio-recorded practice interviews with fifty college students conducted by teacher-trainees during two four-day workshops in 2011 (Ilieva 2012). The goal was to examine the characteristics of the oral performance of Hindi and Urdu HL learners and compare them with those of the FL learners when rated at the Intermediate level on the ACTFL scale. Intermediate is the most common proficiency level rating during these practice interviews, and in many cases, it is the HL learners' usual entry-level into formal language education among Hindi and Urdu speakers. Certain important differences were discovered in the oral production of these two groups regarding the following assessment criteria: (a) functions and global tasks referring to what learners do with the language; (b) content/context comprising the circumstances or setting; (c) components of accuracy including fluency, grammar, sociolinguistic and pragmatic competence, and vocabulary; and (d) text type related to speech organization and quantity (Swender and Vicars 2012, 11–14).

Findings suggested that the HL learners tended to be more skilled navigators or survivors in interactive situations within the test. This characteristic is likely attributable to the prevalent personal engagement with the target culture through their family, which allowed the HL learners to be more skillful in negotiating ambiguity and using guessing strategies. Students' linguistic performance was described using the framework of the three modes of communication—interpretive, interpersonal, and presentational (ACTFL 2012a). In the interpersonal mode, HL learners were generally able to hold on and did not display linguistic breakdown when speaking to others, whether complications were introduced or not. However, when HL learners in the study were given a task engaging the presentational mode, the ceiling was more easily established. In contrast, the interviewers established the FL learners' ceiling more easily through the interpersonal mode of communication.

Second, the HL learners consistently opted to speak about personal topics in which they could perform relatively well. Because their prior language learning had taken place primarily in the domestic environment around family and friends, they demonstrated more intuitive insider knowledge of religious festivals and elements of popular culture such as music, fashion, cinema, social habits, and customs. In spite of the interviewers' attempts to rephrase the questions in a more formal style and to veer the discussion toward sociological, historical, or media topics, references to personal and kinship experiences dominated the discussion, resulting in the test taker consistently using a colloquial register. This pattern of interaction presented challenges to the raters in the probing of higher proficiency levels. On the other hand, the FL learners in the study tended to independently choose to speak about academic topics related to their studies, directing the discussion toward geography, history, or politics, which they frequently could not sustain due to a lack of language skills. In these cases, the interviewers often attempted to bring the conversation back to more personal contexts in order to establish their floor.

Third, the HL learners' articulation and intonation were characterized by native-like intraphrase articulation and intonational contours as well as by ellipsis, interjections, body gestures, interphrasal pauses, and readymade chunks of language. HL learners tended to pay less attention to monitoring grammatical and linguistic accuracy; they seemed to have an intuitive sense of the language in terms of what was correct or understandable and often used guessing strategies and native-like space fillers. In addition, they used simplification, circumvention, approximation and avoidance strategies (lexical, syntactic, topic), stalling and time-gaining techniques as well as code-switching or code-mixing, as is typical of urban native speakers. They sounded fluent and showed control over complex syntactical structures and discourse strategies usually considered indicative of Intermediate High level or above (ACTFL 2012c). At the same time, however, they lacked a mastery over basic morphological forms and structures, such as subject-verb agreement in present tense or noun-adjective agreement, which are usually produced with some consistency at Novice High or Intermediate Low levels. Conversely, FL learners tended to sound less fluent because their articulation and intonation were characterized by phonological features that carried English language characteristics. They tended to use fewer interjections and body gestures, and, while speaking, they created newly developed strings of discrete elements and, hence, used more intraphrase pauses. Throughout their interviews, they monitored their accuracy consciously through self-correction and frequently used repetitions and false starts within the course of the oral performance. Unlike the HL learners, they did not use simplification; in fact, they even caused complication during the conversation. They tended to use more silence instead of fillers and did not resort to English code-switching to keep their speech flow. At times they exhibited signs of hesitation, frustration, or embarrassment and gave nonverbal signals or explicit language to discontinue a topic or made requests for reiteration and reformulation.

Considering this particular context and the prevalence of the OPI in the field of language assessment, the question becomes: how well do established scales of evaluation capture the distinctions between FL learners and HL learners? Looking first to the performance indicators from ACTFL, the specifications explicitly identify the target population: "The ACTFL Performance Descriptors for Language Learners are designed to describe language performance that is the result of explicit instruction in an instructional setting" (ACTFL 2012a, 3). Since it is well documented that HL learners do not first acquire their language in an instructional setting, the appropriateness of these descriptors, which have been designed for FL learners, seems doubtful when evaluating most HL learners' language proficiency.

Similarly, the OPI Familiarization Manual effectively sidesteps an explicit division between HL learners and FL learners in the ways language learners acquire their skills. It states: "The OPI assesses language proficiency in terms of a speaker's ability to use the language effectively and appropriately in real-life situations. *It does not address when, where, why, or the way in which a speaker has acquired his/her language*" (ACTFL 2012b, 4, italics added). This statement suggests that these assessment criteria function equally well for all test takers, HL learners and FL learners alike. The fact that these measures have been designed to describe the abilities of FL learners likely explains, at least in part, the difficulties in administration and score interpretations for HL learner populations. Failure to consider or recognize the identifying features of HL learners' language calls into the question the utility and validity of these measures when assessing them.

Along the same lines, the ACTFL Proficiency Guidelines (ACTFL 2012c) do mention the strengths and weaknesses particular to the HL learner profile in a general way in relation to the interpretive, interpersonal, and presentational modes of communicative competency:

> The modes of communication provide educators of heritage speakers with a useful analytical tool to determine an instructional emphasis. Interpersonal communication and interpretive listening tend to be strengths for many heritage speakers. At the same time, some heritage speakers may benefit from focused support in the modes of presentational writing and interpretive reading if prior language experiences were not in an instructional setting (ACTFL 2012c, 13).

The acknowledgment of the established learning profiles of HL learners is encouraging; nonetheless, parallel, discrete descriptors describing the unique learning characteristics of HL learners along the four modalities of speaking, listening, reading, and writing would be a welcome next step in test design. With similar goals in mind, insightful studies have been conducted based on ACTFL-UCLA Heritage Language Project, whose specific objectives were to assess the appropriateness of OPI testing for HL learners to correlate their linguistic, educational, and experiential background with their speaking proficiency. They also progressed toward identifying the specific linguistic features that prevent HL learners from being rated at the next higher proficiency level (Martin, Swender, and Rivera-Martinez 2013; Swender et al. 2014).

Clearly, more investigation into whether and how these scales adequately assess the broad spectrum of FL abilities is warranted. Specifically, new research is needed to inform the ACTFL performance descriptors to differentiate between HL learners and FL learners by offering descriptions of what the two groups of learners tend to do more or less of at each proficiency level, in each mode of communication, and in each comprehension and comprehensibility domain—that is, language control, vocabulary, communication strategies, and cultural awareness. This research will stimulate teachers to design multidimensional tasks and foster learning environments based on differentiation according to the student profiles in their mixed-abilities classroom. By pinpointing the specific features exhibited by HL learners and designing logical scope and sequence progressions exclusively for them, HL learning and assessment needs will be more precisely addressed.

Looking to other types of tests, some HL programs have adapted existing HL learners nonspecific standardized computer tests for the purposes of determining proficiency levels. One example of these tests is the Computerized Assessment of Proficiency (CAP), validated for grades 7–16 for Arabic, Chinese, French, German, Hebrew, Hindi, Japanese, Persian, Spanish, Swahili, Turkish, Urdu, and Yoruba (CASLS 2008). As yet, there are no such tests for other heritage languages, such as South Asian languages (e.g., Bengali, Punjabi, Tamil) or Central Asian languages (e.g., Uzbeki,

Tajik, Armenian). There are several other computer-based standardized proficiency tests of Spanish, Korean, Japanese, and other languages with listening, grammar, and reading comprehension sections. These tests are largely composed of selected-response and multiple-choice tasks, and in some cases they require the speaking and writing sections to be completed online and rated by human raters (see Fairclough 2012a; Kondo-Brown 2005).

CAP allows technological innovations to assist in the process of assessing students' language ability. Computer-adapted tests (CAT) are tests that are individualized by ability level with differentiated item order based on whether a test taker produces a correct answer. A moderately easy item is the starting point; if a student answers correctly, the next item will be at a similar or more difficult level. This model of increasing difficulty is followed until the questions inevitably become too difficult for a particular test taker and a level is established (Brown and Abeywickrama 2010).

CATs have many advantages for HL learners' testing. The individualized nature of the tests can better identify HL learners' learning strengths and weaknesses by zeroing in on a level more precisely than typical multiple-choice and other selected-response tasks. CAT testing may provide a platform in which greater information about student proficiency can be gained through ready-made, highly practical, multiple-choice computer assessment.

Nonetheless, selected-response formats should be supplemented by constructed response tasks such as those required in speaking and writing. In fact, studies have revealed that HL learners are more test-wise and have more skills to predict and guess answers correctly, scoring particularly high on tests that focus on the traditionally receptive skills of reading and writing (Kondo-Brown 2005; Kondo-Brown 2010; McGinnis 1996). In addition, test administrators should be cautious when giving tests that are focused on evaluating only one set of skills since they cannot provide ample evidence for what HL learners can do with the language in real contexts.

Diagnosis and Placement Tests

Diagnostic and placement procedures are widely documented and debated in the field of HL education (Harding, Alderson, and Brunfaut 2015; Fairclough 2012a, 2012b; Fairclough, Belpoliti, and Bermejo 2010; Tucker 2005). Diagnostic assessment focuses on evaluating learners' strengths and deficiencies and is set apart from other types of assessment (Alderson et al. 2015). In fact, diagnostic tests have been said to focus more attention on weaknesses of test takers than on strengths, which can be seen as different from the goal of proficiency tests (Alderson and Huhta 2011). Placement assessment is typically implemented to sort candidates into different levels of programs of instruction. Although the uses of diagnostic and placement tests seem intuitive, there is a great deal of complexity surrounding this debate.

J. Charles Alderson and colleagues (2015) have said that diagnostic assessment has been "inadequately theorized" (1), and point out that proficiency tests are often used in diagnostic or placement capacities, suggesting that the delineations between the uses of proficiency, diagnosis, and placement tests are not easily defined or mutually exclusive.

In placement assessment specifically, its ultimate purpose is to serve as a tool to decrease the diversity in the language classrooms and provide more responsive instruction for students with more homogeneous abilities and interests (Carreira 2012; Otheguy and Toro 2000). Procedures for placing FL learners in language levels tend to be more formulaic than for HL learners, especially when the students have little to no knowledge of the foreign language before they come to class. The FL learner profile is more definable and measurable, especially since these students are often categorized as brand new beginners and in general are frequently placed in the first level of FL study. Nonetheless, some FL learner variability can be attributed to linguistic experiences from other educational institutions or from language study abroad, which can result in appropriate placement of these students in higher levels. In these cases, their learner profile is often determined based on a few specific and quantifiable factors, such as number of years or semesters of study, number of courses completed, number of hours per week, or number of textbook chapters and material covered. In addition to collecting this information, programs use tests designed in the context of the so-called micro or bottom-up framework of instruction and curricula development to evaluate their language skills (Celce-Murcia and Olshtain 2000; see Carreira, this volume [2016], for an explanation of micro versus macro approaches).

In addition, form-focused assessment has been shown to be beneficial (Spada and Lightbown 2008), especially when making placement decisions; however, more research is needed to establish the best strategies to integrate form-focused assessment into HL classrooms. One criticism of form-based, discrete point assessment is that it is not authentic; that is, it does not represent any task that a language learner will need to complete in the target language-use domain (Bachman and Palmer 2010, 60). Perhaps the best way to develop and evaluate HL learners' language skills is by engaging them in authentic contexts that enrich their cultural and global competency. Ideally, grammatical assessment needs to be integrated into real-life performance tasks (Norris et al. 1998; Sandrock 2010), which is possible by transforming real-life tasks into pedagogical ones, especially in the case of HL learners (Polinsky and Kagan 2007; Kagan and Dillon 2001). These practices will assist in the placement of HL learners in appropriate learning levels.

Placement of HL learners within programs, however, can be a complex process since individual learner profiles can be difficult to define and diagnose. HL learners' language learning profiles, including their history, language-use habits, and culture, illustrate the wide range of diversity and language skills that they have already developed before starting their formal education. Although there are common threads in the understanding of HL learners' profiles, HL learners themselves form a heterogeneous group with many subgroups representing a wide spectrum of skills (for a detailed profile of the HL learners, see Zyzik, this volume [2016]). In the last two decades, in an attempt to separate HL Learners from FL learners, numerous programs in the United States have developed placement tests for HL learners as a necessary and essential first step toward their formal language study. Some institutions, in response to larger registration numbers, use placement practices to further sort and group HL learners with a similar level of proficiency together, allowing for instruction and assessment to be more keenly directed toward students' needs.

There is no doubt that diagnosis and placement of HL learners have emerged as central points of discussion among HL professionals, although dwelling on whether a test is intended to identify strengths (Kagan 2005; Polinsky and Kagan 2007) or to unveil deficiency and diagnose weaknesses (Alderson et al. 2015; Alderson and Huhta 2011) may not be a meaningful exercise. Rather, looking toward how language assessment sensitive to HL learners' needs can best inform curriculum design, instruction, and student autonomy (Brown and Abeywickrama 2010; Fairclough 2012b; Fairclough et al. 2010), with HL learners' needs at the forefront, may be the next dynamic frontier in language teaching and learning.

NEW DIRECTIONS IN HL LEARNER ASSESSMENT

The Role for Multiple-Measure Tests

To broaden the accuracy of assessment for all language learners, many institutions have adopted or developed alternative examinations to selected-response tasks (Fairclough 2011). These newly conceptualized tests (e.g., Carreira 2012; Kagan 2005; Thompson 2014) are often composed of tasks allowing for multiple linguistic competencies to be measured to ascertain a test taker's true abilities. What exactly these components need to be and how assessments can be designed to measure HL learners' particular learning profiles accurately are still in exploratory phases; however, these studies are worthy of discussion because they reflect an effort to outline the most effective components of placement assessments, which are designed by taking into account and factoring in the unique and complex profile of the HL test takers, their attitudes, and their motivations (Beaudrie and Ducar 2005).

In a recent study, Gregory Thompson (2014) described a complex placement procedure for Spanish HL learners at the university level. It included a survey with ten questions, followed by a test with three sections—(a) Language Awareness, with ten questions about general language knowledge answered in English or Spanish; (b) Bilingual Skills, with translation of ten sentences targeting specific language structures; and (c) Short Composition. The study revealed that, measured against the results of the test, the questionnaire itself is a reliable tool, especially because it collects information distinguishing between specific domains that HL learners are exposed to as well as the contexts in which they use the language. Thompson (2014, 18) concludes that "productive use of language is definitely a determinant of language level and thus, could be used for placement even in self-reported data."

Another multicomponent exam for HL learners has been suggested as a reliable measure of proficiency (Kagan 2005). It includes an oral interview, informed by the OPI as designed by ACTFL, a biographic questionnaire, and a short essay for Russian learners with some literacy. This is similar to the exam for Spanish HL learners described by María Carreira (2012) in which the third component is an essay based on a reading prompt to assess reading skills as well.

Based on the analysis of student oral and written production during the placement test administered to Russian HL learners, Olga Kagan (2005) provides evidence that even the least proficient group of Russian HL learners displays abilities in global competency. Her findings suggest that these HL learners can handle some real-world listening and speaking tasks from the very beginning, grammar mistakes and limited vocabulary notwithstanding. Her study shows that besides producing relatively rapid fluent speech, "HL learners can perform globally, on a macro level, i.e., negotiate meaning in a large variety of situations," that students' overall competence demands a curriculum guided by a macro approach, characterized by "cognitively rich, global tasks" (Kagan 2005, 218). Most importantly, Kagan advocates for the macro approach to be used both in assessment and in curricular design for the HL classroom. This design involves the employment of top-down strategies in the language teaching of even discrete language elements, representing a departure from a traditional micro or bottom-up approach most used in the FL classroom (Shrum and Glisan 2010; Celce-Murcia and Olshtain 2000).

Furthermore, two measures have been suggested as predictors of proficiency across different heritage languages (Polinsky and Kagan 2007). Speech rate, defined by words per minute in spontaneous speech, and lexical proficiency, based on the Swadesh two-hundred-word basic vocabulary list, were found to predict different aspects of proficiency. The Swadesh list includes pronouns, basic verbs, a few conjunctions and adverbs, and nouns related to geography, food, clothing, body parts, and time, among others. The first component is focused on speech rate by prompting the use of global speaking skills. The second component entails a discrete-item test, which is also a reliable and measurable tool. Placement assessments that include evaluation of the HL learners' lexical knowledge have yielded valid results especially in the case of lower proficiency level learners (Fairclough 2011).

In relation to the HL learners' distinct linguistic profile, Marta Fairclough (2012a) asserts that, ideally, tests need to focus on the students' receptive, productive, and creative abilities and that "the holistic approaches leaning towards authentic, open-ended types of assessment would be more appropriate for HL learners given the naturalistic fashion in which they usually acquire the HL" (2012a, 126). She also suggests that a balance of both approaches will produce the most complete picture: open-ended tasks (e.g., essay, oral interview) are useful measures to evaluate what students can do, whereas discrete items (e.g., fill in the blanks) address particular aspects of the language and probe problematic areas (Fairclough 2012b, 263). These multimodal tests are particularly relevant when assessing HL learners because they tap into HL learners' unique linguistic formation in more comprehensive ways and provide a larger picture of what HL learners can already do and suggest directions for where instruction and assessment should point next.

Performance-Based Assessment as a Formative Model

Formative assessment, often conceptualized as a classroom model of assessment with a larger goal toward learning (Brookhart 2007; Stiggins 2007), consists of multiple modes for evaluation to assess individual competencies. Carreira (2012) supports this notion by arguing that varied and rigorous formative assessment deals efficiently with student diversity in HL classes. Her list of most effective strategies in formative assessment in the HL classroom supports these efforts: (1) ongoing feedback, (2) flexibility and effort reward system, (3) authentic texts used as standard for quality and multiple assessors, and (4) reflection on one's own learning (Carreira 2012, 104–105). Implementing academic tasks such as journals, portfolios, surveys, oral interviews, exit cards, presentations, and re-do assignments provides a platform through which regular and detailed feedback can be given to both students and teachers. By engaging in these formative tasks, guidance, practice, and preparation toward performance on larger summative assessments can be incorporated into regular classroom activities. These formative assessment tools and the decisions based on students' performance establish what and how students learn and inform the instructors about strategies and activities that work and don't work. Formative tasks allow for teachers to not only grasp differences among the HL learners' command of grammar, familiarity with formal registers, attitudes and goals but also to "attend to them, and afford them due recognition" (Carreira 2012, 104).

Performance-based tasks can easily be used with HL learners in formative ways. Assessing language use through simulations of real-world tasks can accompany standardized examinations and allow for linguistic competencies to be tested in more authentic ways (Brown and Abeywickrama 2010). By implementing low-stakes performance tasks in class, teachers can create an excellent learning environment that boosts student motivation and positive attitudes toward learning the language.

Two projects directed toward HL learners' language proficiency have been designed around formative performance assessment. Kean University's STARTALK Intensive Summer program for Hindi and Urdu, housed in the School of Global Education and Innovation, uses global project-based learning with secondary or early postsecondary HL learners. In this curriculum, learners' proficiency levels are challenged daily through activities such as creating storyboards, conducting daily Skype meetings and interviews, and preparing TED Talks related to issues of activism, human rights, and sustainability. The final task is to use newly acquired language, information, and ideas and to present a product to an audience of community members and invited dignitaries. The goal of this project is ultimately to heighten awareness, advocate, and promote culturally sensitive, viable solutions to these issues. Students' progress toward performing these tasks is monitored through extensive formative assessment and abundant feedback through the development of their multimodal performances. Clearly, student work is performed in interpretive, interpersonal, and presentational modes of communication, which has been determined as the most effective sequence in student learning (Clementi and Terrill 2013) and is assessed in appropriate ways according to these modes.

Similarly, Hindi HL learners at New York University have shared enthusiasm for project-based learning (Ilieva 2008). In this model, group projects are built through using authentic materials, in most cases a combination of a classical text and related film in Hindi. The formative assessment is a continuous, multipronged process resulting from the efforts of teamwork. Rubric- and checklist-based assessment; self, peer, and teacher reviews; reflective journals; and community partners' feedback all play an important role in a formative evaluation process. At the end of the project, each learner submits her portfolio, including all the notes, homework, essays, assignments, redos, journal entries, checklists, and written script for the final project. These portfolios are then assessed holistically for completeness, richness, and effort, and they inform further instruction toward the next project design and student role distribution.

These examples provide a context in which to think about performance assessment as authentic assessment, especially in its foregrounding of formative assessment through learner-centered, project-based tasks. By integrating language, culture, and content and by requiring the use of authentic materials and real language in the target language-use domain, HL learners can progress in their developing proficiency. These programs illustrate the kind of performance that can distinguish the linguistic proficiency that HL learners possess from that of their FL learner counterparts and can address the gaps and weaknesses in their language though real-world tasks.

RECOMMENDATIONS AND SUGGESTIONS

This chapter has drawn attention to some of the current gaps between valid and reliable assessment practices and HL learner populations. As the number of HL learners in FL classrooms rises, the tools and scales used to evaluate HL learner proficiency must be further honed in order to describe the specific needs and competencies of this particular group of learners. Here we make a series of related recommendations at the intersection of HL learner assessment and instruction.

Beginning with the ACTFL Training Manual and Proficiency Guidelines and their application to the HL field, we offer the following suggestions:

- The ACTFL Proficiency Guidelines for each language need to be expanded to address the distinction between FL learners and HL learners, including a comparative description of the oral performance of HL learners versus that of FL learners at each proficiency level. These guidelines should also address each assessment criterion—namely, task types and functions, context and content areas, accuracy, and text type.
- The guidelines need to include detailed separate outlines for HL learners and FL learners of breakdown characteristics during OPI testing.
- The ACTFL OPI Manual needs to offer differentiated strategies for raters in terms of level checks and probes used to establish ceiling and floor when testing HL learners.
- Modifications to OPI training are also needed to include a discussion and sampling of HL learner and FL learner interviews to further facilitate the process of rating and rater norming.

By developing more extensive guidelines, proficiency levels of HL learners can be more precisely captured, which will help language programs meet the needs of these learners. These modifications and additions will allow the OPI to be a more accurate measure of HL learners' skills and will lead to better decision making based on scores.

Finally, given the heterogeneous nature of the HL learner population, we propose an organically integrated assessment model for the evaluation of HL learner language skills. This model is a responsive selection of assessment measures implemented to uncover or highlight nuances of HL learner language proficiency that are not sufficiently captured in more formal assessments. It incorporates multiple modality assessment strategies and is constituted by the following principles:

1. Centrality of authentic contexts: Assessment of HL learners should be integrated when possible in project-based, performance-based, and/or student-centered learning that is consistently anchored in real-life contexts. HL learners' performance quality should be purposefully and methodically

modeled after and measured against authentic samples, with emphasis on raising awareness toward variety of registers and styles.

2. Multiplicity of measures: Assessment of HL learner language proficiency should integrate a variety of strategies to efficiently gather evidence to support claims of language learners' ability. Rigorous, formal and/or informal assessment tools should be employed for diagnostic and placement purposes, as well as throughout the course of instruction, to evaluate HL learners' diverse skills, knowledge, proficiencies, and progress.

The following components should be considered when designing such a model of assessment. They can be compiled in a student portfolio and inform programmatic decisions related to HL learners.

A. Questionnaires focused on students' unique backgrounds. These documents can provide a lot of pedagogically significant information related to place of birth, age of acquisition of English and/or of the target language, language(s) spoken at home, amount of schooling, situations when target language is used, and expectations for what the student wants to learn and expectations for difficulty. These questionnaires can provide a context for learning and guide appropriate assessment.

B. Essays to assess literacy skills. The prompts can elicit writing on a variety of topics. One suggestion is within the narrative genre—for example, an open-ended essay question about family, school, or a favorite celebration. Another suggestion is an essay responding to one or more reading prompts that requires an integration of language learning skills. These should be evaluated according to established criteria of writing and must be closely aligned to the purposes of the program.

C. The Swadesh list. If the specific language program or institution has a developed lexical proficiency test based on the Swadesh list for that language, this test can be a possible source of proficiency information as well.

3. Diversity of feedback: Abundant formative feedback based on varied samples of students' performance and ongoing guidance should be integrated in the process of teaching and learning. In addition, feedback needs to be provided from multiple sources including instructors, peers, self, and native-speaking partners. The native speaker relationships can be fostered through in-person connections in the home heritage community or through technologically assisted connections through virtual partnerships or online pen pals from the target country.

4. Reliance on research: A descriptive taxonomy of the categorical strengths and weaknesses of HL learners in language learning needs to be developed. If the learning profiles of HL learners are truly distinct from that of FL learners, then the intrinsic characteristics of these profiles need to be determined through large-scale data collection of HL learners' language learning skills at various stages of their language acquisition processes. If consistent linguistic patterns emerge in the participants, then valuable targeted instruction and assessment could easily follow.

These principles and strategies are important not only for assessment but also for pedagogy in that they support the quality of HL assessment and education in general. Varied, contextually embedded tests allow HL learners the opportunity to display their linguistic abilities by performing authentic global tasks before starting training in a formal classroom and throughout their language study.

CONCLUSIONS

Evaluating student achievement, performance, and proficiency in appropriate ways is an integral part of any language classroom or program. Assessment informs practitioners, researchers, learners, and various stakeholders at all stages of the learning process. It supports language educators to diagnose what learners can do with the language, to identify what they have learned and what needs to be worked on, and to provide feedback or to place them in a course continuum. It reveals how effective both classroom practices and instruction are in meeting the curricular goals and advises how to further facilitate and advance student learning. Assessment also provides the basis for a constructive dialogue with relevant stakeholders, such as parents, schools, community members, and professionals about instructional needs, funding, and policy decisions. In addition, it allows students to know what language skills they have and what kind of progress they have made, to set up personal goals, to gain confidence and motivation, and to become independent learners (Bachman and Palmer 2010; Cohen 1994; Shrum and Glisan 2010).

Undoubtedly, the HL field has made great progress to better understand the HL learners' language abilities in relation to the specific domains and settings of their language acquisition. These positive steps have improved assessment and classroom practices tremendously for HL learners as a whole. New innovations are being explored as to how to expand the notion of testing into arenas of real-life communicative situations and exploratory tasks, purposefully measured against authentic oral and written texts. These models involve self-, peer, instructor, and community evaluation based on criteria articulated in rubrics created specifically for HL learners.

Nevertheless, plenty remains to be explored as to how to better address HL learners' needs, especially in the area of assessment of HL learner–specific language abilities. Research focused on what HL learners and FL learners do similarly and differently needs to inform existing language proficiency frameworks and scales that are created for the FL students but are currently used to assess HL learners as well.

The organically integrated assessment model suggested in this chapter offers a more robust picture of HL learners' abilities in the target language. By measuring HL learners' competencies through multiple measures in real-life contexts and giving abundant feedback, instructors will be more informed when planning what kind of instruction, topics, and structures they need to present to HL learners next. This model also leaves room for future large-scale studies to develop a more consistent diagnostic profile of HL learner strengths and weaknesses, which will inform both instructional and assessment procedures implemented specifically for HL learners. Having more information about students' proficiency from a variety of different sources will improve the reliability and validity of the inferences made. All of these deliberate measures will function to reduce the unintended consequences of incorrect HL learner placement in language programs or HL learner frustration with language learning as a whole.

Future assessment projects also need to take into account the growing numbers of HL learners in foreign language classrooms and differentiate consistently in content and procedures for HL learners and FL learners. More research needs to be conducted relating to how assessment measures can be affected by HL learners' specific attitudes, motivations, and aptitudes. Furthermore, language-specific research needs to identify collectively the most common combinations of language abilities and strengths of HL learners to subsequently inform how to meet students' needs. Creating these models will bring us a better understanding of HL learner learning pathways and give practitioners and assessment specialists the tools to design assessments especially for HL learner populations. Continued efforts to improve existing practices and develop new valid assessment tools will naturally lead to better learning environments for all learners. After all, successful students with excellent outcomes are the best ambassadors of HL education.

NOTE

1. STARTALK is a federal grant currently supporting eleven critical languages, managed by the National Foreign Language Center at the University of Maryland, a national program for critical language education K–16, professional development for critical language teachers, and resources for the world language teaching and learning field.

REFERENCES

ACTFL. 2012a. "Performance Descriptors for Language Learners." http://www.actfl.org/sites/default/files/pdfs/PerformanceDescriptorsLanguageLearners.pdf.

———. 2012b. "ACTFL Oral Proficiency Interview Familiarization Manual." http://www.languagetesting.com/wp-content/uploads/2012/07/OPI.FamiliarizationManual.pdf.

———. 2012c. "ACTFL Proficiency Guidelines." http://www.actfl.org/sites/default/files/pdfs/public/ACTFLProficiencyGuidelines2012_FINAL.pdf.

Alderson, J. Charles, Tineke Brunfaut, and Luke Harding. 2015. "Towards a Theory of Diagnosis in Second and Foreign Language Assessment: Insights from Professional Practice across Diverse Fields." *Applied Linguistics* 36, no. 2: 236–60. http://dx.doi.org/10.1093/applin/amt046.

Alderson, J. Charles, and Ari Huhta. 2011. "Can Research into the Diagnostic Testing of Reading in a Second or Foreign Language Contribute to SLA Research?" In *EUROSLA Yearbook 11*, ed. Leah Roberts, Gabriele Pallotti, and Camilla Bettoni, 30–52. Amsterdam: John Benjamins. http://dx.doi.org/10.1075/eurosla.11.04ald.

Bachman, Lyle, and Adrian Palmer. 1996. *Language Testing in Practice*. Oxford: Oxford University Press.

———. 2010. *Language Assessment in Practice*. Oxford: Oxford University Press.

Beaudrie, Sara. 2011. "Spanish Heritage Language Programs: A Snapshot of Current Programs in the Southwestern United States." *Foreign Language Annals* 44, no. 2: 321–37. http://dx.doi.org/10.1111/j.1944-9720.2011.01137.x.

Beaudrie, Sara M., and Cynthia Ducar. 2005. "Beginning Level University Heritage Programs: Creating a Space for all Heritage Language Learners." *Heritage Language Journal* 3:1–26.

———. 2012. "Language Placement and Beyond: Guidelines for the Design and Implementation of a Computerized Spanish Heritage Language Exam." *Heritage Language Journal* 9:77–99.

Beaudrie, Sara M., and Marta Fairclough, eds. 2012. *Spanish as a Heritage Language in the United States: The State of the Field.* Washington, DC: Georgetown University Press.

Brookhart, Susan M. 2007. "Expanding Views about Formative Classroom Assessment: A Review of the Literature." In *Formative Classroom Assessment: Theory into Practice*, ed. James McMillan, 43–62. New York: Teachers College Press.

Brown, H. Douglas, and Priyanvada Abeywickrama. 2010. *Language Assessment: Principles and Classroom Practices*. 2nd ed. White Plains, NY: Pearson/Longman.

Brown, James Dean. 2014. *Testing in Language Programs*. New York: McGraw-Hill.

Carreira, María. 2012. "Formative Assessment in HL Teaching: Purposes, Procedures, and Practices." *Heritage Language Journal* 9, no. 1: 100–120.

———. 2016. "Supporting Heritage Language Learners through Macrobased Teaching: Foundational Principles and Implementation Strategies for HL and Mixed Classes." In *Innovative Strategies for Heritage Language Teaching: A Practical Guide for the Classroom*, ed. Marta Fairclough and Sara M. Beaudrie, 123–42. Washington, DC: Georgetown University Press.

Celce-Murcia, Marianne, and Elite Olshtain. 2000. *Discourse and Context in Language Teaching*. Cambridge: Cambridge University Press.

Center for Applied Second Language Studies (CASLS). 2008. "Computerized Assessment Proficiency Test Specifications." https://casls.uoregon.edu/pdfs/cap/CAPTestSpecs.pdf.

Clementi, Donna, and Laura Terrill. 2013. *The Keys to Planning for Learning: Effective Curriculum, Unit, and Lesson Design*. Alexandria, VA: ACTFL.

Cohen, Andrew D. 1994. *Assessing Language Ability in the Classroom.* 2nd ed. Boston: Heinle/Cengage.

Elder, Catherine. 2000. "Is It Fair to Assess Native and Non-Native Speakers in Common on School Foreign Language Examinations?" In *Fairness and Validation in*

Language Testing: Selected Papers from the 19th Language Testing Research Colloquium, Orlando, Florida, ed. Anthony J. Kunnan, 82–104. Cambridge: Cambridge University Press.

Fairclough, Marta. 2011. "Testing the Lexical Recognition Task with Spanish/English Bilinguals in the United States." *Language Testing* 28, no. 2: 273–97. http://dx.doi.org/10.1177/0265532210393151.

———. 2012a. "Language Assessment: Key Theoretical Considerations in Academic Placement of Spanish Heritage Language Learners." In *Spanish as a Heritage Language in the United States: The State of the Field*, ed. Sara M. Beaudrie and Marta Fairclough, 256–77. Washington, DC: Georgetown University Press.

———. 2012b. "A Working Model for Assessing Spanish Heritage Language Learners' Language Proficiency through a Placement Exam." *Heritage Language Journal* 9, no. 1: 121–38.

Fairclough, Marta, Flavia Belpoliti, and Encarna Bermejo. 2010. "Developing an Electronic Placement Examination for Heritage Learners of Spanish: Challenges and Payoffs." *Hispania* 93, no. 2: 270–89.

Harding, Luke, J. Charles Alderson, and Tineke Brunfaut. 2015. "Diagnostic Assessment of Reading and Listening in a Second or Foreign Language: Elaborating on Diagnostic Principles." *Language Testing* 32, no. 1: 1–20.

Ilieva, Gabriela. 2008. "Project-Based Learning of Hindi: Managing the Mixed-abilities Classrooms." *South Asia Language Pedagogy and Technology* 1:24–33.

———. 2012. "Hindi Heritage Language Learners' Performance during OPIs: Characteristics and Pedagogical Implications." *Heritage Language Journal* 9, no. 2: 18–36.

Kagan, Olga. 2005. "In Support of a Proficiency-Based Definition of Heritage Language Learners: The Case of Russian." *International Journal of Bilingual Education and Bilingualism* 8, no. 2–3: 213–21. http://dx.doi.org/10.1080/13670050508668608.

Kagan, Olga, and Katherine Dillon. 2001. "A New Perspective on Teaching Russian: Focus on the Heritage Learner." *Slavic and East European Journal* 45, no. 3: 507–18. http://dx.doi.org/10.2307/3086367.

———. 2006. "Russian Heritage Learners: So What Happens Now?" *Slavic and East European Journal* 50, no. 1: 83–96. http://dx.doi.org/10.2307/20459235.

Kondo-Brown, Kimi. 2005. "Differences in Language Skills: Heritage Language Learner Subgroups and Foreign Language Learners." *Modern Language Journal* 89, no. 4: 563–81. http://dx.doi.org/10.1111/j.1540-4781.2005.00330.x.

———. 2010. "Curriculum Development for Advancing Heritage Language Competence: Recent Research, Current Practices, and a Future Agenda." *Annual Review of Applied Linguistics* 30:24–41. http://dx.doi.org/10.1017/S0267190510000012.

Lacorte, Manel, and Evelyn Canabal. 2002. "Interaction with Heritage Language Learners in Foreign Language Classrooms." In *The Sociolinguistics of Foreign-language Classrooms: Contributions of the Native, the Near-Native, and the Non-Native Speaker*, AAUSC Issues in Language Program Direction, ed. Carl Blyth, 107–29. Boston: Thomson Heinle.

Llosa, Lorena. 2014. "Assessing Heritage Language Learners." In *The Companion to Language Assessment*, ed. Anthony J. Kunnan, 440–53. Madden, MA: Wiley-Blackwell.

Lynch, Andrew. 2008. "The Linguistic Similarities of Spanish Heritage and Second Language Learners." *Foreign Language Annals* 41, no. 2: 252–381. http://dx.doi.org/10.1111/j.1944-9720.2008.tb03292.x.

MacGregor-Mendoza, Patricia. 2012. "Spanish as a Heritage Language Assessment: Successes, Failures, Lessons Learned." *Heritage Language Journal* 9, no. 1: 1–26.

Martin, Cynthia L., Elvira Swender, and Mildred Rivera-Martinez. 2013. "Assessing the Oral Proficiency of Heritage Speakers according to the ACTFL Proficiency Guidelines 2012 – Speaking." *Heritage Language Journal* 10, no. 2: 211–25.

Martínez, Glenn. 2016. "Goals and Beyond in Heritage Language Education: From Competencies to Capabilities." In *Innovative Strategies for Heritage Language Teaching: A Practical Guide for the Classroom*, ed. Marta Fairclough and Sara M. Beaudrie, 39–55. Washington, DC: Georgetown University Press.

McGinnis, Scott. 1996. "Teaching Chinese to the Chinese: The Development of an Assessment and Instructional Model." In *Patterns and Policies: The Changing Demographics of Foreign Language Instruction*, ed. Judith E. Liskin-Gasparro, 107–21. Boston: Heinle and Heinle.

Norris, John M., James Dean Brown, Thom Hudson, and Jim Yoshioka. 1998. *Designing Second Language Performance Assessments*. Honolulu: University of Hawaii Press.

Otheguy, Ricardo, and Jeanette Toro. 2000. "Tests for Spanish-for-Native-Speaker Classes." In *Spanish for Native Speakers*, AATSP Professional Development Series, vol. 1, ed. Lynn A. Sandstedt, 91–98. New York: Harcourt College Publishers.

Polinsky, Maria, and Olga Kagan. 2007. "Heritage Languages: In the "Wild" and in the Classroom." *Language and Linguistics Compass* 1, no. 5: 368–95. http://dx.doi.org/10.1111/j.1749-818X.2007.00022.x.

Potowski, Kim, ed. 2010. *Language Diversity in the USA*. New York: Cambridge University Press. http://dx.doi.org/10.1017/CBO9780511779855.

Potowski, Kim, and María Carreira. 2004. "Teacher Development and National Standards for Spanish as a Heritage Language." *Foreign Language Annals* 37, no. 3: 427–37. http://dx.doi.org/10.1111/j.1944-9720.2004.tb02700.x.

Sandrock, Paul. 2010. *The Keys to Assessing Language Performance: Teacher's Manual*. Alexandria, VA: ACTFL.

Shrum, Judith, and Eileen Glisan. 2010. *Teacher's Handbook: Contextualized Language Instruction*. 4th ed. Boston: Heinle/Cengage Learning.

Spada, Nina, and Patsy M. Lightbown. 2008. "Form-Focused Instruction: Isolated or Integrated?" *TESOL Quarterly* 42, no. 2: 181–207. http://dx.doi.org/10.1002/j.1545-7249.2008.tb00115.x.

Stiggins, Richard J. 2007. "Conquering the Formative Assessment Frontier." In *Formative Classroom Assessment: Theory into Practice*, ed. James H. McMillan, 8–28. New York: Teachers College Press.

Swender, Elvira and Robert Vicars. 2012. *ACTFL Oral Proficiency Interview Tester Training Manual*. Yonkers, NY: ACTFL.

Swender, Elvira, Cynthia L. Martin, Mildred Rivera-Martinez, and Olga E. Kagan. 2014. "Exploring Oral Proficiency Profiles of Heritage Speakers of Russian and Spanish." *Foreign Language Annals* 47, no. 3: 423–46. http://dx.doi.org/10.1111/flan.12098.

Thompson, Gregory L. 2014. "Understanding the Heritage Language Student: Proficiency and Placement." *Journal of Hispanic Higher Education* 13, no. 5: 1–15.

Tucker, G. Richard. 2005. "Innovative Language Education Programmes for Heritage Language Students: The Special Case of Puerto Ricans?" *International Journal of Bilingual Education and Bilingualism* 8, no. 2–3: 188–95. http://dx.doi.org/10.1080/13670050508668606.

Valdés, Guadalupe. 2006. "The Teaching of Heritage Languages: Lessons from California." In *Developing Minority Language Resources: The Case of Spanish in California*, ed. Guadalupe Valdés, Joshua Fishman, Rebecca Chávez, and William Pérez, 235–69. Clevedon: Multilingual Matters.

Zyzik, Eve. 2016. "Toward a Prototype Model of the Heritage Language Learner: Understanding Strengths and Needs." In *Innovative Strategies for Heritage Language Teaching: A Practical Guide for the Classroom*, ed. Marta Fairclough and Sara M. Beaudrie, 19–38. Washington, DC: Georgetown University Press.

11

Technology-Enhanced Heritage Language Instruction

Best Tools and Best Practices

Florencia Henshaw
University of Illinois, Urbana–Champaign

It is undeniable that technology-enhanced foreign language (FL) instruction has become mainstream. The role of technology in language courses ranges from being a supplemental component (e.g., assignments completed with the help of Web-based resources) to serving as either a partial replacement of instructional time, as in the case of hybrid courses, or the sole means of instruction, as in fully online courses. Technology allows for immediate and individualized feedback, it gives learners and instructors access to authentic oral and written input, and it helps to connect learners with each other and with native speakers, thus extending their opportunities for meaningful communication in the target language. Synchronous and asynchronous interaction outside of the classroom has certainly been made more attainable thanks to Web 2.0 tools, which allow learners to create and share content online (e.g., wikis, blogs, podcasting, video chat, social media sites).

The affordances of technology as a tool for language learning have been documented in the literature for over three decades. In a review of 350 empirical studies on the effectiveness of technology use in second language (L2) teaching, Ewa Golonka and colleagues (2014) found strong support for the claim that technology—particularly text-based computer-mediated communication (CMC)—can help to increase the amount and the complexity of learner language production. Research has suggested that text-based CMC might have a facilitative role for L2 development by promoting negotiation of meaning and form (Blake 2000; de la Fuente 2003; Smith 2004; Zeng and Takatsuka 2009). A number of studies have also reported that synchronous written CMC may lead to greater oral proficiency development than face-to-face discussions (Blake 2009; Payne and Ross 2005; Sykes 2005).

Perhaps the most distinct affordance of technology is the ability to make learning ubiquitous and personalized by allowing learners to advance at their own pace and access content and practice any time, any place. For language program administrators, this advantage has translated into the development of hybrid and online courses to satisfy student demand while maximizing instructional resources (for guidelines on program administration issues, see Beaudrie, this volume [2016]). Despite faculty concerns over the potential impact of decreasing the number of contact hours on oral proficiency development, a growing body of research has indicated that technology-enhanced FL classes, including those delivered completely online, may be as effective as traditional courses. Overall, findings from research comparing traditional and hybrid sections have consistently yielded no significant differences in performance between those two delivery modes (Chenoweth, Ushida, and Murday 2006; Murday, Ushida, and Chenoweth 2008; Rubio 2012; Scida and Saury 2006; Young 2008), and, in some cases, the writing skills of L2 learners in hybrid sections improved significantly more than those in sections without an online component (Thoms 2012). Similarly, Blake and colleagues (2008) found that that there were no significant differences in oral proficiency development between students in online sections of an introductory Spanish course and their traditional counterparts, suggesting that learners in technology-enhanced courses are not at a disadvantage in terms of language development. With respect to student perceptions and attitudes toward computer-delivered instruction, research has shown that students are highly satisfied with hybrid and online FL courses and in some cases prefer it over traditional instruction (Bañados 2006; Blake and Shiri 2012; Strambi and Bouvet 2003; Murday, Ushida, and Chenoweth 2008).

Even though the vast majority of research on computer-assisted language learning (CALL) has focused on L2 teaching and learning, many of its advantages could also apply for heritage language (HL) instruction. In fact, the National Heritage Language Resource Center (NHLRC 2013) acknowledges that "computerized materials will help educators to accommodate the diversity within a classroom and the conditions under which HL study may be pursued." Under the assumption that HL learners constitute a heterogeneous group not only with respect to their degree of bilingualism but also in terms of attitudes, goals, and preferences, technology may offer educators the opportunity to successfully meet different students' needs in the HL classroom, given that one of the main advantages of CALL is that it allows for more individualized instruction and personalized learning. The flexibility of Web-based courses also offers a possible solution to overcoming logistical obstacles when offering separate face-to-face courses for L2 and HL learners is not a viable option. Furthermore, electronic literacy in the heritage language plays a pivotal role in directly meeting many of the goals for HL instruction, particularly HL maintenance, cultivation of positive attitudes toward the heritage language, and development of cultural awareness (Martínez, this volume [2016]). As Michael Fitzgerald and Robert Debski (2006, 97) remark, "the ways in which immigrant and ethnic communities use media can influence the status of community languages, human attitudes towards them, and the practices in their teaching and learning." Considering the veritable influence of the Internet on interpersonal communication and transmission of information, integrating Web-based tools and resources in HL education seems essential to achieve the goal of maintaining and expanding the learners' use of their home language.

Despite these clear benefits, technology integration in the HL curriculum has remained largely unexplored. In this chapter, I first discuss the current state of the field, focusing on affordances and limitations of online materials for HL learners. I then propose some basic guidelines for HL educators to bear in mind when considering integrating technology in their curriculum. Last, I explore the most useful Web 2.0 tools for the HL classroom and provide practical examples for implementing authentic synchronous and asynchronous online communication. To conclude, I offer suggestions for future research to continue expanding our understanding of the role of technology for HL learning and maintenance.

ADVANTAGES OF TECHNOLOGY USE FOR HL LEARNERS

To date, very few research studies have explored the use of technology in HL courses, and most have been small-scale descriptive studies evaluating the usefulness of certain tools within the context of L2 courses rather than specially designated courses for HL learners. Nonetheless, results suggest that technology may offer several benefits specific to HL instruction, in addition to the many other advantages of CALL reported for L2 learning.

Carla Meskill and Natasha Anthony (2008), for instance, evaluated the benefits of asynchronous text-based discussions among four Russian HL learners and a visiting international student from Russia. Students were required to post between three and five postings per week on topics designed to emphasize academic discourse, especially cross-cultural comparisons. Researchers analyzed the data from both the online postings as well as the interviews conducted by the instructor of the course at the end of the semester. Students reported that participation in the online discussions strengthened their lexical repertoire, their spelling skills, and their composing and editing abilities. Moreover, the exchange of ideas with other HL learners gave them the opportunity to reflect on their identity and share perspectives and experiences unique to their linguistic and cultural backgrounds. The researchers concluded that asynchronous CMC may be "a viable tool to help heritage learners increase their lexical range and command of written registers in the home language" (Meskill and Anthony 2008, 16).

Similar linguistic benefits were reported in a case study of two Korean HL learners who participated in online blogging (Lee 2006). In addition to learning new words and mastering new syntactic structures, "the flexibility and creative means of expression commonly found in electronic literacy practices also lowered their inhibition about writing in Korean" (Lee 2006, 109). Furthermore, Lee's results underscore the role of Web 2.0 tools, particularly social media and blogs, in serving as a forum for HL learners to reinforce their linguistic and cultural identity. Blogging in Cyworld, an authentic platform of considerable popularity in Korea, allowed participants to form social networks with other Korean speakers, which strengthened their connection to their cultural heritage and motivated them to continue learning the language.

Another advantage of the online modality for HL learners is that it may be less anxiety-producing. Joellen Coryell and colleagues (2010) interviewed seven HL learners enrolled in a fully online Spanish course intended for FL learners. The researchers found that the online environment may be appealing to HL learners as it promises "a safer space for them to wrestle with feelings of linguistic and cultural incompetence" (Coryell, Clark, and Pomerantz 2010, 465). The flexible and individualized nature of Web-based courses allows learners to review the material as much as needed without feeling inadequate in front of their peers or their instructor and to complete assignments at their own pace without feeling that their Spanish is either "too good" or "not good enough." Likewise, Jin Sook Lee (2006) reported that students found online blogs to be a comfortable environment to communicate and experiment with language use without feeling constrained to orthographic conventions.

From a practical standpoint, the use of technology allows language program administrators to maximize resources. As Melissa Bowles and Silvina Montrul (2014, 119) point out, when it comes to face-to-face courses, "scheduling constraints are a real logistical problem for heritage-language courses, and many times conflicting schedules preclude students from taking a heritage-speaker course who would otherwise do so." Since it is almost always the case that the population of HL learners is significantly smaller than that of L2 learners, the scheduling options for HL courses tend to be limited. It is inevitable that some HL learners would be unable to enroll in the specially designated courses. Offering fully online or hybrid courses with fewer weekly meetings may be a feasible way to have classes for HL learners that do not create conflicts with their existing schedules. Florencia Henshaw (forthcoming) describes a fully online Spanish composition course for HL learners developed and implemented at the University of Illinois, Urbana–Champaign. The author reported that students were satisfied with both the format and the content of the course, likely due to the abundant feedback and guidance they received from the instructor on an individual basis as well as the fact that the online activities aimed to help students improve their writing and spelling skills, which HL learners tend to identify as one of their main learning objectives (Bowles and Montrul 2014; Mikulski 2006). Furthermore, the scheduling flexibility afforded by the online format helped to avoid the issue of low enrollments, which had been the cause of HL courses being cancelled in previous years.

In institutions that lack sufficient resources or student demand to offer separate courses for HL learners, as is the case with most universities (Beaudrie 2012a), Web-based materials might help instructors meet the individual learning needs of HL learners even when they enroll in the same FL courses as L2 learners. One way in which technology facilitates differentiated instruction is, for instance, by allowing instructors to control learner access to different assignments. Most course management systems (e.g., Blackboard, Moodle, Desire2Learn) include an "adaptive release" feature that allows the release of content to specific users based on criteria established by the course administrator. This way the instructor can create virtual "centers" in the form of folders with reference materials, tutorials, and practice that target different learners' needs, which would be visible only to certain students as determined by the instructor (see Carreira 2012 for specific examples).

POTENTIAL PITFALLS OF TECHNOLOGY FOR HL TEACHING

Even though the benefits of technology integration in the HL curriculum are numerous, there are some drawbacks that have been pointed out in the literature. As rich as the Internet is as a source of authentic written input, it is impossible for instructors to control the quality of the texts students might encounter online. Donald Loewen (2008) expresses some concerns about exposing HL learners to alternative spellings commonly found in discussion forums or comments posted by Internet users. While Loewen focuses on Russian, that phenomenon is not foreign to other languages. Lee (2006), for instance, explains how nonstandard orthography is a key characteristic of Korean Internet language use. Although Loewen does not conclude that this issue is serious enough to deter instructors from using online resources in their HL courses, he does warn instructors that websites may contain "almost exactly the fundamental mistakes that we are trying to help our heritage learners overcome" (Loewen 2008, 33), suggesting that special caution should be exercised when assigning Internet research projects to HL learners. Loewen recommends preparing students through class discussions and activities that prompt them to notice differences between standard spelling conventions and Internet language use.

With respect to the use of computerized assessment and instruction, such as quizzes and tutorials, Coryell and Carolyn Clark (2009) point out two limitations that affect HL learners in particular. First, the inherent rigidity of the preprogrammed answer key of computer-graded activities reinforces the notion that there is only one correct way of expressing something in the target language. The constant pressure to produce correct forms may be especially detrimental to the HL learners' confidence and linguistic identity. Second, the individualized nature of online instruction and practice runs the risk of making it difficult to foment a sense of community among learners. In the case of HL learners, this feeling of isolation may be particularly problematic, considering that previous research has shown one of the main reasons why they study the language is to form part of a linguistic and cultural community (Alarcón 2010; Bowles and Montrul 2014; Carreira and Kagan 2011; Coryell and Clark 2009).

For instructors, the biggest obstacle in implementing the use of technology in the HL curriculum is the scarcity of publisher-provided online materials that meet the needs of HL learners. There is a staggering difference between textbooks for L2 learners and those for HL learners in terms of availability of online ancillary materials. One would be hard-pressed to find an FL textbook, especially of a commonly taught language like Spanish, that did not include any digital content. On the other hand, the majority of textbooks for Spanish as a heritage language of various levels do not include online activities but rather have companion websites with supplementary materials (e.g., files with activities for instructors to print out) or external links and topics for Internet research projects. In some instances, grammar tutorials originally developed for L2 learners are available as additional practice, an option that seems more problematic than convenient, considering that L2 and HL learners differ considerably in their linguistic and pedagogical needs. A recent survey of thirteen universities in the Southwest revealed that the lack of online materials suited to meet the needs of HL learners is one of the main areas of dissatisfaction with textbooks for Spanish as a heritage language (Guzmán 2013). The situation is undoubtedly more dire for languages with a much smaller market share.

Other limitations to the integration of technology in any language curriculum, whether a heritage language or second language, are related primarily to the availability of resources and the experience of the learners. In some institutions, mainly at the K–12 level, access to the Internet might be restricted, and even at the college level it may not always be possible for students to complete online assignments from home. The 2013 report on computer and Internet access conducted by the US Census Bureau revealed that a little over 25 percent of households do not have Internet access (File and Ryan 2014). Instructors should take into account their students' circumstances prior to assigning tasks that require the use of Web-based tools, and they should always offer alternative ways to access information or completing projects.

Another key factor in determining the successful implementation of technology-enhanced courses is the students' adaptability and receptivity to using new technologies for educational purposes. Although the vast majority of students now in college were born at a time when Internet use was commonplace, instructors cannot assume that "digital natives" are technology experts; in fact, they might only be familiar with a limited number of sites and tools (Margaryan, Littlejohn, and Vojt 2011). Educators need to dedicate considerable time not only to learning how to use different tools themselves but also to training their students. Requiring the use of online tools to complete class projects without first providing adequate training as well as a clear explanation of the distinct advantages of technology will likely lead to frustration and resistance. Adaptability on the part of the instructor to the ever-changing technology landscape is equally important: as new online tools are made available, others cease to exist. Therefore, it is important for instructors either to choose tools that are likely to endure from one academic year to the next (e.g., Facebook, Pinterest) or to be aware of alternative tools with comparable functions.

PRACTICAL CONSIDERATIONS AND BEST PRACTICES

Even though publisher-provided online materials are scarce, there are many Web 2.0 tools that can be used for HL courses. When trying to determine which tools are the most appropriate, many of the same factors that apply to the selection of technological tools for L2 learners, such as cost, user-friendliness, accessibility, and reliability, also apply. Perhaps the most important tenet when it comes to selecting technological tools, especially in the case of HL instruction, is to keep the learners' needs in mind. As Christopher Blake (2013, 12) states, "technology is theoretically and methodologically neutral." In other words, technology is only a tool that has the potential to facilitate language development; it is the instructors' responsibility to ensure it is being used in a pedagogically sound way. In the case of HL courses, educators should consider the pedagogical practices and goals proposed in the literature (e.g., Beaudrie, Ducar, and Potowski 2014; Carreira and Kagan 2011; Martínez, this volume [2016]) when determining the extent to which a particular technological tool would enhance HL teaching and learning.

Based on the advantages and drawbacks uncovered by emerging research on technology use with HL learners, and based on what the literature on HL teaching has suggested with respect to the students' needs, motivation, and goals, the following best practices are suggested for incorporating technology in the HL curriculum:

1. Favor instructor-graded tasks over computer-graded quizzes. As Coryell and Clark (2009) point out, relying on computer-graded activities may not only lead to frustration when students struggle to understand why their answer is incorrect but, more importantly, it may have a negative effect on the learner's linguistic identity. Without the guidance and contextualization

afforded by instructor feedback, computer activities that are limited to accept specific, preprogrammed correct responses may inadvertently send the message to HL learners that their language varieties are unacceptable. Although computer-graded activities can be designed to facilitate the expansion of their bilingual range and acquisition of academic skills in the heritage language (e.g., quizzes on technical vocabulary, reading comprehension questions), they should not be the main source of practice and assessment in HL courses. At the very least, automatic feedback should offer the type of explanations and guidance that a real-life instructor would, as opposed to only "right" or "wrong" indicators.

2. Foment electronic literacy by embracing learner autonomy. While it is certainly true that all learners benefit from the fact that the Internet allows them to explore a myriad of topics relevant to them, establishing a personal connection to the language and culture is even more crucial to support HL maintenance, one of the goals of HL instruction (Martínez, this volume [2016]). Empowering learners in the process of discovering and selecting materials not only increases their motivation to continue learning but also strengthens their identity as members of the target language culture. Seong Park and Mela Sarkar (2007) found that one way that parents helped their children maintain Korean as their heritage language in Montreal was through encouragement of Internet use in Korean. This is not to say that students should be left to fend for themselves in cyberspace. Given that most HL learners are not electronically literate in their heritage language (i.e., they use the Internet in English rather than in their home language), as reported by Maria Carreira and Olga Kagan (2011), instructor guidance is still paramount. However, the starting point in the learning process is not the instructor but rather the learner's own knowledge, preferences, and experiences. Exploring personally relevant online content foments electronic literacy in the heritage language, which in turn validates the social status of their home language.

3. Use tools that allow learners to convey meaningful content to real audiences. As Lee (2006) and Coryell and Clark (2009) point out, technology is only useful for HL maintenance when it provides opportunities to use the language for authentic purposes. Therefore, the online component of HL courses should not be limited to activities where the only participants are the instructor and other classmates. Doing so would overlook the "desire on the part of HL students to connect more directly and more deeply with local and transnational HL communities" (Martínez, this volume [2016]). Although asynchronous discussions like the ones suggested by Meskill and Anthony (2008) are one way to foster student–student interaction and collaboration, forums within course management systems lack authenticity. Instead, technology-enhanced projects for HL learners should require them to engage in meaningful communication with a real audience, including native speakers of the heritage language. Specific examples of tasks that involve meaningful synchronous and asynchronous online communication are provided in the next section.

4. Capitalize on the text-based nature of online materials. Considering that there is a close relationship between reading and writing (Beaudrie 2012b; Templeton and Morris 2001), and that most HL learners do not spend much time reading in the heritage language (Carreira and Kagan 2011), the predominance of written communication in the online environment (e.g., blog posts, comments, websites, articles) might facilitate the development of their literacy skills and the expansion of their bilingual range. Although Loewen's (2008) concerns regarding nonstandard orthography should be taken into consideration, an important best practice when it comes to incorporating Web-based materials in the HL curriculum is precisely to expose students to written input of diverse registers and dialects. In fact, the authenticity of Internet materials, including nonstandard spelling or punctuation, is perhaps the greatest advantage of technology use in the HL curriculum, as it validates how learners speak or write as a context-specific form of communication. Rather than confining students to a limited selection of websites where a specific register or language variety is used, instructors should "invite students to explore the notion of language variation and to appreciate the importance of developing broad-based linguistic competencies" (Coryell, Clark, and Pomerantz 2010, 466). Acknowledging that language usage in Web pages is not bad input but rather real input helps HL learners understand that there are no right or wrong varieties, and it cultivates a positive attitude toward all varieties of the heritage language, one of the main goals of instruction (Martínez, this volume [2016]).

TECHNOLOGICAL TOOLS FOR THE HL CLASSROOM

CALL researchers have evaluated the advantages and disadvantages of a myriad of tools for L2 learning, ranging from computer-delivered tutorials to Web 2.0 tools, such as blogs, wikis, social media sites, podcasting, screencasting, and videoconferencing, among many other applications. In some cases, the benefits of certain tools for L2 learners may be directly applicable to HL learners as well. The question that arises is which tools are best suited for enhancing HL learning in particular. Taking into account the goals of HL education and the best practices outlined in the previous section, Web 2.0 tools would be the most appropriate because they encourage authentic language use, promote learner autonomy, and facilitate linguistic and cultural explorations through the exchange of ideas not only among learners but also with native speakers of the heritage language. In this section I offer examples of how different Web 2.0 tools may be used in the HL classroom. The majority of the tools and tasks suggested in this section are more appropriate for higher-education settings; that being said, instructor discretion should ultimately determine whether the ideas presented here can be adapted to their own contexts.

Asynchronous Communication and Collaboration

The inherent community-building nature of social media sites like Facebook and Twitter makes them excellent forums for meaningful dialogue and collaboration, thus increasing students' motivation and interest in the language and culture. Emerging research has shown how social media tools may contribute to L2 development, especially with respect to writing skills, by offering increased opportunities for communication outside of the classroom (Lomicka and Lord 2012; Wang and Kim 2014). Although the focus on written communication is also beneficial to HL learners, the benefits of using social media as a tool for HL courses extend far beyond serving as a class discussion forum. As HL learners express their ideas, react to what others are saying, share information, join groups, like pages, and connect with other speakers of the heritage language worldwide, their identity as members of that linguistic community is reaffirmed. Nicole Mills (2011), for instance, explored how Facebook allowed intermediate L2 learners of French not only to learn about French cultural products from information posted in special interest groups but also to become active participants in online francophone communities. Similarly, HL educators can design projects that require students to explore the linguistic and sociocultural aspects of social media use within the target culture. Even more pertinent to the HL classroom would be to have students participate in social media sites that are popular among native speakers of the heritage language: Tuenti (Spanish), VK (Russian), Kakao Story (Korean), Renren (Chinese), and so on. Social media sites like those are a direct connection to the target culture and possibly one of the most effective ways to promote electronic literacy in the heritage language. It would be insightful for future research to explore the impact of social media use on HL learners' perceptions and attitudes, particularly with respect to their motivation to continue using the language.

Other tools for social sharing and collaboration are content curation sites, like Pinterest (http://www.pinterest.com), Scoop.It (http://www.scoop.it), and Pearltrees (http://www.pearltrees.com), among many others. Content curation consists of creating collections of digital content either selected from existing material online or from original files uploaded by users. Collections can be organized thematically and made available to other users, thus facilitating the process of sharing information with members of the online community who have similar interests. Directing students to research a topic online can result in an overwhelming experience; instead, instructors can use online curation sites to encourage collaboration not just among students but also with other users. Although content curation also has benefits for L2 learners, HL learners may benefit even more, as they would be able to identify and thoroughly review a wider range of authentic sites in the target language on their own, which could be an intimidating task to L2 learners. For HL learners, the curation of content related to subject matter that is personally relevant to them helps them to develop greater social attachment to the language and culture since it encourages them to engage with the language and content in a real and meaningful way as they review and filter their selections to form a coherent and varied collection. Furthermore, learners can be instructed to provide a summary and comments on the articles, videos, websites, or images in their collection, putting their writing skills into practice.

There are many different ideas for using content curation sites in the language classroom. One that may be especially good for HL learners is the creation of a collection that represents who they are. Instructors can invite students to reflect on their own bilingual and bicultural identity through the process of selecting images, quotes, news stories, blog posts, videos, music, social media groups, and other online content personally relevant to them. Crucial to the pedagogical success of this task is to have learners write comments explaining how the different components of their collection reflect their personality, ideology, goals, and life experiences. Another example of a more elaborate project involving online curation tools is the creation of a collection of stories related to immigration, and each group of students can be assigned either a particular area of the world or a particular media format. The collection as a whole could then be used to analyze the content from ethnographic and linguistic perspectives. Other users, such as instructors and HL learners, would be able to access the collection and post comments or use it as a source of information for their own projects, fostering the sense of a global learning community.

Similar projects may be carried out with other curation sites that organize the content in the form of a digital magazine or newspaper, such as Paper .li (http://paper.li) and Zinepal (http://www.zinepal.com). Students can create their own news sites based on articles, blog posts, and rich media content from Internet sources selected by them. Unlike static collections, like those in Pinterest, students can choose to have their news stories update on a regular basis. This way students can continuously learn more about a topic of interest to them in the target language, as if they had their customized online newspaper delivered to them every morning, which would surely increase their motivation to read in the heritage language. Sites like Paper.li and Zinepal would be ideal to help students become experts on a particular topic, especially related to their home communities or to current events in the HL-speaking world, over the course of the semester. At the onset of the project, students would select the topic and sources. The instructor should guide them in the selection of reliable sources that expose students not only to different points of view but also to a variety of dialects and registers in the heritage language. Throughout the course, possibly on a weekly basis, students would be required to read and learn from the news stories that appear in their sites. In the final part of the project, they could demonstrate what they have learned and share their newfound knowledge with their classmates implemented in the form of student-led discussions and activities.

Whereas sites like Paper.li and Zinepal generate e-magazines based on existing online content, there are many free tools that allow users to create their own digital magazines with original content. Students can use sites like Openzine (http://www.openzine.com) and Issuu (http://issuu.com) to design and publish a professional-looking magazine with images, text, and video. For instance, a project could consist of students working in groups to publish a special issue of their e-magazine that revolves around a topic of their choosing and of relevance to the HL community (e.g., "the language issue," "the family issue," "the health issue"). Students would produce texts of a variety of genres (expository, argumentative, narrative) as well as visuals to accompany them (e.g., pictures, videos, cartoons). The main benefits of a project like this for HL learners are twofold: it emphasizes the multifaceted nature of language as a meaning-making tool highly dependent on audience and intent, and it foments multimodal communication, particularly audio, visual, and spatial patterns of meaning. This type of project would be most appropriate within a multiliteracies approach to HL teaching, as described in Malena Samaniego and Chantelle Warner's chapter in this volume (2016).

Synchronous Communication

Although the tools and projects described so far provide HL learners with opportunities for real-life, meaningful communication, the most direct and effective way for them to connect with the language and culture is through real-time interaction with other speakers of the heritage language. It is widely accepted that ethnographic projects such as interviewing family members are beneficial for exploring issues of identity construction as well as engaging in meaningful use of the heritage language (for ideas on ethnographic projects, see Leeman and Serafini, this volume [2016]). However, it is not always feasible for students to carry out interviews in person or even to have access to relatives who speak the heritage language. Students may also want to branch out of their social circles and expand their knowledge of other communities of speakers of the heritage language. Through Web-based videoconferencing, language instructors now have access to platforms that allow for synchronous communication with native speakers worldwide. Since one-to-one Internet-mediated conversation exchanges can be tailored to the interests, goals, and proficiency level of each learner, projects that incorporate Web-based videoconferencing are appealing and beneficial to both L2 and HL learners, making them ideal for instructors who teach mixed classes.

There are different options when it comes to implementing Web-based videoconferencing, depending on the language and the availability of resources. One possibility is to establish a partnership with an institution abroad, which Robert O'Dowd (2005) describes. Marquette University, for example, works within a consortium of universities to offer conversation exchanges via Skype for students of French, Spanish, Arabic, and Italian. Although this option offers a cost-effective and safe way to conduct Internet-mediated conversations, establishing and maintaining these partnerships is labor intensive. An alternative for instructors and program directors who might not be able to partner with international institutions is to use free Internet platforms designed to connect language learners around the world, such as the following:

- Conversation Exchange: http://www.conversationexchange.com
- The Mixxer: http://language-exchanges.org
- We Speke: http://en-us.wespeke.com
- My Language Exchange: http://www.mylanguageexchange.com
- iTalki: http://www.italki.com/partners

Many of these sites also allow for users to engage in text-based chat, which has some advantages for both L2 and HL learners in terms of language development: it allows them "to perceive visually the utterance they are creating," and it "gives heritage speakers more production time to search their lexicon" (Blake and Zyzik 2003, 540–41).

Instructors should keep in mind the following two caveats: it might not be possible to find conversation partners for all languages, and the quality of the interaction might not always be up to par. Since these platforms are free and open to the public, instructors have little control over the length of the interaction or the background of the conversation partner. To reduce some of the unpredictability of open-access platforms, instructors may opt for paid services, such as Talk Abroad (https://talkabroad.com), which offers thirty-minute conversations by appointment with native speakers of Spanish, French, and Chinese. Michigan State University, Duke University, and the University of Illinois at Urbana–Champaign are some of the institutions that currently use Talk Abroad as supplementary conversation practice for students of Spanish. In addition to being more reliable than free platforms, another advantage of Talk Abroad is that conversations are automatically recorded. HL instructors could assign students to conduct ethnographic interviews of their conversation partners, and the audio-recorded answers would then be transcribed to produce a written interview, which would help HL learners notice differences between oral and written language (e.g., punctuation, orthographic conventions).

As with any other tasks, the use of technological tools that allow for synchronous communication should be integrated within the curriculum. In other words, learners should not be instructed to merely have a conversation or chat; rather, they should be provided with "explicit guidance in developing cultural awareness" (O'Dowd 2005, 116). The videoconference should only be one part of a larger project relevant to the course content, with specific tasks to be completed before and after the conversation. For instance, in preparation for their interview, learners could review a transcript of an ethnographic interview, receive some basic training on how to craft ethnographic questions, and discuss strategies to overcome certain challenges related to the pragmatics of interacting with a stranger from another culture (e.g., how to start the conversation, how to change topics, how to keep the conversation going, how to ask for clarification or more details). After the interview, class discussions should focus on how to properly interpret the information provided by the conversation partners, emphasizing intercultural appreciation rather than cultural comparisons. O'Dowd (2007) discusses different models for Internet-mediated telecollaboration projects, and offers recommendations for organizing, facilitating, and assessing these projects as well as keys for overcoming the challenges they present.

CONCLUDING REMARKS

Whereas the use of technology in FL instruction is now the norm, technology-enhanced HL courses remain the exception, likely due to the scarcity of computer-delivered materials that meet the needs of HL learners. In this chapter I have argued that HL teaching and learning may be enriched with the sound use of the technological tools available. I have also put forth a number of practical suggestions for the use of innovative technologies in the HL courses in the form of tasks or projects aimed to achieve the goals of HL education, especially with respect to language maintenance, development of literacy skills, expansion of the learners' bilingual range, and the promotion of positive attitudes toward the heritage language and culture.

Although this chapter contributed to furthering our understanding of the advantages and challenges of technology-enhanced HL instruction, more research is needed on the pedagogical and affective dimensions of the integration of technology in the HL curriculum. As suggested earlier, research should explore the role of social media as a way to promote electronic literacy in the heritage language. It would first be necessary to determine current practices when it comes to HL use online. The results of the 2007–2009 NHLRC survey suggested that almost 85 percent of HL speakers rarely, if ever, accessed the Internet in the heritage language (Carreira and Kagan 2011). A more in-depth investigation of online language use by HL learners according to language and age of arrival to the United States would be warranted, especially considering the social media boom in the years that have passed since the survey was conducted.

Furthermore, future work should shed light on the nature of Internet-mediated conversational exchanges between HL learners and other speakers of the heritage language from both interactional and sociocultural perspectives. It would be particularly worthwhile to compare learning gains between oral and written chats for HL learners. To date, only Robert Blake and Eve

Zyzik (2003) have reported on the use of synchronous CMC with HL learners, and their study was purely descriptive. It is yet to be determined whether the results of CALL studies comparing written CMC with face-to-face oral interaction between L2 learners would also hold true for HL learners. Further research is also needed to determine the advantages and disadvantages of Web-based instruction for HL development. It would be insightful to compare traditional, hybrid, and fully online HL courses not only in terms of linguistic outcomes, as Blake and colleagues (2008) did with L2 courses, but also with respect to learner perceptions and anxiety, building on Coryell and Clark's (2009) findings. Exploring the positive and negative aspects of different delivery modes for HL instruction would help to inform the decisions of textbook publishers and program administrators.

In both the L2 and HL curriculum, the integration of technology needs to be carefully planned, taking into account not only the availability of resources and potential pitfalls of using technology, such as those outlined in this chapter, but more importantly the learners' goals and needs. In the case of HL instruction, technology should serve to promote authentic language use, develop translingual and transcultural awareness, and increase motivation through learner autonomy. Considering that a successful HL program "requires innovative and flexible curricula that are adaptable to diverse needs" (Beaudrie 2012a, 215), it is logical to predict that technology will soon be at the core of HL instruction. Therefore, exploring its affordances and limitations for HL courses in particular is imperative. Proper implementation of technological tools and features such as the ones suggested in this chapter would help instructors meet the needs of their students, and it could motivate learners to become life-long users of their heritage languages.

REFERENCES

Alarcón, Irma. 2010. "Advanced Heritage Learners of Spanish: A Sociolinguistic Profile for Pedagogical Purposes." *Foreign Language Annals* 43, no. 2: 269–88. http://dx.doi.org/10.1111/j.1944-9720.2010.01078.x.

Bañados, Emerita. 2006. "A Blended-learning Pedagogical Model for Teaching and Learning EFL Successfully through Online Interactive Multimedia Environment." *CALICO Journal* 23, no. 3: 533–50.

Beaudrie, Sara M. 2012a. "Research on University-Based Spanish Heritage Language Programs in the United States: The Current State of Affairs." In *Spanish as a Heritage Language in the United States: The State of the Field*, ed. Sara M. Beaudrie and Marta Fairclough, 203–21. Washington, DC: Georgetown University Press.

———. 2012b. "A Corpus-Based Study on the Misspellings of Spanish Heritage Learners and Their Implications for Teaching." *Linguistics and Education* 23, no. 1: 135–44. http://dx.doi.org/10.1016/j.linged.2011.09.001.

———. 2016. "Guidelines for Building a Heritage Language Program: Guidelines for a Collaborative Approach." In *Innovative Strategies for Heritage Language Teaching:*

A Practical Guide for the Classroom, ed. Marta Fairclough and Sara M. Beaudrie, 80–98. Washington, DC: Georgetown University Press.

Beaudrie, Sara, Cynthia Ducar, and Kim Potowski. 2014. *Heritage Language Teaching: Research and Practice*. New York: McGraw-Hill.

Blake, Christopher. 2009. "Potential of Text-Based Internet Chats for Improving Oral Fluency in a Second Language." *Modern Language Journal* 93, no. 2: 227–40. http://dx.doi.org/10.1111/j.1540-4781.2009.00858.x.

Blake, Robert. 2000. "Computer Mediated Communication: A Window on L2 Spanish Interlanguage." *Language Learning & Technology* 4, no. 1: 120–36.

———. 2013. *Brave New Digital Classroom: Technology and Foreign-Language Learning*. Washington, DC: Georgetown University Press.

Blake, Robert, and Sonia Shiri. 2012. "Online Arabic Language Learning: What Happens After?" *Journal of Linguistics and Language Teaching* 4, no. 2: 230–46.

Blake, Robert, Nicole L. Wilson, María Cetto, and Cristina Pardo-Ballester. 2008. "Measuring Oral Proficiency in Distance, Face-to-Face, and Blended Classrooms." *Language Learning & Technology* 12, no. 3: 114–27.

Blake, Robert, and Eve Zyzik. 2003. "Who's Helping Whom? Learner/Heritage-Speakers' Networked Discussions in Spanish." *Applied Linguistics* 24, no. 4: 519–44. http://dx.doi.org/10.1093/applin/24.4.519.

Bowles, Melissa, and Silvina Montrul. 2014. "Heritage Spanish Speakers in University Language Courses: A Decade of Difference." *ADFL Bulletin* 43, no. 1: 112–22. http://dx.doi.org/10.1632/adfl.43.1.112.

Carreira, Maria. 2012. "Meeting the Needs of Heritage Language Learners." In *Spanish as a Heritage Language in the United States: The State of the Field*, ed. Sara M. Beaudrie and Marta Fairclough, 223–40. Washington, DC: Georgetown University Press.

Carreira, Maria, and Olga Kagan. 2011. "The Results of the National Heritage Language Survey: Implications for Teaching, Curriculum Design, and Professional Development." *Foreign Language Annals* 44, no. 1: 40–64. http://dx.doi.org/10.1111/j.1944-9720.2010.01118.x.

Chenoweth, Ann, Eiko Ushida, and Kimmaree Murday. 2006. "Students Learning in Hybrid French and Spanish Courses: An Overview of Language Online." *CALICO Journal* 24, no. 1: 115–45.

Coryell, Joellen, and Carolyn Clark. 2009. "One Right Way, Intercultural Participation, and Language Learning Anxiety: A Qualitative Analysis of Adult Online Heritage and Nonheritage Language Learners." *Foreign Language Annals* 42, no. 3: 483–504. http://dx.doi.org/10.1111/j.1944-9720.2009.01037.x.

Coryell, Joellen, Carolyn Clark, and Anne Pomerantz. 2010. "Cultural Fantasy Narratives and Heritage Language Learning: A Case Study of Adult Heritage Learners of Spanish." *Modern Language Journal* 94, no. 3: 453–69. http://dx.doi.org/10.1111/j.1540-4781.2010.01055.x.

De la Fuente, María. 2003. "Is SLA Interactionist Theory Relevant to CALL? A Study on the Effects of Computer-mediated Interaction in L2 Vocabulary Acquisition." *Computer Assisted Language Learning* 16, no. 1: 47–81. http://dx.doi.org/10.1076/call.16.1.47.15526.

File, Thom, and Camille Ryan. 2014. "Computer and Internet Use in the United States: 2013." *American Community Survey Reports, ACS-28*. Washington, DC: US Census Bureau.

Fitzgerald, Michael, and Robert Debski. 2006. "Internet Use of Polish by Polish Melburnians: Implications for Maintenance and Teaching." *Language Learning & Technology* 10, no. 1: 87–109.

Golonka, Ewa, Anita Bowles, Victor Frank, Dorna Richardson, and Suzanne Freynik. 2014. "Technologies for Foreign Language Learning: A Review of Technology Types and Their Effectiveness." *Computer Assisted Language Learning* 27, no. 1: 70–105. http://dx.doi.org/10.1080/09588221.2012.700315.

Guzmán, Sergio. 2013. "Textbooks in SHS Programs: What Has Been Adopted and Why." Paper delivered at the ACTFL Annual Convention, Orlando, FL, November 22–24.

Henshaw, Florencia. Forthcoming. "Online Courses for Heritage Learners: Best Practices and Lessons Learned." In *Advances in Spanish as a Heritage Language*, ed. Diego Pascual. Studies in Bilingualism series. Amsterdam: John Benjamins.

Lee, Jin Sook. 2006. "Exploring the Relationship between Electronic Literacy and Heritage Language Maintenance." *Language Learning & Technology* 10, no. 2: 93–113.

Leeman, Jennifer, and Ellen Serafini. 2016. "Sociolinguistics for Heritage Language Educators and Students: A Model for Critical Translingual Competence." In *Innovative Strategies for Heritage Language Teaching: A Practical Guide for the Classroom*, ed. Marta Fairclough and Sara M. Beaudrie, 56–79. Washington, DC: Georgetown University Press.

Loewen, Donald. 2008. "Overcoming Aural Proficiency: Pitfalls for Heritage Learners in Russian Cyberspace." *Heritage Language Journal* 6, no. 1: 23–39.

Lomicka, Lara, and Gillian Lord. 2012. "A Tale of Tweets: Analyzing Microblogging among Language Learners." *System* 40, no. 1: 48–63. http://dx.doi.org/10.1016/j.system.2011.11.001.

Margaryan, Anoush, Allison Littlejohn, and Gabrielle Vojt. 2011. "Are Digital Natives a Myth or Reality? University Students' Use of Digital Technologies." *Computers & Education* 56, no. 2: 429–40. http://dx.doi.org/10.1016/j.compedu.2010.09.004.

Martínez, Glenn. 2016. "Goals and Beyond in Heritage Language Education: From Competencies to Capabilities." In *Innovative Strategies for Heritage Language Teaching: A Practical Guide for the Classroom*, ed. Marta Fairclough and Sara M. Beaudrie, 39–55. Washington, DC: Georgetown University Press.

Meskill, Carla, and Natasha Anthony. 2008. "Computer Mediated Communication: Tools for Instructing Russian Heritage Language Learners." *Heritage Language Journal* 6, no. 1: 1–22.

Mikulski, Ariana. 2006. "Accent-uating Rules and Relationships: Motivations, Attitudes, and Goals in a Spanish for Native Speakers Class." *Foreign Language Annals* 39, no. 4: 660–82.

Mills, Nicole. 2011. "Situated Learning through Social Networking Communities: The Development of Joint Enterprise, Mutual Engagement, and a Shared Repertoire." *CALICO Journal* 28, no. 2: 345–68. http://dx.doi.org/10.11139/cj.28.2.345-368.

Murday, Kimmaree, Eiko Ushida, and N. Ann Chenoweth. 2008. "Learners and Teachers Perspectives on Language Online." *Computer Assisted Language Learning* 21, no. 2: 125–42. http://dx.doi.org/10.1080/09588220801943718.

NHLRC. 2013. "Instructional Materials." Curriculum Guidelines for Heritage Language Classrooms at the University of California. http://web.international.ucla.edu/nhlrc/page/curriculumguidelines/materials.

O'Dowd, Robert. 2005. "The Use of Videoconferencing and E-mail as Mediators of Intercultural Student Ethnography." In *Internet-Mediated Intercultural Foreign Language Education*, ed. Julie Beltz and Steven Thorne, 86–119. Boston: Cengage.

———, ed. 2007. *Online Intercultural Exchange: An Introduction for Foreign Language Teachers*. Clevedon, UK: Multilingual Matters.

Park, Seong, and Mela Sarkar. 2007. "Parents' Attitudes toward Heritage Language Maintenance for Their Children and Their Efforts to Help Their Children Maintain the Heritage Language: A Case Study of Korean-Canadian Immigrants." *Language, Culture and Curriculum* 20, no. 3: 223–35. http://dx.doi.org/10.2167/lcc337.0.

Payne, Scott, and Brenda Ross. 2005. "Synchronous CMC, Working Memory, and L2 Oral Proficiency Development." *Language Learning & Technology* 9, no. 3: 34–54.

Rubio, Fernando. 2012. "The Effects of Blended Learning on Second Language Fluency and Proficiency." In *Hybrid Language Teaching and Learning: Exploring Theoretical, Pedagogical and Curricular Issues*, ed. Fernando Rubio and Joshua Thoms, 137–59. Boston: Cengage.

Samaniego, Malena, and Chantelle Warner. 2016. "Designing Meaning in Inherited Languages: A Multiliteracies Approach to HL Instruction." In *Innovative Strategies for Heritage Language Teaching: A Practical Guide for the Classroom*, ed. Marta Fairclough and Sara M. Beaudrie, 191–213. Washington, DC: Georgetown University Press.

Scida, Emily, and Rachel Saury. 2006. "Hybrid Courses and Their Impact on Student and Classroom Performance: A Case Study at the University of Virginia." *CALICO Journal* 23, no. 3: 517–31.

Smith, Bryan. 2004. "Computer-mediated Negotiated Interaction and Lexical Acquisition." *Studies in Second Language Acquisition* 26, no. 3: 365–98. http://dx.doi.org/10.1017/S027226310426301X.

Strambi, Antonella, and Eric Bouvet. 2003. "Flexibility and Interaction at a Distance: A Mixed-Mode Environment for Language Learning." *Language Learning & Technology* 7, no. 3: 81–102.

Sykes, Julie. 2005. "Synchronous CMC and Pragmatic Development: Effects of Oral and Written Chat." *CALICO Journal* 22, no. 3: 399–431.

Templeton, Shane, and Darrell Morris. 2001. "Reconceptualizing Spelling Development and Instruction." *Reading Online* 5 (3).

Thoms, Joshua. 2012. "Analyzing Linguistic Outcomes of L2 Learners: Hybrid vs. Traditional Course Contexts." In *Hybrid Language Teaching and Learning: Exploring Theoretical, Pedagogical and Curricular Issues*, ed. Fernando Rubio and Joshua Thoms, 177–95. Boston: Cengage.

Wang, Shenggao, and Deoksoon Kim. 2014. "Incorporating Facebook in an Intermediate-Level Chinese Language Course: A Case Study." *IALLT Journal for Language Learning Technologies* 44, no. 1: 38–78.

Young, Dolly. 2008. "An Empirical Investigation of the Effects of Blended Learning on Student Outcomes in a Redesigned Intensive Spanish Course." *CALICO Journal* 26:160–81.

Zeng, Gang, and Shigenobu Takatsuka. 2009. "Text-Based Peer–Peer Collaborative Dialogue in a Computer-Mediated Learning Environment in the EFL Context." *System* 37, no. 3: 434–46. http://dx.doi.org/10.1016/j.system.2009.01.003.

AFTERWORD

Curricularizing Language

Implications for Heritage Language Instruction

Guadalupe Valdés
STANFORD UNIVERSITY

In the last several years, the field of heritage language (HL) teaching and learning has grown and changed in important ways. The stepchild status of HL programs within foreign, national-language literature departments is still an issue in some contexts, but the role and contribution of these programs to the education of young, non-English-background Americans has been transforming over time in a world that is characterized by globalization, superdiversity (Blommaert and Rampton 2011) and transidiomatic practices (Jacquemet 2005). Not surprisingly, discussions in the field go far beyond where we started many years ago. For example, there is a growing awareness that a large number of American students have a personal connection with a language that is part of their heritage (recent or distant) and a strong desire to reacquire, strengthen, and develop this "beloved language" (Fishman 1997). This is an important part of their birthright and legacy and a fundamental element of their past, their present, and their future.

As a result, the field has grown rapidly in the last several years, engaging the attention of scholars and practitioners in the examination of HL instruction in a number of both commonly and uncommonly taught languages. The body of knowledge that informs the broad field of HL teaching goes beyond applied linguistics and language pedagogy and includes discussions of language ideologies (Leeman 2005; Leeman and Martínez 2007; Showstack 2012), identity (Potowski 2007; Potowski and Matts 2008), assessment (Fairclough 2006, 2011; Malone, Peyton, and Kim 2014), and demographics (Potowski 2014). More importantly, perhaps, we are beginning to engage in debates about difficult theoretical issues such as "incomplete acquisition" (Benmamoun, Montrul, and Polinsky 2013; Montrul 2002, 2008; Pascual y Cabo and Rothman 2012; Otheguy, 2013).

This volume is a major and singular contribution to the field of HL instruction. It moves the field many steps forward by drawing from previous work carried out over decades as well as by critiquing and interrogating understandings of issues, questions, and challenges surrounding the teaching and learning of heritage languages. Contributors to the volume include scholars and researchers committed to improving the practice of HL instruction in a variety of languages and in a number of settings.

In the introduction to the volume the editors state their goals clearly:

- To present "a state-of-the-art overview of current practices in HL teaching in the United States based on cutting-edge knowledge drawn from extant research";
- To advance "a working model for the HL classroom in each of the key instructional areas informed by research on heritage languages from linguistic, sociolinguistic, psycholinguistic, and educational perspectives";
- To include "an overview of the types of challenges faced by initiatives to transfer findings from research to teaching"; and
- To offer "suggestions on how to overcome practical problems associated with the implementation of innovative teaching approaches."

In meeting these goals, the volume's main emphasis is *innovation*, defined as including ideas, processes, and products that are original, groundbreaking, pioneering, or improved. The chapters that make up this book, therefore, focus on theoretical and instructional innovations and program designs aimed at creating and ensuring student involvement, engagement, and lifetime commitment to the development of multicompentence (Cook 1996).

The editors have asked that my contribution to the volume address current innovations and future possibilities for the field of HL learning. In so doing, I draw from a framework (more fully developed in Valdés [2015]) for thinking about the challenges that are faced by policy makers, researchers, and practitioners who are engaged in language-teaching program design, evaluation, and study. I focus specifically on HL teaching and learning but draw from my current work on bilingualism and second language (L2) acquisition more broadly to examine the intersecting mechanisms that are involved in what I refer to as *curricularizing* language (Kibler and Valdés, 2016).

CURRICULARIZING LANGUAGE

I use the phrase "curricularizing language" to refer to the process of organizing and selecting elements from a particular dialect or variety of a language (e.g., Spanish, French, German, Chinese) for instructional purposes as if they could be arranged into a finite, agreed-upon set of structures, skills, tasks, or functions. When language is curricularized, its "teaching" is approached as if it were an ordinary academic subject, the learning of which is parallel to learning science, history, or mathematics. It is assumed that "language" can be "taught" and "learned" in classroom settings, its "study" awarded units of credit, and its "learning" generally assessed by paper and pencil examinations. Concentrating most often on standardized or prestige varieties of language, such curricularization is informed by conceptualizations of language drawn from informing disciplines and theoretical perspectives, by ideologies of language, by traditions of instruction, by existing textbooks and materials, and by language policies that define unit/credit institutional requirements. Figure A.1 depicts the various mechanisms involved.

As depicted in figure A.1, the curricularization of language—that is, the design and implementation of language-teaching programs—is part of a multi-element system composed of a number of mechanisms. Designing a language curriculum in the United States is directly informed by language policies that are enacted at multiple levels (state, school district, institution) and regulate foreign or world language instruction. These policies establish the specific languages that are offered as subjects in schools and universities as well as the outcomes of elementary, secondary, and postsecondary foreign or world language instruction. These policies also establish expected competencies and proficiencies, implement standards of various types (e.g., ACTFL Standards), align secondary programs with higher education entry and credit-granting regulations and guidelines, and ensure the implementation

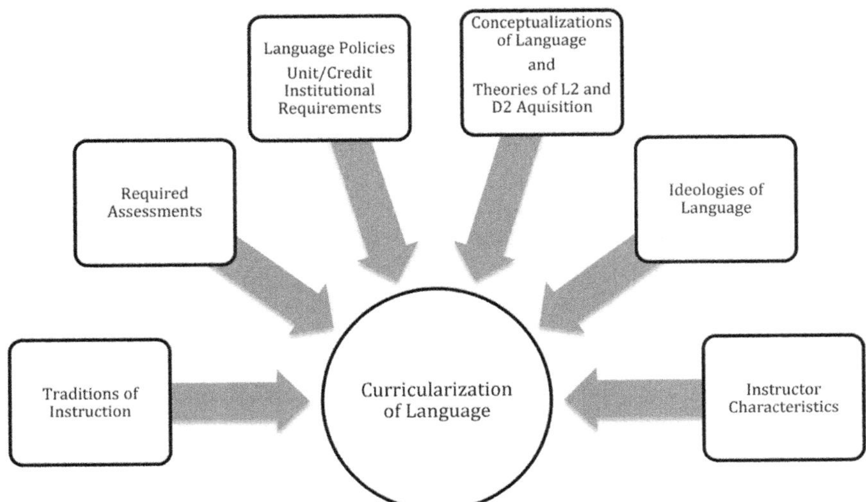

Figure A.1. Mechanisms Involved in the Curricularization of Language in the United States

of curricula and instructional practices that can provide students with the preparation they will need to complete: secondary-level foreign language requirements mandated by the state, courses required for college entry, and units needed for fulfilling college and university graduation requirements.

The process of curricularization also draws from traditions of instruction that include

- the identification of student levels and placement procedures,
- agreement on elements to be covered,
- decisions on approaches and methods to be used in instruction, and
- decisions about the selection of textbooks and other instructional materials selection.

The identification, categorization, and conceptualization of language learners are particularly noteworthy because these processes are uniquely shaped by formalized language instruction. Such instruction both creates and requires the social construction of language-learner categories that, while they may appear to be neutral and common sense descriptions of student characteristics (McDermott 1996), nevertheless deeply affect the academic lives of students who are sorted and categorized in ways that seriously impact their lives (Kibler and Valdés, 2016; Valdés, Poza, and Brooks, 2014).

As is suggested by figure A.1, required assessments are also an essential part of curricularization processes. These assessments are intended to determine the degree to which students have acquired the required knowledge or the functional proficiency expected. Assessments include formative procedures that provide information for teaching as well as end-of-course and end-of-program summative examinations to measure program outcomes as mandated by relevant language policies.

Equally important in the process of curricularization are instructor characteristics. Inevitably, the language proficiencies, background, and preparation of available instructors have a strong impact on program design. It matters how well instructors speak the language, what varieties of the language they are familiar with, and how knowledgeable they are about second language and/or second dialect acquisition theories and with particular pedagogies informed and supported by these theories.

The design of language curricula is also influenced by ideologies of language, that is, by largely unexamined ideas and beliefs that shape people's thinking about language and about those who use language. Language ideologies—often multiple and conflicting—help compose the institutional and social fabric of a culture (Kroskrity 2004, 2010; Woolard and Schieffelin 1994) and include notions of what is "true," "morally good," or "aesthetically pleasing" about language, including who speaks and does not speak "correctly." They also inform conceptualizations of what language is and how it is acquired and the construction of both heritage and foreign language learners (Kibler and Valdés, 2016). In the case of Spanish HL learners, their construction is influenced by the backgrounds of their instructors (Valdés 2006; Valdés et al. 2008), including whether they are speakers of Peninsular or Latin American Spanish or are anglophone individuals who have acquired Spanish as a second language. Instructors' comfort with their ascribed identities as hispanophones in the United States also matters, as does their acceptance or challenge of hegemonic ideologies of *hispanofonía* (Del Valle 2006, 2007, 2009; Mar-Molinero and Paffey 2011; Paffey 2007, 2012; Urciuoli 2008).

As is also noted in figure A.1, conceptualizations of language have a direct impact on the design of instruction. The ways in which program language policy makers, language researchers, and language instructors conceptualize language defines the specific content of the instruction and the goals and outcomes of the teaching and learning enterprise. Conceptualizations and definitions of language vary in important ways, however. To illustrate the profound differences in existing conceptualizations of language, Cook (2010a) provides various definitions of language, including

1. A human representation system, a species-unique format for representation and an abstract external entity, a set of rules similar to other rule systems (e.g., chess, football).
2. A set of actual or potential sentences, patterns of data internalized in usage models of language.
3. A social phenomenon, a cultural product, the possession of a community.
4. The knowledge in the mind of an individual, "a mental state, consisting of rules, weightings, principles, or whatever, which constitutes their language" according to Chomsky's views of language competence.
5. A mode of action, a set of observable actions that people use in order to *do* things, rather than a simple mode for transmitting information, a vehicle for carrying out speech acts (e.g., requesting, challenging) in the external world.

These definitions are clearly different and give rise to dramatically dissimilar assumptions about both "teaching" and "learning" languages. Cook (2010b) argues, therefore, that because discussions of learning in second language acquisition (SLA) depend on often contradictory definitions of language, arguments about language learning are generally unwinnable because individuals taking one perspective on language (based on a particular conceptualization of language) cannot account for aspects of language the existence of which the other side denies.

Teaching language, however, as emphasized by recent work in applied linguistics (e.g., Seedhouse, Walsh, and Jenks 2010) requires agreement on

- What we mean by language;
- What it is that has to be learned/taught given that definition of language;
- What it is that needs to be taught given different learner characteristics and goals;
- What we know (and don't know) about how those aspects of language are learned; and
- What we know about how teachable these aspects of language are learned or acquired in a classroom context.

For example, in designing language programs and classes, we can conceptualize language as a set of building blocks (pronunciation, vocabulary, grammar, and meaning) acquired one block at a time through direct instruction; ways of speaking and writing that can be classified as correct or incorrect, standard or nonstandard, native and nonnative; or a communicative repertoire (Rymes 2010) acquired in actual use, which includes a number of styles and registers of one or more language(s) (e.g., colloquial, presentational, intimate, casual, and more literate-like varieties of language). There are significant differences between these three orientations, and teaching programs defining language in these three ways will organize instruction in very dissimilar ways.

Conceptualizations of language also directly inform views and theories about the language acquisition process—hence the importance of SLA in the process of curricularizing language. The HL teaching field, for example, because of its close relationship with foreign language teaching, often looks to the field of SLA for theoretical grounding on the process of acquisition and for theories about the characteristics of ultimate attainment. Importantly, in the last decade, the field of SLA has been divided into two opposing theoretical perspectives, characterized as incommensurable by some scholars (Ortega 2013; Zuengler and Miller 2006). Mainstream SLA takes the position that what is to be acquired is the abstract grammatical system of the target language, and it views language acquisition as an individual cognitive process that results in a change in a learner's mental state. Whether in naturalistic or instructed settings, the ultimate goal of L2 acquisition for cognitivist-oriented scholars is the "native-like" internalization of the target language's grammatical system in its entirety (Larsen-Freeman 1997). The socially oriented SLA position considers that the process of acquisition—rather than focusing exclusively on the developing linguistic systems of learners—is concerned with understanding how speakers of one language become users (speakers, writers, readers) of a second language. From the social perspective, the goal of second language learners is not necessarily to become like native speakers of the language but to use the language to function competently in a variety of contexts for a range of purposes.

Chaos and Complexity Theory (Larsen-Freeman 2002, 2003, 2010, 2012; Larsen-Freeman and Cameron 2008) and Dynamic Systems Theory (De Bot et al. 2007) have raised additional questions about the nature of language acquisition and have emphasized the centrality of variability in the SLA process. Within this theoretical perspective, SLA is a complex adaptive process that is itself self-organizing and intrinsically variable. Interacting elements constantly change, and language forms are considered to emerge in language use. Individual variability is considered central, and, as Diane Larsen-Freeman (1997) has argued, no single "end-state" is expected as the result of the process of SLA.

In addition, the cumulative scholarship on individual and societal bilingualism (Auer 2007; Bialystok 2009; García and Wei 2013; Grosjean 1985, 1989, 1997, 2010; Heller 2007; Otsuji and Pennycook 2010; Wei 2013) has established that

- Bilinguals are specific speaker-hearers;
- Bilinguals are not two monolinguals in one;
- Bilinguals use their multiple linguistic repertories in a variety of ways in order to meet their communicative needs;
- Bilinguals do not normally have the same levels of proficiency in all language modalities (speaking, listening, reading, and writing) in each of their languages; and
- Bilinguals should be compared only to other bilinguals and not to monolinguals in any one of their languages.

Stephen May (2013) has referred to these changing theoretical perspectives as directly informing the "multilingual turn" in applied linguistics. This shift in orientation is seen as a natural consequence of a progressively more globalized world in which the acquisition and use of subsequent languages has been found not to lead to monolingual-like usage. It also is a product of the growing problematization and rejection of the tendency to view individuals acquiring a second language as failed native speakers (Bonfiglio 2010; Canagarajah 1999; Cook 1999; Davies 1991; Doerr and Lee 2013; Kramsch 1997; Leung, Harris, and Rampton 1997; Ortega 2013).

Currently, outside of mainstream SLA, there is increasing agreement on the following points:

- SLA is a highly variable process.
- SLA is not linear.
- Ultimate attainment for most L2 learners does not result in monolingual-like language, even when the L2 is acquired by young children (Ortega 2009).
- Teaching may not cause learning (Larsen-Freeman 2013).

Lourdes Ortega (2013) in a provocatively titled article, "SLA for the 21st Century: Disciplinary Progress, Transdisciplinary Relevance and the Bi/Multilingual Turn," draws attention to the difference between SLA and second dialect acquisition, challenges the "straight jacket of the comparative fallacy" present in SLA (Bley-Vroman 1983; Klein 1998; Cook 1992), and calls for a reframing of the field that moves it away from the target deviation perspective that has been dominant.

LOOKING TOWARD THE FUTURE: THE UNIQUE CONTRIBUTIONS OF THIS VOLUME

The implications of the theoretical shifts that I have summarized above for the field of HL learning are clear. What we know and think about L2 acquisition has shifted significantly. This means that that our examination of the process of HL teaching and learning must also shift, as must our expectations of the "ultimate attainment" of HLs. This volume makes unique contributions to our understanding of the various aspects of the process of curricularizing language as I have outlined it and offers the field important directions for the future. Chapters address the several mechanisms of HL curricularization, clearly illustrating how the teaching of heritage languages operates while making evident the various challenges that are still before us.

Categorizations of learners, for example, matter. In chapter 1, Eve Zyzik attends specifically to the important issue of the greater "variability" of HL learners in comparison to "native speakers." Dismissing narrow views of proficiency measured in numerous disparate ways, Zyzik proposes a prototype model based on implicit knowledge as a key attribute in understanding the population of HL students. She draws from other recent research to identify factors (e.g., number of different speakers that regularly use the heritage language with particular individuals) that might affect students' distance from the prototype. Glenn Martínez (chapter 2) also addresses the issue of learner categorizations and program learning goals in a particularly novel way by proposing the notion of "capabilities" rather than competencies. Explaining that capabilities refer to what an individual is able *to do* and *to be*, he argues for HL instruction that has a much broader agenda and is deeply embedded in community-based learning, within which the heritage language is used for a broad number of purposes and goals.

Jennifer Leeman and Ellen Serafini (chapter 3) address ideologies of language and propose a critical model of HL program design that challenges monolingual normative models including well-meaning perspectives on language appropriateness. They argue for instruction that allows students to study contextual and stylistic variation. Similarly, María Luisa Parra (chapter 8) presents a critical model of HL instruction informed by sociolinguistic knowledge and a multiliteracies framework. She, too, advocates for the implementation of community service–learning programs through critical dialogues informed by the recent multilingual turn in applied linguistics and problematizes notions of standardness and native-like production. These two perspectives are congruent with socially oriented views of HL acquisition that are parallel to those found in nonmainstream orientations in SLA. Malena Samaniego and Chantelle Warner, in chapter 9, expand further on the challenge of responding pedagogically to current deficit perspectives present in the HL field. Focusing on the difficulties of helping students develop "academic" literacies without degrading vernacular varieties, these authors propose a multiliteracies framework that can help students to understand linguistic choices in writing and to develop strategies for redesigning existing genres to voice their own meanings powerfully.

Marta Fairclough, in chapter 7, and Maria Carreira, in chapter 6, illustrate to some degree the presence and use of both mainstream and socially oriented SLA perspectives in heritage language acquisition in establishing instructional goals for HL students. Fairclough addresses both ideologies of standardness as well as theoretical mechanisms and conceptualizations of language that have traditionally informed the field. She focuses on the process of second dialect acquisition, seeking to understand the trajectory of the acquisition of standard varieties by HL learners by drawing from work on second dialect acquisition among African Americans. Carreira focuses specifically on the teaching of the linguistic system (grammar) to HL learners, building from Olga Kagan's views on macro- versus micro-based pedagogies. Comparing both approaches, Carreira describes the use of macro- and micro-based teaching approaches in mixed classes and the benefits and limits of form-focused instruction given the particular needs and backgrounds of both groups of students. She takes into account the established expected outcomes of HL study in traditional departments of foreign language.

Other key issues that are central to the curricularization of language are also addressed in the volume. Program design and program evaluation are examined and problematized by Sara Beaudrie in chapter 4, making evident the challenges of establishing quality HL programs by providing examples of existing well-conceptualized initiatives. Manel Lacorte, in chapter 5, addresses the enormous task of preparing HL instructors. His discussion is informed by both the L1 and L2 acquisition fields and by current work in multiliteracies and translanguaging. He presents a thorough blueprint for HL teacher development that is both theoretically and pedagogically grounded and urges attention to ideological, cultural, and socioaffective considerations. Finally, the important issues of assessment and materials selection (chapter 11) are included. Gabriela Ilieva and Beth Clark-Gareca (chapter 10) provide an overview of the very serious existing challenges of assessing both proficiency and progress in HL learning. In so doing, they outline an agenda for developing empirically based language progressions, for experimenting with computer-adaptive assessments, for challenging the limitations of OPI-type assessments for HL, and for developing valid and reliable placement procedures. In chapter 11, Florencia Henshaw examines the problem of appropriate materials selection in language curricularization by describing the benefits and limitations of technology integration in HL instruction. She provides an overview of recent research including both benefits and pitfalls, and she comments that an important challenge to be surmounted is the availability of appropriate online materials. The article offers a set of examples of various uses of technology as well as tools and projects that can be used in meaningful, real-life communication with other HL speakers.

In sum, this new and much-needed volume focusing on HL teaching and learning makes unique and essential innovative contributions to the field of HL learning and to the understanding of what I have characterized as curricularizing language in the field of HL instruction. The chapters focus on the future both directly and indirectly and offer new perspectives and new orientations to those seeking to develop HL programs, to prepare instructors to work with HL learners, to assess progress and proficiency, and to engage in groundbreaking pedagogies building on the sophisticated language resources of HL students. The contributors to this volume point out the limitations of existing approaches; they describe new solutions, and they interrogate ideologies and deficit thinking that have made the teaching and learning of HLs a particularly difficult enterprise. As one who continues to follow the field closely, I am grateful to the editors and the authors for moving us forward in significant ways.

REFERENCES

Auer, Peter. 2007. "The Monolingual Bias in Bilingualism Research, Or: Why Bilingual Talk Is (Still) a Challenge for Linguistics." In *Bilingualism: A Social Approach*, ed. Monica Heller, 320–39. London: Palgrave.

Benmamoun, Elabbas, Silvina Montrul, and Maria Polinsky. 2013. "Heritage Languages and Their Speakers: Opportunities and Challenges for Linguistics." *Theoretical Linguistics* 39, no. 3–4: 129–81.

Bialystok, Ellen. 2009. "Bilingualism: The Good, the Bad, and the Indifferent." *Bilingualism: Language and Cognition* 12, no. 1: 3–11. http://dx.doi.org/10.1017/S1366728908003477.

Bley-Vroman, Robert. 1983. "The Comparative Fallacy in Interlanguage Studies: The Case of Systematicity." *Language Learning* 33, no. 1: 1–17. http://dx.doi.org/10.1111/j.1467-1770.1983.tb00983.x.

Blommaert, Jan, and Ben Rampton. 2011. "Language and Superdiversity." *Diversities* 13:3–21.

Bonfiglio, Thomas Paul. 2010. *Mother Tongues and Nations: The Invention of the Native Speaker*, Trends in Linguistics, Studies and Monographs series, 226. Berlin: Walter de Gruyter. http://dx.doi.org/10.1515/9781934078266.

Canagarajah, A. Suresh. 1999. "Interrogating the "Native Speaker Fallacy": Non-Linguistic Roots, Non-Pedagogical Results." In *Non-Native Educators in English Language Teaching*, ed. George Braine, 77–92. Mahwah, NJ: Lawrence Erlbaum.

Cook, Vivian. 1992. "Evidence for Multi-Competence." *Language Learning* 42, no. 4: 557–91. http://dx.doi.org/10.1111/j.1467-1770.1992.tb01044.x.

———. 1996. "Competence and Multi-Competence." In *Performance and Competence in Second Language Acquisition*, ed. Gillian Brown, Kirsten Malmkjaer, and John Williams, 57–69. Cambridge: Cambridge University Press.

———. 1999. "Going Beyond the Native Speaker in Language Teaching." *TESOL Quarterly* 33, no. 2: 185–209. http://dx.doi.org/10.2307/3587717.

———. 2010a. "Prolegomena to Second Language Learning." In *Conceptualizing "Learning" in Applied Linguistics*, ed. Paul Seedhouse, Steve Walsh, and Chris Jenks, 6–22. New York: Palgrave.

———. 2010b. "The Relationship between First and Second Language Acquisition Revisited." In *Continuum Companion to Second-Language Acquisition*, ed. Ernesto Macaro, 137–57. London: Continuum International Publishing.

Davies, Alan. 1991. *The Native Speaker in Applied Linguistics*. Edinburgh: Edinburgh University Press.

De Bot, Kees, Wander Lowie, and Marjolijn Verspoor. 2007. "A Dynamic Systems Theory Approach to Second Language Acquisition." *Bilingualism: Language and Cognition* 10, no. 1: 7–21. http://dx.doi.org/10.1017/S1366728906002732.

Del Valle, José. 2006. "US Latinos, la hispanofonía, and the Language Ideologies of High Modernity." In *Globalization and Language in the Spanish-Speaking World: Macro and Micro Perspectives*, ed. Clare Mar-Molinero and Mirand Steward, 27–46. London: Palgrave Macmillan.

———. 2007. "Embracing Diversity for the Sake of Unity: Linguistic Hegemony and the Pursuit of Total Spanish." In *Discourses of Endangerment: Ideology and Interest in the Defence of Languages*, ed. Alexandre Duchene and Monica Heller, 242–67. London: Continuum.

———. 2009. "Total Spanish: The Politics of a Pan-Hispanic Grammar." *PMLA* 124: 880–86.

Doerr, Neriko, and Kiri Lee. 2013. *Constructing the Heritage Language Learner: Knowledge, Power and New Subjectivities*, Contributions to the Sociology of Language series, 103. Berlin: Walter de Gruyter. http://dx.doi.org/10.1515/9781614512837.

Fairclough, Marta. 2006. "Language Placement Exams for Heritage Speakers of Spanish: Learning from Students' Mistakes." *Foreign Language Annals* 39, no. 4: 595–604. http://dx.doi.org/10.1111/j.1944-9720.2006.tb02278.x.

———. 2011. "Testing the Lexical Recognition Task with Spanish/English Bilinguals in the United States." *Language Testing* 28, no. 2: 273–97. http://dx.doi.org/10.1177/0265532210393151.

Fishman, Joshua A. 1997. *In Praise of the Beloved Language: A Positive View of Positive Ethnolinguistic Competence*. Berlin: Walter De Gruyter. http://dx.doi.org/10.1515/9783110813241.

García, Ofelia, and Lee Wei. 2013. *Translanguaging: Language, Bilingualism and Education*. London: Palgrave Macmillan. http://dx.doi.org/10.1057/9781137385765.

Grosjean, Francois. 1985. "The Bilingual as a Competent but Specific Speaker-Hearer." *Journal of Multilingual and Multicultural Development* 6, no. 6: 467–77. http://dx.doi.org/10.1080/01434632.1985.9994221.

———. 1989. "Neurolinguists, Beware! The Bilingual Is not Two Monolinguals in One Person." *Brain and Language* 36, no. 1: 3–15. http://dx.doi.org/10.1016/0093-934X(89)90048-5.

———. 1997. "Processing Mixed Language: Issues Findings and Models." In *Tutorials in Bilingualism*, ed. Annette M. De Groot and Judith F. Kroll, 225–54. Mahwah, NJ: Lawrence Erlbaum.

———. 2010. "The Bilingual as a Competent but Specific Speaker-Hearer." In *Multilingual Norms*, ed. Madalena Cruz-Ferreira, 19–32. Frankfurt: Peter Lang.

Heller, Monica. 2007. "Bilingualism as Ideology and Practice." In *Bilingualism: A Social Approach*, ed. Monica Heller, 1–22. London: Palgrave. http://dx.doi.org/10.1057/9780230596047.

Jacquemet, Marco. 2005. "Transidiomatic Practices: Language and Power in the Age of Globalization." *Language & Communication* 25, no. 3: 257–77. http://dx.doi.org/10.1016/j.langcom.2005.05.001.

Kibler, Amanda, and Guadalupe Valdés. 2016. "Conceptualizing Language Learners: Socio-Institutional Mechanisms and Their Consequences." *Modern Language Journal* 100, no. 16: 96–116.

Klein, Wolfgang. 1998. "The Contribution of Second Language Acquisition Research." *Language Learning* 48, no. 4: 527–49. http://dx.doi.org/10.1111/0023-8333.00057.

Kramsch, Claire. 1997. "The Privilege of the Nonnative Speaker." *PMLA* 112: 359–69.

Kroskrity, Paul V. 2004. "Language Ideologies." In *A Companion to Linguistic Anthropology*, ed. Alessandro Duranti, 496–517. Oxford: Blackwell.

———. 2010. "Language Ideologies–Evolving Perspectives." In *Society and Language Use*, ed. Jürgen Jaspers, Jan-Ola Östman, and Jef Verschueren, 192–211. Amsterdam: John Benjamins. http://dx.doi.org/10.1075/hoph.7.13kro.

Larsen-Freeman, Diane. 1997. "Chaos/Complexity Science and Second Language Acquisition." *Applied Linguistics* 18, no. 2: 141–65. http://doi.org/10.1093/applin/18.2.141.

———. 2002. "Language Acquisition and Language Use from a Chaos/Complexity Theory Perspective." In *Language Acquisition and Language Socialization*, ed. Claire Kramsch, 33–46. London: Continuum.

———. 2003. *Teaching Language: From Grammar to Grammaring*. Boston: Heinle and Heinle.

———. 2010. "Having and Doing: Learning from a Complexity Theory Perspective." In *Conceptualizing "Learning" in Applied Linguistics*, ed. Paul Seedhouse, Steve Walsh, and Chris Jenks, 52–68. New York: Palgrave.

———. 2012. "Chaos/Complexity Theory for Second Language Acquisition." In *The Encyclopedia of Applied Linguistics*, ed. Carol A. Chapelle. Oxford: Wiley Blackwell. http://dx.doi.org/10.1002/9781405198431.wbeal0125.

———. 2013. "The Standards and Second Language Development: A Complexity Theory Perspective." Paper presented at the TESOL Annual Meeting, Dallas, Texas. March 21–23.

Larsen-Freeman, Diane, and Lynne Cameron. 2008. *Complex Systems and Applied Linguistics*. Oxford: Oxford University Press.

Leeman, Jennifer. 2005. "Engaging Critical Pedagogy: Spanish for Native Speakers." *Foreign Language Annals* 38, no. 1: 35–45. http://dx.doi.org/10.1111/j.1944-9720.2005.tb02451.x.

Leeman, Jennifer, and Glenn Martínez. 2007. "From Identity to Commodity: Ideologies of Spanish in Heritage Language Textbooks." *Critical Inquiry in Language Studies* 4, no. 1: 35–65. http://dx.doi.org/10.1080/15427580701340741.

Leung, Constant, Roxy Harris, and Ben Rampton. 1997. "The Idealised Native Speaker, Reified Ethnicities, and Classroom Realities." *TESOL Quarterly* 31, no. 3: 543–60. http://dx.doi.org/10.2307/3587837.

Malone, Margaret E., Joy Kreeft Peyton, and Katie Kim. 2014. "Assessment of Heritage Language Issues: Issues and Directions." In *Handbook of Heritage, Community, and Native American Languages in the United States*, ed. Terrence G. Wiley, Joy Kreeft Peyton, Donna Christian, Sarah C. Moore, and Na Liu, 341–69. New York: Routledge. http://dx.doi.org/10.4324/9780203122419.ch33.

Mar-Molinero, Clare, and Darren Paffey. 2011. "Linguistic Imperialism: Who Owns Spanish?" In *The Handbook of Hispanic Sociolinguistics*, ed. Manuel Díaz-Campos, 747–64. Malden, MA: Wiley–Blackwell. http://dx.doi.org/10.1002/9781444393446.ch35.

May, Stephen. 2013. "Disciplinary Divides, Knowledge Construction and the Multilingual Turn." In *The Multilingual Turn: Implications for SLA, TESOL, and Bilingual Education*, ed. Stephen May, 7–31. New York: Routledge.

McDermott, Raymond. 1996. "The Acquisition of a Child by a Learning Disability." In *Understanding Practice: Perspectives on Activity and Context*, ed. Seth Chaiklin and Jean Lave, 269–305. New York: Cambridge University Press.

Montrul, Silvina. 2002. "Incomplete Acquisition and Attrition of Spanish Tense/Aspect Distinctions in Adult Bilinguals." *Bilingualism: Language and Cognition* 5, no. 1: 39–68. http://dx.doi.org/10.1017/S1366728902000135.

———. 2008. *Incomplete Acquisition in Bilingualism: Re-Examining the Age Factor*, Studies in Bilingualism, 39. Amsterdam: John Benjamins. http://dx.doi.org/10.1075/sibil.39.

Ortega, Lourdes. 2009. *Understanding Second Language Acquisition*. London: Hodder Education.

———. 2013. "SLA for the 21st Century: Disciplinary Progress, Transdisciplinary Relevance, and the Bi/Multilingual Turn." *Language Learning* 63, no. s1: 1–24. http://dx.doi.org/10.1111/j.1467-9922.2012.00735.x.

Otheguy, Ricardo. 2013. "The Linguistic Competence of Second Generation Bilinguals: A Critique of Incomplete Acquisition." In *Romance Linguistics 2013: Selected papers from the 43rd Linguistic Symposium on Romance Languages (LSRL), New York, 17–19 April 2013*, Vol. 9. Amsterdam: John Benjamins.

Otsuji, Emi, and Alastair Pennycook. 2010. "Metrolingualism: Fixity, Fluidity and Language in Flux." *International Journal of Multilingualism* 7, no. 3: 240–54. http://dx.doi.org/10.1080/14790710903414331.

Paffey, Darren. 2007. "Policing the Spanish Language Debate: Verbal Hygiene and the Spanish Language Academy (Real Academia Española)." *Language Policy* 6, no. 3–4: 313–32. http://dx.doi.org/10.1007/s10993-007-9064-5.

———. 2012. *Language Ideologies and the Globalization of 'Standard' Spanish*. London: Bloomsbury Publishing.

Pascual Y. Cabo, Diego, and Jason Rothman. 2012. "The (Il)Logical Problem of Heritage Speaker Bilingualism and Incomplete Acquisition." *Applied Linguistics* 33, no. 4: 450–55. http://dx.doi.org/10.1093/applin/ams037.

Potowski, Kim. 2007. *Language and Identity in a Dual Immersion School*, vol. 63. Clevedon; Buffalo: Multilingual Matters.

———. 2014. "Spanish in the United States." in *Handbook of Heritage, Community, and Native American Languages in the United States*, ed. Terrence G. Wiley, Joy Kreeft Peyton, Donna Christian, Sarah C. Moore, and Na Liu, 90–100. New York: Routledge. http://dx.doi.org/10.4324/9780203122419.ch9.

Potowski, Kim, and Janine Matts. 2008. "MexiRicans: Interethnic Language and Identity." *Journal of Language, Identity, and Education* 7, no. 2: 137–60. http://dx.doi.org/10.1080/15348450801970688.

Rymes, Betsy. 2010. "Communicative Repertoires and English Language Learners." in *The Education of English Language Learners: Research to Practice*, ed. Marilyn Shatz and Louise C. Wilkinson, 177–97. New York: Guildford Press.

Seedhouse, Paul, Steve Walsh, and Chris Jenks, eds. 2010. *Conceptualising "Learning" in Applied Linguistics*. London, New York: Palgrave Macmillan. http://dx.doi.org/10.1057/9780230289772.

Showstack, Rachel E. 2012. "Symbolic Power in the Heritage Language Classroom: How Spanish Heritage Speakers Sustain and Resist Hegemonic Discourses on Language and Cultural Diversity." *Spanish in Context* 9, no. 1: 1–26. http://dx.doi.org/10.1075/sic.9.1.01sho.

Urciuoli, Bonnie. 2008. "Whose Spanish? The Tension between Linguistic Correctness and Cultural Identity." In *Bilingualism and Identity: Spanish at the Crossroads with other Languages*, ed. Mercedes Niño-Murcia and Jason Rothman, 257–77. Amsterdam: John Benjamins. http://dx.doi.org/10.1075/sibil.37.16urc.

Valdés, Guadalupe. 2006. "The Spanish Language in California." in *Developing Minority Language Resources: The Case of Spanish in California*, eds. Guadalupe, Valdés, Joshua Fishman, Rebecca Chávez, and William Pérez, 24–53. Clevedon: Multilingual Matters.

———. 2015. "Latin@s and the Intergenerational Continuity of Spanish: The Challenges of Curricularizing Language." *International Multilingual Research Journal* 9:253–73.

Valdés, Guadalupe, Sonia González, Dania López.Garcia, and Patricio Márquez. 2008. "Ideologies of Monolingualism: The Challenges of Maintaining Non-English Languages through Educational Institutions." In *Heritage Language Acquisition: A New Field Emerging*, ed. Donna. M. Brinton and Olga Kagan, 107–30. New York: Routledge.

Valdés, G., L. Poza, and M. Brooks. 2014. "Educating Students Who Do Not Speak the Societal Language: The Social Construction of Language-Learner Categories." *Profession*, October 9, https://profession.commons.mla.org/2014/10/09/educating-students-who-do-not-speak-the-societal-language/.

Wei, Li. 2013. "Conceptual and Methodological Issues in Bilingualism and Multilingualism Research." In *The Handbook of Bilingualism and Multilingualism*, 2nd ed., ed. Tej K. Bhatia and William C. Ritchie, 26–51. Oxford: Wiley Blackwell.

Woolard, Kathryn A., and Bambi B. Schieffelin. 1994. "Language Ideology." *Annual Review of Anthropology* 23, no. 1: 55–82. http://dx.doi.org/10.1146/annurev.an.23.100194.000415.

Zuengler, Jane, and Elizabeth R. Miller. 2006. "Cognitive and Sociocultural Perspectives: Two Parallel SLA Worlds." *TESOL Quarterly* 40, no. 1: 35–58. http://dx.doi.org/10.2307/40264510.

Contributors

Sara M. Beaudrie is an associate professor of Spanish linguistics in the School of International Letters and Cultures at Arizona State University, where she directs the second language and heritage language programs. Her research focuses on heritage language pedagogy and development, heritage language maintenance, and heritage language program and curriculum development. She is the co-editor of *Spanish as a Heritage Language in the United States: The State of the Field*, published by Georgetown University Press in 2012, and coauthor of *Heritage Language Pedagogy: Research and Practice* (McGraw-Hill, 2014) as well as numerous book chapters and scholarly articles.

Maria Carreira is the codirector of the National Heritage Language Resource Center at UCLA and a professor of Spanish at California State University, Long Beach. Her research focuses on Spanish in the United States, heritage language teaching and learning, and the education of US Latinos. She is the coauthor of four Spanish textbooks published by Cengage (*Nexos*, *Alianzas*, *Cuadros*, and *Sí se Puede*) and *Voces: Latino Students on Life in the United States* (Praeger, 2014), which offers an intimate view of what it is like to grow up Latino in this country, focusing on the intersection of language, culture, and education. Maria Carreira served as chair of the Spanish SAT Committee.

Beth Clark-Gareca, PhD, is a lecturer in the TESOL/Applied Linguistics program and the head of the TESOL K–12 Certification Track at Teachers College, Columbia University. Her research focuses on classroom-based assessment for emergent bilinguals and teacher education in K–12 contexts. She has taught English as a second language, English as a foreign language, and Spanish as well as teacher professional development in a variety of contexts for over twenty years. In 2015 she was granted a Fulbright Scholar Award in Argentina.

Marta Fairclough is an associate professor of Spanish linguistics and director of Spanish Heritage Language Education at the University of Houston. She previously served as department chair and director of undergraduate studies. Her research focuses on heritage language education and US Spanish. She has published a book (Iberoamericana, 2005) and a co-edited volume (Georgetown University Press, 2012) as well as numerous book chapters and articles. In 2012 she received the Provost Teaching Excellence Award, and in 2013 she was granted a Fulbright Scholar Award to Croatia.

Florencia Henshaw earned a PhD in second language acquisition and teacher education from the University of Illinois, Urbana–Champaign, where she is now the director of Advanced Spanish. Her research interests focus on evaluating the extent to which different pedagogical tools and practices may be beneficial to second language and heritage language learners not only in terms of linguistic gains but also with respect to the learners' perceptions and attitudes. She has also authored two Spanish textbooks: one for grammar review courses and one for composition courses.

Gabriela Ilieva is a clinical professor of South Asian Studies and coordinator of the South Asian Languages Program at the Department of Middle Eastern and Islamic Studies, New York University (NYU). She has been the academic director of the Hindi and Urdu Teacher Training Summer Institute, funded by the STARTALK grant since 2008. She has received the NYU Golden Dozen Teaching Excellence Award and Program Excellence Award, University Continuing Education Association (UCEA) Mid-Atlantic Region. She has published research on Hindi and Urdu heritage speakers and on project-based learning as well as on the construction of gender identity in Sanskrit.

Manel Lacorte is an associate professor of Spanish applied linguistics, director of the Spanish Language Program, and director of the Master's in Hispanic Applied Linguistics Program at the University of Maryland. He is also associate director of undergraduate studies at the Spanish School, Middlebury College. His research and publications focus on L2 pedagogy and teacher education, classroom interaction and context(s), applied linguistics, and sociopolitical issues in L2 and heritage language teaching and learning. He is a co-editor of the Theory and Practice in Second Language Classroom Instruction series (Pearson) and associate editor of the *Journal of Spanish Language Teaching*.

Jennifer Leeman is an associate professor of Spanish at George Mason University and research sociolinguist at the Center for Survey Measurement at the US Census Bureau. Her research focuses on critical approaches to heritage language education; ideologies and representations of language, race, and nation in the United States; census questions on race and language; and language policy. She has published numerous journal articles and book chapters and co-edited the volume *Spanish in the US and Other Contact Environments: Sociolinguistics, Ideology and Pedagogy* (Iberoamericana 2009) with Manel Lacorte.

Glenn Martínez is a professor of Hispanic linguistics and chair of the Department of Spanish and Portuguese at the Ohio State University. His research focuses on language policy in the United States, Spanish in health care settings, and heritage language education. He is the author of *Mexican Americans and Language* (Arizona University Press, 2006) and coauthor of

Recovering the US Hispanic Linguistic Heritage (Arte Público, 2008). He has published numerous book chapters and scholarly articles and has served as principal investigator on research and education projects from the National Institutes of Health, the US Department of Education, and the National Endowment for the Humanities.

María Luisa Parra is a Spanish senior preceptor and undergraduate advisor in Spanish, Latin American, and Latino studies at the Department of Romance Languages and Literatures at Harvard University. She pioneered the first Spanish-language sequence for Latino students at Harvard and directs the RLLs' initiative on the teaching of Spanish as heritage language. Her research interests focus on pedagogy for Spanish as a heritage language, bilingualism in Latino children, and the impact of immigration in Latino children's process of school adaptation (Paidós, 2005). She has published in the *Heritage Language Journal* (2013) and the AAUSC series Issues in Language Program Direction (2013 and 2015).

Ana Roca is a former professor of Spanish and linguistics at Florida International University and is now an independent scholar and consultant. Although recently retired, she continues to focus on and publish in the areas of Spanish-English bilingualism in the United States and the teaching of Spanish as a heritage language at the college and secondary levels. She has numerous publications in her field and is currently working on the fourth edition of *Nuevos mundos* (Wiley), a college text for heritage learners, and an edited volume on bilingualism and sociolinguistic research on Spanish in contact.

Malena Samaniego is an assistant professor in the English Pedagogy Program at the Universidad Austral de Chile in Valdivia. She is currently a PhD candidate in second language acquisition and teaching at the University of Arizona. Her dissertation research focuses on the politics of translation studies as it is played out in education, particularly on the assumptions by educators as well as students on translating and translator education. At Universidad Austral she taught Spanish as a heritage language as well as translation and interpretation in the Spanish and Portuguese Department. Her research considers translation pedagogy from multiple perspectives, including teacher and student beliefs about language and translation, multiliteracies approaches, and language development in individual and societal contexts of languages in contact.

Ellen J. Serafini is an assistant professor of Spanish at George Mason University. Her research explores the role of learner internal and external factors in instructed second language and immersion settings, critical approaches to heritage language pedagogy, and task-based approaches to curricular design in specialized contexts. She has published several journal articles and book chapters in these areas.

Guadalupe Valdés is the Bonnie Katz Tenenbaum Professor of Education at Stanford University. Working in the area of applied linguistics, she has focused much of her work on the English-Spanish bilingualism of Latinos in the United States and on discovering and describing how two languages are developed, used, and maintained by individuals who become bilingual in immigrant communities. Valdés has carried out extensive work on maintaining and preserving heritage languages among minority populations since the 1970s. Her early publications in this area include a co-edited volume of articles entitled *Teaching Spanish to the Hispanic Bilingual: Issues, Aims and Methods* (Teachers College Press, 1981). In the last several years her work has included a book on Spanish in California titled *Developing Minority Language Resources: The Case of Spanish in California* (Multilingual Matters, 2006). She was awarded the Joshua Fishman Award for Outstanding Contributions and Leadership in the Heritage Language Field from the National Heritage Language Resource Center at UCLA in 2010.

Chantelle Warner is an associate professor of German studies and second language acquisition and teaching at the University of Arizona. She is codirector of the Center for Educational Resources of Language, Literacy, and Culture, a Title IV National Language Resource Center, and also directs the language program for German at the University of Arizona. Her research is in second language learning and teaching, literacy studies, and discourse stylistics, with particular interest in the aesthetic and affective dimensions of language use.

Eve Zyzik is an associate professor and chair of the Department of Languages and Applied Linguistics at the University of California, Santa Cruz. She has published on a variety of topics related to Spanish as a second language, Spanish as a heritage language, and also more general issues such as language-focused instruction in content courses. She published an advanced-level textbook, *El español y la lingüística aplicada*, with coauthor Robert Blake.

Index

Figures and tables are denoted by f and t following the page numbers.

CPSIA information can be obtained
at www.ICGtesting.com
Printed in the USA
BVOW11s0726090817
491533BV00021B/351/P